THEIR

EARTHSHAKING

NEWS

THEIR EARTHSHAKING NEWS

WHEN SCIENCE AND THEOLOGY

SPEAK

THE SAME URGENT LANGUAGE

by
Helen Tzima Otto

The Verenikia Press
2680 Camelot Drive
Rock Hill, S.C. 29732-9405
Ph.: (803) 327 9637; Fax: (803) 327 0467

031384

December, 1995

Library of Congress Cataloging-in-Publication Data

Otto, Helen Tzima 1946-

THEIR EARTHSHAKING NEWS:
WHEN SCIENCE AND THEOLOGY
SPEAK THE SAME URGENT LANGUAGE

Includes bibliographical references.
Includes Index.

ISBN 0-9639553-4-9 (paperback)
1. Religious Prophecy.   2. History.   3. Current Affairs.   4. Volcanology.
5. Archaeology.   6. Cometary Astronomy.

printing number

1 2 3 4 5 6 7 8 9 10

Published by   The Verenikia Press
                      P.O. Box 35799
                      Houston, Tx. 77235-5799

Library of Congress Catalog Card Number: 95-62058

to the memory of my father

Apostolos Spyrid. Tzimas

Acknowledgements

I cannot find enough words to express my intellectual debt and my gratitude to all those who in the words of Henry Wadsworth Longfellow

> still achieving, still pursuing
> learned to labor and to wait.

Yet, anybody who willingly accepts to labor and to wait for results that may only begin materializing long after he is gone, does so out of love for the human race, does so out of willingness to share his riches with generations as yet born. In a way, by a conscious choice he willingly relinquishes his property rights.

It is due to the conscious decisions by such men and women that our libraries are filled today with so much nourishing material for the spirit and the soul, and with so much vital knowledge and information, which can practically mean the difference between life and death for the current generation. It is to the Saints and Seers and Prophets of God, to the scholars and researchers, to the men and women of the Investigating Habit, to such silent heroes of the Legend, who are not truly dead but merely patiently waiting in the pages of a book, waiting till a future generation heeds their messages and benefits from their advice. They wait for such kisses of resuscitation that they may be brought back to life. To such enchanted creatures the study before you owes its existence.

To those heroes of silent battles, to those illustrious champions of yet unsung victories, to those lovers of mankind and of the pursuit of knowledge and understanding, who labored and waited, may Heaven grant all the blessings of Elysium. And to those who are still alive and keep on pressing their footprints on the sands of Time, may God grant His guidance and inspiration through the great perils of the age. Each time their work is remembered, each time their intellectual efforts and achievements appear in the body and in the footnotes of a book, those footprints on the sands of Time may reveal a path for a fellow wanderer and assist him in breaking from a vicious circle.

To this great solidarity between souls which had never met in person, to this silent network of great communicators across geography and time, to this patient, unselfish laborers for a better world, no gratitude, admiration and respect are adequate. May God grant it, that they may also know, that if we make it through this Age of Great Tribulations, we shall owe it to a great extent to the lifelines they have been casting out for us from Beyond.

TABLE OF CONTENTS

PREFACE

A few words to the reader:

Albert Einstein was convinced that *God does not play dice with the universe*. Once the previously unquestioned, original form of the theory of Evolution of Charles Darwin came under attack by geological and historical evidence supporting the theory of Catastrophism, scientists began questioning the validity of Einstein's dictum.[1] They articulated a suspicion that *apparently Einstein was wrong: God does play dice, at least when it comes to slinging asteroids and comets toward the living Earth.*[2]

In this study we will show that **God does not play dice**, and even when He slings asteroids and comets towards a living earth inhabited by the pugnacious Homo Sapiens, **He gives ample advance notice!** In fact, the evidence of such premonitory intelligence is democratically distributed across the globe and truly overwhelming in its power and detail.

The Almighty God has been forewarning us regarding our proximate close encounter with a body from outer space since the time of the Hebrew Prophets and the Greek Sibyls (at least as far as the History of Judeo-Christianity is concerned). I suspect that holy persons in India, China, and elsewhere have received analogous intelligence a long time ago, as well. Consider the following words from the Bible:

And I will show wonders in the heavens above, and signs on the

---

[1] As early as 1973 the space scientist and Nobel Laureate Harold C. Urey suggested that impact events from outer space have indeed marked the boundaries between the geological ages and have wiped out large numbers of species and can explain the sudden global changes in sedimentary behavior and in the fossil species preserved in the rocks. However, in the 1940s, Immanuel Velikovsky using different analysis was essentially ushering the notion of Catastrophism as corroborated by the Bible and other ancient writings. The Darwinian Theory, by contrast, advocated a cosmically uneventful and smooth and very slow process of evolution of the species upon the earth without the interference of exogenous factors, such as comets and asteroids.

[2] See William K. Hartmann, [1991].

x

Earth beneath; blood, and fire, and vapor of smoke. The sun shall be turned into darkness, and the moon into blood, before that great and notable day of the Lord comes. And it shall come to pass that whoever calls upon the name of the Lord shall be saved. (Originally appearing in Joel 3:3-5, repeated by St. Peter and incorporated in Acts 2:19-21).

The great and notable day of the Lord, **is not the Second Coming**, but rather an event preceding it, and it will arrive before the year 2000 A.D. The Almighty God and Lover of Mankind not only has given us ample advance notice before the next major killer comet will be slung towards the living Earth, He also tells us what technology will be effective and salutary against such eventuality! Consequently, the fear and suspicions of scientists are exaggerated and must be modified through the words of the Holy men and women of God, who have been speaking about this dreaded phenomenon more or less since the very beginning of written History.

As it happened in the times of Noah, the Flood (a catastrophe of immense global proportions) did not obliterate the human race. Noahs in every country and locus of civilization were spared and told us subsequently all about it through their national myths and legends adding their national evidence to the words of the Hebrew Book of Genesis. Again, the Elect will be spared from the catastrophes looming over our horizon, provided they follow the divine precepts and the advice of the prophecies.

This book, as its title suggests, will be a work of synthesis of solid scientific evidence publicly available to us, with the Word of God through the mouths and the pens of God's holy men and women, derived through publicly available sources, as well. The reader will be soon convinced that, indeed, we have been given a tremendous amount of specific information. If we fail to heed the messages we will have only ourselves to blame for the consequences for our lives in this world and the next.

For, we are free to shape our own destiny within the constraints prescribed by God. We have been given many opportunities to count ourselves among the Elect if we so choose, depending on the use we shall make of that great freedom of ours. It is not predestination that makes us (or fails to make us) members of the Elect group, it is only the self-selecting process we are engaging in during the course of our entire earthly existence, and whose activities and consequences are going to be of more vital importance between now and the end of this decade.

The forewarning and data-points for most of our analysis come directly from above, from the Father of Lights, and are unadulterated, direct, unembellished and free from editors' intervention. In jargon that is both austere and provocative, those who never spoke under condition of anonymity (regardless of the consequences for their personal safety) will tirelessly repeat to those who have ears to listen and minds to understand what must be done so that the tremendous perils of our proximate future become mitigated, if not partially averted. The message of the prophets is universal and all-encompassing. What will happen to the Earth before the year 2000 A.D. will leave not even a single human being untouched and unscathed, and only by our prayers, repentance, and other prescribed acts of reparation can we positively influence the outcomes.

This book was written with the well educated, socially concerned and spiritually alert audience in mind. The task at hand is a little bit analogous to St. Paul's while addressing the intellectually sophisticated, yet spiritually disabused and disillusioned Athenians of the first century A.D., on the Hill of Areos Pagos. As the reader may remember, St. Paul's introductory words were: *'Men of Athens, I see that in every respect you are extremely religious. For, as I was going about and observing objects of your worship, I found also an altar with this inscription: To the Unknown God.' What therefore you worship in ignorance, that I proclaim to you. (...) The times of our (prior) ignorance God has truly overlooked, but now He calls upon all men everywhere to repent. (...)* Acts 17:22-30.

Mutatis mutandis, the message of our book runs as follows: *Fellow human beings: In your scientifically sophisticated search and analysis of the phenomena of the cosmos you have already reached the correct conclusion that it is merely a matter of time before a major comet (or an asteroid in Earth-crossing path) delivers a devastating blow to our civilization. Your brilliant scientists have already written numerous books and articles debating all the parameters for such an event and its consequences for life on this planet. This comet, which your instruments cannot yet detect, and which in your heart you already expect with trepidation and worry, this comet which God has already launched on an Earth-approaching trajectory, this comet, which you already have been speaking about while ignoring its particulars, this is the comet which I will present you in this book, based on the evidence showered upon us by the Almighty.*

I would also add: Now is not the time for retrenching in our ideological, political, and religious niches and revert to a self-defeating tribalism of the spirit and the soul. Tribalism is division, and those who can exploit the divisiveness can conquer without much trouble (*divide et rege*, was the motto of the Roman rulers). The agents behind this extremely dangerous tendency towards tribalism so pervasive in our societies (and those within the Western Democracies and the Christian fold in particular) have been many and varied. In fact, to analyze these phenomena and their hidden and not so hidden causes, a separate study would be necessary. Yet, we are going to suffer tremendously in the foreseeable future from the consequences of that tribalism amongst our ranks, at the same time that the dreaded comet will make its uninvited visit. Now more than ever, the intellectually sophisticated and spiritually alert contemporaries of ours are called upon to follow the Divine precepts, in order not only to save their own body and soul and be counted among the Remnant, but also to assist in the deliverance of as great a portion of the rest of humanity as possible.

When evil is very powerful and abounds in the world, so does also Divine Grace. In this sense, the frequency with which the apparitions of the Most Blessed Virgin Mary Theotokos have been registered all over the world during the past decades are indicative of both the intensification of the evil, but also of the intensification of the Grace emanating from Heaven to assist us in dealing with the perils. This book will provide, therefore, ample testimony of the love of God for mankind and the ways the Elect have **already been empowered** in their combat against evil in all its manifestations.

We will invite the readers to corroborate the findings through their own independent research. If they can detect mistakes in our logic or analysis, we hope that they will inform us accordingly in a timely fashion, so that they may be corrected and the public be properly informed. Never before did we have so little time available to change gears and drastically modify the course of our existence. The words of the prophets are the life-saving road-signs placed along the perilous highways of the *status quo* and the *ceteris paribus*, of ignorance and complacency, of mental paralysis fomented by a continuous bombardment of trivia and the trite concerns of daily pursuits. All these lead to a precipice of no return. We are on the verge of a major Paradigm Modification in human existence. Let us heed the signs on the way and dodge the precipice while we still have a chance.

CHAPTER ONE

INTRODUCTION

From the Devil, the Turk and the Comet,
Good Lord deliver us. Pope Calixtus III.

Introduction

Constantinople fell to the Ottoman Turks on May 29, 1453 A.D. The conquest of the Byzantine empire being now almost complete, the Turks turned towards the rest of the Peninsula of Haemus and the European lands beyond. By 1456 A.D. they had led siege to Belgrade. The Christians of Europe, finally realizing that their previous assistance to the Ottomans in the capacity of mercenaries, artillery experts and assorted 'military advisors' had proved counter-productive and self defeating, began preparations for defense. Pope Calixtus (Callistus) III (1455-1458 A.D.) sent a force of 40,000 Christians to defend Belgrade against the armies of Mohammed II. During that same year (1456 A.D.) a great comet was seen both in Europe and in China.

Comets, which even to this day exhibit a peculiar tendency of coinciding with fateful events such as wars, famines, and deaths of princes, (quite oblivious to, and unperturbed by the derision of certain modern scientists) did not fail to shake the self-confidence of the belligerent parties observing them from below. This was the case in the siege of Belgrade also. Legend has it, that Pope Calixtus ordered that the following prayer be inserted into the 'Ave Maria': **"From the Devil, the Turk, and the Comet, Good Lord, deliver us"**.

The comet that so impressed the world in 1456 A.D. was Halley's Comet in one of its periodic visits to our inner Solar System. Legend further has it (or rather the Marquis de Laplace, who gave us that story) that Pope Calixtus III excommunicated the Comet whose evil apparition coincided with an Islamic advance at the expense of (his) Christian Europe. And although written evidence of such a step against a Comet has not been yet located in the Vatican archives, the legend would not likely have persisted for so long in the absence of any kernel of truth therein.

Calixtus III, an otherwise lackluster Pope of a very short pontificate, obviously had good reasons to be concerned, although in the short run his fears turned out to be a little exaggerated. On the other hand, since History fails to teach us and therefore becomes repeated, we, today, have many more good reasons to be concerned. Like the Hungarian Christian mercenary who fired the Ottoman cannons against the walls of Constantinople merely for money, (and by so doing he precipitated the time when the Ottomans would invade his own country, ravage it completely and keep it under their yoke for long centuries), the Christians of today have been supplying the canons and the powder for a new invasion of Europe and the Middle East to those self-same historical enemies of the West.[1]

The present study will submit evidence to show that our generation has many more reasons than Pope Calixtus III to pray fervently to the Almighty for deliverance from the Devil, and the Turk, and the Comet. And the reasons for such urgency are several. Between now and the end of this century we will be called upon to deal with:

> a) a paroxysm in the various manifestations of evil;

> b) WWIII; a global conflict of unsurpassed destructiveness, in which the Turks and all their blood relatives along with the rest of the Muslim world will attack the lands of Christian Europe and the land of Israel; and

> c) a comet, whose close approach to our planet will unleash a chain of geophysical upheavals of unsurpassed destructiveness within historical memory.

Once these three evils have passed, the world will never be the same; even the physiology of the planet will have changed considerably, including the height of volcanoes, the beds of major rivers, the obliteration of islands and port-cities etc., while the hearts and souls of the Remnant (the Elect, in other words), will have undergone a great purification and chastisement before being allowed to enjoy a prolonged period of peace, prosperity and bliss,

---

[1] This realization will become more pronounced during the Presidential Debates of 1996, considering that so many among our elected Representatives seem to be so anxious to arm and financially support the Bosnian Muslims, the Albanian Muslims and all other assorted declared enemies of Christianity and the West.

the intensity of which, again, the world has never experienced before.

This book provides very detailed information of all major developments on all fronts of the war, waged by the Remnant (of many countries and cultures) against the three formidable enemies, introduced above. This information comes directly from the prophets who have predicted with remarkable accuracy **all** the events of our age. It will also help us identify how we individually, as a human entity, can improve our own chances of salvation and survival, again, by following the specific precepts from Above.

As we have been forewarned ever since the times when Lord Jesus Christ walked upon this planet, in the last times there will rise many Antichrists and many pseudo-prophets. The apostasy will be great and the confusion among the Elect will be manifest in many self-destructive ways. The pseudo-prophets that I have been particularly concerned with in the course of this research are the self-proclaimed interpreters of Biblical and other Prophecies, those instant experts who promote their personal (unlearned) opinions with authority and passion as if they were the ultimate truth. Undoubtedly the reader is already aware of the existence of many accounts predicting even the wholesale catastrophe of the earth before the year 2000.

It is quite possible that the reader have grown weary with the various 'interpreters' of Biblical Prophecy, Nostradamus etc. according to some of whom WWIII was supposed to have finished 20 years ago, or the end of the world took place in September of 1995... So, the initial reaction may be: Oh, Lord, yet another of those books predicting the end of the world!

This book is not predicting the end of the world. And if the reader will read patiently through the pages detailing the further motivation for this study and its research methodology he/she will be convinced that this is not yet another of those books.

On the other hand, there are other more dangerous pseudo-prophets out there who lull our spirit into inactivity and dull our brains with their soothing messages. They appease our worries and disenchantment with the world with their claims that life will go on as usual, there is nothing serious to worry about, and through political debate and legal action we shall manage to resolve all problems currently on the front line of the press. Such persons, routinely claim also that since the fall of the USSR we have a fairly stable universal peace and war will not be an option if we only keep on paying our 'allies' for their acquiescence, chastise the Russians for their

3

'Anti-Western Hysteria', and teach those 'criminal Serbs' a lesson or two and force them to obey the orders of our assorted 'laptop bombardiers' from Washington D.C.[2]   Such remarkable policy makers try to treat the symptoms instead of the underlying disease and in so doing they precipitate the events that will be unleashed upon us before the end of this decade with a cataclysmic fury.

Deliverance from the Devil
The Devil has been present on this world ever since the very beginning of our History. So, why this sudden special concern? For the simple reason that the Devil has been particularly powerful during the 20th century, which can very easily be voted as the most criminal century in the History of the world. Between now and the end of WWIII his activity will become even more noticeable and he will become manifest in many guises. It is not only the exacerbation of man's rebellion against God, it is also the misguidance and the error of otherwise well-meaning people; such errors become exploited and capitalized upon by the 'Prince of this world' and the millions of his disciples.[3]

This century of the Devil will come to a stop after a series of cataclysms (both God-made and man-made) which will change the souls of men along with the shorelines of our countries, the skylines of our cities and the contours of our neighborhoods. As the Spirit predicts, furthermore, the power of the Devil will be crushed for a number of years, and people shall live in peace and security till the advent of the Antichrist. At that time, the Devil will be unleashed once again and will be allowed to ravage the world

---

[2]   This most appropriate term was coined by Mr. A. M. Rosenthal, former executive Editor of the New York Times.

[3] Furthermore, we have to deal also with the attacks by the unseen evil powers, the demons, proper, who will be allowed to torment and harass both the faithful and the unholy for a predetermined period of time during our proximate future, as per the testimony of our prophets. (This attack has already began, as any Orthodox and Catholic priest, called upon to perform exorcisms, would be able to attest). In summary, the Devil will attack us from many quarters and victory against him cannot be achieved without the assistance of the Omnipotent God, His Saints and His Angels. All these terrifying events have been predicted, we expect them to continue happening, but we are also given advance notice on the duration of the torments associated with them as well as the proposed spiritual technology that will bring about their defeat.

before his new defeat and imprisonment for the duration of 1000 years, as specified in the Book of the Revelation and several other sources of eschatological literature.

Considering how much confusion exists in the minds of the general public concerning the timing of the various events predicted by Prophecy, (due among other things to the confusion created by so many 'Biblical interpreters' and Pseudo-prophets in the past) I feel it is important to emphasize this tremendously important distinction right now, before we embark on our more detailed study:

Evil will have a heyday till the advent of the Comet, it will reappear at the time of the Antichrist and will disappear upon Devil's defeat during the Second Coming for the entire stretch of the Millennium. This information comes from the prophecies and it is clear and categorical enough; therefore no misunderstandings and confusion need to enter here.[4]

Deliverance from the Turk

Does this sound like a farfetched scenario considering the hype of our mass media and our Washington lobbying firms promoting at every instant the great merits of our 'staunch ally in the NATO?' Before jumping to any premature conclusions, let us consider for a moment the New World Disorder inherited from the political blunders of the Cold War era and following the Collapse of the Soviet Union. Turkey, which lost an empire in the wake of WWI, would have subsisted as a lackluster, technologically backward and economically poor Islamic country till our days, save for an accident of geography, which placed it at the border of what became the Soviet Union. Although Lenin and Kemal Atatürk were the best friends and allies in the word at the time, things changed after the emergence of the Soviet Empire after WWII. Turkey (which remained neutral during WWII) rose to a 'staunch ally' of the United States, became a NATO country, benefitted immensely from Western military technology and direct economic assistance, and has amassed a tremendous arsenal, compliments of the US taxpayer, primarily.

------

[4] In the event the reader considers such deliberations beyond the scope of standard 'scientific analysis' and rather exotic material for a serious study, I only beg for patience and perseverance, and continuing with the reading of the study. In the course of our analysis this connection of the Devil with the rest of the evils of our age will become apparent.

Although our staunch NATO ally never fought any battle nor won any victory against the Soviets on our account, this and other mercenary nations, which joined the Western block during the Cold War era, have learned the secrets of modern warfare and high-tech mass annihilation. With this know-how they are now ready to turn to their true enemy, the Western System of Values, as a whole, where 'West' should always include the Christian populations of the former Soviet Union, as well as Israel. In this light, it is no wonder that the inimitable Aleksandr I. Solzhenitsyn made note in his historical accounts of an event generally unpublicized in the West, (except for such sources as the Mediterranean Quarterly, Der Spiegel, and a few other well-researched and thorough investigative Journals): '*Almost all Central Asian leaders have already declared the new orientation of their states towards Turkey. Not everybody noticed in December of 1991 a much promising conference in Alma Ata for the creation of a 'Great Turan' destined to stretch from the Peninsula of Anatolia to the Djungarskii Altai mountains. In the 21st century, the Muslim world, which increases numerically at a fast rate, no doubt will assume ambitious tasks for itself, - and who is there to tell us (Russians) not to be concerned?*[5]

Our recent experience with former mercenary and 'friendly' countries such as Iran and Iraq should provide us with sufficient reason for alarm. Our complacent countrymen whose ignorance of historical facts can only be matched by their gullibility to the pronouncements of hired Lobbyists such as Robert Keith Gray, still hold the misguided view that faraway 'friendly' nations pose no military threats to the USA. These voters still take at face value the manufactured reports on all events transpiring in the Balkans, the Caucasus, the Kashmir, and everywhere else where at least one Islamic nation is involved in fighting against a non-Islamic one.

The ranks among Islamic countries are closing everywhere and even Saddam Hussein is making overtures towards his primordial enemy, Iran, for future friendship and co-operation. As a first step to this direction came the accords for the exchange of war prisoners of the Iran-Iraqi war, the first contingent having been exchanged in the summer of 1995.

The beginning of the end of the Soviet Empire marked the rebirth of the regional conflicts along religious lines, in Armenia, the Middle East, North

---

[5] [Russkii Vopros... ("The Russian Question" at the end of the 20th century) reprinted in Le Messager, no. 169, I-II - 1994, p. 258].

Africa, the Balkans, Central Asia, Pakistan, Kashmir, Chechnya, and other places less publicized in the news. Consequently, the "Turk" is rising once again against Christian Europe and the "West" in general. Under the term "Turk" we must also comprise along with the Turks from Turkey all other populations of Tatar-Mongolic and Turkic origin (the Great Turan, in other words), such as those composing most of the Islamic lands of the former USSR. Although the Mongols, Tatars and Turks are not related racially with the Arabs or the Iranians, a major alliance along religious lines and common enmity against the 'Devil residing in the West' (Christians and Jews) is to be reckoned with in our most proximate future.[6]

We must add to the above list the various 'freedom fighters' who have already established terrorist training camps in Muslim Bosnia, and about whose existence even the American public began hearing as of late. With regards to those 'freedom fighters', who till yesterday were Atheist Marxist-Leninists and who upon the dissolution of the USSR suddenly saw the light and overnight were converted into 'warriors of Allah', the truth is that political power is their only target and objective. If the hype about Allah serves this purpose better and draws around them a larger group of the disenfranchised masses who have lost the competition game in the global marketplace, then hot Muslims shall they claim to be, brandishing the Koran in one hand and the Kalashnikov (AK-47) in the other.

Therefore, the term "Turk" will also be used to specify Islamic lands and armies who have exhibited a great resistance, enmity and hatred against the West and its value system; this will comprise Islamic lands stretching from Indonesia in the East to Mauritania in the West.

Besides the loosely defined 'Turks' we will have to add to our list another group, already in residence within Western Democracies: Palestinian Muslims in Israel, legal and illegal Muslim aliens in France, Spain, Italy,

---

[6] Among other things, one only needs to look at what happens in the Balkans today, where not only the Turks, the Pakistanis and the Saudis, but even the geographically more remote Malaysians joined the clamoring for the interests of their Bosnian 'brothers'. The Malaysian Prime Minister Mahathir Mohamad, furthermore, in a recent Interview to Der Spiegel threatened to arm his UN-Peacekeeping contingent in Bosnia (provided the Bosnians would agree, of course) and continue the armed conflict there, over the potential objections of the UN. [Der Spiegel, no. 34/1995, pp. 136-139].

Germany, the British Isles, Kossovo (in former Yugoslavia), Muslim minorities in Bulgaria and the Former Yugoslav Republic of Macedonia, and the countries of the former Soviet Union, notably Russia and the Ukraine. (To a lesser extent Greece with its illegal economic refugees from Muslim Albania and many illegal political refugees from other Islamic lands). The list can be expanded. These and other types of refugees into the lands of America, Europe and Israel will be the spark to start a major conflagration in the months and years to come, and they already warm up to the task with imported terrorist activities from their lands of origin. The US Trade Center bombing and the numerous attacks upon Parisian civilian positions as recently as Fall of 1995 are only cases in point.

The above-mentioned countries, for a number of historical reasons, have amassed sizeable minorities from Africa and Asia, a portion of which is loyal to the country of their adoption and share in its system of values, having voted with their feet against the politics of their land of origin. These people are already apprehensive of the political trends back home sensing the disasters to be unleashed soon, beginning with the 'renegades' who opted for the Western way of living. They are fearful of Islamic Fundamentalism and are understandably against the local corrupt political elites who, despite the overwhelming financial assistance from the West have allowed such economic polarization to take root and such ideologies to take hold and achieve political ascendance.

A sizeable portion of Muslims living abroad, however, consider themselves disenfranchised, ill-treated, and hopelessly non-competitive in a world of high-tech industrialization. Basically most of them are manual laborers in the factories of the second industrial revolution or live from hand to mouth in the various 'service' industries, such as unloading ships at the docks of Marseille, selling cheap clothes in the Metro and shining shoes in Paris and London. High school drop-outs most of them, already view themselves as the hopeless economic pariahs of today and tomorrow. Such groups tend to lend a sympathetic ear to imported Fundamentalist ideologies from the motherland, by analogy to the stupidest of the stupid of the Czarist empire who were promised to live like kings after the destruction of the old order and the re-distribution of wealth.

Nobody can afford to discount the British experience in that respect, where the Pakistanis and other Muslims from the former British Commonwealth of Nations even clamor for the establishment of their own Parliament. They will have nothing to do with British laws and anything Western...[7] The evidence accumulated in this study will be sufficient to convince the alert reader that, indeed, there is a new war coming, whereby the Islamic hordes will attempt the reconquest of Christian Europe, Israel and other lands naturally allied to the West. At the same time, Communist China, in open alliance with Islam, or with its tacit acquiescence, will find its great opportunity of taking care of some unfinished business in Siberia, Inner Mongolia, the Spratly Islands, Hong Kong and Taiwan, South-East Asia and the North Pacific. (China currently maintains very lucrative and friendly economic and military exchanges with Iraq, Iran, Pakistan, and many other Islamic countries whose intentions vis-à-vis the West are unequivocal and very bluntly expressed in speech and writing).

The American public is shielded from much of this information and U.S. aid continues to flow to many of these countries, especially Turkey, thanks to massive lobbying efforts. Lobbying firms in Washington have created this misguided and manipulated image emerging in print today. Those lobbyists who have discovered that *'the wars in the press can be won cheaper than on the battlefield'* and, furthermore, they can be marketed *"just like soft drinks and toothpaste"*[8], are accountable for making the American foreign policy in general and the Balkan one in particular, in the words of Professor Nikolaos Stavrou, "increasingly a hostage to ethnic lobbies and Congressional defenders of the underdog. This (...) is particularly facilitated by the wonders of a system that makes it legal to peddle, buy and exercise influence on behalf of any one with a deep pocket."[9]

Pat Choate, in his *Agents of Influence* [1990], attaches a highly informative *Appendix A*, whose content is of particular interest in the context of our

---

[7] In view of these recent trends of Islamic Fundamentalism at the expense of Britain, one must tip a hat or two to Jean Raspail, whose book, *'The Camp of the Saints'* though a novel was an inspired one and sounded like a prophecy for the events exploding all around us today. That book when it first appeared was not considered 'politically correct' and was read by politicians behind closed doors. Prophecy is rarely considered politically correct, either, when it first becomes promulgated.

[8] the quote is taken from Susan B. Trento, [1992].

[9] "The Balkan Quagmire and the West's Response", Mediterranean Quarterly, (Winter 1993), p. 35.

present study. The reader may wish to consult that list and try to come up with a plausible theory explaining the inordinate amount of millions of US$s yearly invested by Turkey (a relatively poor and neither commercially- nor industrially-developed nation) to purchase representation in Washington.

Susan B. Trento, [1992, p. 210] supplies us with additional food for thought: Robert Keith Gray (of Hill & Knowlton Lobbying 'Power House') "resented being questioned by the media about his *'unsavory'* international clients. *'We don't represent any foreign government without first clearing it with the Secretary of State and the head of the CIA to ensure it is in the best interests of the United States for us to take the case,'* Gray said. Time Magazine wrote: "But how did he know, for instance, that more military aid for Turkey was in the national interest? *'I always check these situations out with Bill Casey,'* says Gray, dropping like a brick the name of his friend the CIA director. For Bob Gray, friendships like that are not just to be made; they can be marketed."

The men and women who worked for Gray, Ms. Trento informs us, *had taken on tough assignments: trying to convince Congress and the American public that countries with abysmal human rights records - Haiti, Morocco, Turkey, China- were misunderstood.'* At times the effort was very strenuous and all absorbing: In the Washington Times column entitled 'Doers Profile' Mr. Gray (who profiled himself in the February of 1992 edition) informed the readers that his preferred vacation spot was Istanbul, Turkey. Yet, Ms. Trento notes that even this was nothing but a calculated answer for effect purposes only, in order to promote the 'unsavory' client. She reports that *the response on the profile that caused the most mirth among Hill & Knowlton, Inc. veterans was his favorite vacation spot, Istanbul.* "They had *to drag him, kicking and screaming, to go to Istanbul at all to see the Turkish client,"* said one. (...) "I mean people broke up. It was faxed all over town because everybody knew,..."[10]

Deliverance from the 'Comet'
As intimated earlier, we have the word of the prophets that a comet will

---

[10] [ibid. p. 393].

make its mark upon our proximate future.[11] It appears, by a thorough scrutiny of the wording of the prophecies themselves, that it will be a comet and not an asteroid.[12] In my previous study, entitled *Our Revelationary Age: The Prophecies for WWIII and the Year 2000*, I referred to this object from outer space and analyzed some of its specifics in a chapter entitled 'The Three Days Darkness'. While in the former study the war was the focus and only peripherally did the study touch upon the geological upheavals, the current one is focused on the comet and its consequences primarily and only peripherally on additional relevant information regarding the military activities of the WWIII.[13]

The contributions by Astronomers and other Scientists have been most instrumental for the feasibility of the present study. Even so, they provided only part of the data necessary for the research. Their literally earthshaking news had to be supplemented by another group and its earthshaking news. Beginning with the Hebrew Prophets and the Greek Sibyls and stretching

---

[11] The Astronomic profession is unable to predict exactly when such an event is bound to occur. Among other things, not all comets are periodic, with a trajectory that has already been computed and whose next perihelion approach can therefore be neatly calculated down to the year and month of its visitation. It may take more than a year between the discovery of a new comet and its approach to our inner Solar system. Comets are invisible in the outer space because the solar heat cannot yet reach them and cause through sublimation their elements to be heated and become visible.

[12] I have been concerned for a while whether it will be a comet, strictly speaking, or an asteroid on an Earth-crossing path, on the basis that since the word 'Asteroid' is a later introduction in the scientific jargon, the prophets might have been constrained to using the closest equivalent available. It appears, however, that the question deals with a comet and not an asteroid, considering the other details such as visible characteristics that cannot be shared by an asteroid (having no atmosphere, for instance and no gases that could sublimate and generate specific visual effects).

[13] When we refer in this study to the 'current generation' we mean all those persons alive today. When the Bible speaks of the 'current (present) generation', however, the meaning is quite different. The Biblical terms refer to all humans to be born beginning with the contemporaries of Jesus Christ and His disciples up untill His Second Coming. After that, a new generation will be born into the Millennial age. Therefore, the terms 'current generation' employed in this study will imply **us**, the mortals living today, unless otherwise specified.

down to our own times, especially through the various intimations by the Most Holy and Blessed Virgin Theotokos since 1846, a voluminous body of prophetic literature became available to us, which, when combined with the fruits of scientific enquiry by the Astrophysicists and other related scientists will convince the reader of the tremendously vital significance of the evidence at hand.

REVIEW OF THE MOST SALIENT POINTS

a)   Prophecy is one of the perfect gifts that comes from the Father of Lights and it is meant for the **betterment, edification, premonition and protection** of the Elect; like the laws of nature we can neglect it only to our peril.

b)   The Almighty has already written our Future History. We can read and profit therefrom in the numerous accounts spread out all over the globe. This study will concentrate (due to time constraints and primarily to the limitations of the expertise of its author) to the evidence from Judeo-Christianity only.

c)   A thorough, multi-disciplinary analysis will reveal that modern science is in full internal consistence with the Theology of Judeo-Christianity and the premonitions of the prophets. With their voices in unison, therefore, it is hoped that they will arouse the interest of even religiously disenchanted and skeptical, yet alert and thinking persons, to the call from Above.

CHAPTER TWO

RESEARCH ISSUES AND METHODOLOGY

Almost always the men who achieve these fundamental inventions of a new paradigm have either been very young or very new to the field whose paradigm they change. Thomas Kuhn.[1]

A brief introduction of the author: I have been trained academically for Business and Economics. My doctoral research was on the Economics of the Construction sector of the USSR and so far I have taught in the Academy Mathematics, Economics and Finance. What possibly could such a pretentious outsider contribute with any degree of authority on the subjects of Comets, Volcanoes and Prophecies? Let us start with the following:

a)   Prophetic evidence is, in a way, a kind of undervalued security waiting patiently to be discovered, capitalized upon and properly incorporated in one's portfolio of assets. There, it will immensely enrich the discoverer(s). In fact, I cannot conceive of a more gratifying and deserving object of scientific research than the pearls and diamonds of the Word of God for the benefit of mankind.

b)   Having been raised in the Greek Orthodox Church, and through my mature years having remained in it by choice, throughout life I had many opportunities to study and observe the various manifestations of direct Divine intervention in the affairs of the Faithful. Such experiences provided from early on a motivation to keep on reading on Theology and Metaphysics, along with other academic subjects. The best educated persons pursued an education that transcended the confines of the specialized training they made their living with.

c)   I am educated in both modern and ancient History and read eight languages. This has enambled me to read many prophecies in their

---

[1] From *The Structure of Scientific Revolutions*, [1970, p. 90], quoted by Martin Bernal, *Black Athena*, vol. I, [1987, p. 1].

original text and identify numerous translation errors, while my knowledge of History has allowed me to see the context within which the prophecies were written.

In conclusion, I am neither the first nor the last person on this earth who at some point in their life expanded their area of interests and saw new areas of research where their tools of analysis could be effectively applied. The world is heading towards a major paradigm shift on a global scale right now. Like millions of human beings before me I began sensing that the inexorable thrust of overwhelming changes emerging in the world had to be addressed and the necessary steps to be taken. A major shifting of gears was called for. For me personally, that moment arrived in the wake of the Chernobyl explosion of April 26, 1986, which essentially ushered in the end of the Old World Order. (Interestingly enough, that disaster was presaged by the perihelion approach of Halley's Comet...)

A few caveats
1) The Voice of one Shouting in the Wilderness

One of the most misunderstood and, therefore, misquoted passages from the Bible deals with *the voice of one crying in the wilderness* which refers to St. John the Baptist. This expression came to be synonymous with an ungrateful, hopeless and completely futile effort and has enjoyed great currency by all kinds of people for quite a long time. This misapplication of a Biblical quote perpetuates the mistaken belief that St. John was basically all alone out there, shouting his admonitions to the four winds.

However, the meaning is quite contrary: St. John the Baptist already **had** a following, and his disciples were the raw material and the seed out of which the initial crowds of Lord Jesus Christ were recruited. *Crying in the wilderness* merely signified that St. John had made the decision to move away from city life and establish his school in the desert of Judaea, instead. In other words, the people came to him to listen to his sermons, there, in the desert, i.e., in the wilderness, away from the noise and the distractions of the city life, and closer to the river Jordan in which his converts were baptized. (Let us also remember that Lord Jesus Christ also came to him, in the desert, to be baptized. It was not St. John the Baptist who came to the Lord, but rather the Lord, like so many others went to him, out there in the wilderness). So, when Prophet Isaiah spoke of *The voice of one crying in the desert (wilderness)*, "*make ready the way of the Lord, make straight his paths*" he wanted first and foremost to differentiate this particular prophet

14

from others, by alluding to his modus operandi.

Consequently, the true meaning of *the voice of one crying in the wilderness* ought to be construed as follows: *be alert for the arrival of a new prophet who holds his sermons outside the towns and is a forerunner of the Lord, who prepares the world for the New Paradigm.* History proves that St. John the Fore-runner **did not** engage in hopeless enterprises by just uttering futile shouts and recriminations in the middle of nowhere with no audience listening to him and hence no attitudes to be modified. Furthermore, such assertion would have been in most glaring and direct contradiction with the belief that the Almighty God dispatches His prophets to the world for the benefit of mankind.

This persevering misapplication of a famous Biblical passage was brought up in order to show how misunderstood and under-appreciated the formidable power of prophecy remains to this day with the general public. Let us preserve the image of St. John delivering his sermons to an elite who came all the way to his habitat in order to hearken to his sermons. All great progress in mankind begins with an initially small group, a self-selecting elite, a sensitive, alert and dissident minority, dissatisfied with the status quo, thirsty and hungry for the new truth. This elite appreciates the words of the prophet, rallies around him, carries his message to the world and eventually becomes the path breaker. (In this specific case, it makes straight the way of the Lord).

And another caveat
2) The Debate on what constitutes
a legitimate book of genuine Prophecy

The Sibylline Oracles:
Another sorely misunderstood body of vast value and importance for the researcher are *The Sibylline Oracles*. This (for the purposes of our current study) must be differentiated from the *Libri Sibyllini*, its Roman counterpart, which included predictions focusing on the future of the Italian peninsula, proper. The *Sibylline Oracles* are a collection of books and fragments mainly from Greek Antiquity. The Oracles contain a number of prophecies which have already materialized, as well as a famous acrostic poem dealing also with the earthly career of Lord Jesus Christ. The theory has been advanced that the poem was too exact and on target to be prophecy, hence, it must have been written ex post facto, when the events were already history. According to this theory, it was promoted as prophecy by

early Christians who felt the need to add legitimacy and weight to their new religion. The corollary from such a theorizing is that since 'apparently' the poem is history and not prophecy, and hence 'spurious' all Sibylline Oracles better be treated as spurious as well.

The next step of such 'rotten-apple' school of thought was a logical one: forget about the Sibylline Oracles, they are spurious anyway.

The Book of Revelation:
The same kind of 'superior' logic has plagued the study of the Book of Revelation. Just because one of the many possible versions in interpreting the number 666 (the number of the Beast, hence Antichrist and by extension, eschatology) has been *Nero Caesar*, the 'instant experts' among the Biblical Scholarship establishment again jumped to the conclusion that the Roman Emperor Nero (who was already dead when St. John wrote the Apocalypse) **is** the Antichrist of St. John's prophecies. Hence, why bother, since under the light of such remarkable logic the entire book looses its character as the Prophecy par excellence of the New Testament and becomes de facto demoted into one more 'metaphorical' and 'poetic' chronicling of the troubles of Christianity under the Roman Empire during the first centuries of our era!...

Nostradamus:
The study of the prophecies by Nostradamus, like so many other prophetic texts, exhibits wide variations in the quality of research and the efficacy of interpretation. Normally, it takes a long and painstaking effort to produce any thorough study, while presenting merely personal opinion and speculations requires only a fraction of the time necessary for the former case. Therefore, ceteris paribus, for every thorough analysis of prophetic texts in general, (and in our case, Nostradamus exegeses in particular), there correspond several volumes of the hastily prepared and speedily promoted competitors.

Unfortunately, the excellent books are usually sold alongside the not-so-excellent ones and to the unsuspecting reader they appear as close substitutes, out there on the shelf. Considering that the non-serious studies quantitatively overpower the books of scholarship on the subject, there emerges a crowing out effect, where the weighted average of the efficacy of all books read on the subject is pulled down. Many readers begin suspecting the Originator instead of the Interpreters. Overwhelmed by speculative pronouncements which invariably failed to materialize, the readers begin losing confidence on the value of Nostradamus himself, rather than that of his 'experts'.

The fact that even good commentators sometimes throw the towel and begin shifting the burden of proof on a dead man who cannot defend himself, does not improve an already difficult state of affairs. Suspicions have been aired that perhaps Nostradamus occasionally delighted in writing *retroactive prophecies*, and of having great lacunae in his knowledge of History and Geography. I hold the greatest respect and admiration for the genius of Nostradamus, and I am convinced that we are doing ourselves a great disservice by not dedicating to his study the best and the brightest that contemporary scholarship has to offer.

And yet another caveat
3) The 'it can never happen to me!' syndrome

'Veritas odium parit'. The Romans used to say, that truth gives birth to hatred. Given the nature of this study and the general tenor of its conclusions, it would be naive and unduly optimistic to expect full and unquestioned acceptance of its conclusions by each and every reader. No matter how ardently authors desire to arouse the interest of their readers to the urgency of their message, predicting dire events for the proximate future is a very risky business and has always been so. After all, the very existence of the term *'vaticide'* ought to temper the most sanguine hopes and desires of any analyst ambitious enough to propound interpretations of prophecies of doom. Vaticide is one who kills a prophet and one kills a prophet because one finds his pronouncements unpalatable. But killing the prophet has never changed the course of History.[2]

An object from outer space pre-destined by God, thousands of years ago, to effect a close encounter with our system will materialize all the same, whether we are willing to think about it and prepare for such an eventuality or not. Blackout by the media, as well, allegedly to avoid the 'premature

---

[2] Ancient civilizations devised remarkably intricate ways to force prophetic materialization on a less painful scale by replicating the conditions of the wording in a more or less controlled environment. They hoped to soften the blow of Heaven and somehow 'trick' destiny. History shows that such attempts were of questionable efficacy, however. (See the analysis of the Roman attempts to manipulation of prophecies by H. W. Parke [1988], among other sources).

and uncalled for spreading of panic among the people' has been tried before with disastrous consequences and it will surely be tried again.[3]

The reader who may be familiar with the controversy during much of the 20th century on the new theory of Plate Tectonics may remember that it was Alfred Wegener (a German scientist with broad interests besides his professional ones in astronomy, meteorology and geophysics) who propounded these views in the 1920s. Yet, the reaction of the professional milieu was cold, to put it charitably, among other reasons because, *if we are to believe Wegener's hypothesis, we must forget everything that has been learned in the past seventy years and start all over again.* This is exactly how R.T. Chamberlin summarized succinctly the dilemma of the status quo in front of a serious challenge during a meeting of the American Association of Petroleum Geologists in 1926.[4]

Alfred Wegener died years before his brilliant theories became corroborated with the assistance of other scientific discoveries and achieved wide acceptance. Our case right now, however, is quite different, because

---

[3] Let us review for a moment the chronicle of events around the explosion of Mt. Pelée in the town of St. Pierre on Martinique on May 8, 1902:

Prior to its explosion, the volcano of Mt Pelée had made its intentions clear: Three days earlier venomous snakes had abandoned their abode and came from the surrounding jungle to take refuge in the town. Also, boiling mud-slide had already poured down one side of the volcano destroying a sugar mill along its path. Although the inhabitants had enough evidence and proof that evacuating the town was the **only** advisable policy, the island's governor had worries that the upcoming elections would be interfered with if the electorate were to vote with their feet against the volcano rather than with their ballots. All that investment in the electoral campaign would be for nothing and a new electoral campaign with its concomitant expenses would have to be re-initiated... No, the city must not delay the elections just because the volcano may erupt at any time!...

The Governor posted troops to prevent people from leaving the city before the elections were over! Such interference with sober logic and solid factual evidence proved fatal for St. Pierre. Of the 30,000 inhabitants of the town only two survived, one of them thanks to the very thick walls of the local prison! One can only hope that the Mt. Pelée paradigm will not be lost on the readers of this study.

[4]Quoted by Hartmann and Miller, [1991, p. 128].

although the Father of Lights is in no hurry, our very chances of survival depend upon the speed with which we are capable of adapting ourselves to the drastically modified rules of the game. It is we, the present mortal generation, who cannot afford to drag our feet like the opponents of all the Wegeners in the History of the world with our tergiversations and arm twisting while considering the evidence at hand.

No matter how much emotional havoc and socio-economic dislocation the verdict of the prophets may imply for our near future, the imperative nature of its messages **must be allowed** to interfere with our future plans, projects, propositions and daily activities.

While oftentimes the Messengers of God fell victims to vaticidal actions and to the apathy and indifference of a generation of skeptics, the alert listeners of God's message, who chose to take corrective action in a timely fashion, managed to survive and tell us all about those who didn't. By the same token, the doctor who tells us how desperate our condition will be if we do not undergo a major surgery and drastically change our diet and modus vivendi right now, will probably save our life, regardless of the tears, the cost and the agony we will go through in the process of complying. We may hate the doctor temporarily, we may call him a quack who knows nothing and probably is sorely mistaken, and most probably we will take the highly recommended step of asking for a second expert opinion. But when the second expert opinion and the third one after that are also in the affirmative, then we must begin doing something about it with no undue delay.

So, before the reader becomes carried away by the cacophony of an entire army of special interest groups expressing strong antipathy for our subject matter, let him and her be reminded of the famous proposal of Themistocles to Eurybiades on the eve of the sea-battle of Salamis. *Beat me, if you feel you must, but listen first to what I have to say.* Πάταξον μέν, ἄκουσον δέ. I only ask that the reader will listen first, and beat me later (and in a public place and on a public forum, if he chooses), if such beating proves warranted by the circumstances.

ON RESEARCH METHODOLOGY PROPER

It is a tenet of those who believe in prophecy that every great event in history has been specifically and often amply foretold.[5]   No diligent student of History would disagree with the above proposition.   Within the Judeo-Christian historical experience there exists a large body of historical evidence on the advance knowledge afforded the Ancients on the outcome of major battles, changes of kingdoms, impeding plagues, and other such events by their Prophets, oracles, and seers. Roman Historians followed suite and increased the body of knowledge with a plethora of data extracted from their own historical experience. It is not at all fortuitous that the Roman counterpart of the Greek *Sibylline Oracles*, the *Libri Sibyllini*, were considered sacred, were kept under lock and key by especially selected priests and were consulted with due diligence when the state experienced a crisis.   The political leadership of the Roman Republic and later the Roman Empire did not find it beneath their dignity to institutionalize the study of prophetic intimations.

Many contemporaries of ours, otherwise well educated and highly trained professionally, have their Weltanschauung distorted by a lopsided and asymmetric situation:

a) on the one hand, the great advances of modern technology and their own scientific training that makes them capable of appreciating those advances and their applicability in everyday life for problem solving; and

b) on the other hand, the neglect by our educational system of anything that would constitute a solid study of History in general and Ancient History in particular. Religious education is absent in the majority of our schools for several reasons whose legitimacy will not be debated here. However, such absence further aggravates the problem we are facing as a culture. Having disassociated the instruction of Theology from the historical study of the Human Experience as currently taught in our schools, the multiple links connecting human activities with Divine intervention since the dawn of civilization, remain unidentified and unappreciated.[6]

Consequently, such scientists with asymmetric training become biased in

---

[5] Henry James Forman, [1936, p. 129].

[6] In Latin religio-ionis signifies a bond, a tying of humanity with God. Our modern cultural Philistines have forgotten even the etymology of the word they enjoy ridiculing.

favor of what they know, at the expense of what they failed to learn. With such a frame of mind, they end up occasionally ridiculing the Greeks and the Romans for their naïveté in attaching any political significance to the oracles. According to them, the Greeks ought to have known better than cross on foot through the inhospitable mountains to Delphi for the sole purpose of consulting the oracles. Half-baked historical instruction, furthermore, already convinced them that the oracles were either a hoax concocted by the priests at the expense of gullible pilgrims or at best ambiguous, ambivalent or merely pulling the leg of the persons seeking consultation...

Let us consider for a moment the following counter-arguments:

a) if those people were so naïve to believe in the Delphic Oracles, they would also act in an analogous manner in the other manifestations of their being. History proves otherwise.

b) Since the Greeks were meticulous with their History reporting, today we have ample evidence of the validity of the oracles **when interpreted properly**. An example may suffice to prove this point: when the Delphi Oracle was asked by the Athenians how to prepare against the Persian invasion, the Priestess of Apollo replied: '*The wooden wall will not be taken*'. Those who interpreted the oracle to mean literally a wooden wall, barricaded themselves behind walls of planks upon the Acropolis of Athens where eventually they were burned alive by the invading Persian armies.

Themistocles, on the other hand, read a different message in the same text: the wooden wall signified the construction of a fleet, which would enable the numerically inferior Greeks to fight wars in those fields of battle where they had a natural and a competitive advantage.

If this detail (reported in Book Eight of Herodotus's *Histories)* is of any vital importance for us today, the moral of the story is obvious enough: *a prophecy's efficacy depends on the ability of the men interpreting it, plus their willingness and preparedness to speedily implement its instructions*. Themistocles was not only sharp in mind and knowledgeable in the arts of naval warfare, he was also willing to assume a huge personal risk in order to turn the prophecy to the advantage of the Greeks: by a ruse he convinced the Persians that if they expedited their attack at the place and time that Themistocles knew was most advantageous for the Greeks, the Persians would win the battle...

The moral of the story is that 1) we need to understand a prophecy correctly; 2) we need to implement it properly, and 3) there usually is no time to waste.

Corollary? The gift from the Father of Lights will be manna from Heaven in the right hands at the right time. Otherwise, it will serve no useful purpose. It is the relative scarcity of interpreters of the caliber of a Themistocles that has turned so many intelligent, well-educated persons of our generation away from the manna from Heaven.

c)   To conclude our plea on behalf of Delphi, suffice it to say, that it persevered till the establishment of Christianity in Greece.[7] But by then, it had already served its purpose. Whether it was an Angel, a holy soul, God Himself intimating the information to the Priestess in Delphi we may never know. In the end, when the heathens needed Pythia no longer, ancient temples were converted into Christian Churches and the oracles became silent. Apollo was superseded by Lord Jesus Christ, and the Holy Spirit found new avenues to reach the Elect in the centuries that followed.[8]

The Hebrews did not need to come to Delphi like so many other peoples of the Mediterranean only because they already had a superior personal

---

[7] One must give the Delphi Oracle its dues, especially since it volunteered the prophecy **predicting its own demise at some time in the future!** Who can expect anything more from an Oracle?

[8] In summary, we tend to underestimate the wisdom and the sagacity of the ancients, only to our own risk. As History testifies, the Oracles (especially of Greek antiquity) were not specializing in predictions of disaster or the outcome of military conflicts, only, but covered most any facet of human life and vital concern. For instance, the specific advice given to the Greeks going abroad in order to establish new colonies, as to the relative merits of the various competing prospects. It was a standard practice for the Greeks to consult the God before founding their new cities. Therefore, Apollo was officially venerated as the 'Founder' by most Greeks, especially those located in Southern Italy and Sicily (Magna Grecia).

relationship with God. They did not need the *Libri Sibyllini* of the Romans, either, because their had their own books of prophets. On the other hand, since God cared about the Romans too, the *Libri Sibyllini* were fulfilling the role of advance warning and premonition for the edification and the protection of the Elect of the Italian peninsula during its pagan ages.

If we are to fully appreciate what the Sibyls predict for us in the years to come, we must first shed our misguided and un-researched views concerning the importance and prestige enjoyed by prophecies in the pagan world. And keeping in mind that the *Sibylline Oracles* are of particular importance for our present study, we must not handle them with the prejudiced and pre-conceived biases handed down to us through a paragraph or a footnote on the subject lost in a college textbook ambitiously covering the History of Western Civilization in one semester.

The truth is that the Ancients were by far more mature, discerning and intelligent than we, today, burdened by Historical ignorance, and inflated egocentrism, seem to recognize. They were astute observers of natural phenomena and had a higher religious sensitivity and awe towards the Divine. The very terminology of the term Sibyl betrays this innate willingness to heed God's precepts. The word comes from the Greek Σίβυλλα, Σιός Βουλή, God's counsel.

Those presumably 'superstitious peoples of antiquity' undertook the meticulous observation and study of phenomena so instrumental to the advancement of modern science. Were it not for the painstaking data collection and analysis by the Chinese, the Middle-Easterners, the Greeks and the Romans concerning, for instance, comets and the phenomena concomitant to their apparitions, cometary research would be different today and many of the recent breakthroughs would have to wait much longer. And if the Ancients persisted in associating comets with wars and catastrophes, they had first class reasons to do so. Up until this day, a persisting pattern of 'coincidence' between trouble and comets seems to obtain. Just because we have so far failed to propose a plausible theory that explains such coincidence does not give us the right to laugh at those who noticed it, recorded it, but failed to advance a theory that **we today** may consider plausible. Let us scrutinize the evidence further, recruiting the analytical tools from additional areas of learning before we label it as superstitious and unscientific and discard it out of hand.

A Short Summary of the Most Salient Characteristics of Prophecies

- Events are often, amply, foretold and as a group they are covered in considerable detail of all their vital specifics. The evidence is all around us, pervasive across prophets, across national borders, across languages, religions and denominations. This, ceteris paribus, alleviates the burden of interpretation, because it supplies us with more plentiful data to be used in the analysis. This wealth allows the researcher to considerably reduce bias and other errors in his work.

- We expect to identify a certain pattern in prophetic utterances promulgated over a long period of time. The most ancient ones are more general predictions with a small percentage of detailed information, and when this latter appears it usually is of a national character; e.g. Hebrew Prophets and the fortunes of Israel, Sibyls and the fortunes of Greece or Rome. This does not mean that Hebrew Prophets and Sibyls cannot be **all-encompassing** and **all-inclusive** in their prophecies as well. However, the Sibyl will refer to the 'Rulers of the West' ($\delta v \sigma \mu \hat{\omega} v$ $\tau \epsilon$ $\delta v v \acute{\alpha} \sigma \tau \alpha \iota$) to incorporate the armies of the USA ad Western Europe fighting in the Mediterranean during WWIII. The USA did not exist when the Sibyl made public her prophecy; although she knew what she was talking about, she had to use such language not to confuse her readers. However, in the last two hundred years prophecies speaking specifically about the USA can call it by name and do not have to use generic and periphrastic terms. Consequently, they can also give lots of details regarding the future of USA.

- As the geography of the world became better known, the deserts, the jungles and the mountains were mapped and the corners of the earth became inhabited, prophecy became more detailed and more specific as well. As human life became more advanced technologically and structurally more complicated, so also prophecies kept pace with the evolution. In other words, the language of the prophecies and their subjects evolved pari passu with humanity. They were meant by the Father of Lights to be used for the benefit of mankind. History provides many incentives for our being immensely grateful for that gift from Above.

- The more complicated a structure is, the more assiduous and painstaking labor it presupposes to be tackled properly. Prophecy interpretation is a most complicated human endeavor. Compartmentalized research, especially along narrowly defined religious denominational lines is not the correct approach to the problem. The narrow fiefs of this or the other church (proclaiming to hold the ultimate answers to all theological issues, including prophecy) are doomed to a crushing defeat, attested to by book after book of predictions which failed to materialize. Cross-fertilization across scientific disciplines is also a sine-qua-non, considering how involved and demanding and complicated the labor at hand truly is.[9]

■ According to the Epistle of James, (1:17), *every good and perfect gift comes from above, from the Father of Lights*. Prophecy is one of the greatest among those perfect gifts, because it can literally achieve the preservation of the life and the salvation of the soul. Hence, from an economical effectiveness point of view, few other topics of human endeavor and of scientific research can compete with prophetical investigation in terms of the expected average rates of return.[10]

■ Since Prophecy is a gift from Above, fully understanding its workings brings us closer to our Creator and strengthens our personal relationship with the Divine. A person familiar with the role of prophecy can never despair of the love of God for His children. For, it is a Loving God who offers such a gift for the **betterment, edification, premonition and protection** of the Elect. Who always gives repeatedly advance notice before the eventual punishment descends; Who can turn even the punishment into a path leading ultimately to salvation.

■ Further, as also Henry James Forman [1936] declared, *prophecy, a*

---

[9] The publishing industry has changed considerably in its driving motives since the era of Aldus Manutius, and the day has not yet dawned when consumer groups will rise to demand a recall by publishers and bookstores of highly deficient products proven 'dangerous to one's spiritual health'.

[10] Plato called it "the noblest of the arts", while Socrates called it θεία μανία (divine inspiration, enthusiasm, madness); yet, he explained, a madness which "was the special gift of heaven, and the source of the chiefest blessings among men".

persisting human inheritance, would seem to fare somewhat like the laws of nature, systematically neglected until the critical time, to mankind's incalculable cost. If the future, as some hold, is the only reality, it can hardly be other than our most prized possession. Hence, the incalculable importance of treating prophecies with great attention and deriving their immensely profitable lessons with a clear head, a dispassionate heart and with **no undue delay**. Treating prophecies lightly smacks of blasphemy to those who truly appreciate their origin and their intended purpose.

■ Prophecy is one of the manifested ways that God uses to write along with us the History of the world. Inability to accept this fact appears to be due primarily to ignorance.

THE PARADIGM OF SIMULTANEOUS EQUATIONS AND THE CLUSTERING OF PROPHETIC DATA ACCORDING TO THEIR MOST LOGICAL PATTERN

So far, I have been speaking of prophecies as being the major source of raw materials for the present study. I selected my samples from as broad a spectrum and as representative of various denominations as feasible. The reader will notice a complete absence of any references to works by Protestant interpreters of Prophecies. The reasons are the following:

Beginning with the Reformation, the Protestants began denouncing the legitimacy of any prophetic pronouncement promulgated after the Apostolic times. They reached the conclusion that the last true prophecy has been already included in the Book of Revelation (the last entry in the Canon), and anything subsequently written is suspicious, non-inspired, and ought to be discarded.

They ended up basically throwing out the baby along with the bath-water when it came to the issue of private revelations. By accepting as genuine only the basic texts of Old and New Testament and completely de-emphasizing the religious literature since the Book of the Revelation, they deprived their scholarship from a tremendous wealth of first class information. By contrast, the Orthodox and the Catholics have embraced the testimony of the last 2000 years as divinely inspired and their research and theology have been, consequently, enriched therefrom. By the same token, the Jews treasure their Tradition besides their official Torah, and their scholarship, augmented by thousands of years of additional contributions have enriched both their religion as well as ours.

The above analysis would suggest, prima facie, that every Scholar within Judeo-Christianity except the Protestants are routinely benefitting from each other's data banks. Unfortunately, this has not been the case during our generation. This most beneficial cross-fertilization that existed in previous ages has been lost in our times of ideological hardening and spiritual tribalism. I will not enter into the debate of whose fault this is. I trust that after the Eighth Ecumenical Council this issue will be resolved in an optimal way by persons more qualified than myself to debate it.

I only notice the problems that this tribalism has generated in the study of prophecies among our contemporaries: a very learned Greek Monk from Aghion Oros (Mount Athos), convinced that he needs to look no further, interpreted the Greek Prophets based on the Bible and the Byzantine and other Greek seers exclusively. His conclusions proved equally erroneous as those of a multi-published Baptist Scholar who relied only on the Old and New Testament (plus what he thought he knew about History, modern warfare and global politics). On the other hand, the Catholics, being convinced that they are the only true Church of Jesus Christ will have nothing to do with the rest of us. Consequently, their prophetic interpretation of **their own** Catholics prophets, proceeding in isolation from the treasures other denominations have to offer, has been impoverished data-wise, and further burdened by their inherent biases. Many contemporary authors, therefore, reached the **same erroneous** conclusions regarding the WWIII and events around it, as did a certain French author who, based on Nostradamus prophecies exclusively (and his own judgement) wrote a voluminous book to the effect that WWIII has already been fought.

The fact, however, that the Holy Spirit is so democratic in the dissemination of prophetic intelligence, should entice us to become more open-minded when processing information from God's chosen ones. The One Holy Catholic and Apostolic Church will be a choice for each one of us at the individual level. In other words, the re-unification of the Christian Churches begins at home. Considering that I emanate from a completely unrelated discipline, I am free to chose my technology without asking permissions for imprimaturs and nihil obstats. At least I do not have to carry over any ideological baggage or dogmatic impediments in my analysis. I bring along, instead, the tools of a rigorous mathematical analysis for my alphanumeric data. I also chose to impose upon my analysis a host of additional constraints which must be satisfied fully, before the system achieves its final solution-values and the research findings see the light of the day. On the other hand, I have relaxed numerous other constraints which would normally inhibit the research of many scholars endemic in the discipline: Not to offend the pet projects of your egregious colleagues by proving their theories untenable, not to disagree with the official stance of your religious superior even though you know he is wrong, not to challenge the shaky arguments which gave full professorships and tenures to those before you, not to make waves, in other words.[11]

Those trained in statistical data analysis are aware of the problems posed by 'outliers'. These extreme numerical values can be treated in different ways, depending on their nature: they can either be disposed of as not pertaining to the body of evidence currently under analysis, or if they are found to pertain to that body, they will be treated as suggestions that the theory currently accepted is an untenable one. The informational content of an outlier, in other words, depends on its origin. If the first case is true, the researcher can take care of the problem posed by such extraneous intruder by simply ignoring its testimony, as irrelevant.

In our specific case, outliers may be caused by a number of reason. Mistakes in transcribing a manuscript. Uncalled for 'editing' by a scribe or a commentator at an early age. Whatever their origin, however, the mere fact that from time to time something spurious and questionable may slip into the body of prophetic evidence does not poison the rest, nor does it constitute an adequate reason for discarding the whole. There are so many highly educated 'quality control engineers' in the discipline, capable of detecting the rotten apples and properly purifying the barrel.

Because the Protestants chose the risk-aversion path, being over-suspicious of potential manipulations by questionable clerics with a special agenda at

---

[11] Hans Georg Wunderlich, a German Orogenist who has advanced the most original and brilliant theory so far, on the link between the transmigration of Middle-Eastern culture into Europe and its Greek metamorphosis, in a book aptly entitled 'Whereto did the Bull carry Europa?' expressed his experience as an outsider breaking new paths in the following words: *Interdisciplinary research often has to contend with wholly unscientific resistance. When revered doctrines of a greatly gifted founder are threatened, defensiveness against the heretical outsider is especially fierce. Perhaps that is because the endangered beliefs cannot be defended with rational arguments.*

some point in the History of Christianity, they de facto reduced their total availability of data. The consequences of such over-reaction have been far-reaching, and can be amply noticed in Protestant prophetical interpretation efforts to this very day.

THE PARADIGM OF SIMULTANEOUS EQUATIONS[12]

Let me elaborate on this issue further with the help of the paradigm of simultaneous equation systems and the techniques available for solving them. Let us take such a system, and let us consider for a moment the simplest available form, that of linear equations. The equations represent information available to us and the unknowns represent questions being asked, whose specific answer will depend upon the nature, quality and availability of acceptable information (the rows of equations). Thus each row is a prophecy and every column is an event being prophesied. Some events may be connected to other events by geography and timing. If we have three equations (three lines of information) and two unknowns (two questions to answer with the help of the three lines of information at our disposal) we are in an advantageous position: we have plentiful information and can answer the questions unequivocally (namely, solve the equations correctly).

If, instead, we have three equations and three unknowns we have just enough information to correctly answer our questions, with no additional information to spare, and no margin for error left in the event of the introduction of speculations on our part. We must utilize fully all the information we have if we are going to satisfactorily answer our questions. This is true, however, only if the lines of information do not repeat the same basic message (linear dependence), but rather they provide three separate pieces of good, non-overlapping, information generated from independent sources, (namely, they are linearly independent). If two of the lines say basically the same thing, we cannot answer three distinct questions with the assistance of basically two lines of data only.

---

[12] I tried to simplify the description of this section for the benefit of the reader without mathematical training. I may have failed in my effort to substitute verbal analysis for simple algebra. Considering that there is no pop quiz waiting the unsuspecting reader at the end of the section, however, it may be worth the effort of persevering with my tortuous arguments for whatever benefit the un-mathematical reader may still derive therefrom. Otherwise, he may wish to skip the entire section.

If now we have three equations and ten unknowns we are in serious trouble: we must **arbitrarily** choose the answers to be given to the majority of the questions (a number $\geq$ 7) and let the total information generated in this manner determine the answer of the remaining questions, with the help of the three equations at our disposal. In that case, we have multiple solutions, and a very large number thereof, indeed. By arbitrarily changing our opinion on some of the values chosen for some of the variables, also the final answer for the remaining variables will necessarily change, each and every time. This can go on and on for a very long time; we obtain what in mathematics is called an infinity of solutions when we have too many questions to answer and too few pieces of information available to answer these questions with.

This is in a most simplified form the prevailing relationship between quantity and quality of available information for the answering of questions regarding things unknown. It appears that if we have to deal with three variables we may wish to have at least three (unrelated) equations to work with, preferably many more. To be certain for our results we would appreciate the availability of more factual information that is relevant to the problem at hand; the more, the better.

The paradigm of the simultaneous equations problem is a very relevant one, because it contains the essence of the problems involved in prophecy interpretation. To be certain that the interpretation of the prophecy is a correct one, my results **must be corroborated** by all other existing prophecies which were originally designed to deal with the **same** set of events, periods, nations and persons. In other words, I must operate under very strict constraints: I must satisfy not only the logic of the particular equation I work with, my solution to the variables of that equation must be exactly the same one that gives the same 'numerical value' to the same variables appearing in all the remaining equations of the system.

In other words, in prophecy interpretation we cannot afford to arbitrarily propose a given value and force the rest to comply with that one arbitrary value of the unknown variable, just because we have too few data available. What does this mean in the present context? The Protestant tradition has eliminated thousands of equations by sweeping clean the slate of prophetic texts generated world-wide within the Hebrew and Christian religions in the last 2000 years. So they are left with the testimony contained in the Bible only. Numerous and extremely valuable as those prophecies may be, they are not sufficient for **unequivocally** answering **all** fundamental questions pertaining to the future of nations and peoples, periods and dynasties, land masses and continents, the fates of men and races. We are only human, we have limited intellectual abilities and we need additional assistance in our search efforts. If we humbly accept the finite nature of our intellect, we may start looking around for additional props and auxiliary media to supplement it. If we feel we do not need anything more to assist us in our labors of prophecy interpretation we have already lost the battle, like those Athenians, who being ignorant of the fact that warships are also constructed with wood, spent their last penny and their last hour nailing planks on the Acropolis of Athens.

To return to the simultaneous equations paradigm, self-sufficiency with Old and New Testament only, (or to the body of evidence generated exclusively within the Orthodox or Catholic domain, for that matter) corresponds basically to trying to solve $n+m$ variables with less than m equations, considering that many prophecies are repeating the same things with different words and through different mouths; hence, the prophecies are not as many as they appear prima facie to be. They are linearly dependent, as the Mathematician would say. God being most generous with mankind, He solved the linear dependency problem for us by plentifully supplying additional information; however, those researchers who have been petrified in their ideological positions will have nothing of this, refuse to accept the additional information as legitimate and stubbornly discard all new pieces that were given to us in the course of the last 2000 years to lit our path as we grope through the darkness of our Future.

So, if I want to resolve optimally my problem I must ask for as much information as possible. Since many prophecies repeat basically the same thing, I welcome them with gratitude because they allow me to **double check** the correctness of my solutions, so far. (Linear dependence, in other words, once correctly identified as such, can prove immensely beneficial! If not identified as such, however, can lead to the wrong conclusions!). If the data from a set of prophecies corroborate my previous findings based on a different set of data, (a different set of rows of information, i.e., equations) so much the better! It means I am on the right track. On the other hand, these prophecies have a limited informational content and cannot answer all questions. Prophecies about the future of Israel may be completely mute about the future of the USA. Hence, I need more data to correctly predict the future of the USA as well, and the Old and New Testament may not suffice when it comes to the specific fortunes of a metropolitan area within a state within a country that is only ca. 200 years old. Hence the voracious need for more and more prophetic raw material.

The non-voracious researchers are apparently content with what they believe they command fully and satisfactorily, so far. But, when you deal with, say, 20 equations in 150 unknowns you get in the end an infinity of solutions that could satisfy your model and **yet disagree** with each other all the same. This happens because you must choose **arbitrarily a set of specific solution values** and force the remaining variables to assume their own solution values subject to the arbitrarily chosen set. So, what many authors have done, is to guess what the prophecy means, and having considered no available information from other sources that would have told them clearly they made an error, they go happily with the writing of their book and the publication of their results, misguide the public and disenchant their readers, who fail to realize that the problem lies with the interpreter and has nothing to do with the prophet or prophetess at all.

Employing the simultaneous equations logic on our prophecy analysis is a most beneficial technique for achieving consistency and plausibility and relevance. It is a form of imposed self-discipline, which (like all forms of self-discipline) may be onerous while it is exercised, yet, it can afford us great rewards in the long run. We are basically trying to fit thousands of pieces in a huge puzzle, where the subset of pieces not only generate a most plausible image, but also they must be harmoniously aggregated to their immediate surroundings and also to the entire design of the puzzle, as well.

Suppose, for instance that a number of pieces in this huge puzzle, properly collated, generate the image of a fresh red rose. A rose could emerge out of the earth, a vase, or be a part of a bouquet. It can also appear on a lapel, behind a dancing Gypsy's ear, as a decor on fabric or wood or gold, or whatever. There is a limitless number of ways a rose would look plausible in a given environment. It would not look plausible emanating from a spewing volcano, however, or adorning the tail of a shark. If such be the case, we were mistaken to take the subset of items constituting a rose and putting them on the fish, or in the volcano. They must be removed and placed elsewhere in the pattern.

It is my humble personal opinion that if any author, despite such impediments imposed upon his labor, manages to strike upon the right answer when attempting the interpretation of a given prophetic text, he must be either extremely lucky, or an unqualified giant of the human spirit. To hit upon the **true** persons and facts and geographical location and year of the prophecy's materialization by sheer good luck, while arbitrarily selecting their joint solutions out of thousands if not millions of competing alternatives, is a mathematical probability whose numerical calculation would tax the best computer algorithm available today.[13]

Consequently, since extreme luck is much more rare than genius, it appears that most of the useful research on the subject of prophecy interpretation will still emanate, (at least as far as the Western literature is concerned), from the intellectual quarters of the Hebrews, the Orthodox, and the Catholics, for the simple reason that their theology affords them the luxury of much richer data bases, **provided they are willing to cooperate with each other, share data bases and openly debate all their differences**.

I trust the above analogy helps explain some of the failures in producing desirable results when trying to predict the future of the world for two thousand years down the line, based on the Book of Daniel and the Book of Revelation, primarily. The analogy is for demonstration purposes only and must be interpreted for what it is: a mere pedagogical tool, a simplified model of reality, and hence an approximation of reality. But I hope it helped vindicate Prophecy in the eyes of those disillusioned and cooled-off readers of so many prophecy-interpretations which failed to materialize. It was not the prophecy that failed them, but rather the technology adopted by the interpreters whose volumes they finished reading.

A corollary of our previous mathematical digression is that there is no such thing as *embarrassment of riches* when dealing with prophetic data. The incorporation of several individual prophecies relating to the same event only serves to clarify its details and underline its significance. The paradigm of the simultaneous equations system addresses only a few of the major difficulties encountered by prophecy analysts. I said nothing yet about the other types of constraints that must also be satisfied, and which may be numerous, indeed:

---

[13] This in no way implies that the Protestant scholars cannot make brilliant contributions in general Theology and Exegesis. I only say that in the domain of Prophecy Interpretation they operate under very onerous self-imposed impediments. What they try to achieve is mathematically impossible, so to say. The probability of their succeeding with the tools of their analysis is for all practical purposes equal to zero.

Historical evidence must not be manipulated to fit a particular solution. (A number of the so called Nostradamus scholars are deficient in their Historical background and when they take upon themselves the formidable task to interpret the **entirety of Nostradamus's prophecies** they bite off more than they can chew. Consequently, in order to fit their pre-conceived ideas of what Nostradamus meant they even insert in his texts words he never intended to use!... At other times they accuse **him** of being historically ignorant because their conclusions do not make much sense. The same observations apply to self-proclaimed Biblical scholars who feed the popular presses with their learned volumes (routinely without bibliographical notes and sources of references). Knowledge of History, therefore, is a sine-qua-non for effectiveness in the task of prophecy interpretation. The benefits derived from such an expertise are manifold and can be grouped as follows:

a)   As intimated above, it sharpens our sensitivity in observing the world around us and appreciating the incalculable contributions of prophetic premonition for the affairs of Mankind; worded differently, History increases our appreciation of the power of Prophecy, by supplying us with a wealth of factual information on the ways it has proved so tremendously efficacious in the past;

b)   Since many a single text of prophecy may cover a long period in time, a good knowledge of History allows us to determine which portion of the text has already materialized and which still lies ahead. So, our overall task becomes better delineated, more limited in scope, more narrowly defined and, consequently, of more manageable proportions. The value of reducing the complexity of any problem can never be underestimated.

As a corollary, I venture to propose that only those cultures exhibiting a deep appreciation for the value of a solid historical education, properly implemented in their school curricula, can hope to generate effective analysts and researchers of Biblical studies and prophetic analysis in particular. In the course of my study on comets and asteroids I had ample opportunity to realize how casual an approach the average cometary astronomer has taken towards the study of History.[14] The unhappy result of such a cavalier approach towards the Human Experience is that our generation discards as 'superstitions and gullibility' the respect of the metaphysical dimensions of our physical universe, so evident in cultures of the past. Such persons, furthermore, look suspiciously upon modern analysts who wish to defend those ancient positions. Such supercilious attitude is fully unwarranted and impoverishes scientific research, instead.

Another imposed constraint is that the message of the prophecy must make sense in today's world, if its message is for the current generation.

One's conclusions must not clash with **scientific evidence**. Consequently, whatever, for instance, Nostradamus proposes that will happen when such and such geological upheaval takes place, must not be contradicted by the scientific evidence of plate tectonics and volcanic eruptions, for instance. In the event it does, we should not blame Nostradamus but our own ignorance and failure in decoding him properly.

What I am basically saying is that the genuine prophecy interpreter knows his limitations, does not attack the prophet or the prophecy for their alleged deficiencies, and abstains from judgement when faced with wording too recalcitrant to his analytical tools. On the other hand, since nobody is perfect, in the event a superior prophecy contains something proven untenable (perhaps for reason completely independent from the prophecy, such as a mistake in copying a manuscript), this 'outlier' can be identified and corrected in the light of information from a plethora of other sources which can help us identify the outlier, evaluate it for what it is and eliminate it from the rest of the prophet's data.

It is better to try only 10% of Nostradamus's quatrains and do a thorough study, rather than undertake the formidable task of 'interpreting' them all in their entirety, without the benefit of checks and balances from the outside.

---

[14] In one of the appendices we submit some evidence of a few indicative faux-pas perpetrated by otherwise acclaimed professionals, merely for purposes of illustration.

Ditto, for all other prophecies and prophets.[15] Optimizing under constraints is the essence of our existence, and this truth should have never been lost on prophecy interpreters, either.

Last and not least, there are many **logical constraints** that must be obeyed. Consequently, 'retroactive prophecy' is a contradiction in terms, and Nostradamus cannot be considered as an evil genius when his whole life and his entire prophetic testament demonstrate the opposite. A house divided against itself cannot stand, as our Lord Jesus Christ forewarned us, when He too was accused of driving out the demons by the power of Beelzebub. Satan wants the destruction of the human race, the prophets fervently desire to preserve it. The potential benefit of Nostradamus's work for mankind is incredibly rich and lamentably underestimated to this day by the general public. Ditto, for all other genuine prophecies.

THE MAJOR SOURCES OF DATA USED IN THIS STUDY

■ The Hebrew Prophets of the Old Testament are invaluable for our analysis because, despite their ethnic focus they give us prophecies spanning millennia, and hence reaching to our present and our future. Furthermore, History suggests that the fates of Israel and Christianity are interconnected *in saecula saeculorum*, and the military and other fortunes of Christians and Jews are intertwined. Knowing what will happen to Israel is also of direct relevance to us since similar things, if not the identical ones, will happen to us also at the same time.

■ The Greek Sibylline Oracles are an extremely valuable source from antiquity. Again, although they exhibit a certain ethnic focus, with mainland Greece, Magna Grecia, Anatolia and the Greek Colonies in Asia Minor and around the Black Sea, the Sibyls can be also comprehensive in their coverage. As we shall see later, they have made several statements of global import and uttered predictions that are all-inclusive and all-encompassing.

---

[15] It is precisely situations such as these that underline the need for a plentiful overall supply of data. An avid amasser of information has prophecies to spare when confronted with occasional impasses. The Father of Lights has foreseen this, and has compensated richly for our deficiencies, through a plenitude of data, which keep on coming to this very day.

36

The Prophecies included in the New Testament are a most valuable source; especially,

-    the Synoptic Apocalypse,
-    the Book of Revelation, and
-    certain specific references contained in the Epistles.

To the above are added the following groups:

-    hundreds of prophecies from the lands of the Catholic West;
-    hundreds of prophecies from the lands of the Orthodox East (particularly the Byzantine era and subsequently);
-    Nostradamus;
-    a collection of prophecies written in Old French and Old Italian existing in various libraries and collated under the title *Les Prophecies de Merlin*. These chronologically precede Nostradamus.[16]

-    The messages through the many apparitions of the Most Holy Virgin Mary Theotokos, who, since 1846 A.D. has been tirelessly forewarning us regarding the perilous times ahead. The Most Holy Virgin has been proposing the detailed steps that need to be taken towards safety and salvation.

The above explicitly mentioned groups are containing rich information across geographical expanses and time periods. (In terms of time-series and cross-sectional analysis, these data are the best sources of our overall

---

[16] It must be stressed at the very start that *Les Prophecies de Merlin*, which will be repeatedly referred to in our study have **nothing** to do with a book of a similar title by Geoffrey of Monmouth. Our *Les Prophecies ...* is a collection of manuscripts from many libraries of Europe, organized and collated by Dr. Lucy Allen Paton. They contain both romantic historical material around King Arthur but also many prophecies unrelated to him and spanning many centuries and many lands. *Les Prophecies...* tend to be verbose, because they are written in the style of an ongoing conversation between the prophet and his scribes. The predictions are delivered in installments, so to say, in the course of this question-answer format. In order to save space and time we shall present the gist of the main message of each prophecy, while eliminating the verbosity that would obtain by the repetition ad infinitum of some basic ever-recurring types of questions and verbal mannerisms.

available information). To these major groups we shall also add many individual prophetic pronouncements and private revelations, which refer to a specific country and a narrowly defined time frame. Such information will allow us to supplement that derived from the larger groups, complete the picture presented by the former, and in this fashion end up by having constructed a stronger total edifice.

REVIEW OF THE MOST SALIENT POINTS

a)   every great event in history has been specifically and often amply foretold. This would suggest that humanity must be for ever on the lookout for prophecy pronouncements that would apply to its own future. This would also suggest that prophetic interpretation ought to be an ongoing quest for mankind, in a way analogous for the search of identifying new minerals, new raw materials and new resources for our livelihood.

b)   a prophecy's efficacy depends on the quality of analysis and judgement invested in its interpretation. Having understood its message correctly is not enough; we must act upon it and implement it properly and without delay.

c)   A thorough historical education is a sine qua non for efficacy in prophecy interpretation. We 'must live in the past' if we are going to have any luck with understanding the present and taking advantage of our knowledge of the future.

d)   We can never have too much information when engaging in the task of prophecy interpretation. For this reason, our loving and caring Father in Heaven has been showering us with data through the ages.

CHAPTER THREE

A BRIEF INTRODUCTION
ON THE PHYSICS OF COMETS

*The astronomer's problem is not a lack of information
but an embarrassing excess of it. His is often a problem of dis-entanglement rather than one of synthesis.*
Sir Fred Hoyle.

<u>Introduction</u>
Throughout History, cultures differentiated by geography, language, religion
and achieved degree of technical sophistication reached a consensus on
their assessment of comets as harbingers of ill tidings. Although a few
comets were considered benevolent, in their majority they were understood
as unequivocal portents of evil. We are for ever in the debt of the
meticulous observations of the Chinese whose reports have expanded our
knowledge back to the 11th century B.C., at least. The civilizations of the
Middle East, capitalizing on their natural advantage of clear nocturnal skies,
contributed further to astronomy and the behavioral patterns of comets
visible to the naked eye, in particular. Greeks and Romans added further
to the body of evidence over the centuries.

<u>The Origin of Comets</u>
A more thorough study on the material composition of comets and other
aspects of their behavior had to wait the technologies of the last few
centuries, and especially the breakthroughs of our age. Spectral analysis,
for one, enabled modern scientists to identify the nature of the various
chemical elements present in a comet, while advanced telescopes and
speedy computers have tremendously increased the vision-range of the
'naked-eye'. Consequently, professional but also amateur astronomers have
increased the numbers of comets already known to man.

The most relevant and indispensable for our study information about comets
is summarized below:

We now believe that comets are composed of the primordial material out of
which our solar system has evolved. The comets have been building blocks

of our solar system that were not utilized ultimately for its construction. They did not manage to graduate into a planet or a sun, and were left like the bricks at a construction site after the building was finished. They have been caught in diverse individual motions by the universal gravitational forces. We believe that their bulk inhabits the edge of our solar system beyond our remotest planet in what is known as the 'Oort Cloud' (named after Astronomer Jan Oort). The Oort Cloud constitutes a sphere enveloping our world, not a disc. As a result, comets can be thrust against the inner solar system from every conceivable point from that huge sphere, dramatically increasing the total potential number of such visitors.

As the entire solar system moves along with the rest of our Milky Way - Galaxy through space, occasional gravitational forces from beyond attract a number of those invisible comets and thrust them towards the sun. For all practical purposes, a major force invisible to us from down here, every so often thrusts into the inner solar system a subset of those comets from the rich inventory of comets in the Oort Cloud.

We may visualize the comets being thrust into our world as something similar to the legendary thunderbolts of Zeus, hurled against an impious humanity in a moment of righteous indignation.[1] Not all such Jovian thunderbolts are invariably lethal and catastrophic, however, and many of the periodic comets have rather innocuous trajectories and never come so close to the earth to give rise to panic and terror; rather, they frequently approach us from a safe distance and from an angle favorable to prolonged observation. We can enjoy their beautiful tails stretching in the nocturnal heavens and their spectacular and elegant motions against the sky.

So, usually the comets presage dire events upon the planet, but do not always cause those events themselves. For the catastrophes that are endogenous to our tellurian system (or to the deficiencies of human nature, such as wars) the comets may act only as forewarning agents. On the other hand, a Jovian thunderbolt, proper, is a comet that strikes the earth, or approaches so very close as to set the stage for a number of geological upheavals, triggered by its gravitational pull.

---

[1] The predilection of thunderbolts from above as a way of retribution for the sins of the world may be nothing more than the collective memory of primordial catastrophes of that nature which persisted through the ravages of the Flood and became finally incorporated into the Olympian Mythology.

As we saw earlier, the theory of smooth, extremely slow, relatively safe, Evolutionism, so central to the theories of Charles Darwin, has been superseded by a theory of Catastrophism. Accordingly, from time to time in the past 4.5 billion years of the earth's planetary career abrupt and drastic changes have been registered by the geology of our planet. As a result, the Earth received its atmosphere possibly from water imbedded in comets (besides that spewed out via volcanism); on the other hand, a number of species became extinct, the weather patterns changed, the axis of rotation of the earth may have shifted several times, and rare minerals (such as iridium) have been deposited on our rocks' strata compliments of interstellar visitors such as asteroids, meteorites and comets.

Furthermore, comets are believed to be a major cause of such impacts while asteroids and meteorites play a relatively minor role, primarily because they are smaller objects travelling at different speeds. The fact that 3/4 of the surface of the planet are covered by oceans inhibits the search of many such impacts, which must have occurred, ceteris paribus, much more frequently on the oceans.

A Brief Digression for Additional Definitions and Clarifications

-       A comet is a sort of planet revolving in very eccentric orbits around the sun. By contrast, the planets of our solar system have elliptic orbits that approach a circle.

-       An asteroid (a.k.a. a minor planet) is either rocky or metallic. It can exhibit very irregular shapes, has no atmosphere and is found in greater numbers revolving in the region between Mars and Jupiter. It appears that the theory that they are the debris of a primordial planet which was broken under the gravitational pull of its neighbors is not supported by scientific evidence currently available.

-       When solid particles from comets or asteroids collide with the atmosphere of the Earth, they burn up and the visual effect is called a *meteor* (a.k.a. a *shooting star*). If such particles manage to reach the surface of the planet before they have burned up completely, they effect a collision with results of varying importance. If they achieve a collision they have graduated into *meteorites*. Most fall in the depth of the oceans (considering the odds). Upon solid ground they can create a crater at the point of impact, and leave behind some of their matter, such as iron.

- Meteorites are believed to result from ancient collisions of asteroids, while the majority of meteors come from comets, (comet dust). The brightest meteors are called *bolides*.

- Astronomers believe that in a more remote antiquity, there has been a higher frequency of impacts with minor bodies from space, notably meteorites large enough and sturdy enough to survive the friction of the earth's atmosphere and still have some of their material left over after the impact. It may also be true that the very first supply of commercial iron ore to our ancestors came through the iron in meteorites, much before they had mastered the technology of smelting iron directly from ferrous-bearing ore. Consequently, in the Greek language the word for iron has always been '*sidiros*' *σίδηρος*. In Latin, *sidus-sideris* signifies a constellation but also a single star, whence terms such as 'sidereal time' have originated. Furthermore, '*sideratio-tionis*' was a blight upon plants supposed to have been produced by the influence of the stars.

The word 'disaster', is a composite of 'dis' and 'aster', namely the workings of an evil star. This would further suggest a very old acquaintance of mankind with impacts from space and their consequences for human life, such as the debris that can reach the ground and cause trouble of some sort. What the present generation discards as semi-savagery and superstition on the part of our forefathers may have been merely a superior understanding that gradually became lost to the world and only vestiges survived here and there in fragments of manuscripts, semi-ruined papyri, linguistic curiosa, legends and myths, the thunderbolts of Jupiter and the fall of Phaethon.

On Cometary behavioral patterns

Once thrust out of the Oort Cloud towards our inner solar system, a periodic comet may exhibit delays or accelerations in its trajectory towards the sun. If during a particular journey it passes closer than usually by our huge gas planets, notably Jupiter, the gravitational attraction exerted by that planet will interfere with the original trajectory. Not all comets are periodic, however, and even those which are may have such long periods that historical observations have failed to record them. Since nobody was collecting data on cometary periods 100,000 years ago, and if they did the evidence was lost during one of the many catastrophic upheavals on the planet, we do not know as much as we would like about comets. Cometary Astronomers are, therefore, apprehensive due to their relatively limited ability to predict in a timely manner a dangerous cometary approach.

First of all, a major and very large comet, either periodic (but with a very long and yet untraced period), or non-periodic, may enter our solar system at any time. It must approach sufficiently close to the sun before its gases and dust particles begin to sublimate and the comet become visible from the observatories of the Earth, (or with any luck, also with the naked eye).[2] It may approach from an angle that is not particularly favorable to observation. This means that it will come dangerously close before the first dependable observation occurs in the countries that have Astronomers trained for the job.

Depending on size, nucleus composition and other characteristics, its acceleration as it approaches the sun increases dramatically. For all practical purposes, by the time our astronomers find it, measure its trajectory, and predict its closest approach to the earth it may be very late for any diverting action to be effectively planned and executed, especially in an era of great social and military upheavals down here. A type of diverting action, already proposed by astronomers, would be to launch a missile (or a number of missiles) ahead of time, and while the comet is still at a safe distance from us, to impact it and make it change its path. 'Persuading' the comet to reconsider its plans must happen in distances which would protect us from the radioactive fallout of the missiles' impact and/or the consequences of a miss. If the approach of the comet occurs in mid-WWIII, for instance, there will be little willingness for a concerted timely effort to launch such a missile. So, even if the technology is available the political will necessary to carry the plan out may be lacking.[3]

---

[2] In a vacuum, ices do not melt to create a liquid. They evaporate at the surface of the snowball. This is essentially the 'sublimation' process. The sunlight begins vaporizing the ice as the comet approaches the sun, and it is precisely this 'sublimation' which generates the spectacular visual effects associated with comets.

[3] According to Dr. Whipple "a wild comet (rather than a tame one or an asteroid with known parameters) could, however, upset our best-laid plans. We might have difficulty in obtaining sufficient advance warning. (...) Protection of the Earth from undesirable impacting bodies is not just a science fiction project for some improbable future. (...) We could choose to protect ourselves from asteroids and comets rather than from each other." [1985, p. 249].

The above scenario, admittedly very bleak and pessimistic, is not the kind of academic exercise astronomers like to indulge in. It is a very real and ominous possibility. The chasm which separates the level of knowledge on comets and their risks and opportunities among the professional astronomers on the one hand, and the ignorance on this subject plaguing the average layman on the other, is a dangerous one.

Among the many professionals who already sounded the bell of alarm (and have produced books that greatly benefit laypersons in understanding these issues), have been Drs. Clark Chapman and David Morrison. Others would include John Keith Davis [1986], Carl Sagan and Ann Druyan [1985], Fred L. Whipple [1985] and Hartmann & Miller [1991]. (A professional Astronomer would be able to expand this list). More recent voices of concern continue pouring in from academic and other presses but also from a few periodical publications. The following reports are cases in point:

a)   March 23, 1989: a comet whose nucleus resembled a tuberous root, about 800 meters long, and travelling at 70,000 km. per hour approached the Earth. (By comparison, the Earth travels around the Sun at over 14 km. per second. Objects in cometary-type orbits, at the moment of collision with the Earth could hit us head-on at speeds higher than 70 km per second). Had the comet been delayed somewhere along its way for a mere couple of hours, the earth would have collided with it. According to Don Yeomans, one of the foremost cometary experts of our times, such a collision would have sufficed to generate hundred-meter-high tidal waves, and among other catastrophes, usher in a new ice-age. To put it charitably, this was quite a close call. However, only a few references that even mentioned this event were found in the popular presses.

b)   February 1, 1994: A meteorite weighing 1,000 tons and travelling at 72,000 km. per hour fell in the Pacific Ocean at the vicinity of the Tokelau Islands, after having been broken into pieces during the latter part of its trip through the atmosphere. Luckily, the area of impact was the open ocean. The only eye-witnesses were fishermen at a safe distance, plus U.S. spy satellites. It appears that the spy satellites are the regular and most dependable observers and reporters of such phenomena, which seem to be rather frequent: Between 1975 and 1992 the satellites have registered about 136 meteorite-explosions in the Earth's atmosphere. Their behavior is very similar to that of atomic weapons' explosions and the military detection equipment currently in use has a hard time differentiating between the two. The inability of our current military technology to safely identify the source of such explosions in a timely manner may have a lot to do with the fact that such events (on the average 8 per year) do not get the broad publicity they deserve.

More on The Heads and Tails of Comets

Assisted by the marvels of modern technology, we now know quite a lot about the physics of comets, (although scientists caution that much remains to be learned concerning comets and asteroids). For instance, astronomers believe that the total repository of comets in the Oort Cloud contains 10^{12} comets. Only a most insignificant portion thereof enters our solar system. It has also been calculated that ca. 500-800 short-period comets cross the Earth's orbit, yet only 20 are known and have been methodically studied, so far. The short-period comets can afford to take trips around the sun more frequently. Considering that they move along the ecliptic plane (i.e., the same imaginary plane of our revolution around the sun) the probability of their eventually impacting the Earth increases.

While asteroids are made of rock and iron, comets are primarily 'dirty snowballs'.[3] The European Space Agency's Giotto spaceprobe, which was launched for a rendez-vous with Halley's comet in 1986, sent back images of a soot-black peanut-shaped nucleus about the size of Manhattan Island. When the comet approaches the sun, the sunlight presses away towards the opposite direction the outgoing material from the head of the comet; the gases and particles become shiny as they become chemically active and are pushed backward by solar wind action. Then, they generate a spectacle analogous to the waters from a fountain that are pushed back by the law of gravitation in an elegant curved motion. It is at this stage that the comet begins exhibiting its spectacular tail. A comet *nucleus* (corresponds to the brain and the skull of a head); a *coma* is the hair that covers the head at sun's approach and so is the *tail*, which is basically the visual result of a hair that grows longer under the pressure of the solar wind.

Both gases and dust particles imbedded in the nucleus begin to warm up

---

[3] Fred L. Whipple, considered the Dean of Cometary Astronomers, was the first to establish the composition of cometary nuclei as a great mass of ices which are embedded with dust or meteoric particles.

and emit colors which will differ according to chemical origin (gases generate different colors from dust particles). The solar wind will push the coma of the approaching comet away from the nucleus, and the coma begins to expand to generate also the tail. In the dark expanses of the cosmos, comets are deprived of comas and tails. They essentially enter a 'hibernation' stage when they return to the Oort cloud. During repeated entries to the solar system, comets gradually lose a portion of their volatile material. After a number of trips they lose enough to become unspectacular and faint.[4]

During the sublimation process (while the chemical elements of the comet begin to evaporate under the pressure and heat from the sun) a certain amount of cometary material is lost into the space. While the earth, in its revolution around the sun, enters a region of the cosmos where a comet left behind through sublimation its cometary debris some time ago, these particles when they come in contact with the Earth's atmosphere begin to activate and we get the regular meteorite showers, some of which occur yearly and others in longer periods of time. (The phenomenon of *Aurora Borealis* is also partially attributed to the solar wind's activating material left behind by a comet in the past).

Comets possess an intriguing variety of shapes and nucleus characteristics. Many comets come with almost round heads (and by extension, comas). The very term *comet* suggests in the Greek the long, beautiful hair, usually associated with womanhood. Many cometary comas are asymmetric and hence associated with a wide variety of tails. A comet that approaches sufficiently the earth to afford us good observation, could exhibit a 'head' 6 times the size of a full moon. The IRAS-Araki-Alcock, 1983 VII comet came close enough to afford us such comparisons.

The tails of the comets fall into three categories. Type I, whose tails are nearly straight, and types II and III, which are hard to tell apart at times. The Type I class of cometary tails comprises most of the spectacular comets.

----

[4] Periodic comets may be compared to vain ladies who are solicitously and regularly visiting the fountain of the elixir of youth (inner solar system) to become rejuvenated again. These regular visits are not free however, what they achieve in good looks they have to pay with reduced overall longevity. They end up unattractive and unspectacular after a few thousand trips to their 'plastic surgeon'. Old age and ultimate death are inexorable facts of life even for comets.

Since in the emptiness of space there exist no forces counteracting the impact of the solar wind on the cometary coma, the tail generated by the wind's action can extend for huge distances into space. In certain instances, tails extended from the horizon to the zenith. The comets whose trajectories bring them very close to the sun are called *sun-grazers*. These can exhibit the most spectacular fountain-type phenomena under the pressure of the solar wind. In a certain case, the coma produced a tail 300 million km. long.

The gases embedded in the nucleus will normally generate a bluish color while sublimating, the dust particles, a yellow shade. The tail may change shape, become separated, break into a number of slimmer tails, under the pressure of the solar wind. Thanks to the meticulous Chinese and other ancient cultures we now know how comets looked like to the naked eye upon the skies of antiquity, untouched by industrial pollution and free from the visual impediments of city lights and other such modern constraints. The following list of observed comets is merely indicative:

- bluish-white broom star comet;
- white broom star comet;
- bushy star comet;
- tailed star comet;
- banner-like comet;
- white vapor;
- loose cotton;
- red broom star comet with pointed rays;
- a celestial magnolia-tree-type comet;
- a comet shaped like a white rainbow;
- lance star;
- sword star;
- yellow-white broom star;
- a comet the size of a peach;
- a comet the size of a large ray;
- etc. etc. etc.

Spinning Comets

We can visualize the nucleus of the comet as either a spherical or as an asymmetrical non-spherical body, moving through space. It may rotate around an axis by analogy to the earth's rotation, or it may not. In the former case, we deal with a *spinning comet*, whose movement will depend

47

on the angle at which its axis of rotation may be tilted vis-à-vis the ecliptic. The average 'cometary day' has been measured to be fifteen hours long. The longest 'cometary day' measured thus far, covers the temporal length of five terrestrial days.

Spinning comets could be of particular interest to us because we have reasons to believe that in the skies of our future signs and wonders will appear which may have a natural cause and be produced by the visual effects of a specific cosmic source. It may be that the specific source will remain a great mystery to us. However, it may also be that the 'marvelous and stupendous' signs in the sky may be produced by an object with a spinning nucleus, of a special shape of that nucleus, of a certain chemical composition and the like. In the chapter entitled 'Sings of the End(s)' we will revisit the paradigm of the spinning cometary nucleus to advance a speculation concerning a most miraculous event to materialize in our most proximate future.

CHAPTER FOUR

THE SIGNS BEFORE THE END(S)

It is a blasphemy against God to ask for His assistance at a moment of danger, having never before in life prayed to Him. Dominique François Jean Arago (1786-1853).

Introduction

Most of the published interpretations of apocalyptic literature appear to have fused all predictions relating to the *End Times* into a single corpus. Since those authors (for reasons expounded in a previous chapter) operate usually under very restrictive data sources, they believe that what they are studying in the Bible refers to the career of the Antichrist and the events surrounding his reign. So, for them, *End times* can mean one thing only: The Second Coming. So, what seems to relate in its description to the phenomena around the Second Coming is automatically assumed to imply that the world will be destroyed soon!

However, as better informed analysts have been suspecting for many ages now, the *End Times* is not a single point on the time line, instead it corresponds to an entire region of points. Consequently, we have already entered the *End Times*, but the Second Coming is still further down the time line, and lies (on the basis of evidence already available to us) beyond the life horizon of the present generation. Also, the death of the Antichrist does not have to coincide with the cosmic phenomena that will mark the end of the age. God the Father alone knows the exact timing of the end of the world.

There are at least **two distinct periods** of time in our future which share common characteristics. The testimony of the prophets is categorical enough and we have no reason to collapse them into a single event. The analytical tools at our disposal afford us the ability to differentiate the data and fully distinguish the periods they refer to.

This chapter sheds light on the causes that led to the confusion prevailing in the popular apocalyptic literature, clarifies with convincing evidence the real issues, and establishes the claims made above. Several chapters that follow will add their own testimony and provide yet additional supporting evidence to corroborate the thesis that our times precede by far those of the Antichrist and the Second Coming. The geological upheavals that will soon occur (horrendous as they may be) precede a second set which will be of such violence and intensity as to completely wash the earthly slate clean for new inscriptions by the Lord of the Universe.

On the sources of the confusion in the literature

Assertions concerning the speedy occurrence of terrifying events that will include natural phenomena such as hail and fire, the rising of the sea, severe earthquakes and inundations, the change of the flow of rivers, plagues of humans and animals and plants, as well as many signs and wonders in the skies, are common to both sets of data, because the cosmic forces that engander them are very similar. This merely indicates that periodic catastrophes have occurred several times in the past history of the Earth and will happen again. There is nothing geologically suspicious, intellectually abnormal or theologically heretical in this assertion. We shall show in this chapter that such phenomena will be brought about as the consequences of (at least) **two** distinct close encounters of our planet with extraterrestrial objects.

The first such encounter will occur **before the end of the 20th century**, and deals with the comet intimated already in the introduction chapter. Its destructiveness, although great, will be limited in astronomical and geological terms and will not eliminate the human race, although civilization, as we know it, will be drastically affected and radically altered. The second close encounter will be much more destructive. In fact, the prophecies indicate that it will be fatal for the present life forms on the planet. The second encounter is the one most closely associated in a temporal sense with the events around the Second Coming.

What we should have already known about such phenomena

There exists no a priori reason to refute the possibility that a comet of a particular mass, composition characteristics, proximity of trajectory to the earth's revolutionary path and similar parameters is more than capable of inflicting extreme damage on the earthly environment. Especially, if it were to crash upon our planet. Approaching us from a dangerously close distance, it can cause major upheavals which could bring about a chain of reactions on the tellurian sphere but would be less disastrous than the upheavals generated by a head-on collision.

An asteroid, being of rock or metal composition is more dense than a comet of similar size and hence it would be much more destructive. Comets in general are much more numerous, larger in size and more unpredictable. However, given that they are composed primarily of ice and dust particles, their composition is less robust than that of an asteroid either on a head on collision, or through the gravitational pull exerted while travelling close to the earth. On the other hand, a comet has many gases imbedded in it. They can release many poisons besides useful minerals and water into our atmosphere if contact occurs. Finally, a meteorite, however large and heavy, can obliterate a sizeable part of the world around its impact point but its damage will not match that of the destruction generated by either a comet or an asteroid.

As stressed already in the previous chapters, the accumulated scientific testimony strongly militates in favor of the inexorability of a close encounter with either an asteroid or a comet in our future. Our cometary scientists, sky watchers, and killer-Asteroid observers may be restricted so far to a tiny, underfunded group, shunned by the mass media and occasionally ridiculed by the ignorant journalistic pundits for their alleged science fiction pronouncements. Yet, their voices are clamoring in remarkable unison with the voice of the prophets, who assert the unavoidability of such an event, plus its imminence!

This danger from outer space had already loomed on the prophetic horizon of our future thousands of years ago! It is only due to our ignorance and our general complacency born out of this ignorance that we underestimate the probability of a too close encounter with a guest from outer space. Lack of funds, equipment, and manpower are to blame in part for the fact that so small a percentage of earth-crossing asteroids have their trajectories already computed and the risk of their encounters with our planet assessed by the astronomers. The cosmos is holding many secrets for us. Cometary science, despite its breakthroughs in the course of our century is still shrouded by the many unknowns.

Practically every *untamed comet*[1] in existence, suddenly appearing in our skies, is a wild risk to be reckoned with, if its trajectory approached ours from too close a distance. Could it collide with us, or travel so close as to generate enormous tidal waves, usher in a nuclear winter, conjure volcanic eruptions from many simultaneous vents, shift the planet from its axis, or all of the above, within a number of hours or days only?

We had a close call with such a potentially lethal comet in the week preceding Easter of 1989, as we noted in a previous chapter. That was a mountain-sized comet which approached us with a speed of 70,000 km/hour. That frustrated rendez-vous, in the words of Don Yeomans, would have been more than sufficient to generate a new ice age, create tremendous firestorms, and raise sea waves 100 meters high.[2]

While the mass media downplay such eventualities, the scientific community as well as the knowledgeable laypersons with astronomical interests are convinced that these are not only possible but very likely and they are bound to occur, sooner or later. The fact that the general public remains ill-informed or even disinformed on this issue, in no way affects the probability of their occurrence. We live in an era dangerously reminiscent of the doomed town of St. Pierre on the island of Martinique, during that fateful morning of May 8, 1902. As the reader may remember, the upcoming elections were the main theme of the media of St. Pierre which down-played all suggestions emanating from the adjacent volcano of noisy and disturbing Mt. Pelée. The net result of that disinformation was the immolation of an entire city to the gods of irresponsible science, cheap journalism and political expediency. It is precisely this St. Pierre syndrome that the current study wishes to guard the reader against. Because, although we sit on the planet with no other obvious place to go, we **do have a choice and a route of escape** as we shall see later on.

To be fair, it is not only the vested interests to blame for our current predicament. There is also the innate self-centered conviction that the Almighty would not dare do any such thing during our own lifetime and thus

---

[1] Such is a comet whose astronomical characteristics are still unknown to us. An example of an untamed comet would be a non-periodic comet or a periodic one, whose last perihelion approach occurred before humans had invented writing.

[2] Der Spiegel, 28/1994, *Der Erde zur Warnung*, p. 140.

interfere with our plans and pet projects. The dictum *man proposes and God disposes* sounds great, pious and plausible when it is applied **to someone else**. When we bring it to bear to our own propositions and expectations, things begin to run afoul. Such things can never happen to **us, personally**.

Clark R. Chapman and David Morrison in their *Cosmic Catastrophes* dedicate an entire chapter along analogous considerations. Entitled "Threat from the Skies: Will a Comet Strike?" the chapter debates the relative risks for dreaded events that can befall us either as individuals or as entities of an ecosystem. The risk of dying from a cometary collision (which will also have catastrophic consequences for our civilization) has been computed to be 2000 times greater than dying from exposure to TCE at the EPA limit, for instance, and ten times greater than dying in a tornado.[3] Reference was also made to a scientific document analyzing these risks and proposing ways to reduce and/or avert them. Evaluating the elicited response to such premonitions, the scientists concluded that **saving our civilization from destruction by an extraterrestrial agent is not high on the list of national or international priorities today**. [Emphasis added].[4]

It is not surprising, therefore, that a report generated after the 1980-NASA symposium on "new directions" was never released to the public. In their majority, cometary scientists agree that the danger of a destruction from outer space has been sorely underestimated, so far.[5]

---

[3] In a later publication for the British NATURE magazine, (January 1994) the authors calculated that death through a comet is more probable than death during an earthquake or by drowning in a flood.

[4] [op. cit., p. 276].

[5] David Rabinowitz from the University of Arizona has concluded after only two years of research that the stony objects of a size at least as large as a house with trajectories close to the Earth's are one hundred times more numerous than it had been previously estimated. The Asteroids and Near Earth Objects that can pose serious threats to our future are very numerous. A death by a comet is equally lethal as the death brought about by a Near Earth Object. Finally, whether the Asteroid which killed us has evolved from dead comets during a remote eon, can be quite secondary to our vital concerns here and now. For all practical purposes, most of the deaths will be caused not by the Asteroid or the Comet, strictly speaking, but by their consequences on the earthly environment.

John Rather of NASA has lamented on how little we really know about the dangers from outer space. And since the bulk of comets enter our system without advance notice, the human race will have very limited time to be timely advised of such a dangerous rendez-vous, and even less time to take any recommended precautions. The risks are compiled further by the realization that even well-known (tame) periodic comets might find their trajectory interfered with by heavenly bodies, and once their trajectory becomes altered they themselves may join the population of the dangerous wild comets whose conduct is unpredictable.

The astronomers, therefore, are currently at a disadvantage. Their voices of warning are overpowered by the clamor of more 'immediate' and 'vital' concerns of mankind. They may be relieved to know, however, that among God's Elect they will find the best natural ally. The prophets **agree** with the astronomers, although their jargon may at times sound remote and apparently unrelated, but this is only a superficial impression. Properly decoded and brought in harmony with modern technological jargon the text of the prophecies could easily find its way into any astronomical textbook dealing with the nature of these phenomena and the probability calculus of their future conduct.

The predictions by the Physicists

From the testimony of David Morrison before Representatives of the US-Congress:

> Suppose a 1.5 km long rock from space were to collide with the Earth. It would create at the point of impact a crater whose diameter could be 16 km long. The dust produced through this collision would cover the earth like a shroud. It would hover in the atmosphere for a month or a year, turning the days dark. Blocking the sunlight for such prolonged a time would precipitate a new ice age. The temperature would fall, the crops would fail. Hunger and epidemics would drastically reduce the population of the earth.

This paragraph encompasses the most salient points generally made by astronomers regarding the immediate consequences of such events. Obviously, the conclusions are sensitive to the change in the parameters:

much more serious results would accompany a bigger object travelling at a higher speed and making land fall in a densely populated area rather than the Marianas Trench in the Pacific Ocean, for instance. What is noteworthy for us, however, is the nature of the phenomena: **prolonged contamination of the atmosphere** that could precipitate tremendous climatic changes and endanger the life of many species, **darkening of the skies** during daytime, **earthquakes and volcanic eruptions** caused by the sudden impact.[6] One must also add that if the gravitational pull of such a body can raise tidal waves in the oceans, it will also raise the waters in rivers and lakes as well, and even reverse the flow of rivers. Earthquakes have been credited with reversal of river flows in the past. It can uproot trees and cause other damage, routinely associated with hurricanes (whose impact, however destructive, will pale by comparison).[7]

The predictions by the Metaphysicists

As noted in a previous chapter our prophetic evidence available for this study is limited to pagan Greece, the Hebrews of the Old Testament and the

---

[6] Although not explicitly mentioned in the above excerpt, earthquakes and volcanic eruptions are a sine-qua-non in the general predictions by astronomical scientists of the consequences of such impacts.

[7] If life for the human race was given a boost in the wake of the mega catastrophe following a cometary impact, there is no reason why the human race (the 'present generation', of the Scriptures) couldn't disappear in a new cometary impact, so that a more advanced form of humanity (the Saints) can begin a new life cycle in the course of the prophesied Millennium in the Book of Revelation. As intimated elsewhere, in the primordial memory of the Greeks, Zeus, the highest deity, was equipped with the thunderbolt, a means of punishment and retribution against his superhuman enemies (Titans, Giants etc.,) as well as the wicked mortals. The thunderbolt may have been merely a surrogate symbol reminiscent of the cometary collisions and close approaches which occasionally played sudden havoc with the ceteris paribus assumptions of the wicked mortals, this way generating for the Creator a clean slate for new evolutionary inscriptions. The very image of the 'flaming sword' brandished by the Angel of the Book of Genesis who was guarding Paradise after Adam and Eve were expelled, may again be a symbol in the collective memory of our remote ancestors of a cometary destruction (a comet can look like a flaming sword and many prophecies describe them as such). In that case, the Fall may have coincided with a catastrophic impact which altered the biological parameters for our Biblical ancestors, who now had to face a much harsher existence and earn their bread by the sweat of their brow.

testimony of the Europeans from the beginning of the Christian Era up until our very own times, as well as a number of private revelations by US seers. My ignorance of the evidence from other cultures and religions is the only reason no such sources have been incorporated here. From the bits and pieces of the Hindu literature that I have seen, I believe that their prophecies would be in great internal consistency with the Western body of evidence, at least with respect to the coverage of the geological upheavals during our near future.

Let us turn to the evidence of the prophetic pronouncements referring to astral phenomena of the same nature as those described above.

The Signs before the End(s)

As intimated in the introduction to this chapter, the confusion around the *Signs of the End* has not been universal. From time to time, perspicacious and knowledgeable researchers noticed that **there obtains sufficient discrepancy** in the description of the phenomena under investigation to support at least a suspicion that the signs fall into two distinct categories: Those preceding the birth of the Antichrist and those following him (or coinciding with his downfall). Consequently, this latter group of phenomena and signs ought to be grouped with the events more or less coinciding with the Second Coming.

Stunning and serendipitous such observations as they may be, they are few and far in between in the current literature; therefore, the greater the credit due to such researchers who made such remarkable distinctions, already. I will be forever in the debt of Richard Kenneth Emmerson, and his *Antichrist in the Middle Ages*, [1981], a book I researched a few years ago for my previous study. I noticed there an obiter dictum by Dr. Emmerson to the effect that the signs that are preceding the Antichrist's birth and/or rise to power **must not be confused with the signs before the second advent of Jesus Christ**.

This short sentence launched me in my new quest. Dr. Emmerson's proposition of the existence of two sets of evidence is a testable one. I only had to accumulate the data and begin testing the hypothesis of two sets of Signs before the End(s).

William W. Heist's *The Fifteen Signs Before Doomsday*, [1952], provided some of the evidence upon which Dr. Emmerson's fortunate observation was resting. William Heist researched a voluminous body of literature, altogether amounting to ninety six (96) versions of the legend of the *fifteen signs before Doomsday*.[8]

Since several of the versions were practically identical forms, the author organized the more unique cases (affording additional bits of information or exhibiting peculiarities in the details) into four major groups.[9] Some of those will be given below under a separate rubric so that the reader can satisfy his/her curiosity on the underlying differences between the two sets.

Our major sources of information
for the Signs before the End (of this Century)

The major bodies of prophecies which incorporate **both** sets of events and

---

[8] His sources emanated from: Latin, English, German, Frisian, Flemish, French, Spanish, Italian, Provençal, Irish, Welsh, Basque, and also included the Latin translation from the Sibylline Oracles, specifically the famous Acrostic Poem of Book VIII. The Acrostic is spelled as follows: ʼΙησοῦς χρειστὸς θεοῦ υἱὸς σωτῆρ σταυρός. (Jesus Christ Son of God Savior Cross).

[9] The interested reader will find *'The Fifteen Signs...'* a most thorough and informative study, always keeping in mind the valuable distinction made by Dr. Emmerson. In fact, William Heist himself supplies a footnote, which at least indicates that he is aware of the prevailing confusion among the scholars, given the great similarities of many signs in the lists. Specifically, on page 39, ft. 17 he writes:

"(...) This part of Lactantius (namely, his work entitled *Divinarum Institutionum*, Lib. VII, cap. xvi and xix, to be found in Migne's Patrologia Latina VI. 791-798) gives many signs that turn up on fifteen-sign lists; but some of these are signs of Antichrist, some accompany Christ in his descent to earth, and some occur at the slaying of the Antichrist. They include these: cities destroyed by fire and sword, earthquakes and floods, diseases, famines,; barrenness of the earth; the drying up of fountains and rivers; the change of waters to blood or bitterness; destruction of birds, beasts, and fishes; signs in comets, sun, moon, and stars; the fall of mountains level with plains; the sea's becoming unnavigable; a trumpet from heaven."

In view of the above, one must assume that William Heist might have been at least aware of the relative temporal distinctiveness of a large group of signs, although he fails to identify our proximate future as a recipient of some of them.

<u>signs are grouped as follows</u>:

Prophecies that speak of astronomical phenomena temporally commingled with man-made catastrophes such as wars and slaughter are relatively plentiful and, to the best of my knowledge, as far the Judeo-Christian tradition is concerned they begin with the Old Testament.[10] Besides the Old Testament [OT] prophets, both sets of events are mentioned in the New Testament; first in the Synoptic Apocalypse but also in the Book of Revelation. Once we establish the arguments supporting this latter claim we shall turn to other prophetic texts from the Christian tradition and complete the data with sources from elsewhere.

The Synoptic Apocalypse and the Signs before the End(s)

The Synoptic Apocalypse appears in three Gospels. Although the Apostle John is mentioned as being present in the gathering of the disciples when Lord Jesus Christ delivered his prophetic pronouncements (later named the Synoptic Apocalypse), his Gospel does not contain a passage that can be easily identified as covering that particular gathering and the pronouncements associated with it. Furthermore, there are small differences in the wording of the three versions of the Synoptic Apocalypse. Although they never contradict each other, they provide bits of additional information that are unique to the specific Evangelist, and this way they increase the total body of information available to us.

The portion of the text most relevant for us now will be reproduced below, to allow us to better follow the temporal sequencing of the prophesied events and to identify the salient points of greatest interest for our generation.[11]

From the Gospel according to Luke

An introductory Remark: In the beginning of chapter 21 there is a prophecy

---

[10] Much of such evidence was presented in *Our Revelationary Age...* and the interested reader may wish to consult that study for material not replicated here. We shall present only new evidence and only occasionally we shall 'borrow' evidence from the previous study for purposes of buttressing our conclusions with the corroborating material the old study provides us with.

[11] The excerpts appearing in this chapter come from the King James Version.

concerning the destruction of the Temple in Jerusalem. This is obviously the reference to the Jewish Wars, when Titus destroyed the Temple (70 A.D.). The Temple prophecy appears in all versions of the Synoptic Apocalypse in the beginning of the relevant chapters. The text continues with the prediction of a number of events which will follow the destruction of Jerusalem by the Romans. The passage we are now interested in begins with:)

Luke 21:11
And great earthquakes shall be in divers places, and famines, and pestilences; and fearful sights and great signs shall there be from heaven. (...)
Chap. 21:20-27.
And when ye shall see Jerusalem compassed with armies, then know that the desolation thereof is nigh. Then let them which are in Judaea flee to the mountains; and let them which are in the midst of it depart out; and let not them that are in the countries enter thereinto.
For these be the days of vengeance, that all things which are written may be fulfilled.
But woe unto them that are with child, and to them that give suck, in those days! for there shall be great distress in the land, and wrath upon this people.
And they shall fall by the edge of the sword, and shall be led away captive into all nations; and Jerusalem shall be trodden down by the Gentiles, until the times of the Gentiles be fulfilled.
And there shall be signs in the sun, and in the moon, and in the stars; and upon the earth distress of nations, with perplexity; the sea and the waves roaring;
Mens hearts failing them for fear, and for looking after those things which are coming on the earth; for the powers of heaven shall be shaken.
And then shall they see the Son of man coming in a cloud with power and great glory.
(...)

From the Gospel according to Mark

Chapter 13:7
And when ye shall hear of wars and rumors of wars, be ye not troubled: for such things must be; but the end shall not be yet.
For nation shall rise against nation, and kingdom against kingdom: **and there shall be earthquakes in divers places, and there shall be famines**

and troubles: these are the beginnings of sorrows.

(...)

13:14-20

But when ye shall see the abomination of desolation, spoken of by Daniel the prophet, standing where it ought not, (let him that readeth understand,) then let them that be in Judaea flee to the mountains:

And let him that is on the housetop not go down into the house, neither enter therein, to take any thing out of his house:

And let him that is in the field not turn back again for to take up his garment.

But woe to them that are with child, and to them that give suck in those days!

And pray ye that your flight be not in the winter.

For in those days shall be affliction, such as was not from the beginning of the creation which God created unto this time, neither shall be.

And except that the Lord had shortened those days, no flesh should be saved: but for the elects' sake, whom he hath chosen, he hath shortened the days.

(...)

13:24-27

But in those days, after that tribulation, the sun shall be darkened, and the moon shall not give her light.

And the stars of heaven shall fall, and the powers that are in heaven shall be shaken.

And then shall they see the Son of man coming in the clouds with great power and glory.

And then shall he send his angels, and shall gather together his elect from the four winds, from the uttermost part of the earth to the uttermost part of heaven.

(...)

From the Gospel according to Matthew

Chapter 24:6-8:

And ye shall hear of wars and rumors of wars: see that ye be not troubled: for all these things must come to pass, but the end is not yet.

For nation shall rise against nation, and kingdom against kingdom: and there shall be famines and pestilences and earthquakes in divers places.

All these are the beginning of sorrows.

...

Chapter 24:14-22:
And this gospel of the kingdom shall be preached in all the world for a witness unto all nations; and then shall the end come.
When ye therefore shall see the abomination of desolation, spoken of by Daniel the prophet, stand in the holy place, (whoso readeth, let him understand:)
Then let them which be in Judaea flee into the mountains:
Let him which is on the housetop not come down to take any thing out of his house:
Neither let him which is in the field return back to take his clothes.
And woe unto them that are with child, and to them that give suck in those days!
But pray ye that your flight be not in the winter, neither on the sabbath day:
For then shall be great tribulation, such as was not since the beginning of the world to this time, no, nor ever shall be.
And except those days should be shortened, there should no flesh be saved: but for the elects sake those days shall be shortened.
(...)
Chapter 24:29-31:
Immediately after the tribulation of those days shall the sun be darkened, and the moon shall not give her light, and the stars shall fall from heaven, and the powers of the heavens shall be shaken.
And then shall appear the sign of the Son of man in heaven: and then shall all the tribes of the earth mourn, and they shall see the Son of man coming in the clouds of heaven with power and great glory.
And he shall send his angels with a great sound of a trumpet, and they shall gather together his elect from the fours winds, from one end of heaven to the other.
(...)
Chapter 24:36:
But of that day and hour knoweth no man, no, not the angels of heaven, but my Father only.
(...)

What are the major messages of the Synoptic Apocalypse for us?

As already noted, the Synoptic Apocalypse differs in length and in the degree of details across the Gospels. Yet, there are certain events that have been marked by more than one Evangelist. Specifically, these events can be organized as follows:

- wars which will coincide with earthquake activity;

- the abomination of desolation spoken of in Daniel, is something capable of **standing** and will be the trigger event for the alert inhabitants of Judaea to flee, and Lord Jesus Christ exhorts them to **flee to the mountains** and not towards the sea or anywhere else. This way the Elect of Israel will survive the catastrophes. The abomination of desolation will be in Judaea **before** the powers of heaven become disturbed. The best interpretation we can offer with the information available so far is that an enemy army will bring something most offensive in the temple before the extra-ordinary events take place. This notion is consistent with every other prophecy covering that period. Also the prophecy predicts that *Mens hearts failing them for fear, and for looking after those things which are coming on the earth; for the powers of heaven shall be shaken. And then shall they see the Son of man coming in a cloud with power and great glory.* This is an additional clue that the fearful events are global (men's hearts in general and not only Judaean hearts). This is another indication that the period referred to has nothing to do with the past wars of the Judaeans and the destruction of Jerusalem by the legions of Titus.

  On the other hand, if the Synoptic Apocalypse were to refer to the Second Coming, per se, it would be futile for the Judaeans to try to flee, since the prophecies of the Second Coming predict the end of life of this planet as we now know it.

- Lord Jesus Christ advises a flight to the mountains, and not towards the sea. Is this because something may be coming from the side of the sea that would be lethal, but can be avoided if one reaches higher ground?[12]

- women with child and mothers in lactation are singled out in all three mentions as the most unfortunate creatures on the run during that time. What does this tell us about the nature of events that would be most onerous if not most lethal for that particular group of humans?

---

[12] I only wish to draw the reader's attention to the fact that a lethal tidal (seismic) wave from the Mediterranean can be escaped by climbing the mountains.

- the number of days of this tremendous suffering will be shortened for the sake of the Elect; otherwise no human being could have survived. This once again suggests that those events will leave a portion of humanity alive by contrast to the events surrounding the Second Coming which will coincide with the destruction of all current forms of life on this planet.

- The powers of Heaven shall be shaken and our own planetary system will show terrible changes, but of short duration.

- The Son of man will appear in glory and will be visible by all the surviving inhabitants of the Earth.

- all three apocalypses continue with the details surrounding the events around the Second Coming which clearly **follows** the above events.[13]

Finally, the time of the Second Coming is known only to the Father. Since in this study our concerns are more immediate, we will use the events surrounding the Second Coming only to the extent that they allow us to delineate more clearly our own proximate future, and differentiate eschatological pronouncements on a temporal basis. Therefore, we shall not cover the details given in the Synoptic Apocalypses surrounding the Second Coming, proper. However, the wording of our Lord Jesus Christ is by no means contradictory to the temporal coincidence of His Second Coming with another astronomical event of immense consequences, (such as the utter destruction of the Earth brought about by a collision with a sizeable comet, a Near Earth Asteroid of some other such object.[14]

Let us return to the various clues afforded us by the individual Gospels and analyze them further.

---

[13] The sign of the Son of man is the cross. This symbol is predicted in many other prophecies as something to be visible as it appears in the heavens, to be seen by every human. On the particular nature of the cross in the heavens we shall have much more to say later on.

[14] This task was taken up by Apostle John, who in his Book of Revelation provides very detailed information on those phenomena, as we shall have opportunity to see in this study.

1)   Lord Jesus Christ mentions signs in the heavens and the altered appearance of stars and planets. "The powers of heavens shall be shaken" after the tribulations of those days which tribulations shall be shortened for the sake of the elect and which tribulations will weigh most heavily upon pregnant women and mothers in lactation. Also, a certain event, central to the period of tribulations, is going to be so sudden that the inhabitants in Judaea are exhorted by Him to not even dissipate the time needed to collect a few provisions and clothing on their way to safety in the mountains.

2)   The preaching of the Gospel to **all nations, throughout the earth**, will precede the end, but will follow the tribulations, the flight to the mountains and the survival of the Elect.   (This is yet another temporal clue for the sequencing of events and in agreement with many prophecies of the Christian Era which predict the end of a global war, the preaching of the Gospel all over the Earth and a period of peace which will end only when the Antichrist rises to power).

3)   In the Gospel according to Luke, the abomination of desolation is not mentioned explicitly, but there will be enemy troops surrounding Jerusalem when those who are in Judaea better flee to the mountains. Ergo, when the time of great tribulations for every living person on the face of the earth sets in, **Jerusalem will be**, once again in its history, **surrounded by enemies**. (This by no means precludes other places from being also surrounded by enemy troops and subject to destruction at the very same time, it merely concentrates the interest and the details of the prophecies contained in the Synoptic Apocalypse to Jerusalem and the Hebrew nation, proper).

4)   As noted earlier, this surrounding of Jerusalem by enemies (the Gentiles) **is not referring to the Roman legions of Titus**, even though, as Historians testify, there were signs in the heavens at that particular time, as well. Flavius Josephus mentioned in his *History of the Jews* that a sword was hanging over Jerusalem for a rather prolonged period. Contemporary astronomers believe that the sword may have been Halley's Comets appearance in 66 A.D. Although other geographically adjacent peoples probably noticed the comet in their skies, the Jews of the period had additional reasons to associate its appearance with their own imminent political fates and

consequently the mention occurs in a Jewish author and not in others.[15]

In summary, when these extraordinary events take place, Judaea will also be in war once again and, furthermore, invaded.

5)   On the abomination of desolation **standing** in the holy place I have no speculation to offer. The exact nature of the abomination remains a great mystery to me, despite the oceans of ink spent on deciphering the *Book of Daniel* and the various interpretations thereof already advanced in the literature.[16]

Let us now turn to the one Evangelist who **did not** include any Synoptic Apocalypse in his Gospel. By contrast, in the Book of Revelation, we have Chapter 11 which again mentions that Jerusalem will be given unto the Gentiles and the holy city shall be trodden under foot forty and two months. This will happen at the time of the Antichrist. Hence, sometime in the relatively remote future. Jerusalem has been trodden by the Gentiles many times throughout its long history. We must not become confused and force a given reference of attack upon Jerusalem by its enemies to any specific historical period we may be familiar with. These enemies have been composed by the most diverse nationalities in the course of the last 3 millennia. Their being regularly referred to in Hebrew prophecies under the term Gentiles has not simplify the prophetic interpretation tasks. As Gentiles qualify nations as different as Assyrians, Babylonians, Egyptians, Greeks, Romans, Arabs, Turks, Mongols, Tatars, Englishmen, and so on and so on.

What I propose, instead, is to consider that Jerusalem in the proximate

---

[15] (By the same token, a comet seen before the fall of Constantinople to the Turks in 1453 A.D., is mentioned by Greek writers and not by Jewish ones who had different concerns of their own at that time. This argument can be extended ad infinitum).

[16] Previous authors have indicated that it will probably be a type of idol, which by its very nature is most abominable to the Jews. Consider, however that the Muslims invade Israel. By being Muslims they do not worship idols, as such. However, a type of weapon, a device of their own religious cult, or even a human being (a most cruel warrior that spreads desolation around him), all these can **stand** and in more than one way can be associated with the abomination of desolation.

future will be attacked and invaded by Gentile enemies. This, however, will be a different attack than the one prophesied in the *Book of Revelation* to coincide with the Antichrist era and the Armageddon battle, and will precede that particular one by several decades, at least.

More relevant for our current study, on the other hand, is the description of the evils to befall mankind detailed in Chapter 16 of the *Book of Revelation*. A cometary astronomer will have no great difficulty identifying *the seven vials of the wrath of God* upon the earth as the concomitant manifestations of a too close encounter with a heavenly body. These vials refer specifically to the seven last plagues to torment mankind before the Second Coming. Therefore, I propose that although St. John the Divine did not supply a Synoptic Apocalypse version for us in his Gospel he did cover the same events following the same temporal sequence like the other Evangelists, in his Book of Revelation.[17]

With that much introduction on this subject from references imbedded in the New Testament, proper, we now turn to other relevant prophecies emanating from the Christian era which lie outside the Canon. Later on, we shall present the testimony of more ancient sources, especially those referring to cometary appearances coincidental with a world war, (as it occurs in the Sibylline Oracles, for instance). It is the nature of the texts themselves which suggested the abandonment of the rule of presenting the material in the strict chronological sequencing of its original creation and promulgation.

Let us now turn to the evidence of the signs **preceding** the Antichrists coming to power, always keeping in mind the valuable observation by Dr. Emmerson that **the General Signs preceding the Antichrist should not be**

---

[17] In *Our Revelationary Age...* I dedicate several chapters showing that we are currently in chapter 9 of the Book of Revelation. I also show that our era **precedes** very distinctly the advent of the Antichrist. We shall also further establish this fact with material presented in the current study. Many Christian era prophets indicate that the end of the WWIII will be followed by an era of peace lasting about 55 years, before the humans revert back in their old evil ways and start bringing new catastrophes upon themselves. The Antichrist will make himself manifest during those years of degenerate living and the cooling of religious fervor. We do not know what length of time will stretch between the fall of the Antichrist and the Second Coming, or between the Second Coming and the Commencement of the Millennium. This is guarded by the Father of Lights.

confused with the 15 Signs before Doomsday as they are detailed in so many apocalyptic texts.

THE GENERAL SIGNS P R E C E D I N G THE ANTICHRIST

We shall present the individual data followed by commentary.

Marie Julie Jahenny de la Fraudais (1891 A.D.).
"There will come three days of continuous darkness. The blessed candle of wax alone will give light during the horrid darkness. One candle will last for three days, but in the houses of the Godless they will **not** give light. During those three days the demons will appear in abominable and horrible forms, they will make the air resound with shocking blasphemies. The lightning will penetrate the homes, but will not extinguish the light of the blessed candles: neither wind nor storm nor earthquake will extinguish it. Red clouds like blood will pass in the sky, the crash of thunder will make the earth tremble; lightning will flash through the streets at an unusual time of the year: the earth will tremble to its foundations; the ocean will cast its foaming waves over the land; the earth will be changed to an immense cemetery; the corpses of the wicked and the just will cover the face of the earth. The famine that follows will be great. All vegetation will be destroyed as well as three-fourths of the human race. **The crisis will come all of a sudden and chastisement will be world wide.** [Emphasis added].

Commentary
One of the implications of the above prophecy is the inability to generate light through any gadget of modern technology which is dependent upon electricity, tele-systems of power grids and the like. Obviously, electricity will be out world-wide, and only those means which can function independently from any disturbances of the electromagnetic field of the earth can still afford illumination in the homes of the faithful. This piece of information is further corroborated by the intimations of the Most Blessed Virgin, Herself, given during her Garabandal apparitions, speaking of a time of sorrows and tribulations when *no motor will run the world over*. Under the term motor we primarily understand a piece of machinery, an engine, activated by electric power and converting electrical energy into mechanical one. This is a further suggestion that electricity will be out when these events take place, paralysing other forms of energy production, transportation, computers, telecommunications, mechanical motion, etc. etc.

I trust, cometary Astronomers will not fail identifying in the above prophecy the makings of a close encounter with a dangerous body from afar. They may feel at odds with the insertion of a prediction that the demons will also appear in abominable and horrible forms, etc., especially if they have not been religiously instructed by Orthodox or Catholics. However, in several other prophecies we are informed that God has allowed the demons to come and collect their own during those Three Days of Darkness. It will be a time of infernal harvest, in other words, quite literally. As for the faithful, the only way to ward off the horror of the demons will be praying to the Omnipotent God, to the Virgin Mary and to the Archangel Michael.[18]

A few additional remarks on the angelic presence: Padre Pio, a Capuchin priest who exhibited all the charismatic gifts and thaumaturgic powers known and who remains the most popular saintly figure in Italy after St. Francis of Assisi has received many revelations from Lord Jesus Christ during his lifetime (1887-1968). We shall have opportunity to study some of his prophecies elsewhere but one in connection with the days of

---

[18] Those brought up in the Orthodox and the Catholic traditions are already familiar with the power of prayer to ward off demonic influences. Their church history and Tradition are filled with instances of the miraculous assistance from Above against such attacks. Although there exist several prayers, the one given by the Virgin Mary to a Bernadine sister during this century has already proven most efficacious. (See also Culleton, [1974], pp. 227-228). The text of the prayer is as follows:

> August Queen of Heaven! Sovereign Mistress of Angels! Thou who from the beginning has received from God the power and mission to crush the head of Satan: we humbly beseech Thee to send Thy holy legions, that under Thy command and by Thy power, they may pursue the evil spirits: encounter them on every side: resist their bold attacks and drive them hence into the abyss of eternal woe. Amen.

The demons will make their deepest mark during the Three Days Darkness. That period will be essentially their Gran Finale. Cases of demonic possessions have multiplied exponentially in the last 10 years. While fewer and fewer clergymen are being trained in this tremendously important function, the need among the Christian population has dramatically increased. (These concerns about the asymmetry between needs and means have also been aired in recent television programs). It is only through prayer that the faithful can sustain the horror of the demonic attacks through the days of darkness. Fervent prayer, as the Lord Jesus Christ demanded in several of His intimations, and the Most Blessed Virgin Mary has been re-iterating in all Her recent apparitions.

darkness given in 1950, is in order here.

(...) This catastrophe shall come upon the earth like a flash of lightning at which moment the light of the morning sun shall be replaced by black darkness. No one shall leave the house or look out of a window from that moment on. I Myself shall come amidst thunder and lightning. (...) Those who shall fight for My cause shall receive grace from My Divine Heart; and the cry: WHO IS LIKE UNTO GOD! shall serve as a means of protection to many. (...) In the days of darkness, My Elect shall not sleep, as did the disciples in the Garden of Olives. They shall pray incessantly, and they shall not be disappointed in Me. I shall gather My Elect. Hell will believe itself to be in possession of the entire world, but I shall reclaim it.

I believe that the Lord Jesus Christ is suggesting in the above prophecy that the Archangel Michael will be directly connected with the events and his name will be invoked as a means of protection to many (but not all; hence to the Elect, specifically). The word *Michael* derives from the Hebrew and translates into *who is like unto God*, or, *who is as God*. St. Michael ranges as the first among all angels. He is the chief of the Archangels and performs a great many important functions. It is plausible that the salutory cry may be an invocation to the specific intercession of St. Michael and his Angels along with the Angels of the Most Blessed Virgin Mary against the demons during the Three Days Darkness.

In the *Dead Sea Scrolls* there exists a passage to the effect that St. Michael is given three names: Michael, Prince of Light and King of Righteousness. But we know from our Christian teachings that Lord Jesus is the King of Righteousness, our Melchisedek, (St. Paul's Heb. 5,6, and especially 7). It appears that the names/titles of Archangel Michael become fused with the names of Lord Jesus as the Prince of Light and the King of Righteousness. St. Michael is also considered the guardian Angel of Israel. Christian prophecies explicitly state that through his intervention the Muslims will be driven completely out of Europe, etc.

Therefore, it seems that St. Michael will appear as a plenipotentiary of the Holy Trinity, so to say, and lead the battle as the champion of Jews and Christians and all the *sons of Light* against the Angels of Darkness under the command of the Prince of Darkness, Belial.[19]

---

[19] See also R. H. Eisenman and M. Wise, [1992, pp. 152-156].

The above intimation by Lord Jesus Christ to Padre Pio, therefore, may be more than a linguistic 'coincidence'. We shall be calling upon God Almighty from whose name Michael's name derives, and we shall experience the very presence of the Prince among the Angels fighting for us, while praying incessantly to Lord Jesus Christ behind locked doors and closed windows.

As a final observation, it is plausible that not only blessed candles but also the traditional lampions of the Orthodox East, which are fed with olive-oil (hence independent of electricity and high-tech) could provide illumination. The olive-oil lampions are a sine-qua-non of every Christian house in the Orthodox world. Blessed candles, on the other hand are consecrated in the churches during the celebrations of the Holy Week, and especially during the night of the Resurrection.

I would like to add a few additional pieces of evidence on the pregnant women and their future troubles:

a)   St. Cosmas the Aetolean (a major prophet of Greece since the fall of the Byzantine empire, whose work was covered in the previous study to a greater extent). Prophecy no. 64: *So many events will take place, that women, due to the prevailing terror, will give premature birth.*

b)   Nostradamus, in his letter to Henry II, King of France:
(in a passage that applies to the WWIII and the fight between Western armies against Muslim ones, Nostradamus speaks of the Holy Sepulchre of Lord Jesus Christ and its future conversion (during a stage of the war) into profane uses.[20]   And then he continues: *Oh, what a calamitous time shall then be for pregnant women!*

Since both predictions are imbedded into material clearly indicating a major conflict between Christians and Muslims, these are yet another proof that

---

[20] Could that qualify for the 'abomination of desolation' we mentioned earlier? Considering that Muslim armies will invade Israel, and considering that the Muslims are the enemies of both Jews and Christians during WWIII, it is very plausible that they will profane both Hebrew temples and Christian churches located in the land of Israel. So, the abomination of desolation can apply to both Judaism and Christianity and the treatment of their holy places by the enemy troops.

they are contemporaneous with the events prophesied in the Synoptic Apocalypse.

Let us now continue with the celebrated Apocalypse of Thomas, believed by many authors to belong to the general phenomena associated with the Second Coming, namely the *15 Signs before Doomsday*, proper. I submit instead, that such belief is unwarranted by the text of the Apocalypse of Thomas, when studied with scrutiny. (Once again, I take the liberty of emphasizing certain passages).

The Apocalypse of Thomas:[21]
"Hear thou, Thomas, the things which must come to pass in the last times: there shall be famine and war and earthquakes in diverse places, snow and ice and great drought shall there be, and many dissensions among the peoples.

At that time shall be **very great rising of the sea**, so that no man shall tell news to any man. The kings of the earth and the princes and the captains shall be troubled, and no man shall speak freely. Grey hairs shall be seen upon boys (...). After that shall arise another king, a crafty man, who shall hold rule for a short space: in those days there shall be all manner of evils, even the death of the race of men from the east even unto Babylon. And thereafter death and famine and sword in the land of Channaan even unto Rome. **Then shall all the fountains of waters and wells boil over and be turned into dust and blood. The heaven shall be moved, the stars shall fall upon the earth, the sun shall be cut in half like the moon, and the moon shall not give her light.**

On the fourth day at the first hour, the earth of the east shall speak, the abyss shall roar: then shall all the earth be moved by the strength of an earthquake. In that day shall all the idols of the heathen fall, and all the buildings of the earth. These are the signs of the fourth day. And on the

---

[21] The Apocalypse of Thomas is an apocryphal work existing in Latin in a number of manuscripts beginning with the fifth century of our era. *The Last Times*, (or The End Times) as we said earlier is a rather comprehensive term that can stretch to an entire century or even longer. *The Last Times,* have already begun but their portion referred to in the Apocalypse of Thomas and hundreds of other prophecies should not be construed to indicate the events immediately preceding the Second Coming.

fifth day, at the sixth hour, **there shall be great thunderings suddenly in the heaven, and the powers of light and the wheel of the sun shall be caught away and there shall be great darkness over the world until evening, and the stars shall be turned away from their ministry.** In that day all nations shall hate the world and despise the life of this world. There are the signs of the fifth day.

After a little space there shall arise a king out of the east, a lover of the law, who shall cause all good things and necessary to abound in the house of the Lord: he shall show mercy unto the widows and to the needy, and command a royal gift to be given unto the priests: in his days shall be abundance of all things."

In the last times there shall be ... many dissensions among the peoples, blasphemy, iniquity, envy, and villainy, indolence, pride and intemperance, so that every man shall speak that which pleaseth him. And my priests shall not have peace among themselves, but shall sacrifice unto me with deceitful minds: therefore will I not look upon them. Then shall the priest behold the people parting from the House of the Lord and turning unto the world, as well as transgressing in the House of God... The House of the Lord shall be desolate and her altars be abhorred... The place of holiness shall be corrupted, the priesthood polluted, distress shall increase, virtues shall be overcome, joy perish, and gladness depart... In those days evils shall abound: there shall be respectors of persons, hymns shall cease out of the House of the Lord, truth shall be no more, covetousness shall abound among the priests; an upright man shall not be found." [Emphasis added].

Commentary
The reasons I believe this prophecy refers to our times, namely before, during, and after WWIII and not during the Antichrist time can be grouped as follows:

1)   Since there will be two encounters with comets, the wording in the *Apocalypse of Thomas* could very well refer to the first comet which will not destroy all life on the planet. This is evident by the wording, which further on specifies the coming of a great ruler who will bring peace and abundance.   The entire text has great internal consistence with hundreds of other prophecies I have investigated and included in *Our Revelationary Age...*, as well as those incorporated in the present study.

2)   The astronomical events **will coincide** with a war. (...even the death of the race of men from the east even unto Babylon). It is most appropriate for a prophecy referring to WWIII to mention Babylon, Channaan and Rome and the race of men from the east, all at the same time. Therefore, I consider this reference to be yet another clue that the *Apocalypse of Thomas* deals with events of our times, and more specifically the events preceding and/or coincidental with major battles of WWIII, a close encounter with an extra-terrestrial body and the subsequent blessed era of peace given to world by a great king (the lover of the law). His reign will precede the times of the Antichrist, and during whose reign there will abundance in all things, again, a prophecy consistent with hundreds of others analyzed so far.

3)   One might argue that Armageddon, the Gentiles (Babylon by extension and many such things), are also consistent with the time of the Antichrist, the Second Coming and the Second disastrous impact with a foreign body from outer space. But these similarities are not justifying our becoming confused and jumping to the conclusion that the text of the *Apocalypse of Thomas* is referring to the period immediately before Doomsday. The Gentiles, Babylon, Rome and armies from the East have been correlated with the fates of Israel many times already in the past. Furthermore, after the fall of the Antichrist the *Book of the Revelation* does not promise any prolonged period of peace for the generation still alive at that time. On the contrary, disasters pile upon disasters and the end will be closing in precipitously.

4)   The specific clues of the second paragraph in the *Apocalypse of Thomas* are of particular interest to us, since they are corroborated by another celebrated prophetic text which further assists us in our temporal ordering of events to come. Specifically "the signs in the heavens and upon the earth are **contemporary to** "*all manner of evils, even the death of the race of men from the east even unto Babylon. And thereafter death and famine and sword in the land of Channaan even unto Rome*" as they are found in the *Fourth Book of*

Ezra.[22]

The relevant text of *4Ezra*, 15:34-64 runs as follows:

"Behold, clouds from the east, and from the north to the south; and their appearance is very threatening, full of wrath and storm. They shall dash against one another and shall pour out a heavy tempest upon the earth, and their own tempest; and there shall be blood from the sword as high as a horse's belly and a man's thigh and a camel's hock. And there shall be fear and great trembling upon the earth; and those who see that wrath shall be horror-stricken, and they shall be seized with trembling. And after that, heavy storm clouds shall be stirred up from the south, and from the north and another part from the west. And the winds from the east shall prevail over the cloud that was raised in wrath, and shall dispel it; and the tempest that was to cause destruction by the east wind shall be driven violently toward the south and west. And great and mighty clouds, full of wrath and tempest, shall rise, to destroy all the earth and its inhabitants, and shall pour out upon every high and lofty place a terrible tempest, **fire and hail and flying swords and floods of water, that all the fields and all the streams may be filled with the abundance of those waters. And they shall destroy cities and walls, mountains and hills, trees of the forests, and grass of the meadows, and their grain. And they shall go on steadily to Babylon, and shall destroy her. They shall come to her and surround her; they shall pour out the tempest and all its wrath upon her; then the dust and smoke shall go up to heaven, and all who are about her shall wail over her. And those who survive shall serve those who have destroyed her.**

And you, O Asia, who share in the glamour of Babylon and the glory of her person -woe to you, miserable wretch! For you have made yourself like her; you have decked out your daughters in harlotry to please and glory in your lovers, who have always lusted after you. You have imitated that hateful harlot in all her deeds and devices; therefore God says, "I will send evils upon you, widowhood, poverty, famine, sword, and pestilence, to lay waste your houses and bring you to destruction and death. And the glory of your

---

[22] The core of the Fourth Book of Ezra (henceforth 4 Ezra) is believed to have been written by a Hebrew of Palestine around the year 100 A.D. See also *The Old Testament Pseudepigrapha*, vol. 1, pp. 517-559, 'A new Translation and Introduction by B. M. Metzger'.

74

power shall wither like a flower, when the heat rises that is sent upon you. You shall be weakened like a wretched woman who is beaten and wounded, so that you cannot receive your mighty lovers. **Would I have dealt with you so violently," says the Lord, "if you had not always killed my chosen people, exulting and clapping your hands and talking about their death when you were drunk?** Trick out the beauty of your face! The reward of a harlot is in your bosom, therefore you shall receive your recompense. As you will do to my chosen people," says the Lord, "so God will do to you, and will hand you over to adversities. Your children shall die of hunger, and you shall fall by the sword, and your cities shall be wiped out, and all your people who are in the open country shall fall by the sword. And those who are in the mountains and highlands shall perish of hunger, and they shall eat their own flesh in hunger for bread and drink their own blood in thirst for water. Unhappy above all others, you shall come and suffer fresh afflictions. **And as they pass they shall wreck the hateful city, and shall destroy a part of your land and abolish a portion of your glory, as they return from devastated Babylon.** And you shall be broken down by them like stubble, and they shall be like fire to you. And they shall devour you and your cities, your land and your mountains; they shall burn with fire all your forests and your fruitful trees. They shall carry your children away captive, and shall plunder your wealth, and abolish the glory of your countenance."

Commentary
Admittedly, the above prophecy is rather long, rather esoteric and full of what appears to be vague terminology and nondescript poetic jargon. However, once we decode it, the text assumes a different countenance. A few observations are in order before we begin our task.

1)   Through the evidence submitted in *Our Revelationary Age...* it is easy to identify Babylon with modern Iraq. In that study I show that a major catastrophe from Above (besides a military defeat inflicted by Christian armies) will befall Iraq in the course of WWIII. The text of 4Ezra further corroborates these sets of events. The first lengthy paragraph given above, therefore, deals with military events (the various winds and tempests moving across the globe) at the same time of the occurrence of natural catastrophes: Let us review the relevant text:

        And great and mighty clouds, full of wrath and tempest, shall rise, to destroy **all the earth and its inhabitants**, and shall pour out upon every high and lofty place a terrible tempest, fire and hail and flying swords and floods of water, that all the fields and all the streams may be filled with the abundance of those waters. And they shall destroy cities and walls, mountains and hills, trees of the forests, and grass of the meadows, and their grain. And they shall go on steadily to Babylon, and shall destroy her.

Since the clouds are rising to destroy all the inhabitants of the earth, it is clear they are not caused by a portion of humanity in the course of military activities. Also, the rest of the above paragraph is clearly made up of natural phenomena and not human actions. Man has not yet devised a way to flood all the streams and fields simultaneously with an abundance of waters. They also seem to describe phenomena associated with the effects of massive gravitational pull, violent volcanism, etc. Also, those natural calamities will destroy Iraq (q.e.d). (...) **then the dust and smoke shall go up to heaven, and all who are about her shall wail over her. And those who survive shall serve those who have destroyed her.** This is a clue that natural calamities and war will happen at the same time. A further clue is that this does not relate to the Second Coming: those who survive shall serve their victors.

2) The next paragraph speaks of *Asia*. *4Ezra* was written in the first century of our era, as was noted above. Asia at that time was the official name of the Roman Province of Asia Minor. Many centuries later a nomadic people from Central Asia began a series of invasions which culminated in the ultimate destruction of the Byzantine Empire and the establishment of the Ottoman rule in the Middle East, the Balkans, much of Central Europe, the region around the Black Sea, North Africa and, of course, the land mass of Asia Minor which became known as Turkey after the abolition of the Ottoman Empire in our century. The Turks, besides being a belligerent people who adopted Islam, are notorious throughout their history for savagery and persecutions inflicted upon Christian populations, and to a lesser extent against the Jews (who have not been spared of persecution in our century, anyway, and consequently only a very small number thereof remains in Turkey today).

The massacres and the genocides inflicted upon the Armenians and the Greeks during this century are the first holocausts of the 20th century and constituted only the last set of such persecutions against the chosen people for the simple reason that a massive population exchange spared the remaining Christians of Turkey from complete obliteration by fire and sword under Kemal Atatürk's new political order. Those few Greeks still remaining in Constantinople today are only a shadow of their earlier numbers and subject to continuous harassment and persecution.

This marvelously informative prophecy speaks of the **future** persecution of the chosen people by Asia. *As you will do to my chosen people," says the Lord, "so God will do to you, and will hand you over to adversities.* The prophecy was written ca. eight centuries before the Turks had any opportunity to do such things to the chosen people. However, a plethora of prophecies emanating from many other sources indicate that in the course of WWIII the Turks and their Muslim allies will inflict once again death and destruction upon the Christian populations of Europe (at the same time when Babylon will attack the land of Israel).

With these historical digressions in mind, it becomes easier to see that this prophecy from *4Ezra* deals with a number of events some of global consequences and others centered on the Middle East. Since the main task undertaken in the present chapter is to speak of the extra-terrestrial occurrences, no more analysis of political and military events will be given here. The reader may wish to keep in mind the remainder of the text of *4Ezra* and return to it after reviewing additional prophetic evidence on the future fate of Turkey and Iraq which is included in other chapters of our current study.

From a revelation given by Lord Jesus Christ to a holy person in Europe, about the year 1965 A.D.:[23]

The Divine fire and the fire of hell will arrive and last during the days of darkness indicated by all the saints. My luminous cross will appear in the sky. It will be the sign that the final events are close and will remind all of My terrible Passion, so that they will have time to reflect, for I shall not punish the world without previous announcement. All will have time to comprehend the significance of that cross in the sky, and

---

[23] Also included in *The Three Days of Darkness* by Father Albert J. Hebert.

every one shall see it. All will know, even those who reject it that this My Cross will be the sign that a Redeemer came once to bring salvation and pardon. My Cross will be honored as never before.

Commentary
In this revelation there is yet another reference to the sign of the Cross becoming visible to **every person in the world**, and becoming visible around the timing of the days of darkness. In other words, something which cannot be mistaken as representing the sign of a Cross will be seen in the skies.

As we know, a *dirty snowball* (a comet) becomes visible only after it has sufficiently approached the sun for its surface ices and dust particles to begin sublimating. In a non-spinning comet, the solar wind will push against the coma of the approaching comet to generate a specific visual pattern; a spectacular elongated tail will be produced, which will go on increasing in length and brightness as the comet continues approaching the sun in its perihelion motion; this is the long hair of the comet, the more frequently observed phenomenon. In other words, while the comet approaches the sun the tail will be formed uniformly always **behind** the nucleus. Once it reached perihelion and begins its return journey to cosmos the tail will gradually rotate so as to always be pointing away from the sun. This is often similar to a sword or a flaming sword.

I can only advance a speculation at this point, considering that I lack sufficient specific information about the very nature of this phenomenon: As cometary scientists have shown, a comet whose nucleus is a spinning one, can generate the visual image of a cross or an ogee while it approaches the sun and its various gases become sublimated. In fact, a few researchers (notably Carl Sagan and Ann Druyan) have advanced the hypothesis that the symbol of the swastika (which is a cross whose branches are either crooked in right angles, or slightly curved in an ogee), are primordial symbols common to all civilizations and emanate from the visual effects of comets in the skies, observed with the naked eye by many civilizations around the globe. The nuclei of such comets spin in such a manner as to generate such visual images. Although the swastika has been associated in our century with the Nazis and their sinister ways, the symbol per se in the collective memory of mankind did not have an evil connotation during the past millennia and it occurs simultaneously in many cultures which were separated geographically and hence unable to communicate directly and borrow this symbol from each other. Hence, it was not copied from one culture by another through conquest, trade or cultural exchange, but rather each one of them independently noticed it in their heavens and immortalized it in its own art and literature.

Carl Sagan and his wife Ann Druyan, in their book entitled Comet, [1985], present the remarkable research on the swastika subject by an earlier writer, Thomas Wilson, [1896], who had already noticed the universality of that symbol since early antiquity. Their insight on this subject is that the swastika was 'originally something in the skies, something that could be witnessed independently by widely separated cultures...'. *(...) The swastika form is not very different from the pinwheel structures seen in many comets, and brought out in short exposure photography with a large telescope. Comet Bennett 1970 II is a recent example. For Comet Bennett, at least, the color of the pinwheel was yellow, implying that the structure is in the dust part of the comet. You look at these forms and perhaps you will grant at least that if enough spinning, jetting, comets pass by the Earth, sooner or later there will be one that presents something like a swastika to view. (...)* '.[24]

The design of a swastika may be more exotic and more rare to achieve, however, than the design of a cross with arms extended in right angles, namely, the symbol we associate so intrinsically with the Christian religion. In the above work by Sagan and Druyan as well as in several other books by cometary astronomers, who have been reproducing pictures of comets from old texts (several of them emanating from antiquity) the sign of the cross and/or of a swastika are time and again crowning the head of a comet. Furthermore, the verbal description often accompanying the pictograph of the comet includes the word 'cross'. Such evidence is amply included in Don Yeoman's book, [1991], and several others available to the general public today.

Again, it is only a speculation on my part that the sign of the cross will be generated by the jetting of sublimated gases from the nucleus of a comet. On the other hand, another phenomenon completely unrelated with the comet may occur at the same time, such as a sudden burst of activity in a solar system remote from our world. But of such intensity and of such magnitude as to generate a phenomenon in agreement with the prediction handed down to us by Lord Jesus Christ. Perhaps, we shall not know for

---

[24] [op. cit., pp. 185-186].

certain until the event happens and we are among the lucky survivors witnessing it, but happen it will![25]

Consequently, if my speculation is a fortuitous one, the sign of the Cross would be generated by the visual effect of the spinning patterns of the extraterrestrial body (a comet or something else) appearing on the heavens and becoming visible by all human beings alive at the time. On the other hand, its nature may be of a completely different origin and be generated by a miracle of Jesus Christ disassociated from all other signs and wonders in the skies, for which we happen to have detailed prophetic indications.

Interestingly enough, the sign of the cross in the sky, which will become diluted and change in appearance over time is a theme re-emerging in Byzantine prophecies of phenomena contemporary with a major military conflict over Constantinople. Such prophecies will be analyzed in great detail later on, but their very wording will intrigue the cometary astronomers as few other known prophecies may have in the past.

From the Revelations of the Most Holy Virgin Mary at la Salette-Fallavaux[26]

Introduction to the text
In the course of Her apparition, the Most Holy Virgin Mary delivered a long prophecy of future events to befall mankind with specific references to a number of European countries. The portion of the prophecy that refers to our own times deals with civil wars, world war, and natural catastrophes. She said specifically that *France, Italy, Spain and England will be at war*. It appears that the wars, at least in France and Italy will be civil ones, although the context seems to indicate that all four will begin as civil wars. Then, the

---

[25] As the Earth rotates around its axis, every person gets a chance to see a given phenomenon in the skies. (Of course, if it is a fixed far-away star visible only from the Northern Hemisphere right now, our TV screens can make it available to the inhabitants of the Southern Hemisphere also, in a split of a second. So, the statement 'all the people will see it', in our high-tech world is an appropriate one, whether the object in question has been captured in orbit around the Earth's Equator, for instance, or it relates to a tremendous astrar birth somewhere in the cosmos.

[26] This occurred on September 19, 1846, when She spoke to two shepherd children, Maximin and Melanie.

war will generalize into a global one which will be a terrifying one (épouvantable). The slaughter will be tremendous.

The Holy Virgin then continues as follows: *At the first strike of his thundering sword the mountains and the entire nature will tremble with fear, because the disorders and the crimes of men have pierced the vault of heaven. Paris will be burnt and Marseille will be swallowed by the waves; many large cities will be broken to pieces and foundered due to earthquakes; people will believe that everything is lost; (...) At that point, Jesus Christ, through an act of His justice and His great mercy for the just ones will command His angels to put to death all His enemies. All of a sudden, the persecutors of the Church of Jesus Christ and all men given to sin will perish and the earth will become like a desert. (...)*

And then the prophecy of the Most Holy Virgin continues with the blessed era of peace that will follow the end of these calamities. Peace and plenty will last for a number of decades but then people will fall once again into their evil ways and the time of the Antichrist will approach.[27]

As we can see, we have been blessed with a plethora of information on the terrible things to come from the mouth of the Most Holy Virgin, as well. Her numerous apparitions and Her advice to us on how to prepare and avert the catastrophes to occur soon, come as additional evidence of the highest order. She elucidates and corroborates the text from older revelations and She adds vital additional information that makes clear the nature of the events, their likely timing and their consequences. I invite the reader to pay particular attention to the wording of the Most Holy Virgin Mary:

> thundering sword; mountains and nature tremble; cities collapse under the sea; earthquakes; people will believe this is the very end of the world.

I wish to venture the speculation that the thundering sword is a metaphor of a destructive comet which will cause geological upheavals, one of which is the sinking of entire large cities at the bottom of the sea. Comets look very much like swords when their gases become sublimated as they jet out from the nucleus. Not only astronomy books depicting comets have lots of

---

[27] The entire text of the above prophecy of the Holy Virgin can be found in several publications. For a full text in French see also J.K. Huysmans, [1965].

images of swords in them, but prophecies and historical texts in general often referred to them as *swords in the sky*. The Blessed Virgin speaks of the thundering sword of Jesus Christ (son épée foudroyante), intimating also its generating a terrible sound; if a supersonic plane can have a thundering sound, how much more could a comet moving close to the earth at a great speed?[28]

This initial sample of prophetic evidence on signs well before the Antichrist's times is now completed. Below we shall present the signs before the end, proper, (i.e., those immediately preceding Doomsday).

The Fifteen Signs before Doomsday

1)   From a prophetic text given in William W. Heist's above-mentioned book, (a Latin version of Peter Comestor's text running as follows):

Jerome, moreover, discovered in the *Annales Hebraeorum* the signs of fifteen days before Judgment Day, but whether these days are to be continuous or discontinuous he does not say. On the first day the sea will raise itself forty cubits above the height of the mountains, standing in its place like a wall. On the second it will sink so that it can hardly be seen. On the third the sea monsters appearing on the sea will give roars as far as heaven; on the fourth the sea will burn, and the waters; on the fifth the herbs and trees will give forth bloody dew; on the sixth buildings will fall; on the seventh the stones will strike against one another; on the eighth there will be a general earthquake; on the ninth the earth will be leveled; on the tenth men will issue from caves and will go like madmen, nor will they be able to speak together; on the eleventh the bones of the dead will rise and stand on the tombs; on the twelfth the stars will fall; on the thirteenth the living will die, that they may rise with the dead; on the fourteenth the heavens and earth will burn; on the fifteenth a new heaven and a new earth will be made, and all will arise.[29]

---

[28] As our evidence on the specifics of the war against the Devil, the Turk, and the Comet accumulates, it may be useful to return to the above prophecy of the Most Holy Virgin and review it again and again.

[29] [op. cit., p. 26].

2)   From Margaret Enid Griffiths's *Early Vaticination in Welsh...*, [1937], pp. 45-46:

(...) The fifteen signs occur on the fifteen days before the day of judgement, and may be summarized thus:

1.   Rising of the sea as a wall.
2.   Sinking of the sea from sight.
3.   Return of the sea to its normal level (this is sometimes omitted).
4.   Fish and inhabitants of the sea come to the surface and make a great noise.
5.   Burning of the sea.
6.   Trees and plants will be full of dew like blood.
7.   Falling of buildings.
8.   Stones and rocks smite each other.
9.   Trembling of the earth.
10. Hills and valleys become one level plain.
11. Men come out of their hiding places in caves and shall be as madmen.
12. Falling of the stars and the "signs" of the heavens.
13. Rising of the dead.
14. Death of the living.
15. Burning of the world.

3)   Lucy Allen Paton's, *Les Prophecies de Merlin*, vol. 2, pp. 198-199, referring to the version attributed to Jacobus de Voragine, gives the following additional details:

(...) Moreover, five terrible signs will precede the judgement; compare with Luke xxi: There will be signs in the sun and the moon and the stars and upon the earth distress of nations bewildered by the roaring of the seas and the waves. Three signs are determined by the wording of Apocalypse chapter vi: The sun will become black like a sackcloth of hair: and the moon will be as if made of blood, and the stars will fall upon the earth as the fig tree sheds its unripe figs when it is shaken by a great wind...

(...) during the first day, the sea will rise .xl. cubits[30] above the height of mountains, remaining in the spot as if it were a wall. During the second day, it will descend so low, in that way as it scarcely can be seen. During the third day, the large animals of the sea will appear on the surface of the sea and will make noises all the way to the heavens, and only God will understand their groaning. (...)[31]

4) From the Greek Acrostic Poem on Christ, ΙΗΣΟΥΣ ΧΡΕΙΣΤΟΣ ΘΕΟΥ ΥΙΟΣ ΣΩΤΗΡ ΣΤΑΥΡΟΣ, SibOr. VIII (verses 217-250).[32]

Jesus Christ, son of God, savior. cross.
The earth will sweat when there will be a sign of judgment.

---

[30] .xl. cubits signifies 40 cubits, a cubit being an ancient measure of length about 18-22 inches. The term appears quite often in the texts of the Hebrews and other Mediterranean cultures. An inch measures 2.54 cm. Consequently, 40 cubits would correspond to waves at least 18 meters high.

[31] The Latin original is given below:
Signa autem terribilia praecedentia iudicium ponuntur quinque. Luc. xxi. Erunt signa in sole et luna et stellis et in terris pressura gentium prae confusione sonitus maris et fluctuum. Tria signa determinantur Apocal. vi. Sol factus est niger, tanquam saccus cilicinus: et luna facta est sicut sanguis, et stellae ceciderunt super terram... Quintum signum scilicet confusionem maris quidam existimant esse, quod mare cum magno fragore peribit a pristina qualitate secundum illud Apocal. xxi: mare iam non est; vel secundum alios ille somnus erit, quoniam non sine murmure magno .xl. cubitus super montes elevabitur et postea deprimetur... Prima die eriget se mare .xl. cubitus super altitudinem montium stans in loco quasi murus. Secunda die tantum descendet ut vix videri possit.
Tertia die marinae belluae apparentes super mare dabunt rugitus usque ad coelum earum mugitus solus Deus intelliget." (...)

The complete coverage of the Jacobus de Voragine list from the *Annals of the Hebrews* can be found in his own book entitled *The Golden Legend*, by Arno Press [1969], p. 4.

[32] See also *The Old Testament Pseudepigrapha*, vol. 1, pp. 423-424, translated by J.J. Collins, as well as Johannes Geffcken, *Die Oracula Sibyllina*, [1902], verses 217-243, for the Greek text and a Latin translation by St. Augustine.

A king will come from heaven who is to judge
all flesh and the whole world forever when he comes.
Both faithful and faithless men will see God
the Most High with the holy ones at the end of time.
He will judge the souls of flesh-bearing men on the tribunal
when the whole world becomes barren land and thorns.
Men will throw away idols and all wealth.
Fire will burn up land, heaven, and sea,
pursuing the hunt, and will break the gates of the confines of Hades.
Then all the flesh of the dead, of the holy ones, will come
to the free light. The fire will torture the lawless forever.
Whatever one did secretly, he will then say everything,
for God will open dark breasts with lights.
A lament will rise from all and gnashing of teeth.
The light of the sun will be eclipsed and the troupes of stars.
He will roll up heaven. The light of the moon will perish.
He will elevate ravines, and destroy the heights of hills.
No longer will mournful height appear among men.
Mountains will be equal to plains, and all the sea
will no longer bear voyage. For earth will then be parched
with its springs. Bubbling rivers will fail.
A trumpet from heaven will issue a most mournful sound,
wailing for the defilement of limbs and the woes of the world.
The gaping earth will then show the abyss of the nether world.
All will come to the tribunal of God the King.
A river of fire and brimstone will flow from heaven.
There will then be a sign for all men, a most clear seal:
the wood among the faithful, the desired horn,
the life of pious men, but the scandal of the world,
illuminating the elect with waters in twelve streams.
An iron shepherd's rod will prevail.
This is our God, now proclaimed in acrostics,
the king, the immortal savior who suffered for us.[33]

The above representative sample of prophecies concerning the catastrophic events which will usher in the Second Coming is, let it be re-iterated, consistent with the text of the *Book of Revelation,* chap. 16, onwards. The

---

[33] The original text of the acrostic poem will be found in an appendix containing other Greek prophetic texts.

reader of the *Book of Revelation* should not be confused, however, by the mention of Babylon and its destruction and coverage by the waves of the sea! This Babylon (whose fate is detailed in chap. 18) is **not the one located in Iraq**. Since these chapters of the Book of the Revelation are much beyond the scope of the present study we shall not dwell on them. Suffice it to say, that the Babylon of chap. 18 is a major sea-port while the original Babylon in Iraq is not. Furthermore, Iraq will be severely destroyed in the course of WWIII and it is most unlikely that after that war the city of Iraqi Babylon will be rebuilt and manage to rise in splendor as per the wording of the *Book of Revelation*. Suffice it to say that the predictions of the relevant chapters of that book refer to a time in the future beyond our own life horizon. Speculations about the identify of that last Babylon have been advanced already by previous authors. I will submit to the scrutiny of the reader a famous Byzantine era prophecy on that future Babylon, later on. All we desire to underline in this chapter is that the very wording of the Revelation's text is very suggestive of collisions of heavenly bodies with the Earth, a shower of stones, tremendous tidal waves and earthquakes generated by the gravitational pulls exerted, and overall, its wording is most consistent with what astronomers expect to happen under such conditions.

REVIEW OF THE MOST SALIENT POINTS

a)   With regard to the *Signs of the End*: Comets have paid disastrous visits to our planet many times before and they will do so in the future; the most imminent one, furthermore, will occur very soon, in the course of a terrible world war. Also, although we can not exclude meteorites and other minor disasters over time, a major and most lethal encounter is expected by the Prophets to coincide with the general period associated with the Antichrist.

b)   the comet of our proximate future began its appearance in the prophetic literature **always in association with tremendous war and other upheavals** already in the Hebrew Prophets, the Greek Sibyls, and possibly also in very ancient prophecies of several Asiatic peoples.

c)   The context of the prophecies reviewed in this chapter indicate that the comet will be temporally associated with a war which will also involve Israel and Europe, explicitly mentioned.

d)   Our Lord Jesus Christ and His Most Blessed Mother have added their own testimony for the sake of the Elect above and beyond the information afforded us already through the Synoptic Apocalypse; in fact, the revelations They shared with humans since 1846 A.D. continue supplying us with most vital information concerning these events.

e)   We have reasons to believe that the comet (or some other object in addition) will appear like a sword and a cross; a sword, technically, looks like a cross with its two arms of uneven lengths intersecting each other at right angles. We also have seen our first piece of evidence that Devil will be defeated in the course of the apparition of the comet on our skies (all enemies of the Church of Jesus Christ, as well as **all** men given to vice). More on this issue will follow in the chapter dedicated to the testimony of the Most Blessed Virgin, as well as in other chapters.

In summary, the dichotomy of the body of evidence on the Signs Before the End, suggested some time ago by Richard Kenneth Emmerson, is fully corroborated by **all other relevant prophecies** collected and analyzed for the present study. The signs preceding the appearance of the Antichrist and those following the apex of his career will have some common physical characteristics, because they will have similar origins, i.e., major geological upheavals brought about by cosmic phenomena. Also military adventures occur at the same time. It was precisely such commonality in some of the wording and the external similarity of the descriptions of the events which led, as mentioned earlier, so many commentators to confuse the evidence as pertaining to a single set of phenomena, and thus to move forward the timing of the Second Coming to the year 2000 A.D...

CHAPTER FIVE

MICHAEL NOSTRADAMUS, THE SIBYLS, 'MERLIN', AND THEIR FRIENDS ON THE COMET AND THE EARTHQUAKES OF OUR NEAR FUTURE

> *And I have made my prognostications concerning events in times to come (...) using the past and understanding the present for thus shall one know the future by the course of time through all regions.*
> Nostradamus, in his letter to Henry II, King of France.

Introduction

Considering the tremendous and universal importance of events soon to materialize, it is no wonder that Nostradamus (1503-1566) too, would have put additional weight to our own times in his prophecies. He has literally showered us with evidence; not only those relating to the military activities during WWIII, but also the geological disturbances, the signs in the sky, earthquakes and disasters. All these have been covered both in his quatrains (where the time sequence has been scrambled for his own protection against the Inquisition) and in his famous letters to his son Caesar and the King of France, where the events are presented in a strict chronological order, as well as in other of his writings.

In this chapter we shall concentrate only on those prophecies that are deemed to be of the most immediate and direct relevance to our present study, which emphasizes the comet event rather than WWIII. Nostradamus's source of inspiration has been very generous with us. (In his letter to Henry II, he maintains that *I cannot err in my calculations since they are done by astronomical rule and according to the Sacred Scriptures.*[1]

Faithful to our simultaneous equations paradigm, we will corroborate **every**

---

[1] In a different passage in the same letter he reiterates that all his astrological computations are in harmony with the Sacred Scriptures.

quatrain with evidence from additional sources. Either additional quatrains from great Nostradamus himself, or from the Sibylline Oracles, Les Prophecies de Merlin, and other sources will also be included. We shall also include testimony from men and women of science, archaeology, and other relevant domains of learning, whose research findings are in complete harmony with the information specified in the prophecies, and who in effect are the best defense witnesses for Nostradamus and his allies. I beg the reader to be patient with this lengthy chapter. It had to be long a) because I wish to defend every position I am taking (which may also disagree completely with previous Nostradamus interpreters) and b) in order to do so, I have brought additional background material that will facilitate our better understanding of his messages and our appreciation for his genius. In the meantime I ask only that the reader listen first and beat me later if he/she must.

A few writers have ridiculed Nostradamus as a quack because he treated Astrology as a serious domain deserving scientific research. Let us remember that the early astronomers such as Nicolaus Copernicus, Tycho Brahe, Johannes Kepler and Isaac Newton were avid students of the 'ancient science', as well. They would very eagerly second Nostradamus's respect for the 'Chaldean Science'. Let us also remember that when in 1660 A.D. Isaac Newton applied to Cambridge University and was asked what area of study he desired to pursue, his prompt answer was: *Mathematics, because I wish to test judicial astrology.* Judicial astrology (considered by many to be the most effective branch of Astrology, provided it is performed by true professionals) is the elaborate (astronomical/mathematical) study of the heavens at the moment of one's birth as a tool of predicting some of the traits to be observed later in the character of the new-born child. The Greek Geographer and Historian Strabo, (book Seven of his Geography), calls the Chaldean Astrologers *Genethlialogists*, namely scientists of the birthdays. The British Astronomer Percy Seymour [1992, p. xii], cautions us not to discard as 'abominable superstition' theories and ideas which have not yet been researched adequately. We should not rush to premature conclusions like those reached by Galileo Galilei who dismissed as 'occult nonsense' the idea that the Moon could influence the tides and, consequently, our climate and the very possibility of life on this planet.

I trust that the reader will submit Nostradamus's words to thorough scientific scrutiny before discarding the evidence given to us by one of the greatest minds of the past 2000 years. It is not Nostradamus's fault if his interpreters and commentators failed to decipher him properly. A few commentators even took the liberty of inserting text into Nostradamus's letter to the King of France, words which simply **did not exist in the original**. They did so under the erroneous assumption that they had already deciphered all major players of our future and they began editing Nostradamus to make him more 'plausible' and 'easier to understand'. It is such initiatives and their less than satisfactory consequences that have turned so many brilliant and well educated contemporaries of ours apathetic if not outright hostile vis-à-vis the great repository of vital information contained in Nostradamus's work.

A few notes on Methodology
I have reviewed all quatrains that appear to refer to cometary phenomena and 'signs in the sky' destined to occur at the same time with a) major geological upheavals upon this planet, and/or b) major military conflict.

Then I selected those which appear to satisfy all imposed constraints, such as relevance to our times and internal consistency with all other information available. As we already saw in the chapter of the 'Signs before the End(s)', we must expect more than one comet (or asteroid) between now and the Second Coming to cause tremendous consternation to mankind. There will again be at some future time 'signs in the sky'. So, one would say, the danger always exists that some of these comets may have been yanked out of their frozen recesses in the cosmos prematurely, so to speak. The suspicion would then be formulated that I may have thrust them in our Solar System much earlier than the Almighty intended to. To reduce as much as possible such potential source of bias a sizeable body of prophetic evidence has been researched. This chapter will be more pedantic and more detailed than usual and some of the more speculative material will be marked with an asterisk.

A few final remarks on the technology of investigation of the Nostradamus's quatrains included in this study:

a)   Nostradamus was an extremely well educated person in the History and Geography of the ancient world; he even undertook the translation of Greek texts at some point in his life. We must, therefore, assume that he was quite familiar with the jargon and the terms used by Strabo, Polybius and the Roman authors of antiquity on issues of the geography of the world as it was known to them.

b)   Nostradamus was careful to avoid further persecution by the Roman

Catholic Church and the various vaticides in the Inquisition. Consequently he took certain measures, such as confusing the chronological sequence in the quatrains. But he did not play any ugly joke on posterity by confusing us with puns and unnecessary word constructions.[2] His purpose was not to make the quatrain hopelessly unintelligible, because that is self-defeating for any prophet. Consequently, when we see the word Arethusa, (or Arethuse), we must not conclude (as a few commentators have) that this must be broken down into 'Areth' and 'USA' and then treat 'Areth' as Ares (the God of War) and 'USA' as the United States of America. The Quatrains are not meant to be stretched out on Procrustean Beds of researchers to be edited and 'supplemented' by wild speculations and preconceived ideas and to be rendered unrecognizable, as a result.

c) Considering the enormity of successfully deciphering such a voluminous body of information, I honestly believe that nobody, acting in isolation and working independently from other researchers or without the benefit of additional material from other sources, will ever be able to adequately decipher Nostradamus within a few years of study. I do not believe that one can be solely a 'Nostradamus Scholar'. One must 'solve his equations' in conjunction with other prophecies by other sources, which seem to apply to the same chronological periods and events as Nostradamus's. Only then there exists hope of 'unique solutions' that can be accepted by all and used to advantage by our generation.

I take the liberty of marking with bold lettering certain passages, to facilitate the reader's referring back to them as our study progresses.

NOSTRADAMUS ON FIRE FROM HEAVEN AND SIGNS IN THE SKIES

Century I: quatrain 20:
Tours, Orléans, Blois, Angiers, Reims & Nantes,
Cités vexées par **subit changement**:

---

[2] Even so, his books were on the Vatican Index of Forbidden Books for centuries. But as Stalin used to say, facts are obstinate things, and the genius of Nostradamus could not be suppressed in view of his overwhelming ability to predict so many major political events in France and elsewhere in the past 400+ years.

Par langues estranges seront tendues tentes,
Fleuves, dards, Rennes terre & mer tremblement.

Translation and suggested interpretation:
This quatrain predicts that the above 7 French cities will be vexed by **a sudden change**, which will occur while foreign troops will have made their tends (expedition and invasion of the territory) and again, at the same time, the land and the sea and also the rivers will be subject to trembling (earthquake activity) and to 'dards', namely darts (from above?). Looking at the map of France, we can see that Tours, Blois, Orléans, Angers and Nantes are close to each other and all situated along the great river *Loire*. Rennes, by contrast, is situated on the confluence of two lesser rivers, (l' *Ille* and the *Vilaine*) although not far from the rest. General area indicated in the quatrain is the French Brittany and immediate vicinity.

Century I: quatrain 46:
Tout auprès d'Aux, de Lestoure & Mirande,
Grand feu de ciel en trois nuicts tombera:
Cause adviendra bien stupende & mirande,
Bien peu après la terre tremblera.

Translation and suggested interpretation:
Aux, Lestoure and Mirande are the old French names corresponding respectively to Auch, Lectoure, and Mirande (modern towns in the region of Gers in SW France); the quatrain predicts that **for the duration of three nights great fire will fall upon them from the sky** in the immediate vicinity of that region; a very stupendous and admirable thing will 'arrive'; shortly after the fire begins descending, the earth will tremble.

And another prophecy on the same cities:

Century VIII: Quatrain 2:
Condom & Aux & autour de Mirande,
Je vois du ciel feu qui les environne:
Sol Mars conjoint au Lion, puis Marmande
Foudre, grande gresle, mur tombe dans Garonne.

Verbatim translation:
In the towns of Condom and Aux and all around Mirande, (which are in the Department of Gers as we saw above) coming from the sky I see a fire which envelopes them: The Sun will be in Mars conjoined with Leo; then, in

Marmande (a town situated on the river Garonne, in the Department Lot-et-Garonne) a bolt of thunder, great hail, and the wall falls into the river Garonne.

Suggested Interpretation:
It is my conviction that the two previous quatrains cover the consequences of exactly the same events. They are internally consistent; for a wall to fall into the river we expect an earthquake of major proportions, a suggestion already included in the previous quatrain (the earth will tremble). This tends to add validity to our thesis that our great benefactor Nostradamus would not leave us in the dark. He richly supplies information and all important events are covered in at least two quatrains for our assistance, occasionally in more than two. In fact, the more important the prophesied event, the larger the number of quatrains supplying its details.

Century II: quatrain 81:
Par feu du ciel la cité presque aduste;
L'Urne menace encore Deucalion:
Vexée Sardaigne par la Punique fuste,
Après que Libra lairra son Phaëton.

Verbatim Translation:
Aduste comes from the Latin verb aduro=to set fire to, to consume by burning. *Urne*, from Latin urna, may mean (besides a pitcher) the zodiac of Aquarius or generically the rivers, personified as deities. *Deucalion* in Greek Mythology is the son of Prometheus and the husband of Pyrrha. Kings of Thessaly, they were saved from the Deluge and managed to repopulate the Earth with a most peculiar fashion suggested by the Gods. *Punique fuste* signifies a punic beating stick.[3] Basically it means that something emanating from Northern Africa (and specifically from Tunisia, where Cartago, Carthage, a Phoenician colony and a great rival of both Greece and Rome was located in antiquity, and whose ruins lie just outside the modern capital, Tunis) will 'vex Sardinia', the Italian island, lying closest to Tunisia, just on its north. Therefore *punic fuste* may imply either a man made "club" or a different type of catastrophe emanating from Tunisia. I prefer the military option, given our information from other sources. *Phaeton* can be construed as simply an epithet of the Sun, (the shining one, from the

---

[3] Our English 'fustigation' derives therefrom and denotes a whipping, a flogging. Fustigation was an established form of punishment in the Roman army.

Greek word for light, φάος, φῶς, Φαέθων).

So, the translation goes: Through fire from heaven the city is almost completely burned. There shall be wave activity and inundations reminiscent of the Flood. The island of Sardinia at the same time is vexed by North Africans when Libra has left the Sun (or the sun has moved from Libra in late fall).

Suggested interpretation:*
There is little we can say on this quatrain, taken in isolation, considering we do not know which city will become almost burned. So, let us keep it in the back of our portfolio for the time being.

Century I: quatrain 91:
Les Dieux feront aux humains apparence,
Ce qu'ils seront auteurs de grand conflict:
Avant ciel veu serein, espée & lance
Que vers main gauche sera plus grand afflict.

Verbatim translation:
The Gods will make their appearance to the humans, who (humans) are the agents of a great conflict: Before the skies are serene again, one will see in them swords and javelins and because of them (swords and javelins) towards the left hand there will be a much greater affliction.

Suggested Interpretation:*
The Gods appearing to the humans is consistent with prophecies from other sources that we shall hear the voice of our Lord Jesus Christ deep in our heart and His sign (the sign of the cross) on the skies. Also, there will be Angelic powers in our midst, as numerous prophecies predict, hence the plural (Gods). Nostradamus belonged to a Monotheistic religion (Christianity), coming from another Monotheistic religion (Judaism). We shall have more to say on the sign of Lord Jesus Christ later.

So, the Holy Ones will appear at the time of a great conflict caused by humans (WWIII?) Before the skies clear up again, we shall see in them sword (a name frequently given to comets since antiquity) and spears (visually reminiscing of elongated 'ballistic missile' of warfare in centuries past). However, these swords and lances (spears) will **fall from the sky** and will cause the greatest damage to the geographical areas located at the left hand. It may appear that this interpretation is too speculative. Granted.

94

But let us not discard it outright now; rather keep it on the back burner until more direct evidence becomes available.

NOSTRADAMUS ON VOLCANIC ERUPTIONS
THE TIDAL WAVES AND THE TSUNAMIS THEY MAY CAUSE[4]

Century I: Quatrain 87:
Ennosigée feu de centre de terre.
Fera trembler autour de cité neufue:
Deux grands rochers long temps feront la guerre,
Puis Arethuse rougira nouveau fleuve.

Verbatim translation:
Ennosigaeus fire from the center of the earth. It will make the new city to tremble all around. Two great rocks will make war for a long time. Then Arethusa will turn red by a new river.

Suggested interpretation:
Ennosigaeus, earth-shaker, was another title for Neptune (Poseidon), the god of the Seas.[5] So far, the first verse indicates that there will be somewhere in the world an earthquake emanating from the center of the earth but it also hints to a violent activity on the part of the sea, since he speaks of Ennosigaeus, Neptune. The second verse informs us that this earthquake will make the 'new city' to tremble all around. Since the 'new city' appears on the same quatrain making reference also of Arethuse, we should restrict our search for the geographic location of that specific one. So, it is obvious that the word Arethuse holds the key to the deciphering of this quatrain.

---

[4] Tsunami is Japanese for *'wave in the port'*, from tsu = harbor and nami = wave. It is popularly but inaccurately called also "tidal wave". Tsunamis are huge sea waves caused by submarine disturbances, like those due to volcanic eruptions and earthquakes. Most earthquake-induced waves are produced directly by the changes in the sea floor which result by the fault movements, themselves. The sea floor may be uplifted by several meters as the faults move and they can cause enormous disturbances in the ocean around them. In the open ocean tsunamis are invisible, although they involve the entire mass of water; approaching the littoral, they slow down, bank up and rise to heights greater than 10 m (33ft).

[5] (ἐνοσίχθων and ἐνοσίγαιος are epithets frequently used by Homer).

Arethusa: in mythology, a nymph of Elis who was changed by goddess Diana into a fountain. Diana further made the fountain disappear in Elis and rise again in the island of Ortygia, near Syracuse, on the island of Sicily. *Arethusa*: in history, a spring in the Island of Ortygia, overlooking the great harbor of the city of Syracuse. To my knowledge we have at least two very detailed reports on this specific Arethusa:

a) Strabo, (book vi of his Geography) who speaks in detail on the Arethusa spring on the island of Ortygia (a.k.a. Nesos). He specifically says that "Ortygia is connected with the mainland, near which it lies, by a bridge, and has the fountain of Arethusa, which sends forth a river that empties immediately into the sea.[6] He then chides those ancient writers who believed that the river Alpheios in Peloponnesus could disappear underground to reappear in Sicily and for believing such a story based on the evidence that the water of the fountain was discolored.[7] (Strabo employs then his analytical skills to settle this issue). But for the purposes of our study, we know now that the waters of Arethusa were turning red even in antiquity, although we are not fully knowledgeable of the geological origins of such metamorphosis.

b) On a much more contemporary level we have the research of Dora P. Crouch, an architectural and urban historian. Besides a detailed hydrogeological map of the ancient city and other types of information on water supply and springs' network Dr. Crouch informs us that *at the very edge of the water on the west side of the original island site of Ortygia, the spring of Arethusa still bubbles up'. (...) Since Syracuse is essentially a great dish of limestone, the inland waters flow down the dip as the strata become the sea floor, only to escape upward in wells on Ortygia and springs at the edge of the island, and become wasted in submarine springs within the harbors. The karst origin of Arethusa is indicated by the citations in ancient*

---

[6] ἡ δ᾽ Ὀρτυγία συνάπτει γεφύρᾳ πρὸς τὴν ἤπειρον πλησίον οὖσα, κρήνην δ᾽ ἔχει τὴν Ἀρέθουσαν, ἐξιεῖσαν ποταμὸν εὐθὺς εἰς τὴν θάλατταν.

[7] Those very ancient authors argued that this was the result of the sacrifices of oxen at Olympia which the Alpheios river, via a subterranean passage, managed to carry all the way to Arethusa, wherefrom the river would re-surface again.

authors.....[8]

The fountain Arethusa was especially honored in antiquity for its vital contribution to life and happiness in the new lands. The Syracusans first colonized the island of Ortygia (attracted by its water resources) and on a silver tetradrachm (namely, a coin worth four drachmae) dating at least from 485 B.C., we can see the nymph Arethusa surrounded by dolphins on the one side and a chariot symbolizing the International Games at Olympia and elsewhere on the other.[9]

Cité neufue simply means new city, in Greek antiquity these words merely translate as *Neapolis*. The Italian Napoli was the ancient Greek colony Neapolis; there have been many Greek cities named Neapolis, but the one in question, appears to have been located in Sicily: Syracuse, the most celebrated city of Sicily, founded about 732 B.C. by Corinthians, was a huge and opulent city with two harbors, and Strabo [op. cit.] tells us that 'in olden times it was a city of five towns, namely, Nesos (Ortygia); Achradine (Acradina); Tyche (Tycha); Epipolai (Epipolae, a district little inhabited), and Neapolis. So, at least there has been a Neapolis in Syracuse as well. *Deux grands rochiers*, (two great rocks) I believe, makes allusion to the straits between Sicily and Southern Italy, which in antiquity were called the rocks of Scylla.[10]

By now we have de-coded all three toponyms, namely, Neapolis, Scylla and Arethusa and we have been able to locate them on Sicily and the environs of Syracuse, in particular. Sicily has the volcano of Etna, while not too far north we find the small islands-volcanoes of Lipari, Vulcano and Stromboli, among others. These three islands are much closer to the Straits of Messina (the Scylla and Charybdis) than to Syracuse. Now, in the event of a chain of volcanic eruptions from under the earth (and the sea) around this general area it is quite probable that both Sicily and South Italy will shake

---

[8] [1993], pp. 94-96, and elsewhere.

[9] See also Peter Levi, [1984, p. 102, and elsewhere].

[10] In fact, on the Italian side there still exists a town named Scylla. These rocks along with the whirlpools of Charybdis on the cost of Sicily caused great heartache to Ulysses, [The Odyssey, Book 12, v. 85], and thousands of other navigators. As Geologists can attest, at some remote point in the history of the planet, Sicily was connected with Southern Italy.

for a prolonged period of time. This suggests that the earthquake in question is bound to be very serious. All of these geological disturbances will cause the earth to crack and a new river to flow through the spring of Arethusa, whose color will be red, possibly due to the chemicals emanating from deep down, and/or the red color from the fire of the volcano spewing lava and minerals over the skies of Sicily.

One may ask at this point: All right, why should such a catastrophe have anything to do with a comet? Aetna (Etna) is known to have had many eruptions before during its very long career, and is discharging lava and ejecta at the time of this writing in 1995. The objection is well taken. True, the above quatrain is not so explicit and categorical on the ultimate causal source of the catastrophe. But we must continue with our search for additional clues; when we juxtapose this information with other bits from Nostradamus and elsewhere, the overall picture begins to look like a major catastrophe brought about by an agent of a specific magnitude that by far surpasses the rumblings and explosions of a single volcanic eruption, even of one that would combine the actions of Tambora, Krakatoa and Mt. St. Helens put together. Since we have to obey the simultaneous equations model at all points of our analysis, we need to look to the next equation, which will receive the 'solutions of this one' and help us identify a few more variables. To this task we now turn, with a minor diversion before we proceed with more data from Nostradamus, proper.

The following is extracted from the vast collection of prophecies written in Old French (repeatedly referred to in the course of this study) under the title *Les Prophecies de Merlin*.[11]

Prophecy no. **lxxxix, (f. 72a)**, entitled: *De Mongibel qui fondra. Et de l'eave chaude et froide qui est devers Chatame*.[12] I will only present the translation of the text ushered in by a few etymological details:

Mongibel, Monsgibel, Moncibel, Mont Gybel, is a composite word. (Latin

---

[11] The reader may be reminded that this collection has nothing in common with the work by Geoffrey of Monmouth's work on Merlin.

[12] Lucy Allen Paton, [1926], vol. 1, pp. 144-145.

mons-montis and Arabic Gibel, Jebel. Both words mean 'mountain').[13]
This Mongibel (namely, mountainmountain) as any linguistically sophisticated Sicilian will attest, is none other than the Volcano of *Aetna* (Etna, Aitna), which assumed this new name during the Islamic onslaught on the island.

Chatame, on the other hand is one of the several phonetic adaptations of *Catania* (Katana, Katania). Catania was originally founded at the very foot of the volcano as a colony of settlers from Chalcis (on the Aegean island of Euboea) in the year 753 B.C.[14] A large and opulent city, it suffered tremendously from the eruptions of Aetna. It was rebuilt as *Aitna* by Hiero I in 475 B.C. after a major catastrophe.

The summary of the translation of the text of the above prophecy **no. lxxxix, (f. 72a)** runs as follows: Mt. Etna will essentially become liquified under the caloric energy of the volcanic eruption. The flames will reach the heavens. This event has been prophesied repeatedly, and allusion is made to the psalms of David predicting that *we shall go through this age by means of fire and water*.[15] The fire will go through the city of Catania. As for the water, there will a co-mingling of hot and cold water. The hot water most likely will come from the steam spewed out by the volcano. The prophecy specifies that the cold water will spring out of a cave, following the collapse of Aetna.

Now, the big question is: when will this terrifying event take place? In the prophecy just preceding this one, **lxxxviii, f. 71d**, entitled *De la mer morte qui se partira d' illec ou elle gist*, we are informed that the Dead Sea in Israel will disappear at that very same time of Aetna's demise and that particular

---

[13] Compare with Jebel Tarik, Gibraltar, the mountain of Tarik, the leader of the Muslim hordes erupting into Spain in the eighth century.

[14] (the self-same year Rome was founded)

[15] Psalm 65, 12 actually speaks of the events around Exodus: *you let people ride upon our heads, we went through fire and water but you have led us out to refreshment.* Maybe this is an allusion by the prophet of the Merlin collection that once again this will occur as it did during the time of the Exodus.

geological upheaval will happen 'after the death of the dragon of Babylon.'[16]

Let us now go back to Nostradamus:

Century VIII: Quatrain 16:
Au lieu que Hieron feit sa nef fabriquer,
Si grand deluge sera & si subite,
Qu'on n' aura lieu ni terres s'attaquer,
L'onde monter Fesulan Olympique.

Verbatim translation:
In the place where Hieron had his boat constructed there will occur such a great and such a sudden deluge that people will be unable to find a place and solid ground to attach themselves and the waves will be of such a height that they could have reached the hill upon which Fiésole is built. (*Fiésole = Fesulae = Faesulae* in ancient Etruria, modern Central Italy. Fiésole is a beautiful modern Italian town just outside of Florence, practically within its metropolitan confines).

Suggested interpretation:
First of all, we again see the term 'subite' sudden; (see above **Century I: quatrain 20**, subit changement, sudden change). It will happen at the place where *Hieron II* had his fabulous yacht built under the instructions of Archimedes! Hieron II was a most enlightened ruler of Syracuse, who ruled for fifty-four years according to the Historian Polybius *without killing, exiling,*

---

[16] In my previous study, I identify this Dragon of Babylon with Saddam Hussein, the present leader of Iraq, whose death is predicted to occur in Israel, during a terrible earthquake which will be of **global proportions**, during the course of WWIII. This material came primarily from my analysis of Ezekiel's chaps. 38 and 39, which provide most specific references to these events.

Certain previous authors have confused the prophetic references to a 'dragon de Babilloinne', with the Antichrist, proper, and consequently they failed to notice the imminence of the events prophesied and their relevance to our proximate future. My position is that there have been many Antichrists in the course of the last 2000 years (as the New Testament attests, besides Nostradamus who has counted eight in total). Yet, the one of most immediate interest to us comes from Iraq and the Antichrist of the *Book of Revelation*, who is expected to appear later, will emanate from a clan whose roots began in Babylonia.

100

or injuring a single citizen, which indeed is the most remarkable of all things. When he died at the ages of 90, (in 216 B.C.) he was mourned as a father and a friend by the entire population. Syracuse at that time was the most populous and prosperous city in the Greek world. It was during the benevolent ruling of Hieron II, that great men like Archimedes thrived. Archimedes supervised the construction of a yacht of immense proportions, and a true marvel of the ancient world, incorporating all the art and science available at the time.

Considering the formidable historical erudition of Nostradamus, we must assume that he knew about that ship from his readings of the Greek authors. The boat was 407 feet long, had a sports deck with a gymnasium and a large marble bath; a shaded garden deck with a great variety of plants; it could carry 300 passengers or mariners; it had sixty cabins very tastefully appointed with the art treasures of the day; it could be converted into a battle ship if need be; it could carry 3900 tons of cargo; its own weight was 1000 tons. Being too expensive to maintain, Hieron II decided to offer it as gift (filled with corn and fish) to the Egyptians during a famine.

Consequently, we must concentrate once again our attention to Syracuse and Sicily as the locus of the prophesied destructions, and not to Jason and Thessaly as previous commentators declared, unperturbed by the term *Fesulan Olympique*. They concluded that the Olympus in Greece is referred to by Nostradamus. Yet, Olympus in Thessaly is 9,570 ft. high, while the one in Fiésole is but a low and humble hill, by comparison.

A sudden deluge, and a great one at that, in Syracuse and vicinity is understandable under the conditions of earthquake disturbances of the great volcanoes of Sicily (Etna) and possibly chain reactions through the adjacent Liparian islands and the tsunamis they can put in motion. The waves are expected to rise:

a)   either to a height that would exactly correspond to the height of the hill of Fiésole, or,

b)   the tidal wave born in this region would perturb the Mediterranean so strongly as to make the waters of the Ligurian Sea in North-Western Italy to reach inland until Florence and Fiésole. In either case, we are talking about a major geological catastrophe within the Mediterranean basin.

Although it has been calculated that a comet with a head as large as the earth, traveling at a distance of 13,290 lieues, or ca. four diameters of the earth would raise ocean tides 2,000 'toises' or ca. four kilometers high, we can only hope that the dreaded comet will not be as large, nor have such a potency.[17] In conclusion, I am inclined to place the Nostradamus's prophecy in Sicily and Central Italy in this specific case, since we are given explicit hints on Hieron (II) and his famous boat and we must not import any Thessalian Procrustean Beds for wildly imaginative transformations.

Century V: Quatrain 31:
Par terre Attique chef de la sapience,
qui de present est la rose du monde:
Pont ruiné & sa grande preeminence,
sera subdite & naufrage des undes.

Verbatim translation:
Across the territory of Attica (Greece), which is chief in wisdom, and which at the present time is the rose of the world, a pont will be ruined and its grand preeminence will be subdued and become a wreck by the waves.

Suggested interpretation:
Again, it appears that some tremendous geological upheaval will cause at some point in the future the collapse and destruction (naufrage) of a portion of Attica under the waves. 'Pont' in the original may be a Latin root (a bridge) or a Greek root (pontos, Πόντος, the sea). There is a chance that there has been a misreading in the manuscript (intending port and having been misread as pont), which was perpetuated in subsequent printings. Then, the prophecy may refer to the port of Piraeus, the greatest in Greece and a city that is by now completely joined to Athens.[18] In that much bleaker scenario, it appears that Piraeus will be the direct victim of the geological upheaval. If, on the other hand, we take 'pont' to give the Greek meaning of a sea, again we are told that terrible geological upheavals may even change the configuration of the Saronic Gulf.

---

[17] See J. Lalande in *Abrégé d' astronomie*, (1795) p. 340, quoted by Immanuel Velikovsky in *Worlds in Collision*, p. 71, ft. 1.

[18] In such an eventuality, 'its great preeminence' may refer to the fact that Piraeus is the preeminent port in all of Greece.

When could such an event occur? Obviously, the above quatrain does not provide exact timing, but again, we have other sources we can juxtapose this prophecy to and 'solve simultaneously'. Such prophecies are copious, indeed: Besides the many references of our Most Blessed Virgin Mary, we have St. Cesar's (Caesar) prophecies on the future of France (and its Mediterranean ports), Les Prophecies de Merlin (speaking explicitly of Greek geological upheavals, earthquakes, which cities will survive and which only partially, etc. etc.), and a host of other sources.[19]

Let us go back to *Les Prophecies de Merlin* for a moment. In various prophecies, too numerous to treat individually (they would deserve a study of their own) we hear of geological/oceanic upheavals in Greece; many lands in Northern Africa, the British Isles, India, the Middle East, Northern Italy and France, among others. But let us concentrate our study in the Mediterranean and consider prophecy cccxx f. 107d with the expressive title *Des villes des Griffons qui serons abatues une grant part*. Here we learn that about the time of 'the death of the Dragon of Babylonia' a sizeable portion of several Greek towns on the mainland and the Island of Euboea will survive the massive earthquakes which will have destroyed a good part of many other Greek cities and towns.

From the Sibylline Oracles (henceforth **SibOr**) of Greek antiquity:[20]

In **Book III**, vs. 335-351 and again vs, 363-366 we learn that many cities will founder with all their inhabitants. And how?
In the West there will shine a star, which they will call comet; it will be for the mortals a sign of swords, hunger and death, of destruction of leaders, of great and important men; and all of a sudden the greatest signs will appear among the humans.[21] And then the Sibyl begins detailing toponyms and

---

[19] Accordingly, we know from elsewhere that Marseilles, for instance, will completely disappear under the waves, along with many other major cities not mentioned explicitly in the Virgin Mary's prophecy at La Salette.

[20] An English translation with an Introduction to the Sibylline Oracles has been contributed by J. J. Collins, in *The Old Testament Pseudepigrapha*, vol. 1, pp. 317-472.

[21] ἐν δὲ δύσει ἀστὴρ λάμψει, ὃν ἐροῦσι κομήτην,
ῥομφαίας λιμοῦ θανάτοιό τε σῆμα βροτοῖσιν,
ἡγεμόνων τε φθορὰν ἀνδρῶν μεγάλων τ᾽ ἐπισήμων.

what exactly is going to happen there. **SibOr3, Book III**, verses 341-349 refer to major earthquakes that will level simultaneously a number of cities: Specifically, the Sibyl predicted the following:

(...) There will again be very great signs among men.
The deep-flowing Tanais will leave Lake Maeotis
and there will be the track of a fertile furrow down
the deep stream, while the immense current occupies a narrow channel.
There will be chasms and yawning pits. Many cities
will fall with their inhabitants: in Asia: Iassus,
Cebrenia, Pandonia, Colophon, Ephesus, Nicaea,
Antioch, Tanagra, Sinope, Smyrna, Maros,
prosperous Gaza, Hierapolis, Astypalaea;
of Europe: famous Cyagra, royal Meropeia,
Antigone, Magnesia, divine Mycenae.
Know then that the destructive race of Egypt is near destruction
and then for the Alexandrians the year which has passed will be the better
one.

Tanais is the river Don and Lake Maeotis is the Sea of Azov. Iassus (Iassos) (island and town of the same name on the coast of Caria on the Aegean), Cebrenia (a town on the Troad, Asia Minor). Except for Pandonia and Tanagra which are still unidentified, the rest, namely, Colophon (city of Ionia, Asia Minor, close to the Aegean), Ephesos, Nicaea, Antiochia, Sinope, Smyrna and Maros, are all located in Asia Minor).[22] Gaza is in Palestine and Hierapolis in Syria, near the Euphrates river. Antigone can be a little difficult to place, because, once again this name appears repeatedly on Greek toponyms. The two most likely (currently nonexistent) cities by that name located on Greek soil would be Antigone on the river Echedorus (Gallikos) (in the vicinity of modern Salonica) and Argyrocastron (in North Epirus, currently in Albania known as Gjirokastra). Magnesia refers to a Thessalian toponym. Astypalaea is much more tricky, because there were several toponyms with that name in Greek antiquity:

σήματα δ᾿ἔσσεται αὖτις ἐν ἀνθρώποισι μέγιστα· (...)

[22] I know only of the Tanagra on Boeotia, which is very close to the island of Euboea, and the Straits of Euripus. That would not be included among the Asia Minor Greek cities, however.

- Astypalaea, ancient city of the Coans, on the Island of Cos. However, this belongs to Greece and not Asia, as the Sibyl specified her Astypalaea to be;

- Astypalaea, a cape in Caria, Asia Minor;

- Astypalaea, (modern Haghios Nicolaos), a cape in Attica, Greece;

- Astypalaea, one of the Sporades Islands in the Carpathian Sea, hence in Greece;

- Astypalaeans also settled Polium on the Simoeis river in the Troad, in Asia Minor;

- Astypalaea, one of the Dodecanese, located between Cos and Carpathos, hence in Greece.

Since Astypalaea is the last entry of 'Asian' cities before starting with European ones, we must search for that particular one in the Troad or in Caria. On Greek territory, Κύαγρα κλύτος, (unidentified so far); βασιλὶς Μερόπεια, i.e., Royal Meropeia, (we shall identify it in a later chapter after additional material has been collected and evaluated). Ἀντιγόνη and Μαγνησία have been already treated; Μυκήνη πάνθεια (Mycenae, on Eastern Peloponnesus, not too far from Corinth).

Later on, in vs. 363-366 the Sibyl uses a famous wordplay to complete the oracular utterance on the destructions (which will precede a blessed era of peace and plenty. We will see this connection again several times in the course of our study). Accordingly,

a) Samos will become flattened and become like sand;
b) Delos will disappear;
c) Rome will become a street; and
d) Smyrna will become so destroyed as never again to become worthy of mention. Following the above, life in Europe will become most happy, plentiful and peaceful, when even the weather will be

different.[23]

All these catastrophes, according to the Sibyl will occur at the same general period of time.

Another Sibyl, (**SibOr, Book VII**, vs. 1-7), informs us that the island of Rhodes (Rodos) will be worthy of our tears, for, it will perish first, the island of Delos will swim upon the waters in a most unsteady fashion, Cyprus will be covered by the waves and Sicily will be burned by the fire that comes out of its interior![24]

The Sibyl drops a most important term to finish up the above prophecy: *This I say (will be caused) by the terrible water of God which, additionally, will arrive from elsewhere.* (As if it were an immigrant and a foreigner). I can only speculate that this reference to an 'immigrant water' ἐπήλυτον ὕδωρ, is a suggestion to the seismic wave (tidal wave) which will transport the destructive energies originating somewhere else (i.e., the epicenter of the eruption of an explosion-type volcano in a different part of the Mediterranean). We must keep in mind, that the Mediterranean Sea is basically a lake with three very narrow conduits to other bodies of water: The Bosphorus, the Suez, and Gibraltar. In the event of major **simultaneous** geological upheavals in several volcanoes, the sum total of seismic waves and tsunamis can be very devastating, when compared with similar events in the open Pacific Ocean, for instance.

Furthermore, the Sibyls provide us with a most valuable clue: These catastrophes are **not the ones that will immediately precede the Antichrist or those which will coincide with the Second Coming**. The

---

[23] SibOr. III, vs. 363-370: ἔσται καὶ Σάμος ἄμμος, ἐσεῖται Δῆλος ἄδηλος, καὶ Ῥώμη ῥύμη· τὰ δὲ θέσφατα πάντα τελεῖται. Σμύρνης δ᾽ ὀλλυμένης οὐδεὶς λόγος. (...) Εὐρώπη δὲ μάκαιρα τότ᾽ ἔσσεται, εὔβοτος αἰθὴρ πουλυετὴς εὔρωστος ἀχείματος ἠδ᾽ ἀχάλαζος πάντα φέρων καὶ πτηνὰ καὶ ἑρπετὰ θηρία γαίης. (...) Geffcken, [1902, pp. 65-67].

[24] Ὦ Ῥόδε δειλαίη σύ· σὲ γὰρ πρώτην, σὲ δακρύσω· ἔσσῃ δὲ πρώτη πόλεων, πρώτη δ᾽ ἀπολέσσῃ, ἀνδρῶν μὲν χήρη, βιότου δέ τε πάμπαν ἀδευκής· Δῆλε, σὺ μὲν πλεύσεις καὶ ἐφ᾽ ὕδατος ἄστατος ἔσσῃ·
Κύπρε, σὲ δ᾽ ἐξολέσει γλαυκῆς ποτε κῦμα θαλάσσης· Σικελίη, φλέξει σε τὸ καιόμενον κατὰ σοῦ πῦρ. τοῦτο λέγω, τὸ Θεοῦ φοβερὸν καὶ ἐπήλυτον ὕδωρ. Geffcken, [ibid. p. 133].

Sibyls let us know most categorically that the catastrophes we mentioned above are going to be followed by a happy era of joy and plenty, an idea most consistent with every other prophecy we have been treating in this study; this is yet another indication that they pertain to our proximate future and the next 5-6 years, most specifically.

The prophecies included in this chapter are by no means the only references of the Sibylline Oracles to the geological upheavals of our proximate future, but I hope this small sample suffices for our current purposes of analysis and comparison.

We have every reason to suspect that the geological upheavals are going to engulf the Mediterranean and the Black Sea and will reach beyond, such as the seas around India (for which we also have explicit European prophetic references, such as *Les Prophecies de Merlin*). The scope and vast expanse of these upheavals suggests most clearly the direct intervention of the Almighty God. Humans have not devised yet mechanisms capable of raising waves that high, causing tsunamis and bringing about inundations of such massive scope in so many far away places, all at the same time. Besides, the prophecies themselves speak of natural causes and not of human action in the bringing about of those catastrophes. It is my belief that the prophecies simply give us the bits of information, few at a time, each seer concentrating on a small corner of the globe and analyzing its fate with considerable detail, while expecting us to put the evidence together into an organic whole and thus generate a tapestry of global proportions, by synthesizing all the evidence at hand.

Let us also consider the following predictions from sources not explicitly treated in this chapter:

a)   Japan will be largely submerged (but not entirely) during a wave of earthquakes. (We shall see relevant prophecies, in a different chapter).

b)   There is an already sizeable and ever increasing body of evidence in the USA indicating the imminence of major geological upheavals, particularly in the Western States.[25] In fact, many seers predict the disappearance of a sizeable portion of California (except for a number of islands remaining) as well as of other parts of the USA's shoreline.

c)   In a subsequent chapter we shall investigate the prophetic evidence on the geological upheavals around the British Isles and Northern Europe.

The prophetic terminology advises us to look for a major natural cause. Their allusion to Noah's times, to a new age ushered in through fire and water, to the approach of the **great and eminent DAY OF THE LORD** all these suggest that our immediate future will be of extreme importance in the history of this planet, besides its obvious relevance for our particular destinies at the individual level. So, let us study further with due diligence the Word of the Spirit. Back to Nostradamus:

Century V: Quatrain 90:
Dans les cyclades, en perinthe & larisse,
Dedans Sparte tout le Peloponnesse:
Si grande famine, peste par faux (feux) connisse,
neuf mois tiendra & tout le cheronnesse.

Verbatim translation:
In the Cyclades Islands, in Perinthus, and Larissa, in Sparta and the entire Peloponnesus, such a great famine and a pestilence will be caused by a false powder (or fiery powder), that it will last for nine months and force an increase in the price of everything.

Suggested interpretation:*

---

[25] In this context the future map of the United States elaborated by Gordon Michael Scallion (Earth Changes Report via the Matrix Institute) as well as of several other US-authors, appears to be in agreement with forecasts from other sources. These U.S. authors, whose reputation has not yet been established throughout Christendom, considering that their work is so much recent vis-à-vis the main body of prophetic literature, deserve our attentive ear. They share with us their visions and information received directly from the Holy Ones, concerning geological upheavals in the USA. The famous US 'sleeping prophet', the late Edgar Cayce is reported predicting also that lands in the Western portion of America as well as a major part of Japan *will go into the sea* at some future time.

As the asterisk suggests, what follows is somewhat speculative, but still intriguing enough in its similarities with what we have studied so far. This quatrain predicts in various places of Greece a great famine and pestilence caused by *a false powder (fiery powder)*, which will last for nine months and will subject everything to price inflation. The areas explicitly mentioned are:

the islands of the Cyclades in the Southern Aegean Sea (between Eastern Peloponnesus and Western Asia Minor);

Perinthe (Perinthus, Perinthos, an ancient name for a town located not too far from the Dardanelles, within the Sea of Marmara (Propontis).[26] During later ages its name changed into Heraclea. The Turkish name of Perinthus became Marmaraereglisi = the phonetic adaptation of 'Heraclea on (the sea of) Marmara'.

Larissa is a name given to several Greek cities in antiquity. Specifically, to the major city of Thessaly, which although inland is not too far from the Northern Aegean Sea.[27]

Sparta and all of Peloponnesus are the last toponyms mentioned in the quatrain.

We should find intriguing the following items:

- since a Turkish town is included in the list, it appears that the 'false powder' is not going to be from a weapon of the enemy against Greek cities, for in that case the Turks (and their Muslim allies) would try to protect their own. The inclusion of a town currently belonging to European Turkey, therefore prima facie militates against a military/chemical weapon;

- if we assume that the Larissa of the quatrain is not the Thessalian one, then more Turkish towns besides Marmaraereglisi would be involved (if the Larissa of the quatrain corresponds to modern Turkish towns on the Aegean Sea: either near Troad or near

---

[26] A few previous authors stretched this word on their procrustean beds and concluded that Nostradamus must have meant Corinth even though he wrote down Perinthe (Perinthus)...

[27] Besides a second Larissa in Thessaly (Larissa Cremasti), there were ancient cities in Asia Minor south of Troy, on the Aegean; near Ephesus on Asia Minor, on the Aegean; another one between Palestine and Egypt; and another on the Tigris river.

Ephesus);

- **all** of the toponyms are on the Aegean Sea and its immediate vicinity in the Propontis and **all** of them are located not too far from the Island/volcano of Thera/Santorini, which is the southernmost island of the Cyclades.

Thera has been associated with one of the most fantastic volcanic eruptions in History. Before collapsing into the sea, the volcano is credited with the destruction of the kingdom of Crete (through tsunamis, firebrands and crop failures); others locate the eruption at the time of the Exodus, and explain the various plagues against the Pharaoh with the side-effects from such a tremendous eruption. This most fascinating subject is covered in many books, so we do not need to repeat its history in this study. It is still a speculation on my part, but let us consider for a moment what would happen in the event of a new eruption from beneath the waters of the Southern Aegean. The 'false powder' (or, rather, fire powder as certain manuscripts suggest, feux connisse and which I would prefer as the appropriate one) could quite possibly indicate the volcanic ash. This, like a hot and poisonous dust, spewed upwards at a great height, will be carried by the wind over a wider radius and will be deposited in the adjacent areas. Nostradamus began naming some of the reluctant recipients of the ash. It is quite logical to expect more information about other reluctant recipients either in Nostradamus or in other authors. But let us stick with the given quatrain for the time being.

The word 'connisse' is a phonetic adaption of the Greek κόνις-κόνεως, which according to the dictionary denotes "all solid substances which have been broken down into most minute particles, commonly, dust". When deposited on crop lands it will ruin the harvest for that particular year (for nine months Nostradamus predicts). It will cause the prices of foodstuffs to go out of the window!, & *tout le cheronnesse*, an indication of cost-push inflation. *Chérot* is a colloquialism denoting something a bit too expensive. Eventually the ash will be washed away and the following sowing season will not be (that much) affected. Under such circumstances, a crop failure could launch a true famine and be followed by diseases in humans, plants and animals (either as a result of the famine, or more directly through the deposition of various poisons present in the hot volcanic ash upon plants and animals, causing burns, blisters, etc. etc.).

As intimated above, if for nothing else, because of space shortage and rhyming constraints, the above quatrain does not mention other areas of Greece as being affected by the 'connisse'. The Ionian Islands, and Epirus are very earthquake-prone but mainly because of tectonic plates and not of submarine or surface volcanoes. Besides, the mountain ridges could afford a certain protection to Western Greece especially if the winds blow in a South-West to North-East direction, depending on the time of the year. The absence of mention of such areas of Greece, in my opinion, lends additional validity to the hypothesis of a Cyclades concentration of the problem and an Aegean concentration of the major consequences. This seems to have been the case during the previous eruption of Thera ca. 3.5 millennia ago, with disturbances in the West having been caused primarily by the tsunamis of the Thera volcano.

Of course, a quatrain is a limited area to squeeze a lot of geographical information, even with Nostradamus's skills. If he had said nothing else (throughout the rest of his work) on the rest of Greece in this connection we would have assumed that the locus of the damage was, indeed, limited. Unfortunately, further research reveals that this is not the case. So, additional information must be culled from other quatrains (and as it turns out from other prophets as well).

But let us first clarify a certain detail of the above quatrain: I would venture the proposition that Nostradamus tends to concentrate geographically his prophecies on a relative narrow geographical area, to the extent possible. This is a rule he rarely breaks. Therefore, we have reasons to believe that the Larissa of the above quatrain is located on Greek territory. It would be especially disastrous, therefore, if the Thessalian Larissa is implied, considering that this city is located in the middle of a major plain and has been the 'breadbasket' of Greece for many centuries. If the 'connisse' destroys the wheat crops of the Thessalian plain, the famine will be a most serious one, indeed, especially in a period of restricted sea trade (such as during a war with its embargoes and blockades, and/or port facilities destroyed at the same time by submersions and tsunamis).

The Greek prophet, St. Cosmas the Aetolean speaks also of a tremendous famine to occur in Greece some time in our future.[28] Consequently:

---

[28] The same prophecy numbering scheme will be preserved, as the one adopted in my previous study, where his WWIII-associated pronouncements were covered.

38.: Many will perish from hunger.
40: One handful of gold will be exchanged for one handful of flour.
53: If they find silver on the road they will not stop to pick it up. However, for a head of corn of wheat they will fight to the death.
75: A sad occurrence I predict for you: today, tomorrow, we are expecting thirst and great hunger, people will give thousands of golden coins and will be unable to find some bread.

Considering that St. Cosmas the Aetolean is the prophet of the terse verse par excellence, he did not try to be poetic with exaggerations and hyperboles. He presented matter-of-factly the relative exchange ratios prevalent in a future barter of money for food. In summary, this *feux connisse (faux connisse)* will indeed cause tremendous suffering and hunger. But notice that St. Cosmas mentions **thirst** too. Could that be due to the potable water becoming temporarily undrinkable because of the ejecta from the volcanoes and other impurities connected with the geological upheavals?

Back to Nostradamus:
Century IX: Quatrain 91:
L'horrible peste Perynte & Nicopolle
Le Chersonèse tiendra et Macédoine.
La Thessalie vastera l' Amphipolle,
Mal incogneu, & le refus d' Anthoine.

Verbatim translation:
The horrible pestilence will reach Perinthus, Nicopolis, the Peninsula of Gallipoli and Macedonia. Thessaly will 'devastate' Amphipolis, the evil has an unknown nature, and the refusal of Anthony.

Suggested interpretation:*
Here we deal with certain common traits and what, superficially, would appear as disconnected and irrelevant verbiage. But Nostradamus is parsimonious and does not waste words. *Nicopolis* is a name commonly used in Greek antiquity. There existed a Nicopolis in Thrace, built along the river Nestos by the Roman Emperor Trajan to commemorate his victory

there.[29] *Chersonèse* is the verbatim translation of Greek *Peninsula*, a most generic term applicable to all peninsulas. However, when used in isolation, it always referred to the Gallipoli peninsula. It is clear and unequivocal that here he refers again to the area around Perinthus, Thrace and Macedonia. *Amphipolis*, was located in Macedonia on the river Strymon, almost halfway between modern Salonica in the West and Kavala in the East; so, all the toponyms mentioned in the quatrain concentrate around the same geographical area, and accordingly we should choose (among all Nicopolises) the one close by, i.e., the Nicopolis of Trajan on the Nestos. Of course, this city exists no more, like so many others in the quatrains, but we are given explicit geographic coordinates to be able to identify the area of prophetic impact.

I have agonized over the expression *le refus d' Anthoine* (the refusal, denial of Anthony). I can only advance a speculation at this point: Marc Anthony was the most famous Anthony ever to be associated with Greek History and to fight on Greek soil. He did so on two occasions:

a)   in the beginning of his military career along with Octavian against Brutus and Cassius, the murderers of Julius Caesar. That took place in Philippi, a Greek city of Macedonia, in October 42 B.C.[30] There, Octavian and Anthony had a glorious victory, and Cassius and Brutus perished.

b)   the second occasion was at the sea-battle of Actium, (31 B.C.). There the joined forces of Anthony and Cleopatra were defeated by Octavian, who commemorated his victory by erecting the Nicopolis

---

[29]   ('Nicopolis'-named cities are victory commemorators as their etymology implies and there have been several such toponyms in Western Greece, in Asia Minor, around the Black Sea on the Russian side, in Israel, Egypt, and elsewhere). The one on the River Nestos would correspond beyond the current Greek borders on the north.

[30]   See Plutarch's *Lives*, under "Marcus Brutus". The reader may remember Plutarch's account of a ghost appearing to Brutus in his tent with the message 'I am your evil genius, Brutus, you shall see me at Philippi'. And Brutus's cool response: "Then I shall see you".

Actia in the vicinity of the ancient fort of Vereniki.[31]

Consequently, the refusal of Anthony may imply the initial military exploits of Anthony in the battlefield of Philippi, an ancient city of Macedonia, located a short distance north-east of Amphipolis, ergo, in the general area under consideration in this quatrain. (On the other hand, if it refers to Anthony's being refused victory at Nicopolis Actia, then we are taken to Western Greece and the Ionian Sea, and a different Nicopolis altogether). I feel, however, that Nostradamus is concerned with Macedonia in this particular occasion. Consequently, this is the second, corroborating, quatrain at our disposal, which enlarges somewhat the total information available to us. I will not advance any more speculations at this point.

Does Nostradamus tell us anything else concerning other portions of the Aegean and its fates in the event of a phenomenon such as a volcanic eruption from Thera? What about Rhodes and Creta and Cyprus, for instance? Or territories south of Thera, towards Egypt, Israel and other lands of the Middle East? Let us continue our search, by excluding all his references to those toponyms in an exclusively military context.

Century II: Quatrain 3:
Pour la chaleur solitaire sous la mer
De Negrepont les poissons demi cuits:[32]
Les habitants les viendront entamer
Quand Rhod & Gennes leur faudra le biscuit.

Verbatim translation:
Because of the solitary (unusual) heat under the sea, the fishes in Euboea will be half-cooked. The inhabitants will come and cut (and eat them) when there will be hunger in Rhodes and Genoa.

---

[31] Also spelled Berenice, and named by Pyrrhus, King of Epirus, after his mother in law, the Queen Berenice of Egypt, of the Macedonian Dynasty of the Ptolemies.

[32] Prima facie the term Negrepont, Negropont would have translated as black bridge or black sea. Yet, it is the vulgarized phonetic adaptation for the Straits of Euripus, and by extension the island of Euboea. Εἰς τόν Εὔριπον, στόν ῎Εγριπον, ν ῎Εγριπον, negripon, negropon, negropont. This remarkable transformation comes in additional flavors, but they should not concern us here.

Suggested interpretation:
Solitary heat under the sea is consistent with a violent under-water volcanic eruption in the Aegean. Rhodes and Genoa will suffer hunger at that same time, possibly for similar reasons (crop failure by volcanic 'connisse' and, in the case of Genoa, upheavals again of marine and geological origin.

Other prophecies have more to say concerning the future fate of Greek Islands in the Aegean.

SibOr, Book III, excerpts from vs. 492-519.
*Woe to the race of **Phoenician men and women and all the maritime cities**[33] none of you will come to the sunlight in common light. (...) for God will terribly subdue them with afflictions beyond all the earth, and send a bitter fate upon them, burning their cities from the ground and many foundations.*

Woe to you, Crete, of many sorrows. *To you will come affliction and fearful, eternal destruction (complete deliverance through death). The whole earth will **again see you smoking** and fire will not leave for ever but you will burn.* (Then follows a list of peoples that would today correspond to Muslims of Turkey, Arabia, North Africa, and the Middle East) (...) *Why indeed should I proclaim each one according to its fate? **for, on all peoples, as many as inhabit the earth will the Most High send a terrible affliction.*** [Emphasis mine].

The Sibyl, having gone down the list of geographical areas already known to the Ancients, goes a step further with the all-encompassing and most categorical statement: **for, on all peoples, as many as inhabit the earth.** But let us return to Crete for a moment, where she tells us that the whole earth 'will **again** see it smoking'. Is this, per chance, a reference to the destruction of the Minoan civilization during the previous eruption of Thera? For, this is the only historical prior reference at our disposal of such a major catastrophe through fire.

The fact that the Sibyl also mentions explicitly places in North Africa and the Middle East as being also affected at that time, is most consistent with our theory. A major eruption will spread over a wide radius and cover lots of territory. We get their names repeated again and again, and also the

---

[33] This suggest the coastline of Palestine and Israel and vicinity.

Hebrew Prophets of the Old Testament make pronouncements that are internally consistent with such a scenario.

I wish to call two 'additional witnesses' on the defense stand:

a)   the events surrounding the Santorini eruption during the second millennium B.C.. These are covered in numerous professional studies and scientific papers not only by Archaeologists and Bible researchers but also by Geologists, Volcanologists and Orogenists.

b)   The tremendous similarity of some of Nostradamus's hints with the historical data from the Tambora Island volcanic eruption of 1815 A.D., which ushered in the 'year without summer'.

Let us scrutinize some of the facts of that particular event in some detail:

The sound from the Tambora explosions reached the island of Sumatra situated 970 geographical miles away from its Indonesian epicenter. The ashes from the volcano created such a profound darkness during daytime on the island of Java 'that nothing equal to it had ever been witnessed during the darkest night'. The ash pall turned the days so dark as to be indistinguishable from nights and these lasted for three days following the eruption. The blast involved in Tambora would correspond to detonating three times the nuclear weapons stockpiles available in the world during the 1980s, according to the research findings by scientists. Ash layers ruined the local crops, caused famines and gave rise to diseases. The wider effects killed about eight times more people than the eruption in the immediate vicinity of the catastrophe locus.

As the observers of the more recent Mt. Pinatubo eruption surely can associate with, the ash and dust ejected by the force of the eruption of Tambora reached the higher layers of the atmosphere and traveled around the world. They spread over the Northern Hemisphere, sucked in, so to say, by the jet stream. The reduction of sunlight caused what became known as the 'year without summer' to millions of people who had no idea at the time on what was going on somewhere in the Southern Hemisphere many thousands of miles away. It caused snowfalls in summer time, their crops failed and their sunsets assumed beautiful hues. The crop failures of 1816 raised the price of wheat to heights never again matched except for the period of the early 1970s when crop failures in the USSR and the Oil-Embargo consequences caused a world-wide shortage of grain.

116

William K. Hartmann [1991, pp. 205-206] advanced a very interesting speculation on the wider global effects of the Tambora eruption. In his own words,

> *(...) provocative data suggest that the eruption also led to the first world-wide epidemic of Asiatic cholera, which caused hundreds of thousands of additional deaths from 1816 to 1830. (...) The famine in Bengal in 1816-17 led to another outbreak there. (...) By 1819 cholera was in South India, by 1823 in Turkey and Asia Minor, and by 1830 in Moscow. Some 50,000 people fled Moscow and 200,000 people reportedly died in Pest, Poland. By 1832 cholera had spread into Europe and Egypt, (...) in 1832 the disease showed up in New York City where deaths approached 100 per day, mostly among the poor. (...)*

It is my feeling that the above speculation by Dr. Hartmann supplies us with a most nutritious food for speculative thought. The consequences of a famine-related epidemic could be more disastrous during a war (and the sanitation problems associated with crowding so many persons in the barracks). Also, during a war, the international transportation system may not remain unobstructed by enemy submarines, embargoes and blockades and people will be forced more than ever to subsist on local supplies, in the absence of buffer stocks. If the local crops fail and the increase in prices is too much for the poor to handle, the organism weakens and becomes more susceptible to diseases (old and new and newly discovered, which we are told have developed immunity to our anti-biotics and are bound to wreck havoc in the future).[34]

What Nostradamus refers to so explicitly with regards to Eastern Greece and the Aegean, he also repeats in many of his other quatrains (war and famine at the same time). Now let us see the quatrains which explicitly speak of a 'comet' proper.

---

[34] Excellent studies of such effects are William H. McNeill, [1989], and F. F. Cartwright et all. [1972], among others.

NOSTRADAMUS ON COMETS
AND THEIR CORRELATION WITH WAR, ETC.

Century II: Quatrain 15:
Un peu devant monarque trucidé
Castor, Pollux en nef, astre crinite
L'erain public par terre & mer vuidé
Pise, Ast, Ferrare, Turin terre interdicte.

Verbatim translation:
Crinitus in Latin means hairy, with long hair. A star provided with long hair is most obviously a comet. So, a little earlier the monarch will be killed; Castor and Pollux are in a ship and a comet appears. The public monetary contributions are squandered in land and sea and the North Italian cities of Pisa, Asti, Ferrara and Torino will become forbidden territory.

Suggested interpretation:
Castor and Pollux are the famous Dioscuri, the Gemini of Greek Mythology, the sons of Jupiter and Leda. It may be a reference to two high-born brothers who will be active militarily at that time. All that can be said for now is that during a war (which per force dissipates public money in land and sea) and the death of a King, a comet will coexist with the major destruction of those cities. (Either through war they become off limits or through natural catastrophes. We cannot tell for sure from the information provided to us). We can only return to this quatrain after sufficient additional information becomes available.

Century II: Quatrain 41:
La grand estoille par sept jours bruslera,
Nuée fera deux soleils apparoir:
Le gros mastin toute nuict hurlera
Quand grand pontife changera de terroir.

Verbatim translation:
The great star will be burning for seven days,
a cloud will give the impression that there are two suns in the sky; the great dog will howl all night long, at the time when the Pope will be changing territory.

Suggested interpretation:
I believe that the 'great star' is the comet of our proximate future. From

Byzantine era prophecies, we are informed that a 'certain sign in the sky' will look like a sun with a hallo around it. (See in a later chapter the specifics of that description). We also have been informed from a great variety of sources of the phenomenon of the Three Day Darkness. If we consider a 'day' lasting 12 hours on the average, then 7 days can be 3 days of darkness, 3 nights of darkness and the 7th day when the sky begins clearing up and signs become more visible in the heavens. The fact that the Pope will be forced to abandon Rome during a major conflict, (in fact, literally walking over the corpses of priests and bishops, as certain Catholics predicted) is a theme corroborated by a large number of prophecies, and more will be said in this connection elsewhere in this study.

Century II: Quatrain 43:
Durant l'estoille chevelue apparente,
Les trois grands princes seront faits ennemis:
Frappés du ciel paix terre tremulante,
Pau, Timbre undans, serpent sus le bord mis.

Verbatim translation:
During the appearance of the star furnished with hair (a comet) the three great princes will become enemies. Peace and the earth will tremble being beaten by the skies; in the Italian rivers of Po and Tiber waves will rise and a serpent will be cast out upon the shore.

Suggested interpretation:
Once again a presence of a comet coinciding with military activity (supplying an extra clue to us). Again, the earth will start shaking, but now Nostradamus tells us that the agent of the earthquake activity will come from the sky! Also, waves will rise in unusual places. I find this quatrain impregnated with important messages for us: It appears that the gravitational pull exerted by the comet will cause not only inundations in the sea but also it will raise the waters in the rivers (and in the lakes, too, as we shall see later on). And, once again, this will take place during a period of war because the peace will also be 'tremulante' besides the earth.

Century II: Quatrain 46:
Après grand troche humain plus grand s'appreste,
Le grand moteur les Siecles renouvèlle:
Pluie, sang, laict, famine, fer & peste,
Au ciel veu feu, courant long estincelle.

Verbatim translation:
'*Troche*' comes from the ancient Greek verb τρυχόω, τρύχω, τρύω, to wear out, torment, consume, waste; to vex, distress, afflict, exhaust. Consequently, after a great distress (affliction) an even greater one presses itself upon the human race, the Great Mover is renewing the Ages: rain, blood, milk, famine, iron and pestilence. In the skies a fire is seen, which while running traces behind it a long spark.

Suggested interpretation:
God is renewing the ages, means we approach a new era (the entering of the 3rd millennium?). Again, we are told that the fire in heaven, supplied with a long spark will appear at a time when humanity will have already been subjected to a great affliction (war?). What will those two afflictions bring us: rain (of what?); blood; milk (very interesting, we shall come back to this much later in this study); famine, iron (a symbol for sword and, by extension, war. But also, quite possibly of ferruginous elements spewed out from the volcanoes along with the famous 'connisse', being deposited on crops and causing famine and pestilence).[35]

At the time of the writing of the quatrains the world had already forgotten Santorini, and Pompeii waited patiently under several feet of volcanic ash till the 19th century to be rediscovered. Therefore, such minute reference to the consequences of major natural catastrophes written in the 16th century gives rise to awe and humility. Dr. Robert Muir Wood [1987, pp. 116-117] as if echoing Nostradamus cautions us against too much nonchalance:

Yet volcanoes do not always look like great conical mountains. There are numerous beautiful lakes, surrounded by forested hills and picturesque villages - in Guatemala, in Italy, in Indonesia and in New Zealand - that are really no more than volcanic craters, produced by cataclysmic eruptions which destroyed any pretense of a conical mountain. **Some day, one or**

---

[35] Considering that volcanoes are the industrial complexes par excellence for the recovery of minerals and metals and diamonds, operating with their own energy sources, it is thanks to their 'purification and concentration' processes under the surface of the earth and at high temperatures that we receive the scarce mineral elements so vital for our civilization. Consequently, most of the copper, gold, lead, platinum, chromium, manganese, aluminum, iron, etc. and practically all of the diamonds reach us during this life-giving and life-destroying activity from the bowels of the earth. Other minerals, such as the poisonous sulfur and mercury will emerge in form of gases with the fumaroles.

other of these beautiful lakes will begin to seethe and boil as a new volcano emerges from the depths. [Emphasis added]. (...) While Europeans know all about volcanoes in Italy, few realize that in the center of France there are a series of volcanoes which last erupted a few thousand years ago, and will almost certainly erupt again. Only 30 miles to the south of Cologne, in the industrial heartland of Western Europe, there are volcanic craters which last erupted explosively only 11,000 years ago, depositing a series of ash layers than can be traced from Italy to Finland. (...)

On the other hand, in 1783 in Iceland, the poison fog that came from the fissure eruptions **killed all** vegetation and caused great death rates to animals and humans through disease and starvation. 'The poisoned fog that comes from the north' mentioned in other prophecies (such as St. Hildegard of Bingen) ought to be kept in mind while studying further the evidence.

Now is the time for the four lakes that will burn and also the Bon Mariniers and what will happen to them...

Century III: Quatrain 12:
Par la tumeur de Heb., Po, Tag. Tibre & Rhone
Et par l'estang Leman & Aretin
Les deux grands chefs & citez de Garonne, (Bordeaux Toulouse)
Prins, mortz noyez. Partir humain butin.

Verbatim translation:
Because of the swelling of the rivers Hebro (in Spain), Po (in Italy), Tagus (in the Iberian Peninsula), Tiber (in Italy) and Rhone (in France), and also because of the swelling of the lakes Leman (in Geneva, Switzerland) and Aretin (in Italy) the French cities on the Garonne which are the major ones, namely Bordeaux and Toulouse will be victims of death by drowning. (La Garonne is a river beginning in the Pyrenees and exiting in the Atlantic, which floods frequently; Toulouse and Bordeaux **are** the major cities on the Garonne). The belongings of the population will be divided (not mentioning by whom).

Suggested interpretation:
For the time being we shall concentrate on the fact that several major European rivers and lakes will see their waters rising spectacularly. Also, as it would be expected severe flooding by Garonne, which is also swelling at the same time. We must assume that, for, otherwise Bordeaux and

Toulouse will not have the fate predicted by Nostradamus. We will have to come back to this quatrain when more is known about the behavior of European rivers in the future.

Century II: Quatrain 60:
La foy Punicque en Orient rompue,
Gang, Ind, & Rosne Loyre & Tag. changeront:
Quand du mulet la faim sera repue,
Classe espargie, sang & corps nageront.

Verbatim translation:
Punica Fides means Carthaginian Faith, and was an expression much in vogue with the Romans, their nemesis. They held it for a treacherous kind of faith, accusing the Carthaginians to frequently breaking their contracts and treatises. Consequently, the term *Punica fides* (la foy Punicque) is a suggestion by Nostradamus of a people (or group of peoples) notorious for their bad faith, or an agreement very strongly reminiscent of such dealings. First verse tells us that in the Orient the bad faith will be broken (presumably after a war); the rivers Ganges and Indus as well as Rhone, Loire and Tagus will change their beds.[36] '*Mulet*' can mean two distinct things in French: a) a mule, a quadrupedal animal, and b) a mullet, a sweet-water but also sea-water fish, which lives on plankton.[37] In either case, when the hunger of that animal (mule or mullet, as the case may be) is satiated, the fleet will be scattered over the waves and blood and corpses will swim on the sea. Nostradamus does not say how long after the change of the rivers the hunger will be satiated and the fleet scattered; only that these events will

---

[36] Previous commentators felt that instead of Ind there was a term Iud in the text. They then proceeded transforming this Iud to sound like Iudas, hence the river Jordan in Israel. I have no reasons to believe that the river Jordan will remain unscathed in the event of the geological upheavals that are the focus of our chapter. Especially, in view of prophecies from elsewhere predicting the disappearance of the waters of the Dead Sea. I feel, however, that Nostradamus wrote Ind (which was mistakenly transcribed by some of his original editors into Iud early on). *Les Prophecies de Merlin* speak of major geological upheavals in India. It is very reasonable, therefore, to expect that Indus in the West and Ganges in the East will also be affected.

[37] (If Nostradamus implied the fish, and if this fish exhibits any particular geographical preference, maybe he is trying to tell us something. I am completely unable to propose a plausible theory at this point).

follow temporally.

Suggested interpretation:
Again, we are given several clues: a few of the previously mentioned rivers will not only swell but also change their course; additionally, far away rivers will behave in a similar fashion. This suggests the global scope of the underlying energies that can change the flow of so many rivers. This will happen during a period of war. Not only the 'punica fides' will be broken but a fleet will be destroyed (by geological upheavals, or through military action?) and the dead will float on the water.

Century VI: Quatrain 4:
Le Celtique fleuve changera de rivage,
Plus ne tiendra la cité d' Agripine:
Tout transmué hormis le vieil langage,
Saturn, Leo, Mars, Cancer en rapine.

Verbatim translation and suggested interpretation:*
Celtic river is the Rhenus (Rhine). *City of Agrippina* should be most likely identified with the city of Köln of Germany, itself a phonetic adaptation of Latin *Colonia*. (Colonia Agrippina, or Colonia Agrippinensis) a Roman city named after Nero's mother, because she was born there. Therefore, this being the city of Agrippina par excellence, it may well be the one intended by Nostradamus, who informs us that the flow of the Rhine will change in the future and it will not go through Cologne (Köln) any longer. Also, everything else will be changed except the old language. This will occur when Saturn, Leo, Mars and Cancer are *in plunder*.

Now, a potentially additional clue suggesting that we are speaking about the German Colonia Agrippina, proper, is the prediction that everything except the language will be different after this event which will force the river to change. We know from many other sources, that politically and religiously Germany will be changed after WWIII, for one thing, many prophecies predict the disappearance of Protestantism and the re-unification of Christian churches. Also, the union of Germany with other German speaking European populations in the future, under the Empire of the Great Monarch. Besides, the littoral, the cities horizons, population density, etc. will be affected, like everywhere else in the world, provided we are speaking about the same periods of time and the same joint forces. Having no background whatsoever and no clues to decode the last verse giving us the astrological time-coordinates of the times referred to, I admit inability to speculate any further. However, the reader may wish to keep this quatrain (already marked by an asterisk) in the background, until more evidence becomes available.

Century II: Quatrain 52:
Dans plusieurs nuits la terre tremblera:
Sur le printemps deux effors suite:
Corinthe, Ephese aux deux mers nagera,
Guerre s' esmeut par deux vaillans de luite.

Verbatim translation:
For the length of several nights the earth will tremble:
During springtime there will be two efforts following each other:
Corinth and Ephesus will swim in two seas,
and a war is stirred up by two men valiant in contest.

Suggested interpretation:
I feel that Nostradamus is truly generous with the clues he is providing: He speaks of the length of several *nights*, as if the god of the earthquakes plans to be sleeping during the day and to work only night shifts! This appears to be a clue to 'The Three Days Darkness'.[38] When this phenomenon occurs, it will appear that the earth will be shaking for several 'nights' in a row. He also tells us it will take place in the Spring, when two major seismic waves will follow each other. Corinth being built at the union point between the Corinthian and the Saronic Gulfs, it overlooks two seas, already. But the prophet tells us it will swim in two seas.[39] Is this a suggestion that in the geological upheavals Corinth will be broken up from Peloponnesus and become an island? (We know from other sources that close-by Mycenae will founder; and we already saw predictions about the Saronic Gulf's upheavals).

---

[38] Let us refer to his own prior mention of seven days during which the earth will tremble. At that time I speculated that his length was an indication that days are indistinguishable from nights due to the darkness and can be counted separately as "days".

[39] When dealing with the 'pont ruiné' in the prophecy about Attica, I was wondering if the Isthmus of Corinth was implied. But Attica, strictly speaking, does not reach till the Isthmus, and I abandoned that version for the one involving 'port ruiné'.

Ephesus, furthermore, will swim in two seas as well, and this is more amazing. Ephesus, while the Greeks controlled the area, was a famous *harbor* on the Eastern Aegean at the mouth of the Kaystros River. Today it is located three miles inland, as a result of a silting process that was left to take its course. Between 1450 A.D. and 1950 A.D. (before it was rediscovered by masses of Western Archaeologists and foreign tourists) it lay dormant and forgotten. For Ephesus, therefore, to swim in two seas it will take a bigger trembling than the one around Corinth. The Greek Ephesus was located in the center of a crescent shaped gulf, just opposite to the island of Samos, which our Sibyls predict will become synonymous to sand (Σάμος, ἄμμος). As we remember, this will happen when Delos, after swimming unsteady on the sea will become invisible (Δῆλος, ἄδηλος).[40] We cannot tell for sure from the information in the quatrain who the two valiant men are, but at least we are given an additional hint that we shall have war contemporaneously with the geological disturbances.

Century III: Quatrain 3:
Mars & Mercure & l' argent ioint ensemble
Vers le midy extreme siccité
Au fond d' Asie on dira terre tremble,
Corinthe, Ephese lors en perplexité.

Verbatim translation:
Mars and Mercury and 'silver' joined together
in the south there will occur extreme drought
In the depths of Asia they will say that the earth trembles
and at that time Corinthe and Ephesus will be in perplexity.

Suggested interpretation:
I believe this refers to the same time as the previous one, with the additional clue offered to us now that also in the depths of Asia the earth will be shaking at that time. Corinth and Ephesus will be in perplexity seeing their geological neighborhood being violently transformed under their nose. Silver may be a reference to the moon (the silver disk on the sky), and the first verse being the normal dating system of Nostradamus: when Mars, Mercury and the Moon will be in conjunction.

---

[40] Delos, a tiny island of great historical interest, lies between Mykonos and Rinia. It belongs to the Cycladic group, which brings it closer to the epicenter of our imputed Santorinian source of upheavals and would explain its future demise.

SibOr III, vs. 457-463:
'A sign for Cyprus; an earthquake will destroy the ravines and Hades will receive many souls at once. Trallis[41] will undo by an earthquake her well-made walls, and a people of grave-minded men. **The earth will flood with boiling water, then the earth, weighed down will drink of it. There will be a smell of brimstone. Samos also will build royal palaces in due time.** (...) [Emphasis mine].

Again we have evidence on Cyprus and Ephesus being hit at the same time. It is most interesting to see how the earth will become heavy and founder in the well-established region of Western Anatolia. Could that be a reference to the destruction caused by the volcano in Santorini? Boiling water and brimstone appear to militate for such a theory. Also, Samos, (for which also catastrophe is implied and not spelled out) is given the assurance that after its destruction it will rise again and become a choice real estate in times to be.

And again, **vs. 485-488:** There will be lamentations with many groans among the Galatians. A final but greatest disaster will come upon Tenedus. Brazen Sicyon, and you, Corinth, will boast over all, with howls, and the flute will sound in equal manner.[42]

Tenedus is one of the two islands in front of the Gallipoli Peninsula; they currently belong to Turkey. In this prophecy we get corroboration for something we have been suspecting all along. Namely, if the evil effects of the 'feux connisse' can reach Perinthus, they must pass over Tenedus. *Sicyon*, on the other hand, is on the Northern Peloponnesus, close to the Corinthian Gulf. Ancient Sicyon was a prosperous town and considered the most ancient kingdom in Greece. It was ruled by kings long before Agamemnon added it to his domains.

Once again *Corinth* emerges as a target of dire vaticination. It is worth noting, further, that **all these events are grouped together by the Sibyl into the same body of evidence.**

---

[41] a neighbor of Ephesus,

[42] Γαλάταις δὲ πολύστονος ἔσσεται οἶκτος. ἥξει καὶ Τενέδῳ κακὸν ἔσχατον, ἀλλὰ μέγιστον. καὶ Σικυῶν χάλκειος ὑλάγμασι καὶ σὲ, Κόρινθε, αὐχήσει ἐπὶ πᾶσιν· ἴσον δὲ βοήσεται αὐλός. Geffcken, [op. cit. p. 73].

We shall conclude the testimony of this chapter with a few additional entries from *Les Prophecies de Merlin.*

CCVII, folio 103d: *(...) And at that time, when war will have once again began among the peoples of the earth, they will be able to see both on the sea and on the land one of those miracles performed by God before the Pharaoh, when he was keeping the sons of Israel in servitude. And this will be the beginning of the anger of that war and it will be the Greeks who will suffer from food shortage.*[43]

LI, folio 57b, entitled: *Et des quatre fumees qui sortyront de quatre lacz*: In a summary form, the main messages of that lengthy prophecy which spills over into the equally lengthy one that follows **(LII**, entitled: *Des gens qui istront fors du pais por les fumees)* are that there are four lakes out of which smoke will emanate at some future point in time, and specifically immediately after the death of the Dragon of Babylon (vide supra). The first is located in French Brittany, and the adjacent French cities will be afflicted; the second is in Mesopotamia, and the land will worsen to such an extent as to be affected all the way to the sea; the third will be in the Barbary coast and the land will be affected all the way to the Mediterranean; the fourth will be emanating from the lake Garda in Northern Italy and the damage will cover an area from French Lyon to the territories of Venice. In fact, the Venetians will be forced to abandon their territories (almost to the man) and settle in the islands of the sea (not explicitly named in the prophecy). From the context it appears that those sadder but wiser Venetians are the happy survivors of the disaster and the war, because they will live in a most Christian manner during the rest of their earthly lives.

BIBLICAL REFERENCES TO THE SAME EVENTS
BY THE OLD TESTAMENT PROPHETS

Several OT Prophets have spoken rather extensively on the events of our near future. In fact, there is repeated mention of the 'Assyrian' and his destruction and his land's destruction during a time of invasion against Israel. Many previous commentators have attributed those predictions to past History. But this was unwarranted by the context of the prophecies.

---

[43] Lucy Allen Paton, [op. cit. p. 327].

Let us begin with an obiter dictum by Wilhelm Bousset:[44]

The Assyrians emerge for the first time in the late Apocalyptic literature. Almost always, their name presents a mystery. (My translation).

Considering that we are writing on this subject almost a century after Bousset, the Assyrians should not present a mystery any longer. Regrettably, too many instant experts who have bought the theory that Russia is the Gog and Magog of Ezekiel have brought too much confusion into the research. Whenever the terms Gog and Magog appear in the prophecies they transformed them to read 'Russia'. As a result, one of these days the Soviet Union (sic) is bound to annex Palestine, and needless to say, Russia will burn completely...

Since the identities of Gog and Magog have been fully established in *Our Revelationary Age...* we can now read the prophecies of the OT with reference to the 'Assyrian' and his Muslim allies during WWIII without confusion. We can, therefore, appreciate the many valuable details the Hebrew Prophets offer us to supplement our much more recent prophetic sources.

It appears that Prophet **Isaiah**'s chapters 10 to 26 apply to the events of our near future. This becomes most apparent in the following chapters: 10 (especially vs 23-32); 11; 13 (especially vs 9-15); 14; 24 and 26. The entire chapter 24 is filled with references to the coming terrible Day of the Lord. While chap. 26:20 is particularly interesting: *Proceed, my people, enter into your chambers, and shut your doors behind you; hide yourselves for a little while until the Lord's wrath is past.* It is my belief that the above passage offers advice to the Elect of taking cover and all the necessary precautions during the Three Days Darkness.

Also in **Isaiah 13**, and particularly vs. 9-22: *(...) Behold, the day of the Lord comes! Fierce, with wrath and raging anger, to make the land and the whole earth a desolation, and to destroy out of it its sinners. For the stars of the heavens and their constellations will not give their light; the sun will be*

---

[44] I am indebted for this detail to Paul J. Alexander, [1967, p. 107, ft. 181]. The original remark by Wilhelm Bousset was printed in the Zeitschrift für Kirchenge-schichte, (1900), under the title *Beiträge zur Geschichte der Eschatologie*, p. 104, no. 1.

darkened at its rising, and the moon will not shed its light. (...) Therefore I will make the heavens tremble, and the earth shall be shaken out of its place at the wrath of the Lord of hosts in the day of His fierce anger. (...) And Babylon, the glory of kingdoms, (...) shall be as Sodom and Gomorrah when God overthrew them. (...)

Isaiah, chap. 17:1: *(...) Behold, Damascus will cease to be a city, and will become a heap of ruins.*[45]

The OT prophets have no choice but speak of Babylon and Assyria and Ishmael and the Mede, when they truly mean Iraq, Saddam Hussein and his armies and his allies. If for no other reason, Iraq, as a geographical term and nation's name did not exist when the Pentateuch was being composed. The country of Iraq took its name from a rock and this name dates from the Arab conquest of Mesopotamia, following the death of Mohammed. But, on the other hand, the Prophets of OT become clear and most specific on the modern realities of our world, after we have made the necessary linguistic transformations and established the true contemporary identity of peoples and places.

Going back to the previous reference by Isaiah we see that in the same prophecy we have all the necessary elements: we deal with the day of the Lord; the sinners will be destroyed (and not only the Iraqis and Babylon); a darkness will be cast upon the earth beginning with sunrise; terrifying earthquakes; invasion of Israel; destruction of its enemies; etc.

There are numerous references across Isaiah concerning the horrendous events of our near future. Also, **chap. 34:8-10**: *For the Lord has a day of vengeance, a year of recompense for the cause of Zion. And the streams of Edom shall be turned into pitch, and its dust into brimstone, and its land will become burning pitch. The burning of Edom shall not be quenched night or*

---

[45] The rest of the chapter indicates a major war and great carnage, but also the utter, sudden destruction of Israel's enemies from Above. The prophecy does not specify how Damascus will become a heap of rocks, but we know from another prophecy, a much later one, that during WWIII, *'the young Lion's victories conclude with the destruction of Damascus'*. (Later in the text of that prophecy follows the description of the time of the Antichrist). [W. Bousset, 1896, p. 76]. This young Lion will be a Bourbon, a blood relative to King Juan Carlos I. Damascus is famed as the oldest **continuously inhabited**, city in the world.

day; its smoke shall go up for ever; (...).[46] Consequently, we learn about the impeding destruction of several port cities of Palestine also through the OT. (We saw earlier the Sibyls predicting the same events).

But let us now turn to another OT prophet, and analyze one of his writings in greater detail. Joel is the only prophet speaking of the valley of Jehoshaphat. (See chap. 3, where the term is mentioned repeatedly). Such a place has not been geographically identified yet. The term Jehoshaphat means 'Yahweh judges'; therefore the name may simply indicate a future event to be associated unequivocally with God's judgement. It is also referred to as the valley of decision.[47]

Joel, 3:14-16: *Multitudes, multitudes in the valley of decision! For the day of the Lord is near in the valley of decision. The sun and moon grow dark, and the stars lose their brightness. And the Lord roars from Zion, and utters His voice from Jerusalem. And the heavens and the earth tremble. But the Lord is a refuge for His people and a stronghold to the sons of Israel. And* **3:18 onwards**: *And it shall come to pass in that day, that the mountains shall drop down new wine, and the hills shall flow with milk and all the rivers of Judah shall flow with waters, (...) Egypt shall be a desolation, and Edom shall be a desolate wilderness, for the violence against the children of Judah, because they have shed innocent blood in their land. (...).*

Let us now see whether more recent prophecies can shed any light on that valley of decision: *Les Prophecies de Merlin*,[48] **prophecy CLXII, folio 129c**. The highlights of that long prophecy are as follows:

---

[46] Edom, which translates as 'red' is the name given to the mountainous land of Seir, upon which the Hebrews of the Exodus wandered. Velikovsky, [op. cit. p. 50, fn. 11], believes the name was given precisely because the ferruginous material that covered the landscape during the eruptions and the other geological events associated with the Exodus gave it that unmistakable red color. Since the prophecy of Isaiah was written centuries after the Exodus, we expect the new plight of Edom to occur in the future.

[47] Some scholars have identified it with the valleys of Hinnom or Kidron. When more is known of the details, we may be able to advance our own speculation as to the exact location.

[48] (from the manuscript collection of the Municipal Library of Rennes, from which all our references from *Les Prophecies de Merlin*, included in this study, emanate).

A fire will emanate from heaven and will come upon the sea, and from the sea it will come upon the dry land. But before arriving upon the dry land, that fire will have burnt both land and sea below the waters all the way down to the abyss. A short time afterwards, a sword will descend from heaven upon the plain of Burtumble.[49] This is a place in the vicinity of Jerusalem. More than 200,000 enemy soldiers will have been gathered there, men who have sworn to destroy all Christians. At that time a king will be in Jerusalem, a very evil person. And it must be known that the sword will administer justice on account of him only, because his faith can never be changed. The faith professed by his followers is not as steadfast as their king's. Therefore, at that time, the Lord Jesus Christ will only have to demand in Jerusalem action upon that king only.

This sword will descend from heaven. It will go through those infidels and cut off their heads without effort. Nobody will escape that sword among those present there. Once this action is performed, an angel will descend from heaven, he will retrieve the sword, will go to the pinnacle of the temple and will say openly to all those who happen to be in Jerusalem at that time, to guard against receiving a similar justice for their own evil doings, as those in Burtumble who just now received it because of their sins, their iniquities and their bad faith. And having done this, both the angel and the sword will ascend to heaven.[50]

There is no certainty that the above prophecy is referring to Jehoshaphat, the valley of justice and the valley of decision, spoken by Joel. However, there are certain items that would militate for such a speculation:

■   *And the Lord roars from Zion, and utters His voice from Jerusalem,*

---

[49] This Burtumble is a rather poor phonetic adaptation of Bethenopolis, ca. 7 miles northwest of Jerusalem, in the region known as 'Emmaus'; it is known as Beit Nabala, Beit-Nouba, Neballat, Nevallat, located in central Palestine. In 1192 A.D. a military encounter took place there between the Crusaders under King Richard and soldiers of Saladdin. However, those events were most insignificant by comparison, and no fire came from heaven to the sea and land at that time, nor did any sword and angel descend from heaven.

[50] See also Lucy Allen Paton, [op. cit. vol 1, pp. 209-210].

And the heavens and the earth tremble, says Joel. In Merlin it is the Angel who speaks from the pinnacle of the Temple in Jerusalem, although we are not told which Temple, specifically.

■   Joel speaks of major earthquake and signs in the heavens. Here too, we are told of a fire coming from heaven, burning the sea and the land, reaching into the entrails of the earth and then moving its destructiveness upon dry land and this region outside Jerusalem in particular. One must assume that the enemy troops have been stationed there.

Admittedly, the connection of Beit-Nuba with the valley of decision in Joel is rather speculative. But the entire text of this entry from *Les Prophecies de Merlin* suggests a judgement directly from Above. From the fire that descends, to the sword that descends to the Angel who descends last. This sword may very well indicate the geological consequences of the comet and the explosion and the ejecta from nearby volcanoes (compare the fire that reaches the top of the sea and burns down into the abyss).

I wish to make a final remark: The way of destruction of an infidel army outside Jerusalem (in Burtumble) is most strongly reminiscent of the destruction of Sennacherib's army ca. 687 B.C. The circumstances are very similar. An army of about 185,000 persons died mysteriously within a night from a fire that descended from heaven. Also, a 'blast' is identified as the cause of the deaths. **The host was destroyed while the Hebrews had commenced to sing the Hallel prayer of the Passover service.** This proves that it happened in Spring, and by late March and early April, in particular![51] This 'coincidence' would provide us with some nutritious food for speculative thought.[52]

---

[51] On an interesting theory about the destruction of Sennacherib's army see also Velikovsky, [op. cit. pp. 227-243]. I disagree with some of his positions, although I also believe that the cause of the death was heaven-sent, can be scientifically explained and is extremely similar to what will once again occur in the future as per Merlin's prophecy. Velikovsky has been on target on many of the most important issues.

[52] In another chapter we shall study a specific prophecy by the Catholic seer Palma Maria Addolorata Matarelli d'Oria who lived in the previous century and who specifically mentions the exterminating angel who will replicate outside the city of Rome the destruction of Sennacherib's army!

Compared with many other prophecies we noted in this chapter, the fact that, as Joel predicts, afterwards *mountains shall drop down new wine, and the hills shall flow with milk and all the rivers of Judah shall flow with waters*, reminds us of the repeated references to milk and honey found in Nostradamus and the Sibylline Oracles when speaking of disasters and comets and warfare and a blessed peace that follows. Let us keep these peculiar verses in the back of our mind as we move on to more evidence from additional sources in the chapters that follow.

REVIEW OF THE MOST SALIENT POINTS

a)   We investigated a number of prophets from the Mediterranean world for the intimations they have to offer considering our near future. Specifically, we looked for temporal proximity of geological upheavals coupled with major military engagements around the Mediterranean region.

b)   The consensus of the prophecies suggests that the volcanoes of the Mediterranean will be the cause of major destruction in land and sea. We expect the eruptions to occur in springtime, of a year not stated.

c)   The cause-effect relationships suggested by the prophets can be fully corroborated by the latest findings of modern science. We also got our first hint to the tremendously important past explosion of the Thera volcano and its connection with the beginning of sorrows for the history of Crete.

d)   Although the prophecies we investigated so far had a geographic slant for the lands that border on the Mediterranean, we were able to establish that the phenomena will be of a global character. This indicates that perhaps other prophets with a different geographical or ethnic preference may fill our gaps concerning the rest of the world, were we to look further into the relevant literature.

e)   Our prophets spoke in no uncertain terms of major catastrophes. This suggests that Biblical references to the same phenomena are anything but poetic hyperboles. Rather, they offer the quintessence of objectivity, specificity and realism.

f)   We may have found the connection between the mysterious location of the valley of Jehoshaphat, the timing of the Judgement of the Lord and the events around it. They appear to replicate a similar event from Hebrew History already mentioned in OT, specifically, II Kings 18, II Kings 19:7; Isaiah, 37:7, as well in other sacred Hebrew sources outside the Bible.

CHAPTER SIX

ATLANTIS REVISITED

*The book has been written with the conviction that conjecture, always provided that it be disciplined by fact (...) is a legitimate means for seeking to arrive at the truth. Its object is to open the path for further assumptions that may lead still nearer the goal; the more vigorously it stimulates to a more logical substitute, the more successfully it accomplishes its purposes. As Jeanroy has happily said, **the discovery of the truth is feasible only through the iterative process of testing the most relevant hypotheses which can grip it closer and closer, until ultimately convergence is achieved.*** Lucy Allen Paton.[1]

<u>Introduction</u>
The main focus of *Our Revelationary Age...* being the prophetic evidence on the military side of WWIII and only secondarily and peripherally the geological upheavals and the phenomena of the Three Days Darkness, I neither collected all the data necessary nor tested all propositions concerning the Darkness phenomenon with the same degree of scrutiny. Regrettably, this led to two speculations regarding the Book of Revelation which have been proven unwarranted in the light of the prophetic information currently available. Although they do not change the conclusions of that study, I hasten to rectify them under the light of most recent evidence, and duly apologize to the reader.

More specifically, in chapter 8 of my previous study, entitled The Great River Euphrates, which covers Revelation chapters 8:12-13, and 9, I perpetrated the following two errors:

---

[1] From her preface in *Les Prophecies de Merlin*. Keeping with our simultaneous equations paradigm, we took a minor liberty in translating the Jeanroy text whose original is as follows: *la découverte de la vérité n' est possible qu' après un certain nombre d' hypothèses qui la serrent de plus près.*

a)   I mistook the darkening of the sun and the moon and the stars with the man-made consequences of the rain-forests fires which are a global phenomenon and can generate visual effects as those described in the Apocalypse and also cause considerable damage on our ecosystem in the long run;

b)   I associated the smoke of the bottomless pit in chapter 9, with the fires of Kuwait, and again their ability to 'darken the air and the sun by reason of the smoke of the pit' and cause environmental degradation.

While both interpretations may still look plausible, they have collapsed under the weight of the evidence and the subsequent analysis from a much larger population of data. The ecological consequences of both the Rain Forest burning seasons and the Kuwait oil-wells fires will be **a most trivial phenomenon** in comparison to the events that await us in the proximate future. These much more terrifying events are precisely those covered by the Book of Revelation, as we shall be able to prove below.

As intimated elsewhere in this study, St. John the Divine is giving us fairly detailed description of catastrophes to befall our planet around the time of the Antichrist's death. Mutatis mutandis, by converting the description of the last seven vials of the wrath of God into the happenings of a close encounter of our planet with an extraterrestrial body, we receive a most graphical description of what is bound to happen at that future time.

While collecting the material for *Their Earthshaking News...*, I became aware of the voluminous information available to us which is making explicit references to comets and signs in the heavens. It was only natural to begin wondering why St. John should exclude the geological upheavals of our proximate future from explicit reference in chaps. 8 and 9. It did not take long to realize that he did not!, Instead, it was I who failed to make the necessary connections.

I had correctly identified in his reference to the bottomless pit, a geological entity. But then mistakenly I transferred it to the oil wells of Kuwait and the source of oil emanating from the depths of the earth, (hence the bottomless pit). As it turns out, it is much closer to home, and immensely more globally important than the wells of Kuwait. In order to fully develop the above thesis, we shall need to keep in mind every new piece of information about the future behavior of Thera and other Mediterranean volcanoes from

Nostradamus and his friends. We also need to begin our analysis by taking a historical tour. Let us, therefore, begin our journey.

THE PIVOTAL IMPORTANCE OF THERA'S ANCIENT EXPLOSION

Modern scholarship has upgraded the importance of Thera's explosion during the 2nd millennium B.C., as the second most far-reaching global catastrophe we have detailed historical evidence about. It is surpassed only by the cosmic events which culminated in the extinction of the dinosaurs some 65 million years ago. Thera's explosion created a caldera that can contain 90 square km of sea-water and displaced matter that corresponds to four times the ejecta from the analogous explosion of Krakatoa in 1883 A.D. It catapulted pumice many kilometers away and the seismic wave it produced travelled long distances. Assisted by recent archaeological investigations, excavations on Thera's lost cities, marine archaeology on the bottom of the Mediterranean, dendrochronology, Carbon 14 dating, the comparative study of historical records from far-away cultures, and other contributions from a number of scientific disciplines, we now have a better idea of when Thera erupted, why, how, and what was the overall extent of the catastrophes it unleashed.

'Dissident' outsiders, usually scientists and researchers from disciplines other than archeology, who have attacked the problem from different perspectives and brought, along with the tools of analysis unique to their disciplines, a fresh approach to the problem solving, have made priceless contributions. Therefore, we can now retrieve much of the information lost and reconstruct many portentous events of Thera's past.

As a consequence, the following claims can be made with relative confidence:

1)   It appears that Thera erupted most probably in 1628 B.C. The explosion coincided with the Flood of Deucalion.[2]

---

[2] See, for instance, Martin Bernal, [1991, chap. VII]. Considering how long the debate over the correct timing of the explosion has been raging, and the great resistance of the archaeological establishment to revise their dates, it becomes even more remarkable to notice that the great Greek Historian Constantine Paparrigo-poulos had already suggested a date that agrees more with the modern 'dissidents' who are correct, rather than with the 'establishment', that has been proven wrong!

2) The explosion coincided with the Biblical Exodus. In fact, the plagues of the Pharaoh were caused by the consequences of the explosion in nearby Thera. In this respect, several previous authors (including Archaeologists) have been vindicated by recent evidence. This allows us to better place the correct timing of the Exodus, as a result, and rectify previously proposed datings. Ditto, for the history of Minoan Crete.

3) The consequences of the explosion were global in extent and severity. In fact, as more than one scholar maintains, they brought about considerable changes in many countries wherefrom written historical evidence has reached us. For one, Dr. Bernal (using his expertise as a Sinologist) shows how it led to a major change of political regime in far-away China; since the Chinese kept detailed accounts of their history, our research has also amply benefited therefrom. Other societies were so overwhelmed that they had to start all over again. This was true for the Jews of the Exodus returning to their Promised Land and also for the Greeks.

Before its cataclysmic transformation, the island of Thera, (which was much larger, very scenic, prosperous, and politically ascendant, bore the name of Callista (Calliste, Kalliste, Kallisti) (the fairest one).[3] As Dr. Bernal eloquently proposes, the new name *Thera*, is not from a Greek root (which would have implied the presence of hunting-grounds, a most unlikely derivation considering the geography of the area) but rather it derives from a Canaanite word (kûr) signifying 'smelting pot' or 'furnace'. The Greek name for the neighboring basically uninhabited Cycladic island of Keros certainly adds additional validity to Dr. Bernal's hypothesis.

THE HEBREW TESTIMONY ON THE THERA CATASTROPHE

Immanuel Velikovsky, an inspired scholar of immense erudition has been the first (to the best of my knowledge) ever to connect the Exodus events with

---

In p. 27 of vol. I of his *History of the Greek Nation*, published in 1885, Paparrigopoulos proposed the year 1796 B.C. as the most likely dating of the Flood of Deucalion. His tools were merely very ancient Greek authors and their sources.

[3] Herodotus, [1987, p. 319]. It was also known as Strongyli, due to its circular shape.

geological upheavals which were caused by a close encounter of our planet with an object from outer space. Although much of what he wrote in *Worlds in Collision* became the object of attack and ridicule by the scientific establishment of the time, Velikovsky incorporated in that study many pages of the most brilliant theorizing. Even though some of the conclusions of his analysis may have been unwarranted, Velikovsky hit at the problem specification correctly, and he will be vindicated by the events of our future, warts and all. Dr. Velikovsky, may the reader be reminded, was a dissident par excellence.[3]

In *Worlds in Collision*, he theorized the presence of volcanic eruptions initiating the disasters reported in the Bible. He proposed that the friction of the earth's lithosphere against the lower strata which was caused by the gravitational pull by a comet approaching our planet, gave rise to many volcanic eruptions. He was the first to propose a theory of catastrophism deeply imbedded in the Bible and other sacred books from a variety of cultures.

Following Velikovsky a host of additional researchers, from Egyptologists to amateur archaeologists to professional archaeologists, began proposing the idea that it was precisely Thera's eruption rather than Sinai's exclusively, which may have some major intrinsic connection with the Exodus events. Velikovsky launched the search on the right path; it is the task of our generation, by means of subsequent iterations to approach closer and closer to the final solution of our system of equations and to converge to the ultimate truth regarding one of the most far-reaching occurrences in the history of the planet.

THE GREEK TESTIMONY ON THE THERA CATASTROPHE

The Greek Mythology does not seem to have a memory of the Biblical

---

[3] He had studied natural sciences at the University of Edinburgh, history, law and medicine (M.D.) in Moscow, biology in Berlin, the working of the brain in Zürich, psychoanalysis in Vienna. He was deeply religious and extremely well read. Whatever errors might have cropped in his work, he deserved immensely more recognition that he received in his life time.

Deluge as such.[4] One must assume that any memory of that event was subsequently obliterated, as the Egyptian priests already intimated to Solon during his journey there. The Greek prehistory/genealogy begins with Iapetos (strongly reminiscent etymologically of Japheth, one of the sons of Biblical Noah, the father of the Indo-European nations). Iapetos and his wife Clymene were high born and raised four sons; Atlas, Menoitios, Prometheus and Epimetheus. Prometheus and Pandora became parents to Deucalion; Epimetheus had a daughter, Pyrrha. Deucalion married Pyrrha. It is here that our story begins.

According to the Greek historiographers of old when Ogyges was King of Athens a deluge took place. That deluge was later known also as the *Flood of Deucalion*. The best bet for the timing of that event the ancient Greek writers had to offer was the year 1796 B.C. According to one version of the story, only Deucalion and Pyrrha survived the Flood of Ogyges (the Flood of Deucalion). Prometheus was universally believed to have received the gift of prophecy, and even gods, including Jupiter would consult him as a most infallible oracle.[5] On his father's advice Deucalion built an arc, like Noah and Gilgamesh and many others before him, and like some other surviving Greeks in legends relating events contemporary to Deucalion.

The fact that Deucalion's father was the source of prophetic premonition and hence the son's avenue to ultimate escape from the Flood is paralleled by several Biblical accounts of an Almighty God advising His Elect, ahead of time. (Other cultures have analogous stories of the gods forewarning the local extraordinary personalities). So, here we have a very ancient Greek reference in history on how Heaven can cause catastrophes but is willing at the same time to forewarn humanity in a most salutary manner.

Deucalion and Pyrrha became the parents of the Greek nation primarily

---

[4] Noah's Flood is the Deluge par excellence, the subject of the Genesis account. It is the same phenomenon described also in the Epic of Gilgamesh (derived from a twelve-tablet masterpiece excavated at Nineveh, the capital of the Assyrians).

[5] The very etymology of the word suggests a penchant for providence and an ability to predict and fore-think: $\Pi\rho o$-$\mu\eta\theta\epsilon\dot{\upsilon}\varsigma$, $\pi\rho o$-$\mu\eta\theta\dot{\epsilon}o\mu\alpha\iota$, to consider, or take care beforehand.

through their son Hellen.[6] Pyrrha's name can be easily traced back to 'fire', πῦρ. I propose, that Deucalion's name is also indicative of the human experience of that period: the most likely derivation of *Deucalion* is from a verb which fell into desuetude and only resurfaced in Modern Greek in words such as ἄρδευσις, ἀρδευτικὸν ἔργον, and the like, always implying irrigation.[7] In essence, therefore, the very etymology of the patronymics of the Greek nation were references to the fact that they were born 'through fire and water', literally!

Considering that the eruption of Thera occurred in 1628 B.C., we have many reasons to suspect that Deucalion's Flood was caused by the Thera explosion and the horrendous tsunamis and tidal waves it brought in its wake.[8] In this respect the date of 1796 B.C., proposed by ancient Greek

---

[6] The story says that Deucalion and Pyrrha managed to repopulate the world with a faster technique than direct procreation: Deucalion threw behind him stones at the instigation of the gods, and all of them became men; Pyrrha did the same, and all of them became women. Their own progeny was rather limited: two sons and one daughter, in toto. One day the researchers may successfully decode the meaning of stones being converted into human beings. It may be a suggestion that we arise from Mother Earth and our molecules and atoms are derived therefrom. Also, one cannot fail to notice that Greece is predominantly a mountainous country...

Hellen has bestowed his name to the Greeks. Hellene, Hellenic, Hellenistic are favorable nomenclature in use. The term Greek which had great currency among the Romans, is of Hellenic origin as well, see the most ancient Γραικός. (Con. Paparrigopoulos, *History of the Greek Nation*, vol. 1).

[7] The verb was the transitive δεύω, moisten, wet, water, irrigate, etc.

[8] The periodic destruction of the world through fire and water is not a theme limited to the Greek mythology and the Jewish traditions, however. Martin Bernal, [op. cit. p. 317], says that "in a tradition that almost certainly antedates 1628 B.C., the god of Israel was fundamentally a divinity of turbulence of the type of the Egyptian Seth and the Greek Poseidon. He had a direct responsibility for earthquakes, tidal waves and disasters of fire and water."
Hindu sages speak in similar terms on the destinies of the planet and the Egyptian priest of Neith who conversed with Solon, very categorically stated that 'There have been, and there will be again, many destructions of mankind, of which the greatest are by fire and water and the lesser ones by many other causes. (See Plato's Dialogues '*Timaeus*' and '*Critias*').

writers seems remarkably close to the true figure!

WAS THERA THE ATLANTIS OF THE PLATONIC DIALOGUES?

The legend of Atlantis, which has reached us through two Platonic Dialogues, has fascinated humanity perhaps beyond any other legend. A German author, H. Steuerwald, has researched the number of writings on this subject to date and came up with the egregious estimate of over 20,000 relevant entries. This figure includes at least 7,000 books on the subject of Atlantis. The proposition that the Island of Kalliste (before it collapsed into the caldera of the volcano and became demoted into a 'Thera') **was the Atlantis** of the Platonic Dialogues, has already been advanced in the literature.[9] In 1956, a Greek Seismologist, Angelos G. Galanopoulos proposed that Atlantis was located north of Crete on what used to be the island of Calliste.   In 1969 with the help of Edward Bacon, the Archaeological Editor of the Illustrated London News, Galanopoulos wrote a book entitled *Atlantis*.

Angelos G. Galanopoulos proposed that the numbers given to Plato by the Egyptian priests were subject to a translation error. Specifically, Plato was given the impression that the size of the Atlantean plain was 340 x 230 miles. That would correspond to an area larger than all of Greece. Also, the date of the destruction was assumed to be 9000 years before the time of Solon. Galanopoulos divided the figures by 10 and discovered that now, the dimensions fit rather well with an area corresponding to the size of Thera. As for the timing, he felt that 900 years was the correct figure. This would bring the disappearance of Atlantis much closer to the time that we now know Kalliste disappeared.[10]

---

[9] Immanuel Velikovsky had mentioned the Atlantis connection in *Worlds in Collision*, published in 1950, and he hypothesized that Atlantis and the Exodus apparently coincided. **However, he did not seem to indicate any connection of Atlantis with Thera.**

[10] As for Velikovsky, he initially proposed, quoting a previous author, that Mt. Sinai (being a volcano at some point in its history), was the culprit. I am unaware whether he later included Santorini in his list of usual suspects. Velikovsky had the greatest respect for Plato's story of Atlantis. He considers his reference to the catastrophes as a result of 'the shifting of heavenly bodies' as the words of Plato which received the least attention, though they deserved the greatest. Also, he belongs to the group who consider the number 9000 as too high, to be corrected

Plato's description of Atlantis before its submergence remarkably matches the ancient history of Thera and vicinity derived from the study of Eastern Mediterranean historical texts, as well. Again, the literature on this subject is already voluminous and grows fast. Particularly, some details are worthy of special mention: Plato wrote in *Critias* that the Island of Atlantis abounded in both cold and hot springs, an indication of geysers and fumaroles present around volcanoes. He specifically said: *they used fountains both of cold and hot springs; these were very abundant, and both kinds wonderfully adapted to use by reason of the sweetness and excellence of their waters. They constructed buildings about them, and planted suitable trees; also cisterns, some open to the heaven, others which they roofed over, to be used in winter as warm baths (...).*

Plato also related that *they dug out of the earth whatever was to be found there, mineral as well as metal, and (...) orichalcum was dug out of the earth in may parts of the island, and, with the exception of gold, was esteemed the most precious of metals among the men of those days. (...).*[11] Any volcanologist can attest to the fact that gold, silver, and other precious minerals are concentrated within a volcano, which is essentially a highly efficient production unit for the accumulation and concentration of minerals that naturally occur in relatively small quantities. A volcano with is own 'thermal power' unit, so to say, acts as a distillation plant par excellence. Over ages the minerals become accumulated and purified and finally get squeezed through pressure from underneath towards the surface of the

---

with 900 years instead.

[11] Orichalcum, ὀρείχαλκος in Greek is an alloy of primarily coper with cassiterite, also known as bronze. The Bronze Age (c. 3500 - 1000 B.C.), which was followed by the Iron Age, covers the period of Calliste's history we are dealing with in this study. I do not wish to expand the debate of the location of Atlantis ad infinitum, but I would like to make a comment on a recent theory of its location: A German Geo-Archaeologist, Eberhard Zangger proposed in a 1992 book entitled *Atlantis - Eine Legende wird entziffert* that Atlantis was located in Troy instead of the Cyclades. One of his arguments is that the processing of Orichalcum has been found only in one location: Edremit (Adramyttion) 80 kms southeast of Troy. However, suppose for a moment that Adramyttion learned the art from the Atlantians but had a better chance of survival being located further north. So, its entire population did not disappear overnight and a portion thereof survived along with the know-how. Hence, the art of processing orichalcum survived through them long for us to discover, but this is not enough proof that it originated there.

planet in the course of violent eruptions. The reference to the relative plentiful supply of those metals should give us additional rationale for concentrating the search of Atlantis around major volcanoes.

Another ancient Greek writer, Theopompus of Chios (born around 380 B.C.), (from whose work only fragments have reached us) in his book entitled *Meropidae* relates a conversation between Silenus and the King Midas of Phrygia. Silenus describes an old civilization remarkably reminiscent of Plato's Atlantis and submits the following bits of information:

a)   "the islanders have so much gold and silver that they esteem it less than we do iron".

b)   "In this land, the race known as Meropes occupies several large towns."[12]

On the issue of the gold and silver, I would like to make a few additional remarks:

-       we know from a byzantine prophecy that the 'treasures of the earth' will become unlocked following the end of the catastrophes and the beginning of the era of peace and plenty. (καὶ ἀνοιχθήσονται οἱ θησαυροὶ τῆς γῆς). I have always maintained that the prophets do not engage in poetic hyperboles but tend to speak in terse verse with very literal meaning. It appears that the above sentence makes reference to the treasures in the depths of the earth, namely the precious minerals that will become unleashed through the violent volcanic eruptions. According to the supposition that Byzantine authors may have also concentrated more specifically on the futures of the Remnant among the Greeks, the above prophecy may be a reference to **Greek treasures being unleashed to the surface.**

---

[12] Merops was a king of the island of Cos, who married Clymene, one of the Oceanides, and whose reign was **contemporary** to the flood of Deucalion! Earlier we saw that Iapetos was the husband of Clymene. Is it possible that Iapetos is also called Merops and he was **also** king of Cos, an island not far from Thera?...

On the other hand, Theopompus who as a Historian was compared by the Greeks to Herodotus and Thucydides, indicates that Meropes was a name given to the entire race of those islanders described by Silenus.

Ceteris paribus, this may indicate also the Greek volcanoes which would supply the gold and silver. That speculation, if correct, would supply an additional hint to our Atlantis-Thera connection.

- From the English Prophetess Joanna Southcott's *The New Earth* (Book 44, p. 35): *(...) And if that gold can do you good, I've mines are hid that shall be showed; And in the seas I've hidden store, And then I'll bring it all on shore; And then I'll make all barren lands to bring in glorious crops for man; (...)*

- In *Les Prophecies de Merlin* we have a most specific prophecy applying to the Greeks, who will re-discover lost treasures in the wake of a catastrophe followed by major upheavals in their sea! Specifically, in **LXXXI, f. 69c**, entitled *De la mer de Grece qui seichera et des grans tresors qui seront trouvez*, Merlin advises us that "a little after the death of the Dragon of Babylon, the sea of Greece will dry up and the great cities that existed in the past in that country will become visible. And people will be able to walk on the valleys (that used to be submerged) as they now walk on terra firma." On the query whether any treasures will be found then, Merlin replies: "more gold and silver will be found there than those existing today in the British Isles. The treasures will be found on the bottom of the sea, because since the time of the deluge till today, the sea of Greece has gulped down about 20,000 ships and it will continue gulping them down. Consequently, the bottom of the sea is a great treasure. And also, since the time of the deluge there foundered forty (.xl.) cities, the poorest among which contained greater treasures than those presently existing in the city of London." On the question whether the waters will be returning to the dried up sea of Greece, the prophet responded with a most affirmative 'yes'.[13]

We cannot overemphasize the value of the above prophecy in our search for the Thera link of lost Atlantis. Let us, therefore, analyze it in greater detail:

a) the sea of Greece will dry up (like for example the Read Sea during the Exodus?). **The sea of Greece**, literally, and not the Atlantic

---

[13] See also, Lucy Allen Paton, op. cit. vol. 1, p. 138.

145

Ocean, for instance. This would indicate that a certain geological upheaval (or a series thereof) must be searched in the Eastern Mediterranean, proper, and not beyond the Pillars of Hercules (Straits of Gibraltar). At the end of the prophecy, Merlin tells us that the waters will return. This is most consistent with our theory overall, and this is exactly what happened also in the Red Sea during the previous explosion of Thera, and in the Mediterranean Sea over a large expanse.

b) We are given most affirmative reports of an ancient civilization that flourished before the flood (Merlin does not specify which flood). It had forty very rich cities and the trade in precious metals must have been a very vigorous one, considering the number of precious loads that reached the bottom of the sea in the course of many shipwrecks. (Whether due to violent geological upheavals or simply tempests and other secondary reasons, the prophet does not specify. Probably all of the above contributed to the large number of shipwrecks mentioned).

c) Merlin predicts that the submerged regions will re-surface in the future and people will be able (for a short period of time, anyway) to walk on them as one walks on terra firma. This is an immensely valuable hint when compared with the testimony from other sources, as we shall see later.

d) Finally, the timing of the events is a little after the death of the Dragon of Babylon. Since I maintain that the Dragon is the Iraqi dictator who will find his nemesis upon his invasion of Israel, it becomes clear what the timing of the rest of the prophecy also is bound to be **during our most proximate future, in the course of events preceding the year 2000!**

In conclusion, the above entry from that most valuable collection of prophecies, which the amazing scholarship of Dr. Paton made available to us, provides an additional indication to at least the possibility of a Theran connection with Atlantis. Merlin speaks categorically of *la mer de Grece*; we need to look no further. He mentions a deluge, he mentions a rich and advanced civilization that was submerged and is bound to re-emerge. He predicts that again the water will return. In a sense, the text of the prophecy, (if all our speculations are correct) would add additional support to the propositions of the group of scientists insisting in locating Atlantis in the Eastern Mediterranean rather than the Atlantic Ocean.[14]

HARMONIZING APPARENT INCONSISTENCIES
BETWEEN A THERAN ATLANTIS
AND EDGAR CAYCE'S COVERAGE OF THE ATLANTIS
PAST AND FUTURE

Considering that Merlin predicted the **re-emergence** of a lost civilization can we look for any corroborating evidence in additional sources? Let us return to America's illustrious native son, Edgar Cayce, the Sleeping Prophet (1877-1945):

Cayce had a prophetic dream in 1936. He saw that he was reborn in the year 2100 with the knowledge that he had lived in the past as Edgar Cayce. With a group of scientists he travelled over the USA in an odd shaped aircraft. They landed in a city that was in the process of being rebuilt. He knew that city was once upon a time New York City, which became destroyed at a time many parts of the world underwent similar devastation. Specifically, Cayce knew in that dream that Nebraska had become the West Coast of the USA, that Los Angeles and San Francisco, and parts of Alabama became submerged. Japan also suffered major catastrophes. Parts of the worlds disappeared and new lands emerged from beneath the Pacific and the Atlantic Oceans.

In this apocalyptic vision which predicted that all the above events would materialize around the year 2000, Cayce was also given by the Spirit the information that WWIII would start ca. 1999 A.D., and that the devastations would not only be caused by agents moving in a downward direction from the skies, but also by those moving upwards from beneath the earth.

In a different set of visions Cayce predicted the literal **re-emergence of the**

---

[14] Even the brilliant speculation by Ignatius Donnelly and subsequent authors that the trident of Poseidon signified command of Atlantis's royalty over three continents can be salvaged without any modification in our framework. Although Donnelly and others might have believed the three continents in question to be America, Europe and Africa, (since they placed Atlantis in the Azores and beyond) we now submit that the three continents were Europe, Africa and Asia, instead. Thera is located very close to the borders of all three continents.

lost Atlantis at a time following the destruction of Communism!...[15] The truth is, that Cayce gave a rather lengthy report on the Atlantis past and future. He placed it in the Atlantic Ocean but also in the Mediterranean and adjacent lands. In fact, what he said is that Atlantis began submerging in a series of catastrophes over a very prolonged period of time which spanned millennia. He predicted partial re-emergence of the Atlantis territories in our proximate future **both within the Mediterranean as well as in the Atlantic**.

In fact, Cayce was emphatic that upheavals in the Mediterranean will precede geological upheavals in other parts of the globe. He predicted the **sinking and rising of the Mediterranean**, (an idea already misinterpreted by previous commentators to correspond to minor events already identified in a few Mediterranean (Greek) ports).

The events in the Mediterranean will coincide with signs in the South Pacific, and the appearance of land near Bimini in the Bahamas. At the same time, Cayce said that inundations will take place in the Eastern USA, earthquakes in the West coast and other upheavals in many parts. He mentioned specifically Vesuvius in Italy and Mt. Pelée in Martinique as being future trouble spots of great scope.

He called some of the remnants of Atlantis "Poseidia", a very remarkable connection with many other contemporary scholars following the mythology around Greek Poseidon, god of the seas and presumed at some point a ruler over Atlantis. He also considered the volcanic island group of the Azores as part of the Atlantean mainland of old, and placed the beginning of the end of Atlantis as having preceded by far the Biblical Flood.

Since the death of Communism began in 1986 A.D. and since whatever vestiges thereof surviving in the countries of the world today will disappear with the victory of the Great Monarch and his allies in WWIII, it becomes apparent that Cayce's prophecy is relating to our proximate future.[16] The similarity between Cayce's vision with the prophecy from Merlin should not

---

[15] Among the many sources of this information, see also, A. Hall & F. King, [1991, pp. 119-122], as well as Mary Ellen Carter et. al. [1990].

[16] China, who will fight against the West in WWIII will lose the war. Hence, its Communism also will be eventually defeated.

be ignored. But even so, these are not the only suggestions available to us through the intimations of the Spirit. What we heard from Cayce is not sufficient evidence to connect Thera with any part of lost Atlantis. Yet, there is nothing in Cayce that is directly contradictory to our theory. Let us consider the following interesting facts:

Thera, as we learnt earlier, had a disastrous eruption around the year 1628 B.C. This, however is by no means the first or last time the **active volcano** of Thera made itself known to the world. There is no reason for us to deny the possibility that prior to 1628 B.C. Thera's volcano misbehaved numerous times. In fact, it has done so within historical memory. Any contemporary map of the Thera Island group will show two little islands between Thera in the East and Therasia in the West. Within the caldera of the collapsed volcano, in other words, over the centuries new islands were born; Palaia Kameni (Old Burnt) Island arose from the deep during the upheavals of 197-196 B.C., when "flames rose from the sea". Many centuries later, in 1570 A.D., Little Kameni (Small Burnt) appeared while a Nea Kameni (New Burnt) Island came to join them in 1711 A.D. Since the eruptions of 1925-1926 A.D., the Little Kameni and the Nea Kameni have been fused and they are now visible on the maps under the name 'Nea Kameni'. Consequently, all the islands currently in existence are: Thera, New Kameni, Palaia Kameni, Aspro (the smallest of them all) and Therasia.

In *The Collection of Etchings of the Ionian Bank of Greece* published in March of 1995, in association with the N.P. Goulandris Museum of Cycladic Art, of Athens, Greece, we can see on pp. 16-17 an old map of the Thera group from an original etching by Abraham Ortelius, a very famous Dutch map-maker of the time. Between Thera and Therasia six (6) islands are clearly visible, plus six very tiny ones. The maps were prepared between 1584-1612. One may discount this discrepancy in the data by assuming that map making during those ages was not the exact science it is today, and probably Ortelius was careless. On the other hand, the Dutch were a sea-faring nation and they built an empire by being careful and meticulous with such things as the geography of the world.

Another argument (and this one frequently surfaces in the literature) could be: how come there were six islands but no Historian of the period mentions that number anywhere. To this a plausible reply would be: Those were dark ages, literally, for Greek Historiographers (struggling under the Ottoman Yoke and the intermittent warfare between Turkey and Venice). Consequently, such neglect by the Greek historiographers can be easily explained away. On the other hand, since the Franks and the Venetians had control of the Island for centuries (and in fact its modern name Santorini derives from the Italian phonetic adaptation of *Santa Eirini (St. Irene)*, the Patron Saint of the Island), we must assume that the Venetians would not have been using so diligently Ortelius's map if it were to be so blatantly inaccurate. Both Dutch and Venetians cannot be accused of nonchalance and ignorance in the map-making and map-using areas. Therefore, it is plausible that in this case and over this period of time, it was the map-makers who were writing the History. Ergo, that would indicate additional volcanic activity from the depths of the sea, with some of those smaller islands becoming submerged later on.

Consequently, if the active volcano of Thera can exhibit such activity within historical times, why should it not be very active during an era for which we have no written historical evidence? In fact, it is quite plausible that even its ultimate destruction may have arrived in two installments. So, there is more than meets the eye between the behavior of Kallisti's volcano over the millennia and the story of Atlantis. But there are additional reasons to promote the Thera-Atlantis connections (at least for that portion of old Atlantis which expanded within the Mediterranean sea region, in the eventuality a portion thereof may in fact still be lying somewhere in the Atlantic).

THE KOURION DISASTER AND ITS POSSIBLE THERAN CONNECTION

Ammianus Marcellinus was a pagan historian from Syria writing in the fourth century of our era, when Christianity was struggling against the attempts by Emperor Julian the Apostate to re-introduce paganism in the Empire. He reports a most catastrophic event that occurred on July 21, 365 A.D., which he characterized as *a frightful disaster, surpassing anything related either in legend or authentic history*:

Just after dawn there were frequent flashes of lightning, and the rumbling of thunder. Then the firm and stable mass of the earth trembled and shook, and the sea withdrew, its waves flowing backward. The sea floor was exposed, revealing fishes and sea creatures struck fast in the slime. Mountains and valleys that had been hidden in the unplumbed depths since the creation of the world for the first time saw the beams of the sun. (...) But then the sea returned with an angry vengeance. As if resentful of its forced retreat, the sea roared and rushed through the seething shallows, (...) For, the great mass of waters, returning when it was least expected, killed many thousands of men by drowning (...).

He goes on to report that ships landed upon buildings in Alexandria, Egypt and some were driven inland by almost two miles. Modern researchers, who have excavated the city of Kourion in Cyprus and simulated on computers the events have concluded that:

■ There were three seismic waves. The second thereof delivered more energy than a hundred Hiroshima atom bombs. When the third wave hit few were alive to witness it. Sporadic after-shocks continued for a period of 50 years. (Seismologist Terry Wallace of the University of Arizona calculated that the quake must have registered at least 7 on the Richter scale).

■ Although the epicenter of the quake is still debated, various theories have placed it in Turkey, Crete or Palestine. It may well have been in the sea, 30 miles off Kourion. Further investigations have located the epicenter along the "tectonic battleground" of the Eurasian and African plates. According to David Soren, Professor of Classical Archeology at the University of Arizona in Tucson, who undertook major excavations in the region, *only here would plate interaction produce this level of damage as well as the accompanying tsunami.* Dr. Soren was the first to associate the reference by Ammianus Marcellinus with the earthquake that obliterated Kourion. His excavations in Kourion met with great success, making it the most attractive archaeological site in Cyprus today.[17] Kourion was very old, the town destroyed by the earthquake reported by Ammianus Marcellinus was a later Roman city.

At this point it may be worthwhile to introduce testimony from religious texts whose emphasis was on a quite different issue. The reader may be familiar with the prophecy by Lord Jesus Christ of the impending destruction of the Temple in Jerusalem (which came about during Titus's wars on 70 A.D.). Also, He pronounced prophecies under what terms and conditions the Temple would be rebuilt. Julian the Apostate, purporting to discredit the

---

[17] See Soren & James [1988], as well as Soren's article in National Geographic July 1988, entitled *The day the World ended at Kourion: Reconstructing an Ancient Earthquake.*

Christian religion and prove the prophecy of Lord Jesus Christ wrong, in 361 A.D. gave orders for the reconstruction of the Temple. Many Hebrews arrived from various countries around the Mediterranean to assist in the work. However, the work was abandoned for the following reasons: almost continuous earthquakes; tempests; lightning and fire that issued forth from the foundations of the old Temple and burned down construction equipment and masons. Such phenomena dissuaded Julian and the Hebrews to continue in their efforts, the Hebrews for realizing that such would be against the Will of God.

Historical references for these events can be found in the following authors who wrote over the period from 350 to 450 A.D. (which interestingly enough encompasses the events at Kourion, as well): The Christian authors St. John Chrysostom; St. Gregory the Theologian; St. Ambrose, Bishop of Milan; Socrates, a Greek Historian; also the Historians Sozomenos, Theodoritos and Philostorgios, the Hebrew Rabbi Gedaliah, and the pagan Historian Ammianus Marcellinus![18]

Is there any connection with the natural phenomena in Palestine and the earthquake that obliterated Kourion? And if there is, where was its epicenter? And was it connected with the Will of God and His plans for the future of mankind or was it absolutely due to the 'forces of nature'? This may be an interesting set of questions for the Historians to consider.

ADDITIONAL EVIDENCE FROM ABOVE ON THE FUTURE CAREER OF THERA AND OTHER MEDITERRANEAN VOLCANOES

As we saw already in the previous chapter, through the testimony of Nostradamus and friends, geological upheavals are bound to happen in the Mediterranean during our proximate future. In fact, the events in the Aegean, the Western Mediterranean, Sicily, and many other locales all speak of cataclysmic volcanic eruptions. Besides the intimations of the Most Holy Virgin Mary about the fate of Marseilles and other port cities, and the explicit words by Ezekiel, Isaiah, and other prophets of the Bible, we have several prophecies by Lord Jesus Christ to that effect. Besides those mentioned already in other parts of this study (such as the Synoptic Apocalypse) we have at our disposal additional ones, of a later date.

---

[18] See also, Metropolitan Meletios Kalamaras, [1991, pp. 185-188].

The one presented below refers to a prophetic text of conditional punishment imbedded in the *Epistle of Sunday*, which was delivered in a most miraculous manner to the Christians of Europe, in an early century.[19] Lord Jesus Christ reveals that because of breaching His law, the Christians have already been punished repeatedly in the past with a number of evils: inclement weather destroying the crops, plagues, earthquakes, hail, insects and diseases of every kind.

In the event of continuous non-compliance by Christians with the instructions and commandments detailed in the Epistle, He specifies that the following will happen to the world:

(...) If we continue disregarding these My commandments also and fail to comply, I am not going to address you another epistle, but instead I will open the heavens and I will reign fire, hail, steaming water, and I will cause terrible earthquakes and I will rain blood and oil of myrrh in the month of April and every seed you have sown and every vineyard and every plant I will destroy and your sheep and your animals I will annihilate for the sake of Holy Sunday. And I have got winged monsters to send against you to devour your flesh, so that you will say: 'open up the tombs, you, who have been sleeping therein since the beginning of the ages, so that we can hide from the wrath of the Lord and God the Almighty; and I will turn the light of sun into darkness and I will create darkness, the same way I did against the Egyptians in the past, for the sake of My servant Moses. And I will send against you the people of Ishmael to kill you through sword and through an evil death, to force you into servitude, and you will cry and you will repent. And I will turn My face from you, in order not to listen to you, for the sake of the Holy Sunday (...)

The Lord Jesus Christ predicts rains of fire and hail and steaming water (strongly reminiscent of volcanic eruption and the byproducts thereof); terrible earthquakes and a rain of blood and oil of myrrh. (Oil of Myrrh is

---

[19] It stresses the importance for celebrating Sunday as the Christian day par excellence, it explains why this day is so holy, besides being the day of the Resurrection of the Lord, it specifies the acceptable ways of honoring it, and it provides information not otherwise available of specific important events that happened on the First Day of the Week. The *Epistle of Sunday* **stresses also the great importance** of keeping the Wednesday and Friday fasts.

not in irrelevant insertion due to a typo but a most valuable clue as we shall see later). The winged monsters referred to in the Book of Revelation (chap. 9) are again specifically mentioned here, as are also the Muslim armies which will invade Christendom. (The Ishmaelites are allowed, in other words, to kill and enslave the Christians as a way of punishment of the former for their faithlessness and sins). Finally, an explicit allusion to darkness which will be of the selfsame nature **as that against the Egyptians at the time of the Exodus!**

Clearly, this is the most important prophecy currently at our disposal because it emanates directly from the Savior Himself and it is addressed to the entire Christendom. It will enormously assist us in appreciating the value of so many other intimations of the Spirit from other sources. It will also provide the vital missing links to make our future manifest in all its details. The Epistle of Sunday existed in several vernacular manuscripts within the Christian world; the original was in Greek and it was known in the Church since at least the 6th century of our era and had an extraordinary diffusion among the faithful.[20]

The Lord Jesus Christ speaks unequivocally of earthquakes and volcanic eruptions and failure of crops and war and events that will **parallel and replicate** the events of the Exodus. Also **they will occur in April**. Still, nothing explicit is mentioned to equate the replication of those events with a replay of Thera's explosion and the possible re-emergence of Atlantis except the word σταктήν oil of myrrh, which sounds so unrelated and out of place, prima facie.

The Greek word σταктή comes from the verb στάζειν and indicates a liquid which drops slowly and accumulates in this process, much like the distillation process for the recovery of the oil of myrrh with which the word became associated in antiquity. Since the oil of myrrh is not important commercially in our days, the words associated with it fell in desuetude. A reader with a good knowledge of Greek may assume that there was a typo in the text wherefrom I excerpted the Epistle of Sunday, and most likely σтάκτη was the correct word instead of σταктή. In that case the translation would be *ash* and *tephra* (which although directly associated with volcanic eruptions and hence most plausible within the context of the prophecy)

---

[20] In fact, one could routinely purchase a copy thereof in the bookstores of Athens and Jerusalem as late as 1894 A.D.

would not correspond to oil of myrrh and the proper intended meaning of the word.[21]

My first reaction was exactly that. The first quality control procedure I undertook was to check the translation of the word in the Spanish and see whether they noticed the typo and 'corrected' it. Apparently, they did not! The Spanish text was most clear: *y haré llover sangre y estacte en abril.*[22]

IMMANUEL VELIKOVSKY REVISITED

In *Worlds in Collision*, (p. 133-134), while covering the events of the Exodus, Velikovsky provides the following remarkable details based on his analysis of ancient texts besides the Pentateuch:

The eerie world, dark and groaning, was unpleasant to all the senses save the sense of smell: the world was fragrant. When the breeze blew, the clouds conveyed a sweet odor. In the Papyrus Anastasi IV, written "in the year of misery", in which it is said that the months are reversed, the planet-god is described as arriving with the sweet wind before him. In a similar text of the Hebrews we read that the times and seasons were confused, and "a

---

[21] My personal acquaintance with the Greek Original of the Epistle of Sunday, came through *Los Evangelios Apócrifos*, [1988], Aurelio de Santos Otero's excellent Spanish edition of Greek and Latin originals with their Spanish translation.

[22] Half of the Spanish dictionaries I searched do not even contain the word *estacte* any longer. The ones which do so, translate it as *oil of myrrh*. The Latin dictionary corroborated the Greek root and aromatic meaning of the word and the Webster's even suggested that the word first appears in Exodus 30:34, where the Lord God gives specific instructions to Moses in the desert to prepare a blend of perfumes for making an incense pure and holy and agreeable to Him. I took a sample of the various Bibles to see how this word is translated:
the Greek Septuagint calls it $\sigma\tau\alpha\kappa\tau\dot{\eta}$; ditto, for the Russian and the Spanish (which translates it as *estacte* or *gotas de estacte*). In the Comparative Study Bible published by Zondervan, the King James, the Amplified and the New American Standard speak of *stacte*, the New International calls it *gum resin*. The Catholic Family Edition of the Holy Bible translates it as *storax*. (This may tell us something of the price we have to pay when we begin to 'simplify and modernize' the languages we speak). So, the Holy Bible corroborates the terminology for that mysterious substance which will be rained upon us in the month of April along with fire, steaming water and other catastrophes.

fragrance perfumed all the world", and the perfume was brought by the pillar of smoke. **The fragrance was like that of myrrh and frankincense.** *[Emphasis mine]. "Israel was surrounded by clouds," and as soon as the clouds were set in motion, the winds "breathed myrrh and frankincense."*

(...) The generation of those days, when the star conveyed its fragrance to men on the earth, is immortalized in the tradition of the Hindus. The Vedic hymn compares the fragrance of the star Agni to the scent of the lotus."

Thanks to the erudition and professionalism of Velikovsky we can now capitalize on the evidence he collected from many cultures besides Israel which further suggest that the Exodus disasters were accompanied by the fragrance of myrrh and frankincense. I will not advance any speculations on the nature of the source of this fragrance; whether it will be generated as a chemical compound by means of the eruptions and the ejecta from the volcanoes, whether through an interchange of the comet's atmosphere with the chemicals from the earth's atmosphere, whether it will come directly from Above from the Father of Lights in a purely miraculous fashion, all these are beyond my capacity to answer. I feel, however, that the mention of this phenomenon in a most authoritative prophecy given to the Christians in the last 2000 years, being so similar to historical accounts researched by Velikovsky is not due merely to chance!

Let us consider the following proposition: if the geological phenomena around the Flood of Deucalion and the Exodus can be replicated in our proximate future, **because the same original causes are at work, once again,** we are bound to experience the myrrh also. Or, conversely, if the myrrh accompanies all other natural events, so strongly reminiscent of the eruption of Thera **and** the Exodus, then we can assume that the factors which will create them are the same as those at play in the year 1628 B.C.

This proposition, if correct, has its obvious corollaries: Between 1628 B.C. and 1998 A.D. (the most likely year for the events, as we shall show later on) elapse ca. 3626 years. Let us assume for a moment that this corresponds to an entire cycle of cosmic events (which the Almighty God, in His infinite Wisdom, decided they ought to be repetitive). Maybe, what generates them is the periodic close encounter with an object from outer space. Such close encounters can bring about catastrophes by fire and water, such as the destruction of Thera, the Plagues of the Pharaoh and all the other specific contemporary events immortalized in the literature of ancient cultures.

Since we know that the world has undergone many catastrophes through fire and water in the past (remember what the Egyptian Priest said to Solon in this regard), and since they will occur also in the future, then, it is logical to, at least, assume that before 1628 B.C. a similar and analogous catastrophe might have taken place. In other words, the Biblical Flood at the time of Noah might have been such an event. And the 'decomposition' of Atlantis piecemeal over millennia may have been due to a set of analogous events harnessed by the same causes, reached back into time into an even more remote past than the Flood of Noah.

Therefore, if the cycles I refer to above can be assumed to be of more or less similar length (as it would be the case for instance of a periodic comet or a close encounter with an Earth-crossing asteroid of analogous trajectory parameters) if we were to add 3626 years to 1628 we may get the timing of the catastrophe which preceded the Thera destruction and which may have coincided with the Flood of Noah. That would bring us to 5254 B.C. This lends to an interesting comparison:

a)   Jewish rabbinical calculations indicate that the world began 3,740 years before the Christian Era.

b)   Roman Catholic Tradition based on the Vulgate placed the creation in 5199 B.C.

Every Christian with an interest in science and an inquisitive mind knows for a fact that the Creation did not happen so late in geological time. Rather, what the Church mistakenly took for **the** creation was nothing more than a Remnant of humanity which survived a severe catastrophe and started all over again. In that sense it was a real and most genuine creation, considering the destruction that obliterated the past. But a re-naissance, more likely, rather than a naissance, per se in an absolute sense.

In any case, the fact that our calculation of a plausible length of a catastrophic cycle brings us to 5254 B.C., while the Bible's chronology brings us to 5199 B.C., (considering how small is, percentage wise, the margin of error involved) might provide us with additional food for speculative thought and could launch additional research and co-operative efforts between Christians and Hebrews to improve upon our Biblical Chronologies.

My theory is that Adam and Eve were expelled from the Garden of Eden in the wake of a major geological catastrophe. The Angel of the Flaming Sword chasing them out is strongly suggestive of a comet recruited by the Almighty God in administering His Justice. Nothing extraneous to such a thought, considering our present knowledge of mass extinctions, the dinosaurs disappearance and many other geological upheavals for which we began accumulating hard evidence. Also, the very wording of the Epistle of Sunday suggests that similar events, destined to occur in our future will be clearly directed for retribution for our sins as Christians who have neglected our religious duties and have ignored the very word of our God.

The Adam and Eve event would correspond to a time well beyond the detailed chronology of the Bible, while the Flood of Noah can be more easily timed with the assistance from many sciences besides Biblical Research. (Such as the excavations of Mesopotamia would indicate, which were crowned by the discovery of a local Flood, the discovery of the Gilgamesh Epic, and many other such finds).

Modern scholarship agrees that the catastrophic impact that led to the disappearance of the dinosaurs and the majority of the then living plants and animals occurred 65 million years ago and was caused most probably by an asteroid crashing on the Yucatán Peninsula. Obviously, the expulsion from Eden must have taken place in the wake of another catastrophe many, many million years later. We may never find out exactly how it happened and whether it was caused by a direct impact or a close encounter of lesser severity in its consequences for life on the planet but, again, we may be blessed with such knowledge at some point of time in the future.

The reader may forgive such galloping speculations for events so remote in the life of the planet, but I cannot resist the imagery of the Angel brandishing specifically a flaming sword. We **know**, thanks both to the Christian and the Hebrew Traditions, of the existence of a practical infinity of Angels organized according to function, domain of influence, proximity to God and many such parameters. We also know that as we, human beings, have been assigned an angel, all celestial bodies have been assigned by the Almighty an angel, as well. If suns and planets can have their own angel, why should not the comets? Ergo, what is there in our Religion and Tradition that outright contradicts the existence of an Angel entrusted with the trajectories and particulars of cometary motions? In fact such an Angel over the comets already exists and we know his name: Ziquiel (Zikiel; also

Akhibel).[23]

We have been told numerous times through our Prophets and Saints, and also the Most Holy Virgin Mary, that many of the punishments to befall humanity are conditional. If humanity as a whole were to repent and change its ways, much of the punishment (if not all of it) would be averted. Consider for a moment what that might imply:

A small delay of a killer asteroid or a comet by a few hours somewhere in the cosmos can mean the difference between life and death for our planet. We know that periodic comets have their trajectories interfered with by the gravitational force of the major planets. (We mentioned earlier that Halley's has an **average** period of 74 years, for these reasons. The Astronomers could generate entire lists of similar phenomena and the drastic change in the behavior of certain periodic comets).

So, it is plausible, that even if a comet were initially launched on a trajectory of a rendez-vous with mankind, as a means of Divine retribution for our evil doings (analogous to the Flood of Noah and the Sodom and Gomorrah extinction), our tears, our prayers and all our acts of reparation acceptable to God, might change His intentions. Instead of a pull by planet Jupiter, then, a slight push by the invisible powers and energy sources in the Universe we collectively call Angels might bring about the desired result. The trajectory would be modified, the Earth would be saved, and the astronomers of the future would break their heads to find out what actually happened. While deliberating on the celestial mechanics involved, they would come upon some very interesting path breaking discoveries and would even begin appreciating the meaning of the words of the Bible to the effect that without the consent of God the sun does not rise.

The above deliberations are very speculative to be sure, but they do not try to tax the tolerance of the reader for an indefinite period of time. The events predicted in the prophecies are precipitating around us and they will materialize within our lifetime. As the reader remembers, the Epistle of

---

[23] See G. Davidson, [op. cit. p. 24]. Also, 3Enoch 14: *These are the names of the princes who guide the world: Gabriel, the angel of fire; (...) Ziqiel who is in charge of comets; Ziiel, who is in charge of tremors; (...).* [*The Old Testament Pseudepigrapha*, vol. 1, a new translation and introduction by P. Alexander, pp. 266-267].

Sunday dates at least since the 6th century of our era. How much compliance to the Divine precepts can we observe in the world around us and in the Christian fold, in particular, (since the Epistle was addressed explicitly to them)? Unfortunately, there exist few reasons for optimism. The events cannot be averted completely, only mitigated at the individual level for those who take the necessary steps to comply with the Divine Will.

In other words, this was a conditional prophecy which at the present stage can be mitigated only partially (for the benefit of the Elect, who are the only ones (in all religions) still complying with the Divine precepts). So, the conditional prophecy is less and less conditional and becomes a strict and inflexible prediction of future happenings. Only ca 1/3 of humanity will live to analyze the data ex post facto and draw remarkable conclusions and morally edifying lessons.

THE IMPORTANCE OF APRIL
AS THE FATEFUL MONTH OF OUR FUTURE

The Exodus of the Hebrews from the land of Egypt took place in the Spring. We know that not only through the Hebrew Religion, but also through our own. Since Lord Jesus Christ was crucified during the week of the Pascha, the Passover, (which is the religious Hebrew Holiday commemorating precisely the Passover from the land of bondage), our own religious celebrations of the Easter (Resurrection, Pascha, and all the other terms associated with it) always are bound to happen in Spring as well. The Orthodox Easter is based on a slightly different calculating rule than the other Christian Churches, and although at some years it may coincide with the rest, usually it takes place a number of weeks later. So, it may happen that the Orthodox may celebrate Pascha early in May while Catholics and Protestants have already done so, early in April or late in March.[24]

---

[24] The Orthodox rule chooses every year as Pascha Sunday the first Sunday that comes after the first full moon after the spring equinox. Consequently, their Easter depends on when the full moon occurs, and this is why it can vary so widely over a several week period.

For instance, in 1994, the East celebrated Easter on May the 1;[25] in 1995, the East celebrated Easter on April 23, while the Western Churches on April 16. (The Jewish Passover began at sundown of April 14); in 1996, the East will celebrate Easter on April 14, one week later than the other Christian Churches (April 7). The Jewish Passover will begin at sundown of April 3, 1996. Therefore, although the holidays do not coincide they are very tightly interconnected with a few days or weeks of difference.

Let us see whether these details can help us identify in what year will the prophecies take place. Lord Jesus Christ speaks categorically of April. Yet, the sequence of phenomena we are investigating will take several days to be completed. (For instance, the Three Days Darkness will be followed by days of relative darkness as visibility again increases and we can finally observe the comet and the signs in the sky. Also, the volcanic eruptions, the hurricanes, tidal waves etc. are not going to take place all within the same day, but rather in a sequence dictated by the very nature of the phenomena).

One way to find out more about the year of the comet would be to look at the Easter Calendar of our Churches and see how they move side by side over the next few years. My feeling is, that when Lord Jesus Christ, Who is addressing the entire Christendom with the Epistle of Sunday, speaks precisely of April, this may be an additional hint that during the year in question, no Christian Church will be celebrating its Easter in May, for instance. My theory is that the events will be a replay of the Exodus, the Passover, and the Passion of the Lord Jesus Christ, obeying all details, even the temporal ones. Therefore, I sense that we must search for years which satisfy fully this constraint of temporal agreement of Easter among **all** Christian churches (including the Russian one, which trails behind, considering her attachment to the Julian calendar for religious purposes). Also, the Hebrew Passover must be celebrated within the same overall time frame. This is an additional constraint that must be satisfied by the correct answer to our timing question.

Another source of potentially valuable hints as to the year of the events would be derived through other prophecies, Now it is time to review certain

---

[25] The reader may remember that the Russian church from a liturgical standpoint is still observing the Julian calendar. Hence, it celebrates Christmas and other church holidays with a delay of ca. thirteen days.

vital sentences from the material compiled by Emperor Leo the Wise:

And this is how the king will be revealed to the people: there will be a star which will appear for the duration of three days and in the third hour of the night of the eve of the holiday of the Mother of the Most High, the star will be seen in the middle of the city. And this star is not one of the planets but it will be like the one which made its appearance during the salvation-bringing birth of Jesus.

And again, from another prophecy:
it will be on a Friday, in the third hour of the morning when he will be revealed.... He, who is to be revealed, will be indicated by means of celestial signs.

Now, the eve of the holiday of the Mother of the Most High, can occur several times during the ecclesiastical year. A few most important holidays, however, occur in the spring: The first is the immovable holiday of the **Annunciation**, on March 25. The other major holiday of the Virgin Mary (at least in the Eastern tradition, and let us remember the above information comes from Byzantine prophets) is her celebration as the **Life Giving Fountain** (Ζωοδόχος Πηγή) which always falls on the first Friday following Easter Sunday. While Annunciation always happens in March 25 and can occur any day of the week, the Life Giving Fountain always happens on a Friday and can occur any week of April or early May and only very rarely could fall by the end of March.

Let us compare for a moment the Eastern holidays over the next few years in both the Eastern and the Western Churches:

Year	Roman Church	Greek Church
1996	April 7	April 14
1997	March 30	April 27
1998	April 12	April 19
1999	April 4	April 11
2000	April 23	April 30

From the above list it becomes clear that for **all** the Christian churches Easter will fall in April during 1998 and 1999. These are the only cases guaranteeing the avoidance of a May holiday for a number of the churches. Ditto, for the holiday of the **Life Giving Fountain** in the Greek Church. This is a more important piece of information than meets the eye, prima facie. Let us consider the events of the Exodus once again.

162

The Exodus occurred in the month of Abib (Nisan), the first month of the Hebrew year. Considering that the Hebrews used a lunar calendar at that time, the new month began with a new moon, and ended with the next new moon. The full moon occurred in the middle of the month. The modern equivalent for Abib, therefore, would be March-April. The Greeks had a similar calendar and till the time of Alexander the Great they were also calculating the day from sundown (like the Hebrews) instead of from sunrise (of the following morning). Consequently, when the geological upheavals that facilitated the Exodus took place, the Hebrews had crossed the last half of the month of March and were already in about the 13th of April.

I believe that the drama of Thera will be replayed down to the details of its previous timing! Again, the events will occur in March and April. Again, it will be the period of spring commemorated by the Hebrews with the Passover and by the Christians with the Week of Passion and the Resurrection of Lord Jesus Christ. Again, March and April are the temporal pivots of the events. Even if I have been wrong in identifying the year (1998 or 1999) at least we may rest assured that the most vital months will be March and particularly April.

Prophecies speak of miracles to take place on the *Feast of Our Lady*. They may relate to events other than the ones investigated in this chapter. Conceivably, the end of WWIII, or a most important victory or a most extraordinary celestial phenomenon may also take place on, say, August 15, the day of the Dormition of the Theotokos, namely, another major feast of Our Lady. I cannot speculate further on this issue with the information available right now. On the other hand, the famous Nostradamus prophecy of the great king of terror coming from the sky on July of 1999, can have the following logical explanation: The comet of 1998 does its horrendous damage, continues towards its perihelion, turns around and several months later, on its way back into the recesses of the Oort Cloud 'drops by' once again, while the WWIII is still raging.[26]

---

[26] I am the last person to accuse Nostradamus for making mistakes, especially since he spoke of events relevant to our Exodus-replay as taking place in **Spring**, most explicitly. The only theory I have to offer is one of numbers: The prophecies speak of 'signs and wonders in the skies'. There is no reason to exclude more than one cometary appearance from the beginning of great Troubles to the end of the war. *Qui vivra vera!*...

In order to be able to arrive at the correct identification of the year we shall need to re-examine all other relevant prophecies at our disposal and specifically the information about timing they may be offering to us. So, let us continue with our task.

NOSTRADAMUS AND FRIENDS REVISITED

Let us now review a few famous quatrains by Nostradamus studied in the previous chapter, and introduce later some new ones. Specifically, let us be reminded of **century II, quatrain 52** speaking of two waves of seismic activity **in spring** during which Corinth and Ephesus will swim in two seas... From the context we have reasons to believe that this applies to the Three Days Darkness as we analyzed it already, namely it will happen in the course of the proximate catastrophes.

Joanna Southcott, the celebrated English Prophetess, has predicted also that some great danger threatens England in **March and April** in a year not specified. However, in many of her prophetic poems and texts she speaks of the phenomena of our times in a most unequivocal fashion. She also predicts a terrible flood, the one long prophesied by God, which will also involve England. Joanna also wrote the following prophecy: **As I destroyed the Philistines and Egypt, so will I now destroy the Turks and their land will give into the hands of Israel.**

What strengthens my belief that the timing of the above prophecy coincides with WWIII and the Islamic invasion of Israel is the categorical statement that the destruction of the Turks will be **exactly of the same nature** as that of the Philistines and Egypt. Israel has had numerous enemies in its past who were destroyed. Why choose specifically the Philistines and the Egyptians from the entire group, unless it is meant to give a hint of the nature of the destruction, per se?[27]

Nostradamus, as we saw earlier in **Century II: Quatrain 46** speaks also of milk, amidst destruction, pestilence and death. (rain, blood, milk, famine, iron and pestilence. In the heavens a comet with a long tail is visible). How

---

[27] The reader may wish to consult the data from Velikovsky [op. cit.] where he analyses also the various connections with the History of the Hebrews, above and beyond the Exodus events. They are relevant and helpful in appreciating the above comparison by the English Prophetess.

can we have milk and famine side by side? They seem, prima facie, mutually exclusive. But let us look further, with a quatrain introduced for the first time:

Century I: Quatrain 57:
Par grand discord la terre tremblera,
Accord rompu dressant la teste au ciel:
Bouche sanglante dans le sang nagera
Au sol la face ointe de laict & miel.

Translation:
Because of a great discord the earth will shake. The accord is broken while the head is turned to the skies: the mouth is bloody and it will swim in blood. Upon the soil the face is anointed with milk and honey.

Suggested Interpretation:
The bleeding mouth swimming in blood may be denoting that the two 'bloods' are of different chemical composition. If the comet leaves behind ferruginous powder, the soil and the waters will be covered by a reddish-colored substance. Hence, when the bloody mouth of the killed person falls upon the ground (or the water) it will swim into a new kind of red, blood-resembling, substance. Let us remember also the Lord Jesus Christ in the *Epistle of Sunday*: *and I will rain blood (...) in April...* Yes, but not only blood but also milk and honey and oil of myrrh!

The milk and honey motif re-appears in historical references beginning with Ovid's *Transformations* (*The Metamorphoses*). Velikovsky [op. cit.], suggested that the ejecta from the comet's atmosphere settled upon the land and the waters of the rivers giving upon the latter the appearance of milk, as their oily substance shimmered in the light.[28] This substance was consumed by humans, having the taste of honey. (According to him, that was precisely the manna from heaven that fed the Hebrews in the Desert). Velikovsky may be vindicated even in this point when the future catastrophes befall us. For, how else can we interpret Nostradamus in the present context? The quatrain again suggests that these peculiar occurrences will coincide with military activities (the accord is broken. And

---

[28] He also mentioned the phenomenon of the red substance covering the waters and the land, and the rivers 'turning in blood' in the land of Egypt, and elsewhere.

we have plenty of Byzantine era prophecies speaking explicitly of a broken accord also...).

And a final reference to Nostradamus:

Century 2: Quatrain 62:
Mabus puis tost alors mourra, viendra,
De gens & bestes une horrible deffaite:
Puis tout à coup la vengeance on verra,
Cent, main, soif, faim, quand courra la comete.

Translation:
Let us begin with a few etymological notes: **Cent** may have two different meanings depending on which Latin root Nostradamus used in this case. *Cento-centonis* signified the coverings used by the Roman army to ward off missiles or extinguish fires.

Centum, undeclined numeral was 1) a hundred; and 2) (used hyperbolically) an indefinitely large number. Since both words collapse into 'cent' in Nostradamus's French we cannot be certain which one he intended, and we must search further for the meaning in the overall context of the quatrain. Since in most old editions of Nostradamus which I researched there exists a comma after Cent, I would imagine that the translation cent main, (one hundred hands) is unwarranted here.

Therefore, it would have been better to say that *cent* and *main* correspond to two different notions which, of course, are somehow related. Furthermore, *main* which comes from Latin *manus* can mean several things, besides a hand. It can even signify the trunk of an elephant, but most importantly, a band or body of men, i.e., armed forces by extension. Let us now attempt a verbatim translation.

Mabus then will soon die, there will come a dreadful destruction of people and animals. Suddenly vengeance will be revealed, protection against falling things, armies, thirst and hunger, when the comet will run.

Suggested interpretation:
No previous commentator has been able to offer a satisfactory theory for the identity of this mysterious Mabus. Until recently, the closest I was able to come to a plausible theory on the identity of Mabus was a sinister Dr. Mabuse, the hero of a famous German film I saw in my childhood. This at

least suggested that maybe Nostradamus is merely referring to the name of a certain personage and we need to bring no Procrustean beds here to begin our transformations.

Therefore, there may be no anagram involved here, no cryptic sequence of words whose initials correspond to the letters in the word Mabus, nothing of the sort. Mabus could simply be a straightforward family name like Smith or Borghese or Ivanoff. Right now, the US. Ambassador to Saudi Arabia is a certain Mr. Raymond Mabus. The fact that he is in a high-risk profession in a high-risk region of the world, renders him a potential target of enemy action in the days to come. In such an event, he may be the prophesied Mabus who will have died (by natural causes, or rather killed by the enemies of the USA) by the time the rest of the quatrain materializes. Or there may be another person, also named Mabus who is the target of this prophecy. With our present degree of knowledge this becomes the limit of our speculation.

However, let us consider the following: A dreadful destruction of people and beasts is going to be caused most probably by natural causes rather than killings in a war. (Nature does not show any particular preference in its target when earthquakes, volcanic eruptions, poisonous gases and ejecta are concerned). So, I believe that the 'horrible defeat' will follow the death of Mabus but will be of natural origin. Then will come the vengeance (divine, or human? or both?) and this will happen while the comet will be seen running in the skies. Also, famine and thirst, says the prophet. Could this thirst be caused by the ejecta of volcanoes and/or the comet rendering the waters temporarily non-potable? In any case, the thirst phenomenon recurs in the prophecies and it is by no means a negligible piece of information for our purposes.

A FEW ADDITIONAL MEDITATIONS
ON EARTHQUAKES AND VOLCANOES

Modern scholarship has upgraded the danger of volcanic eruptions and earthquakes in the event of geological upheavals. Among other things because we now know much more of what lies beneath the oceans. According to data recently released for publication from the classified files of the US Navy, the satellite imaging will revolutionize our thinking about the deep. The avalanche of information suddenly facing the consumer has many immediate consequences for our study: Satellite imaging and research of the Earth's oceans has **doubled** the known number of volcanoes beneath the sea. All of a sudden we learn new things about plate tectonics and their behavior and all Internet aficionados can keep up on a daily basis with discoveries of direct and imminent importance to our future. What is bound to happen to the volcanoes we know so much about **but also to those newly discovered ones** as soon as the events analyzed in the current study begin unleashing their force on our planet? Maybe we are blessed with having so much information at our disposal. One can only pray that we shall know how to make good use of it.[29]

THE PROPHET WHO CAME FROM THE COLD

The following material is excerpted from the prophecies of the Scandinavian seer Anton Johanson, received on November 13, 1907 during a vision.[30] His vision contained a great wealth of material on many events to befall humanity in the years following WWI, the majority thereof has already materialized. We shall concentrate on the portion covering geological upheavals only (although he predicted also military events and social upheavals to occur in our proximate future). The reason for this 'bias' is that we already know plenty about the military events of WWIII and because Johanson delivers a very detailed list of the sequencing of geological events, thus rendering that portion of his prophecy of vital importance to us, now. We take the liberty of highlighting certain portions to make them easier for retrieval later on.

(...) **Great earthquakes** *and* **volcanic eruptions** *visited different areas, and also in places that heretofore had been spared. In Italy these became more violent and destructive than ever before. If I remember correctly, I heard about the great new eruption of Vesuvius in this connection. (...) Several mines were filled with water and collapsed, caused by subterranean catastrophes.* **Storms of greater or lesser violence** *and extent raged in several parts of the world. (...) northern Germany, Denmark and southern Sweden were visited in this way. (...)*

(...) One of the first names I heard in connection with the earthquake was

---

[29] See also The Houston Chronicle, Nov. 6, 1995, *'We're having a data feast': Oceanic agency reveals new map with secrets from the deep.*

[30] The full text of the prophecies of Anton Johanson was published in Sweden in 1918 by A. Gustafson.

*Iceland. But if the source of the eruption was at this place or from the bottom of the North Sea, I could not discern so clearly. It surprised me when the Lord mentioned these places, because I did not know that earthquakes or eruptions took place in this part of the world. But the Lord mentioned these places several times distinctly, and later I understood that I had not been mistaken when I saw the disaster and the places where it happened. While it affected all the countries around the North Sea, none seemed to be as hard hit as England, especially on its east coast. The voice said that this came as 'a punishment for England's pride'. **Twilight seemed to extend over this whole area, and no stars were visible in the skies.** (...)*

Then Anton Johanson continues with a description of an earthquake and a **terrible tidal wave** that obliterates several European ports. He explicitly mentions toponyms in Norway, the Eastern shore of England, the Swedish Gothenburg, Malmö and Helsingbord, harbors on the English Channel, Rouen, other north coastal cities in France, Belgium, Germany and the Netherlands. Antwerp and Hamburg are amongst the worst casualties of the tidal wave-instigated catastrophes. London and Hamburg will suffer similar fate. The Baltic sea will be hit next and a little later the Mediterranean.

The earthquake and the tidal wave are followed in Anton's vision by **a terrible hurricane** that brings devastation to the entire globe. The Panama Canal is explicitly mentioned by the prophet as well as several coastal cities in the Gulf of Mexico and the United States. In his own words:

(...) Many vessels were shipwrecked at sea, and others were carried inland over the shores. Harbors and docks were wrecked so badly, that it was doubtful if some of them would be rebuilt, and commerce was ruined for a long time. (...) The storm raged over a wide belt from the Atlantic coast and up over the Mississippi valley, continuing up towards the Great Lakes, where it seemed to gather new strength. Over the Mississippi valley the storm raged just as violently as along the Atlantic coastline, but a belt between these two areas were spared; an area that was more rugged and where the soil was not so rich. I heard Chicago, Minneapolis, Washington and New York City especially mentioned as visited by this great storm. Among the North American cities New York City suffered most. (...) The city of Quebec was mentioned a couple of times in connection with that storm, as badly harassed.

Anton Johanson continues with the career of the storm in Europe: west and southwest are most affected, it enters the Mediterranean and proceeds into the Black Sea. The Crimean Peninsula, Sicily, Vienna and Marseilles are explicitly mentioned as recipients of its brutal force in greater intensity. Spain would suffer also, but evidently nobody as much as England. For several days telecommunications would be disrupted and no telegrams could be dispatched from England after these events.

(...) Now as before, during the effects of the volcanic eruption, England was one of the countries hardest hit by the storm. No country was mentioned so many times in connection with disasters as England.

Johanson continues with description of the impact of those catastrophes on other countries: Norway will be affected by inundations but not so in the mountains; Denmark and Sweden will be flooded; the hurricane will devastate parts of Finland and will invade Russia over Murmansk and Siberia. The severest damages were around the great lakes Onega and Ladoga.[31]

For more than two years I have prayed, with hundreds of thousands of other Christians, that the Lord might spare us from this misfortune, which was said to be coming because of the wickedness of men. And even if these calamities should be delayed, let us not forget to pray that the Lord might protect us, because it seemed sure that they would come. At first I doubted what the Lord said about the volcanic eruptions, and thought to myself that this is not a place where earthquakes usually take place. But the Lord said positively that it would come.

The valuable testimony of the Scandinavian seer lends additional credence to the proposition that no nation upon the earth will be spared the consequences of the events. It is also most remarkable to notice in his words the following:

a)   the power of prayer for mitigating the evil and averting many of the consequences at the individual level;

---

[31] Considering how close to the fateful lakes the city of St. Petersburg is built, it is most peculiar that the prophet does not mention it all. I do not have any prophetic evidence on the city of St. Petersburg. On the other hand, I am aware of at least one prophecy indicating that Moscow will remain the capital of the nation after WWIII and the concomitant catastrophes.

b)   we can expect earthquakes where none was believed feasible before. Of course, Iceland is a volcanic island, and its volcanoes have caused several geological catastrophes during its history expanding over a large geographical area. But what Johanson says is what became corroborated by the satellite imaging recently declassified: There are many more volcanoes at the bottom of the seas whose existence we ignored up until now.

Furthermore, the toponyms mentioned by Johanson fully agree with similar information beginning with the Hebrew Prophets and the Sibylline Oracles (Remember the river Don abandoning the Sea of Azov? But this is in the immediate vicinity of the Crimean Peninsula, as well...).

Johanson further predicted the complete disappearance of Turkey among the nations (in full agreement with countless other prophecies) and the loss of Eastern Siberia from the hold of Russia. The most plausible explanation for this loss would be analogous to the destructions, inundations and submergence befalling so many other places: Eastern Siberia is the heartland of Russian volcanoes. In fact, most of them are concentrated on the Kamchatka Peninsula and the Kuril Islands. Kamchatka counts 22 active ones, while on the Kurils, 40 of the 160 volcanoes present, are still active. It is quite plausible that some of these may share the fate of Etna in the future and that of Thera in the past.

Consequently, the loss of Eastern Siberia may be due to its disappearance from the face of the earth, altogether. We must expect that the 'ring of fire' from Alaska over the Aleutian Islands, down to Siberia, the Kamchatka Peninsula, the Kurils etc. will not remain quiet while the powers of heaven and earth are shaking. I find the above scenario very plausible although I have only two pieces of prophetic evidence to supply: one is the above reference by Anton, and the other comes from a Quaker female seer, dating from 1922. Her vision, described in a letter, among other things relating to WWIII and the geological disturbances, included the following: *I saw the international boundary line disappear as these two governments broke up and dissolved into chaos. I saw race rioting upon this American continent on a vast scale.*[32]

---

[32] From a letter she addressed to the Mormons of Cardston, Alberta Canada, relating her vision while visiting their new temple.

If my speculation is correct, the international boundary line the seer refers to is the date line, an imaginary line that passes through the Bering Straight, and separates day from night in a sense. It is somewhat a line of demarcation between the USA (Alaska) and Russia (Siberia). In the events of the upheavals we are talking about, the geography of the area will change due to violent volcanism and massive earthquakes, most probably with lands submerging and new ones emerging. Hence the boundary line (as we know it) will 'disappear'.

Anton Johanson was most meticulous in detailing the behavior of **a hurricane of global proportions and destructiveness**. What could be the agent giving birth to that hurricane? According to Velikovsky the hurricane is a sine-qua-non along with the volcanic eruptions, the darkness, the boiling waters, the tidal waves etc. In other words, if our speculation is correct and the events predicted to materialize soon will occur sometime in the spring of 1998 (during March and April, specifically) they are going to be a replay of the events coinciding with the Exodus, a hurricane must accompany the other natural forces. Velikovsky found in the writings of many cultures around the world ample testimony to that tremendous hurricane of the past.[33]

Specifically, the highlighted words from Anton Johanson's vision reproduced below read as follows:
great earthquakes; volcanic eruptions; storms; twilight seemed to extend over this whole area, and no stars were visible in the skies; tidal waves; hurricane; inundations.

Contrast them now with the headings from a number of chapters from Velikovsky's book:
(...) darkness; earthquakes; Passover; the hurricane; the tide; the battle in the sky; the comet; (...) boiling earth and sea; (...)

I do not believe for a moment that these similarities are due to 'remarkable coincidences'. The scenario of Anton Johanson is an exact replica of the events described by Velikovsky as contemporaneous to the Exodus and hypothesized by many other researchers as also contemporaneous to the destruction of Thera.

---

[33] See op. cit. especially pp. 67-70.

With so many prophetic hints and data currently at our disposal we finally reached the moment when we can tackle the question raised in the introduction to this chapter: Did St. John the Divine specifically mention the events before the year 2000, and if so, where exactly and how? Let us turn to the Book of the Apocalypse for clues and hints:

ON THE ETYMOLOGY AND MEANING OF ABADDON

Abaddon appears first in Revelation chap. 9: **And the fifth angel sounded, and I saw a star fall from heaven unto the earth; and to it was given the key of the bottomless pit. And it opened the bottomless pit; and there arose a smoke out of the pit, as the smoke of a great furnace; and the sun and the air were darkened by reason of the smoke of the pit. (...) And they had over them a king, the angel of the abyss; his name in Hebrew is Abaddon, and in the Greek Apollyon.**

In Revelation chap. 20: **And I saw an angel coming from heaven, having the key of the abyss and a great chain in his hand. And he captured the Dragon, the ancient serpent, who is the Devil and the Satan, (...) and he put him into the abyss and he closed and sealed over him the abyss (...).**

(Note: This confinement of the Devil will last for one thousand years).

So we have two references to the abyss, a word translated also as a bottomless pit, and a "phrear" (a deep well emanating from the interior of the earth). The former reference is associated with major catastrophes (on the same chapter which also analyses a major war, WWIII), the latter reference appears in chap. 20 and deals with the beginning of the Millennial Age. So, in the first instance it is a **star** which falls from heaven and which star basically has the power to open (as if with a key) the **bottomless pit**. In the second instance we have a most explicit reference that it will be an **Angel** of the Lord (and not a star) who will bind Satan into the Abyss. Because St. John never used his words carelessly (as so many pseudo-interpreters have implied over the centuries) the very distinctions he makes in the wording are going to become the clues necessary for de-coding his messages.

As I proposed in my previous study, the first reference is a clear indication that something which is going to emanate from the depths of the earth, will have nefarious consequences, such as a smoke of a great furnace capable of darkening the sun and the air, (and a number of other evils which are detailed in sequence).[34]

In a Hebrew text entitled *The Greater Key of Solomon*, Abaddon is "a name for God that Moses invoked to bring down the blighting rain over Egypt." In another, *The Thanksgiving Hymns* we read of the "Sheol of Abaddon" and of the "torrents of Belial (that) burst into Abaddon". Finally, in an apocryphal book of the first century of our era, *The Biblical Antiquities of Philo*, Abaddon is definitely **a place** (sheol, hell) <u>not</u> a spirit or demon or angel.[35]

Let us now organize all new information available:

1) Abaddon, which is known as a place, (the Sheol of the Hebrews), the Hades, or Underworld of the Greeks, the recesses of the earth (where the enemies of Jupiter had been confined since time immemorial and where again Satan will be confined in times to be), emerges as a **tool of punishment** under the complete control of an Omnipotent God.

2) Since Abaddon was the name of God the Destroyer who brought down the plights on the Pharaoh during the Exodus, we have our first connection with Thera, its eruption, the consequences of that eruption for the Exodus of the Hebrews from the land of servitude and also a historical reference of the God of Israel as a divinity *"directly responsible for earthquakes, tidal waves and disasters of fire and water."*[36]

3) The torrent of Belial, furthermore, bursting into Abaddon is peculiarly reminiscent of a *tsunami, or any tidal wave for that matter,* and its huge water volumes pouring into a volcanic *caldera* after a fiery eruption and its subsequent collapse below sea level! For, here we have a clear distinction of water and fire and the proper order of their

---

[34] The Hebrew etymology for Abaddon is merely "a place of destruction". It further personified death and the grave. It is also a fiery place, and always lies under God's power.

[35] I am indebted to Gustav Davidson [1967, p. 1], for the above critical information from Hebrew sources.

[36] Vide supra, Martin Bernal, [op. cit. p. 317].

interaction (the torrents burst into Abaddon and not vice versa). While scholars still debate the true etymology of 'Belial' T.K. Cheyne has suggested that it may be traced to the Babylonian goddess of the Underworld, *Belili*. Again we have an allusion to a place, the Underworld, in other words, a specific location to be searched in the entrails of the planet.[37]

4)   In the previous Chapter we saw in *Les Prophecies de Merlin* that at the time of the killing of the 'Dragon of Babylonia' the Dead Sea will disappear, the Mount Aetna will collapse, and new sources of thermal springs will issue forth. Specifically, in **lxxxix, folio 72a** we were told that as the Prophet David predicted that *'one must pass through this age by means of fire and water'*, "this is exactly the road that we must take", (while all these catastrophes rage around us).[38]

Considering that the Dragon of Babylonia (as proven already in my previous study) will be killed while in the land of Israel according to the predictions specified in Ezekiel's chapters 38 and 39, the simultaneous internal consistency of all these pieces of evidence allows us now to propose a new interpretation for the passage from Revelation's chapter 9:

And the fifth angel sounded, and I saw a star fall from heaven unto the earth; and to it was given the key of the bottomless pit. And it opened the bottomless pit; and there arose a smoke out of the pit, as the smoke of a great furnace; and the sun and the air were darkened by reason of the smoke of the pit.

A star will fall from heaven (or will approach us dangerously close; this appears to be a reference to the comet of our proximate future); to this star, in a mysterious way was given the key that unlocks the bottomless pit (the gravitational pull giving rise to a chain reaction of volcanic eruptions and

---

[37] Another interesting peculiarity of Greek Mythology is the assertion that Zeus, after defeating the Giants and the Titans, he confined them into the recesses of the earth. (For instance, Enceladus, a Giant was buried under Mt. Aetna), while the defeated Titans were forced to reside in the depths of the earth. So, in the pantheon of the pagan Greeks as well, their supreme God had full control and command on the happenings beneath the surface of the earth and he would contain all his enemies there.

[38] Lucy Allen Paton, [op. cit. vol. 1, pp. 144-145].

seismic upheavals emanating from the fault lines in our tectonic plates). A smoke will rise like the smoke of a great furnace (a direct reference to the source of the smoke: the furnace burning under the lithosphere); the sun and the air will be darkened (reference to the Three Days Darkness).

The rest of the prophecy up until chap. 9:13 deals with the additional consequences of the great upheavals caused by the interaction of the 'star' and the 'bottomless pit'. They are in harmony with other pronouncements of the famine, the suffering and the diseases that will emerge after the catastrophes, and will coexist with a furious war. I wish to advance no more speculations on why, for instance, some of the torments are going to last five months long.

Let us now go back to the chapter entitled *The Signs Before the End(s)* where we first introduced a private revelation by Lord Jesus Christ to a European of our generation. It began with *The Divine fire and the fire of hell will arrive and last during the days of darkness indicated by all the saints. My luminous cross will appear in the sky...* We speculated then at possible natural phenomena associated with the luminous cross. Now we can review the very first sentence of this private revelation: The Divine fire **and** the fire of Hell. In other words, the Lord Jesus Christ differentiates between two distinct sources of fire which will cause the darkeness. One emanates from Above, the other from beneath the Earth, traditionally associated with the Sheol. This could be construed as yet another reference of a cometary fire joined by a volcanic fire.[39]

---

[39] The science of volcanology informs us of the existence of many types of eruptive volcanoes. (A most informative study is the one entitled Volcano, written and published by the Time-Life Books, 1982). They differentiate between the following: effusive eruptions, steam explosions, submarine eruptions, strombolian type eruptions, plinian explosions, glowing avalanche (nuée ardente), paroxysmal explosions, etc. The scientists also tell us that when the vent of a volcano is sealed by a dome or an accumulation of debris, under this type of obstruction great pressure gradually builds up. As the cap approaches the bursting point, even the tiniest change in the environment may trigger the final explosion.

The scientists identify the slight strain of earth tides from the gravitational fields of the moon and the sun as more than sufficient to trigger such an explosion! One can only imagine, therefore, the chain reaction brought about by a gravitational field such as that of a comet, which can trigger on a global scale the bursting of many volcanoes. Considering the scientific evidence, therefore, one must be filled with

REVIEW OF THE MOST SALIENT POINTS

a)   Additional evidence has enabled us to achieve a more literal translation and a more narrow interpretation of the relevant chapter from the Book of Revelation. Consequently, we have yet another prophecy of the highest importance and prestige indicating catastrophic events brought about by the interaction of a 'star' with the 'underworld'.

b)   Our excursion into the mythology and history of the Mediterranean peoples lent additional support to the theory that Atlantis was connected intrinsically with the Island of Thera before its destruction. Our research about the future of Mankind suggests that Atlantis will rise again, during the repetition of the events that led to its submersion.

c)   We hope to have vindicated some of the positions originally advanced by Immanuel Velikovsky. If the rest of our speculations about predictions materialization prove correct, we hope that posterity will treat his memory with greater respect.

d)   We had additional opportunities to realize that the upcoming destructions are directed towards the sins and evils of humanity. This evidence corroborates a plethora of similar statements found in other sources. The disasters **can** be mitigated at the individual level only, through a life consistent with the Will of God and the necessary acts of reparation. This is yet another indication that the Elect are writing their own future History by the ways they are making use of their freedom as individuals and as spiritual entities.

e)   We may have advanced a plausible theory explaining some of the problems of Biblical datings of History. The Flood of Deucalion is much more recent than the Flood of Noah, and we have no written evidence how many disasters through fire and water preceded the Flood of Noah. (At least not within the Judeo-Christian Tradition).

---

awe before the Word of the Spirit: and to the star was given the key of the bottomless pit...

f)   We discovered a most interesting link between the Explosion of Thera and the Exodus events with the geological events to happen in our own lifetime. This link is the prophesied 'oil of myrrh' explicitly mentioned in the *Epistle of Sunday*, a document of great prestige within the Orthodox and Catholic Traditions and venerated over long centuries (even though not followed by the individual Christians of our generation).

g)   If what we believe to be a correct interpretation of prophecies materializes in acceptable degree of agreement with the ultimate facts, it appears that prophecy, besides providing the services to humanity already detailed in an introductory chapter, can afford us yet another valuable service: allow us to better understand and reconstruct our past.   Specifically, if Thera re-emerges from the depths of the sea, (besides lands around Bimini, as Cayce predicted and other places of the globe for which names have been given already) we can believe the details of the Atlantis story and we can have more reasons to associate its location (partly, anyway) with the Eastern Mediterranean, and the Cyclades in particular. By the same token that it took the technology of satellite imaging to discover from high above what lies in the depths of our oceans, we can use prophecy also in the future to assist us in the reconstruction of the Earth's past. Specifically, archaeology and Biblical scholarship will be enjoying more synergism than ever before. That would not be a small service to humanity!

h)   Our overall research tends to corroborate the thesis that the ancients were extremely sophisticated people. Even the names they chose for peoples and places and heroes and kings and many things were selected in a most genial way.   Mere etymological study and comparative linguistics among the peoples of the Eastern Mediterranean will continue opening new treasure rooms to us on the history of the region which preceded the cataclysmic events of the Thera explosion.

Two relevant Post scripta

Post scriptum 1:
I would like to resuscitate a reference by the Sibyls to the Royal Meropeia, mentioned already in the chapter on Nostradamus and Friends.

In **Book III**, vs. 335-351 and again vs, 363-366 we heard of the comet and the war and the submergence of a number of cities in Asia Minor, Middle East and Greece. While covering toponyms that can be easily identified as European, the Sibyl included the *Royal Meropeia*. I trust that we can now advance a plausible theory on the identity of the mysterious Royal Meropeia, which has remained a puzzle to researchers so far.

The *Royal Meropeia* is squeezed between mentions of toponyms of the Cyclades, the Dodecanese and the Peloponnesus. Studying the very sequence of the words as they appear in the prophecy, one can easily see that the Sibyl begins with the area around the Sea of Azov, goes down the Asia Minor region, moves to the Near East, turns back towards Greece from the islands of the Aegean moving westward to the mainland and then again westward to Italy and Rome. I believe that this sequencing is of importance here, and the *Royal Meropeia* has to be located in the general area in the way the Sibyl's finger moves across the map, more or less. What we know from ancient Greek writers with regards to **Merops**, **Meropeia** and **Meropes** is rather interesting and quite instructive:

We already mentioned earlier the text of Theopompus of Chios, titled *Meropidae*. As the reader remembers, Merops was a king of the island of Cos, who married Clymene, one of the Oceanides, and whose reign was **contemporary** to the flood of Deucalion! The island of Cos neighbors the ancient Kallisti, and Strabo (who did not believe the story proposed by Theopompus) nevertheless informs us that a city on Cos was called *Meropeian* in antiquity, and that the ancient inhabitants of Astypalaea had changed their abode and moved to the present island of Cos. This may suggest that they were forced to abandon their old homes in the wake of geological events.

On the other hand, at least two authors I researched identify an ancient Meropia (Meropeia) with the Island of Siphnos, in the Cyclades. (The Ancient Roman Pliny and the Modern Greek Dr. E. Karpodini-Dimitriadi, an Archaeologist and author of *The Greek Islands...* Her historical coverage of Siphnos begins with the following:

In ancient times Siphnos was extremely wealthy on account of its gold, copper and silver mines. It was first inhabited by Karians and Phoenicians who called it Akys or Meropia. Later it was called Minoa by the Minoans who settled there. (...)

The presence of gold, copper and silver betrays the existence of volcanic veins which bring such treasures from the depths of the earth. Considering that Merops was a King of Cos **and** adjacent territories we can assume that the Meropidae were inhabiting several areas, including Cos and Siphnos. In any case, it may be not too farfetched to propose that the mysterious Royal Meropeia was located in the area over which Merops was the King. The entire geography of the region, however was modified with the events contemporary to the Flood of Deucalion. By the same token, since Cyagra has not been identified yet, it may also refer to one of those famous cities mentioned by Plato which disappeared in the catastrophe of Atlantis; although the Sibyl had ways of knowing this fact, the historiographers were at a loss since no evidence has been unearthed so far to prove unequivocally the existence of such a place. Theopompus might have been right all along, after all. And *Meropes* was in fact the name for the entire race of those islanders who disappeared overnight leaving behind a couple of traces and a handful of survivors only.

Post scriptum 2:
Several prophecies covering the Three Days Darkness explicitly spoke of peculiar thunder and lightning at a strange time of the year. We know that volcanoes can create lightning with no storm in sight. Friction from swirling ash particles in the course of a violent eruption can generate electric discharges.[40] In fact, the astronomy specialists were looking for lightning on the surface of Venus as an indication of volcanic activity on that planet!

Furthermore, volcanic eruptions can produce an ash cloud very strongly reminiscent of the mushroom of an atomic explosion. Such images have already been captured on film, and *The National Geographic* has been among the publications which first produced many such photographs. Therefore, when the prophets speak of a mushroom cloud it will most likely emanate from a massive volcanic eruption, rather than an all-out, wholesale nuclear war! A volcanic mushroom cloud and all the catastrophes in its

---

[40] The reader may have seen the spectacular discharges generated during the eruptions of volcanoes such as Sakurajima (Japan) and Mount St. Helens (USA).

wake can be survived by a great part of the human race. On the other hand, an all-out nuclear war long prophesied by our instant experts on prophecies **cannot** be survived in peace and prosperity by 1/3 of the human race!... The number of the Remnant is given in many prophecies, we can rest assured on the average, across all races and nations it will be 1/3 of the total. Let us also look at **Zechariah 13:8-9**:

> *In all the land, says the Lord, two thirds of them shall be cut off and perish, and one third shall be left. I will bring the one third through fire, and I will refine them as silver is refined, and I will test them as gold is tested. They shall call upon My name and I will hear them. I will say, 'They are My people', and they shall say, 'The Lord is my God!' "*

The great destructiveness of volcanoes is due more to the material blown out rather than to the flowing lava, which can only travel short distances before it congeals. The solid matter, however, may travel widely; in the Krakatoa eruption of 1883, for instance, it was sent 20 miles high into the air. **Torrents of rain, due to the condensation of the escaping water vapor,** often fall with the ashes converting them into a sort of hot fluid mud (such as the lahars of Pinatubo). This material is most destructive in its effects. Many gases and vapors escape in the explosion. (Steam, however, is the most abundant vapor).

Geologists agree that the steam is indeed the principal force in the violent expulsion of materials from the volcanoes of the explosive type. Many of the gases (among them chlorine, sulfur, and carbon dioxide) are poisonous. When steam and ash particles are mixed together, after the vapor solidifies, they can create hail.

With this technical background in mind, let us return to **Ezekiel** chap. 38:22, speaking about the ultimate destiny of Gog in the land of Israel: "And I will come in judgement against him in pestilence and blood; and I will rain upon him, and upon his bands, and upon the many people that are with him, **a cataclysmic rain, and great hailstones, fire and brimstone**. [Emphasis added]. Cataclysm is the Greek word for the Flood and a "cataclysmic rain" ought to be preserved to convey the enormity of the phenomenon, or the relative vicinity of the source and the concomitant huge volume of escaping water steam through the volcanoes). With the data already at our disposal we can speculate that a single event can cause all of the above.

- a cataclysmic rain (caused by escaping steam vapors) along with
- great hailstones; stones of hail, in the Greek, are the rocks that explode along with the vapors, plus the solidified steam captured along with tephra and can travel long distances, as we noticed already
- fire and brimstone (i.e., literally sulphur) which are the ever-present byproducts of volcanic eruptions of the explosive type.

Consequently, the very wording of Ezekiel's most relevant prophecy is a detailed description of a catastrophic explosion of a volcano. The only thing not explicitly mentioned in this case is the oil of myrrh. On the other hand, Ezekiel speaks of the area around the Dead Sea becoming a massive cemetery for the dead of the invading army. In my previous study I wrote that the Dead Sea was a good choice considering its relative economic value vis-à-vis other locations in Israel. We know now that the Dead Sea will disappear in the course of the upheavals and its waters will move elsewhere. Then in the gap of the former Dead Sea the cemetery will be easier erected, and the economic decision for that choice of location will be even more appropriate.

CHAPTER SEVEN

HARMONIZING THE PROPHECIES REGARDING THE FUTURE OF CHRISTIANITY AND ISRAEL THE MAINLY CATHOLIC EVIDENCE

> *A new scientific truth does not triumph by convincing its opponents and making them see the light, but rather because its opponents eventually die, and a new generation grows up that is familiar with it.* Max Planck.

Introduction

An Eastern Orthodox Christian researching prophetic material emanating from the Catholic branch of Christianity will not fail to notice the distortion of Orthodox realities prevailing in much of the Catholic press. This is basically due to historical ignorance of the general public which can be manipulated by special interest groups with their own agendas, or by equally ignorant authors who have already been misguided by such interest groups and thus perpetuate misconceptions and bias. The quality of their own interpretive efforts and scholarship in general falls victim to such biases. They are led to unwarranted interpretations of the texts and further confound themselves and their readers.

Most of the professional analysis of prophetic materials is still confined to academic presses, University professors, their colleagues and their graduate students. The truths they have discovered so far and the historical research they have completed have not been shared by the general public to the degree one would have hoped for. In this chapter we shall attempt to redress some of these wrongs, and particularly to identify the unwarranted discrepancies prevailing in the popular religious literature today.

We shall have opportunity to establish the lack of validity of several interpretations of Catholic prophecies advanced by Catholic authors. This will derive from accumulated historical evidence and from the wording of the Catholic prophets, themselves. For many contemporary Catholic writers it is still an anathema to include the intellectual treasures from the East and many times (one has to assume, quite unknowingly and innocently) they refer to Eastern authors as if they were part and parcel of the Western Tradition.[1] It becomes obvious, that they are operating with a smaller set of sources than could have been feasible. Anybody trained in Statistics would be able to appreciate the inherent risks such an approach entails for the robustness of the conclusions and the informational quality of the findings of a given study.

I do not wish to engage in polemics here. I only desire to clear misconceptions and erroneous conclusions that have crept in the mind of the reader who has read in the past such books. I also wish to show to the readers (regardless of Christian denomination they presently confess to) in what manner the events destined to transpire before the re-unification of the Christians churches will materialize and **under what exact conditions the re-unification of the Christian Churches will take place.** If these issues become clarified, then the text of the prophecies speaking of the future of Christianity will become more plausible and acceptable to the readers, no matter what church they worship in and what dogmatic positions they currently adopt.

---

[1]   Dr. R. H. Bloch, in a recent book entitled *God's Plagiarist...'* supplies interesting evidence on the modus operandi of the Abbé Migne, a major source of many contemporary Roman Catholics. Migne was sentenced for plagiarism repeatedly; except for a minor reference, he never gave credit to the true architect of the Patrologies and major Editor thereof, Dom Pitra. He engaged in many other forms of questionable publishing activity, such as reprinting "recently published works without indicating his sources". (ibidem, p. 65). Dr. Bloch shows that 'a good proportion of the *Patrologie Latine* and the *Patrologie Grecque* was pirated'.

Such shady dealings did not restrain, however, the pious Abbé from boasting that thanks to his efforts, "*In Russia, it is the reading, the translation and the reprinting of these incomparable ancestors which prevents the Greeks, separated from the Church, from withdrawing entirely*". [p. 5]. Which seems to imply that the 'Greeks' (namely the Eastern Orthodox churches) did not withdraw entirely from Christianity and revert to a state of heathen savagery, thanks only to the Latin editions of pirated books already existing in their monasteries and places of safety and worship for more than two thousand years!... Ludicrous as this claim may be to the initiated, most Catholics know very little, if anything, about the Eastern Churches to this day.

A FEW CAVEATS ON THE FUTURE OF PROTESTANTISM
AS SPECIFIED BY THE PROPHETS

Since the Protestants recognize no prophets of their own in the course of the last 2000 years speaking on the future of Christianity, they may feel that prophecies to the effect that *Protestantism will cease* are nothing more than cheap tricks by Non-Protestant churches engaging in unfair competition practices and questionable market penetration techniques. Yet, this is not an accusation that can stand up in the light of evidence. The reasons being, among others, the following:

a)   Many of the prophecies speaking of the eventual disappearance of Protestantism were written **centuries before** Martin Luther was born. They had no axes to grind against the Reformation in the market-penetration sense. They were simply providing a Divine Intimation along with many others concerning the future of the Christian World and of the globe in general.

b)   Many such prophecies come from the Orthodox East. Since the Reformation and the religious wars it engendered were fought against Rome and the Catholic populations of Europe, again, the Orthodox East cannot be accused for foul play, since they did not participate in the fray and had no political and theological differences justifying such a schism. The East, if anything, had its own differences with the Vatican at that time and its theologians were acting quite independently from it. Nobody can accuse the Eastern Churches for sharing in propaganda games with the R.C.C. at the expense of the Protestant churches.

c)   Protestantism was created as a reaction against the abuses of the Papacy as an institution and against the Vatican as a center of secular power. Once the Church of Rome is spiritually renovated from within, there will be nothing to continue protesting against. The future Pope, as the prophecies predict, will be an Angelic Pope and a truly saintly figure. He will renovate the Catholic Church; for example, we learn from the Catholic prophets that the Order of the Jesuits will be for ever disbanded. Many other internal reforms will return the R.C.C. to its essence during the Apostolic times. It will be simply impossible for knowledgeable clergymen of good will to refuse their reunification with the rest of Christianity, once the reasons leading to their initial separation cease to exist. Hence, the protesting action, reaction to Rome, and Protestantism by extension, will have no more theological and dogmatic reason of existence; consequently, Protestantism will cease. This does not mean, on the other hand, that Protestants will all join the Roman Catholic Church as we know it today.

One has to expect a certain degree of structural unemployment being generated in certain circles, and needless to say, a fierce opposition to the above thesis from certain quarters. However, this will be not the first or the last area of human activity that will experience structural unemployment in the years to come, and considering that most of us change our job description and professional career on the average 3-4 times through life, there is, prima facie, nothing sacred about the career of a Protestant preacher or a Doctor of Theology teaching at the Seminary. We live in a world without job security to speak of, and it appears that flexibility and adaptability is the answer. Unfortunately, as Max Planck had ample opportunity to notice and as we saw repeatedly throughout this study, such a flexibility and adaptability comes in very short supply. However, our salvation and survival are matters of personal responsibility; it will serve us little to err and lose our soul and our life and then blame it on the erroneous guidance by misguided advisors, which may include members of the clergy, deeply entrenched in the status-quo and their own biases.

d) The Protestants will have ample opportunity to convince themselves in the course of WWIII, and in view of the overwhelming evidence all around, of the powers of the Most Holy Virgin Mary, the interference of the Holy Ones from Heaven and the many miraculous events which will be due to their intervention. Both Orthodox and Catholics pray constantly to the Virgin Mary and the Saints, never doubting the power of their intercession on behalf of the faithful. They have good reasons to believe to the efficacy of that intercession because their personal lives have been marked by it. The Protestants ignore the existence of such fountains of grace. They fail to drink from them, have no idea how their water tastes and they are as a result suspicious of the intellectual abilities of those 'naive Christians' who still believe in the power of the relics, the intercession of the Saints, and the uniquely privileged position in Heaven and on Earth given to the Mother of Lord Jesus Christ.

Once they realize the consequences of their incalculable loss over the past five centuries of such neglect and error they will be more than eager to join with the rest of us to differentiate between veneration, adoration, latria and doulia.[2] Ditto, for their misguided position regarding the holy relics and the ability of Saints to intervene and shower blessings on the faithful who call to them. Martin Luther may have been right in many of his accusations against exploitative clerics and their manipulation of the religious sentiment of the masses. But this does not mean that all references to miraculous icons, myrrh-gushing tombs and holy relics are for the idiots who refuse to become enlightened Protestants and remain content with being Orthodox and Catholics. There is a point where the truly intelligent Christian can draw the line between outright manipulation and foul play and hard evidence that cannot be denied.[3]

In conclusion, it will be the sheer force of undeniable facts coupled with the genuine Christian sentiment of intelligent Protestants which will lead them to reconsider many of their views and theological positions. In that spirit of re-discovery they will also participate in the Eighth Ecumenical Council. The sweeping changes imposed upon the new age following WWIII will force the survivors to reconsider their value system, the ways of organizing production and distribution, the means of economic survival in the years immediately following the ravages of our times. Many current forms of activity will either disappear completely or will have to undergo major overhaul and re-engineering. It is not only Protestantism which will cease, most of what we are currently engaging in will either cease or become modified, re-

---

[2] According to the Seventh Ecumenical Council, *doulia* (δουλεία) is the type of worship offered to the icons; *hyperdoulia* (ὑπερδουλεία) is the worship offered to the Blessed Virgin Mary; *latria* (λατρεία) is the highest level and is reserved for God alone.

[3] The Komarovs in their book entitled 'Patriarch', (Патриарх), [1994], chronicle the re-discovery of some of the most venerated relics in Russia. Let all the enlightened positivists and 'disabused' Christians of our generation come with a scientific explanation to the effect that the body of a saint dead for centuries and which body has undergone unspeakable neglect in the last seven decades can still be preserved in such perfect condition. While Lenin's mummy, despite the solicitude of an army of professional attendants and the great advances of modern science, not only failed to perform any miracles but also was dependent on regular injections to continue functioning even as a mummy.

engineered or over-hauled. It is just that prophecies speaking of the future of the Churches will concentrate on themes such as Protestantism, re-unification, the Jesuits and such religious concerns. This does not means that nothing else will cease or become modified.

It is extremely difficult to separate prophetic material dealing with the Christian Church in general or the national Christian Churches in particular from the political and economic fortunes of the land in question. Trying to split the prophecies in separate chapters dealing exclusively with the war and the natural catastrophes on the one hand and the fate of the church on the other would be impractical and would entail splitting often a single sentence in several parts. Therefore, in this chapter which primarily deals with the fate of the Church we shall also include additional pertinent material dealing with the fortunes of the country. This will further help us put in context the happenings and the flow of events that lead into the denouement of the religious fortunes of the countries dealt with in the prophecies.

This is not the proper place for introducing the History of the Europe. But a few caveats may be useful to the reader before we embark on the prophecies themselves:

The study of the History of the Byzantine empire having not been part of the Western curriculum (with very few exceptions) one must assume that most of the readers are still completely unaware of the level of culture and civilization achieved by the East of Europe and the Middle East while the West of Europe was going through its Dark Ages. Also, the consequences of the Ottoman and Tatar Yokes to the peoples and the churches of the Balkans, Central Europe and the expanses between the Danube and the Pacific Ocean, are either ignored or down-played.

The Angles, Saxon and Danes invaded the British Isles which were inhabited by Britons, peoples of different ethnic background. Those Britons never abandoned the hope that political control of their Islands will one day revert to them. Therefore, when dealing with Welsh, Irish and Scottish Catholic Prophecies we must keep in mind that the Angles and Saxons are the enemy and the invader who will be removed one day. The original populations never liked the term 'England' having become synonymous with the British Isles in the popular historiography and are looking forward to the time when the Isles will resume their original name.

With respect to England and the British Isles as a whole we must also keep in mind the following clarifications:

- the Romans who invaded most of the Isle named it *Albio* (albus = white, from the white cliffs of Dover). Albio, therefore is the name employed in many prophecies which were written in Latin, the official language of the Catholic Church in the British Isles. In Welsh, different terms, obviously, obtain yet, when translated into English or other languages consistency obtains.

- The history of the British Isles has fomented the generation of several Christian churches competing for supremacy. Besides the Protestant Denominations and the Irish Catholic Church we must remember the Catholic church of England which since Henry VIII does not obey the Pope in Rome, while espousing the Catholic theology in so many ways. Therefore, when prophecies generated in England, proper, speak of 'England returning to the faith' they mean that (when the churches re-unify) the Church of England as a separate and distinct institution will exist no more. Many Catholic authors cannot resist the temptation of presenting anybody who is not a Papist as a person 'who has abandoned the faith'. The historically innocent reader, reading such lines might think that Englishmen today are heathens like the 'Greeks' would have been in the absence of Abbé Migne, and as the Russians are presented to this very day in most of the Catholic Presses. I hope such distinctions in the language of the prophecies will help us further appreciate their meaning and relevance for our generation.

- Let me remind the reader once again that the particular words employed in the prophecies occasionally can be a source of confusion. But we must make allowance for the terminology in vogue at the time the prophets lived and their texts were written down. Consequently, *Turk*, as we note repeatedly elsewhere may also be understood as an expanded term for Muslim enemies. Since for several centuries the Ottoman Empire (the Turks narrowly defined) were controlling many other Islamic lands occupied by Arabs and other nations, the term came easily to be associated in the Western European mind (being geographically separated and unaware of the prevalent variations of features, temperament, origin, background etc.) with the Ottomans. Similar linguistic carelessness, however, can be found in Eastern writers, who use the terms

Saracens, Sons of Agar (Hagar), *Agarenes, Antichrists*, etc., as synonymous.

Greek may also occasionally refer to the entire body of the Eastern Orthodox Churches all of which refused Papal supremacy and to this day refute the infallibility dogma among other 'innovations' introduced by the R.C.C. such as the Society of Jesus.

Israel too, in some of the prophecies, may encompass besides the Hebrews and the citizens of the modern state of Israel, also the Christians. In a religious sense the Christians too constitute God's Chosen People.[4] It is useful to keep such verbal distinctions in mind when embarking upon the task of interpretation.

The same caveats obtain for the geographical terminology in usage at the time the specific prophecy was recorded. Not only did the names of places and lands change over the years as invaders ebbed and flowed across national borders and as wars reconstructed the map of the world repeatedly; one must also expect a prophecy written centuries before Christopher Columbus's time and referring to the United States of America, for instance, to use periphrastic terminology to identify the country and still make all necessary points.

let us now turn to the texts of the prophecies. Occasionally remarks and explanations will be attached at the bottom of the text along with the suggested interpretation. As always, particularly important passages will be highlighted.

THE PROPHECIES

Pastor Hermes (2nd century of our era):
"When these things thus come to pass then He who is Lord, looking upon what is done and opposing His own will to the disorder, He cleanses the wickedness, partly by **inundating the world with much water, and partly burning it with most rapid fire**, and sometimes pressing it with wars and pestilences. He will bring His world to its ancient state.

---

[4] Compare, the role of Lord Jesus Christ as King of Israel in John 1:49; 12:13. See also the expanded notion of Israel in Rom. 9:6-13; 1 Cor. 10:18; Gal. 6:16; Gal. 4:21-31; Heb. 1:1-2, and elsewhere in the New Testament.

On the Fate of England and the British Isles

Ancient Irish prophecy[5]
(...) **The war shall come out of Asia and shall require the aid of every occidental on earth to put down.** England will again injure the Irish. This will be a sign for the frightful punishment of England. She has betrayed all nations. (...) When the world is appalled by the anguish of Britain, the leaders of the dispersed Irish in all parts of the world shall call upon them to kneel in supplication to God for mercy on their fallen enemy. *We forgive her*, they shall say, *Why not you?* And God astonished (so to speak) at finding in any race of men so God-like a quality, rescind His judgment against the English. England suffers the same degradation as she meted out to her neighbor, and for the same length of time. Not the smallest fraction of time in this long period shall be remitted. Often shall she attempt to rise, but each attempt shall fail. Never shall world power be hers again, but she shall do very much for the Faith, once she makes submission to Rome.

Ireland's progress in peace and plenty shall intrigue the world. Many shall come from afar to see that land so blessed. To the end of time no enemy shall ever again set foot on her soil. France restores order in England after her own recovery from a violent revolution. (...)

Old Scottish prophecy
Falsehood shall rule five years, a peace shall be tried out but not last and punishment shall soon come.
The untrue shall tremble - but when venom is banished and right rules, we shall have peace and plenty. **The sun and moon shall no longer be dark.** The dead shall rise and live to comfort a knight whom fortune chooses. **He shall fight in Syria and win the Holy Cross.** The Lion and the Lioness shall reign as Bannister, Ambrose, Merlin, Wigythington and Thomas say. (...)

St. Cesar (470-542 A.D.), was a major French saint who had predicted all great events in French History, including WWI. He also predicted the destruction of Paris by fire during a revolution and a war, the destruction of

---

[5] Only the portion of the prophecy applying to WWIII and its aftermath is given below.

Marseilles and perhaps of Bordeaux.[6] These catastrophes would precede the coming of the Great Monarch and the Angelic Pope, which implies that they will happen either during WWIII or preceding it by a very short interval.

St. Columbkille (a.k.a. St. Columba) (died in 597 A.D.).[7]
(...) Excellent men shall be steeped in poverty, the people will become inhospitable to their guests, the voice of the parasite will be more agreeable to them than the melody of the harp touched by the sage's finger. (...) **The professors of science shall not be rewarded**. (...) The changes of seasons shall produce only half their verdure, the regular festivals of the Church will not be observed; all classes of men shall be filled with hatred and enmity towards each other. (...) **The clergy shall be led into error by the misinterpretation of their reading; the relics of the saints will be considered powerless**, every race of mankind will become wicked! (...) Inclement weather and famine shall come and fishes shall forsake the rivers. The people oppressed for want of food, shall pine to death. **Dreadful storms and hurricanes shall afflict them.** Numberless diseases shall then prevail. Fortifications shall be built narrow during those times of dreadful danger.

Then a great event shall happen. I fail not to notice it: rectitude shall be its specious motive, **and if ye be not truly holy, a more sorrowful event could not possibly happen.**[8]

(...) After the conclusion of a long and bloody rule of Ireland by England the garment of death will descend and the rowing wheels will arrive. Ten hundred compartments shall be in the fleet, and each compartment shall contain ten hundred men. The armament will spread its forces over sea and land and rear up mounds with mangled bones. They will inflict on their enemies a severe, flesh-hewing course of warfare to such a degree that scarce a man of them shall escape. The fleet of rowing wheels will remain

---

[6] See also H. J. Forman, [op. cit. p. 104].

[7] Only those excerpts from his prophecies relevant to our study are given below.

[8] I believe that this refers to the **Three Days Darkness**. As per the explicit exhortations of the Most Holy Virgin Mary in her various apparitions during this century, one must be truly in a state of Grace in order to be protected from the events. It will be too late to discover the power of God at the 12th hour and beg for His mercy. The time for reparation is **NOW!**

two short years and a half.

This fleet that will come across the sea shall consist of ten ships, ten hundred fairy barks, ten hundred boats, ten hundred cock-boats and ten hundred spacious skiffs. The principal seaport belonging to the country abroad shall look to the west. Such a large assemblage of men never before met in the east or west; and never again shall such a muster congregate while Ireland is a seagirt island.

The nobility shall sink into humble life before the great war; that war will be proclaimed against them from beyond the seas, by means of which the frantically-proud race shall be subdued. The enemies of the English shall be aroused into activity - they who reside in the eastern and western parts of the world - so that they will engage in a battle on the circumscribed sea, in consequence of which the English shall be defeated.[9]

A fleet belonging to a foreign country will come hither, manned by the descendants of Golimh of the gold-embroidered garments, they shall lay prostrate the Galls of the ships, and liberate the people who have been held in bondage. This fleet that will arrive here from the east, cannot be impeded on the mighty ocean; through the impetuosity of its noisy breathing, its strange appearance shall be marked by flaming mouths. They will engage in a furious conflict, it shall be a wonder that it will not be a mutual slaughter, the conflict of those who will come hither to sever the intricate knot.

After the English shall be defeated in this battle, they shall be harassed from every quarter; like a fawn surrounded by a pack of voracious hounds, shall be the position of the English amidst their enemies. The English afterward shall dwindle down into a disreputable people, and every obstacle shall be opposed to their future prosperity: Because they did not (rather, so long as they do not) observe justice and rectitude, they shall be forever after deprived of power! **Three warnings will be given them before their final fall, the burning of the Tower of the great kings; the conflagration of the dockyard of the English, and the burning of the Treasury where gold is deposited.**

---

[9] The circumscribed sea is the Mediterranean. This is most consistent with other prophecies. See also *Our Revelationary Age....*

Commentary

It is my position that the warnings time-clock is already ticking, with the first warning intimated in the above prophecy having already materialized! It refers to the burning of the 'Tower of the great kings'. It is my conviction that this applies to the Windsor Castle, which is the largest surviving castle in Europe and also the most imposing royal castle in existence. Windsor castle, situated 25 miles West by Southwest of Buckingham palace is sitting on a 4,800-acre estate. This 'much loved symbol of the British monarchy' was severely damaged by a fire which blazed for seven hours in November of 1992, the *annus horribilis* of the British Royal family].[10]

It was damaged, but not destroyed. Let us concentrate on the prophet's specific terminology: he calls it simply the *Tower of the great kings*. According to the verdict of the fire officers, the blaze was sparked by a halogen spotlight in the Queen's private chapel which overheated a curtain next to the altar. The curtain, probably pushed in that proximity by a large picture frame ignited soon under the heat of the lights. It is believed now that the flames spread first to wood panelling along the walls near the Brunswick Tower and then spread to the roof.

The blaze expanded from there to adjacent halls and corridors setting the carpets ablaze. St. George's Hall and the Grand Reception Rooms were the ones which suffered the most damage, being reduced to the stone. St. George's Hall was the largest room in the entire castle. Named after the patron Saint of the Order of the Garter which was created here in centuries past, its most notable feature was the magnificent ceiling covered with the multi-color shields of more than 900 Garter knights. Before November of 1992, it was there that the Queen gave her State banquets for visiting Heads of State.

Since Windsor Castle is a castle, one expects it to be provided with several

---

[10] It was built by William the Conqueror, who chose the spot because of the commanding chalk heights overlooking the river Thames. At that time the castle was a structure of timber with a mote and bailey design. Over the centuries the wooden structures were replaced by a system of stone edifices, and the castle underwent several expansions and reconstructions. It increased in importance over the years with every new sovereign adding to its functions and splendor. Queen Elizabeth II had chosen Windsor Castle as her preferred residence after Buckingham palace; besides spending weekends there the royal family hosted the Ascot Week as well as the Christmas day celebrations.

towers. Yet, only one, the Brunswick Tower, has been associated with the fire. Furthermore, St. Columba, who lived in an age before the battle of Hastings (1066 A.D.) which established the Norman William the Conqueror as the new ruler over England, would not have named the Castle *Windsor Castle*, for the simple reason this name was given for the first time by William the Conqueror. It was he who established it in its original form along with the trading post that grew around it.

Windsor comes from 'Windlesora', i.e. winding shore, (the shore belonging to the Thames, at that time the primary commercial artery of the land). Furthermore, among all towers of the Windsor Castle, the Brunswick Tower was the closest to the private chapel and the private quarters of the great kings, hence it did qualify more than the rest as **the** tower of the great kings. (Considering the above, one must be dully appreciative of the power of the Spirit which can speak so clearly and with such an amazing factual accuracy more than a millennium ahead of time).[11]

St. Senanus (Irish Abbot, died ca. 544 A.D.)

(...) The clergy of the holy church will be addicted to pride and injustice; the advantage they will aim at shall be the possession of worldly substance. Women will abandon feelings of delicacy, and cohabit with men out of wedlock; they will follow those practices without secrecy, and such habits will become almost unsuppressible. (...) The earth will not produce its fruits for the race of people to whom I allude; full mansions will be deserted, and unpleasant will be the tidings concerning them. Dreadful plagues will come upon all the race of Adam.

The English themselves will betray each other; in consequence of which their sovereignty will be broken; they will stain their swords and battle-axes with blood; - they will be a selfish race devoid of benignity. The son of the King of Saxon will come to join them across the sea; he will part with the sovereignty of the English in the country whence he will come. The English and the Irish of Ireland will unite in one confederation against the forces of the Saxons, their confederacy cannot be dissolved. The king of the Saxon's son will come at the head of his forces; in consequence of the protection he will extend to them, Ireland shall be freed from her fears. One monarch will

---

[11] The interested reader can find more pertinent information on the various castles of the British Royal family (including a very detailed description of Windsor Castle, along with pages of photos and maps) in Jerrold M. Packard, [1981].

rule in Ireland, over the English and the pure Irish; from the reign of that man, the people shall suffer no destitution.

St. Maeltamhlacht (7th century)
In the latter ages destitution will fall upon many people and whenever the English will commit great evils against the children of Eire, then the English will be expelled and Eire become the property of her rightful owners.

Richard Rolle of Hampole (died 1349)
There will be a general defection from the Church near the end of the world, especially regarding obedience to Her.

Mother Shipton: (15th century A.D.)[12]
The famous Mother Shipton was a real person. She prophesied very effectively during her life time and much of what she predicted has already materialized. Later, many other prophecies that have been associated with her name are believed to emanate from anonymous sources.[13]

When pictures look alive, with movements free;
When ships, like fishes swim beneath the sea;
When men, outstripping birds, can soar the sky:
then half the world, deep drenched in blood, shall die."[14]

In Germany begins a dance, which passeth through Italy, Spain and France, but England shall pay the piper.

More From Mother Shipton's prophecies:
(Only those applying to WWIII and its aftermath are included below. I believe

---

[12] She was born in Knaresborough, in Yorkshire, England, in 1486 A.D., during the second year of the reign of Henry VII. She is believed to have died in 1551 A.D. The first collection of her prophecies were published in 1641. The prophecies included in this study come from the 1864 English edition.

[13] It appears that many times, the prestige of a famous person is so great that others would rather have their own work associated with that person and capitalize on the glamour and acceptability associated with the established ones rather than with themselves.

[14] This comes from a tombstone at Kirby Cemetery, Essex, England, but in many writers it is also attributed to Mother Shipton.

the following one applies to the consequences of our close encounter with the comet of our near future).

Waters shall flow where corn doth grow;
Corn shall grow where water doth flow,
Houses shall appear in the vales below,
And covered be by hail and snow.

The time will come, when seas of blood,
Shall mingle with a greater flood.

Great noise there shall be heard, great shouts and cries,
And seas shall thunder louder than the skies;
Then shall three lions fight with three, and bring
Joy to a people, and honor to the King.

Thunder shall shake the earth;
Lightning shall rend asunder;
Water shall fill the earth;
Fire shall do its work;
Men shall _____ he shall _____.[15]

The fiery year as soon as o'er,
Peace shall then be as before;
Plenty everywhere be found,
And men with swords shall plough the ground.

All England's sons that plough the land,
Shall be seen book in hand.
Learning shall so ebb and flow,
The poor shall most wisdom know.
....
Three times three shall lovely France
Be led to dance a bloody dance.
Before her people shall be free
Three tyrant rulers shall she see;

---

[15] These correspond to lacunae in her original text. Either her vision faded and she was unable to identify the details, or for some reason she preferred to leave the words out.

Three times the people rule alone,
Three times the people's hope is gone;
Three rulers in succession see,
Each spring from a different dynasty.
Then shall the worser fight be done,
England and France shall be as one.

....

(...) London shall be destroyed forever after ... and then York shall be London and the Kingdom governed by three Lords appointed by a Royal Great Monarch of the best blood in the world, who will set England aright and drive out heresy, and after this shall be a white harvest of corn gotten in by women. (...)

Sister Rosa Asdenti di Taggia (1847 A.D.).[16]
(...) England will return to the Unity of the Faith.

Fr. Balthassar Mas: (1630 A.D.)
I saw a land swallowed by the sea and covered with water, but afterwards I saw that little by little, the sea retreated and left the land visible, and the upper parts of the towers and turrets of the cities rose and appeared more beautiful than before being swallowed by the sea, and it was told me that was England.

Venerable Bartholomew Holzhauser (died 1658).
(...) [Wedged between information about the Great Monarch] On account of a terrible war Germany will wail, France will be the cause of all the woe, Germany will be miserably wounded, all will be impoverished. **England shall suffer much. The King shall be killed.** After desolation has reached its peak in England peace will be restored and England will return to the Catholic faith with greater fervor than ever before.

When everything has been ruined by war; when Catholics are hard pressed by traitorous co-religionists and heretics; when the Church and her servants are denied their rights, the monarchies have been abolished and their rulers murdered... **then the Hand of Almighty God will work a marvelous change, something apparently impossible according to human**

---

[16] Portions of her prophecies will appear in other chapters also, covering different types of events.

understanding. (...) The sixth period of the Church will begin with the powerful Monarch and the Holy Pontiff, (...) and it will last until the revelation of Antichrist. (...) All nations will become Catholic. Vocations will be abundant as never before, and all men will seek only the Kingdom of God and His justice. (...) They will live under the protection of the Great Monarch and his successors. (...) The powerful Monarch, who will be sent by God, will uproot all republics. He will submit everything to his authority and he will show great zeal for the true Church of Christ. The empire of the Mohammedans will be broken up, and this Monarch will reign in the East as well as in the West. All nations will come to worship God in the true Catholic and Roman faith. There will be many Saints and Doctors on earth. Peace will reign over the whole earth because God will bind Satan for a number of years until the days of the Son of Perdition. **No one will be able to pervert the word of God since, during the sixth period, there will be an ecumenic council which will be the greatest of all councils. By the grace of God, by the power of the Great Monarch, by the authority of the Holy Pontiff, and by the union of all the most devout princes, atheism and every heresy will be banished from the earth. The Council will define the true sense of Holy Scripture, and this will be believed and accepted by everyone.** (...)

Commentary
The wording of the above prophecy provides several insights on the political reorganization also of the world in the future. It appears that the institution of royalty will be re-introduced in many countries (He will uproot all republics). Although the Great Monarch will rule as an Emperor, we can expect individual countries to have their own national heads of state. In other prophecies we are told that the Great Monarch will re-establish the royal houses that were destroyed earlier. This is just another corroboration for such events. He also makes a distinction about the true Catholic and Roman faith. I do not believe the choice of words is fortuitous here.

More Prophecies on the Church

Sister Mary de Agreda (died 1665)
It was revealed to me that through the intercession of the Mother of God that all heresies will disappear. **This victory over heresies has been reserved by Christ for His Blessed Mother.** In the last times the Lord will especially spread the renown of His Mother: Mary began salvation and by Her intercession it will be concluded. Before the Second Coming of Christ Mary must, more than ever, shine in mercy, might and grace in order to bring

unbelievers into the Catholic Faith. **The powers of Mary in the last times over the demons will be very conspicuous.** Mary will extend the reign of Christ over the heathens and Mohammedans and it will be a time of great joy when Mary, as Mistress and Queen of Hearts, is enthroned.
An unusual chastisement of the human race will take place towards the end of the world.

Blessed Louis de Montfort (died 1716 A.D.)
The power of Mary over all devils will be particularly outstanding in the last period of time. She will extend the Kingdom of Christ over the idolaters and Moslems, and there will come a glorious era in which Mary will be the ruler and queen of human hearts. (...) The training and education of the great saints, who will appear towards the end of the world, is reserved for the Mother of God. (...) These great saints, full of grace and zeal, will be chosen in order to oppose the enemies of God who will appear everywhere. By their word and example these saints will bring the whole world to a true veneration of Mary. This will bring them many enemies but also much blessing. (...) **Mary will be terrible to the devil and his followers, like an army set in battle array.**

Jeanne le Royer, Sister of the Nativity (1731-1798).
(...) One night I saw a number of ecclesiastics. Their haughtiness and air of severity seemed to demand the respect of all. They forced the faithful to follow them. But God commanded me to oppose them: *They no longer have the right to speak in My name*, Jesus told me. *It is against My wish that they carry out a mandate for which they are no longer worthy.* (...) I see in God that a long time before the rise of Antichrist the world will be afflicted with many bloody wars. (...) Armies will come into frightful collisions and will fill the earth with murder and carnage. These internal and foreign wars will cause enormous sacrifices, profanations, scandals, and infinite evils, because of the incursions that will be made into the Church. As well as that, **I see that the earth will be shaken in different places by frightful earthquakes. I see whole mountains cracking and splitting with a terrible din. Only too happy will one be if one can escape with no more than a fright; but no, I see come out of these gaping mountains whirlwinds of smoke, fire, sulphur, and tar, which reduce to cinders entire towns. All this and a thousand other disasters must come before the rise of the Man of Sin.**

I saw in the light of the Lord that the faith and our holy Religion would become weaker in almost every Christian kingdom. [The prophetess continues with the events of WWIII and then] I see in God a great power, led by the Holy Ghost, which will restore order through a second upheaval. **I see in God a large assembly of pastors who will uphold the right of the Church and of her Head. They will restore the former disciplines.** I see, in particular, two servants of the Lord who will distinguish themselves in this glorious struggle, and who, by the grace of the Holy Ghost, will fill with ardent zeal the hearts of this illustrious assembly. [She continues with the triumph of the church and the years leading to Antichrist's rise to power...].

Father Nectou, S. J. (died 1772 A.D.)

When those things come to pass which will bring on the triumph of the Church, then will such confusion reign on earth that people will think God has permitted them to have their own contrary will and that the providence of God is not concerned about the world. The confusion will be so general that mankind will not be able to think aright, as if God had entirely withheld his providence from mankind, and that, during the worst crisis, the best that can be done would be to remain where God has placed us and persevere in fervent prayer. (...) At that time there shall be such a terrible crisis that people, frightened by events shall believe that the end of the world is come. Blood shall flow in several large cities. **The very elements shall be convulsed. It will be like a little general judgment.** A great multitude of persons shall perish in these calamitous times. But the wicked shall never prevail. (...) During this revolution, which shall very likely be general, and not confined to France, Paris shall be destroyed so completely that, twenty years afterwards, fathers walking over its ruins with their children, these will inquire what place that was. To whom they will answer: My child, this was formerly a great city, which God has destroyed on account of her crimes.

(...) As when the fig tree begins to sprout and produce leaves, it is a certain sign that summer is near, so when England shall begin to wane in power, the destruction of Paris shall be near at hand. This shall be a sign. England shall, in her turn, experience a more frightful revolution than that of France. It shall continue long enough to give time to France to recover her strength, then she will help England return to order and peace.[17]

---

[17] Henry James Forman, [op. cit., p. 282], has identified at least thirty-five different prophecies of the burning of Paris which, furthermore, are not confined to French seers only.

Joanna Southcott (1750-1825 A.D.)[18]
From prophecies found in her various writings:

-   I will establish the Throne of David in Jerusalem as I have promised.
-   Of France and Spain and every distant coast, I'll save a remnant, but one nation lost, and that should be for the sake of the Jews, that I should destroy the nation that has their possessions.
-   All nations that forget God will be turned into Hell.

Saint Jean-Marie Vianney, Curé d' Ars (1786-1859). (French parish priest of Ars-en-Dombes, patron of the parochial clergy, canonized in 1925).

[On a prophecy referring to WWIII he says the following]: (...) After the victory their enemy shall not quit entirely the occupied country. They shall come back but this time our army shall fight well everywhere. For during the first war our men would not combat well, but in the second war they will fight. O how they will fight!

The enemy will allow the burning of Paris, and they will rejoice at it, but they shall be beaten; they shall be driven entirely from France. Our enemies

---

[18] She was born in Devonshire, England, in 1750 A.D. died in 1825 and was moved to London. She placed her prophecies in a box, which has been entrusted to a series of custodians over the years; it awaits the time when the Church of England fulfills her expressed conditions before the box become unsealed and its contents made public. It was prophesied that at a time of great national danger and in the presence of twenty-four bishops of the Church of England, as well as twenty-four believers in the divine inspiration of this woman, who one day may be honored as the greatest prophetess of England, the box would be finally opened.

It was also predicted that God will manifest Himself at the opening of the box, and nothing but the instructions and advice contained in her prophecies in the box can prevent England from experiencing utter destruction. An attempt was made in 1918 to open the box. Since the bishops refused to accept Joanna's conditions, the secrets therein have not yet been revealed.

The reader may wish to review the previous paragraph, predicting the God will be present in the opening. I interpret this to mean that our Lord Jesus Christ, as intimated in messages given to members of our generation, will be present amongst us in the midst of these terrifying events that will be like a small Final Judgement. We shall see more of her prophecies in other chapters of this study.

shall return, and will destroy everything in their march. They shall arrive near Poitiers without meeting with any serious resistance, but there they shall be crushed by the defenders of the West, who shall pursue them. From other directions their provisions shall be cut off, and they shall suffer very serious losses. They will attempt to retire toward their country, but very few of them shall ever reach it. All that they took from us shall be returned, and a great deal more. The Communists of Paris, after their defeat, shall spread themselves through all France, and will be greatly multiplied. They shall seize arms; they shall oppress people of order. Lastly, a civil war shall break out everywhere. These wicked people shall become masters in the north, east, and southwest. They will imprison very many persons, and will be guilty of more massacres. **They will attempt to kill all the priests and all the religious. But this shall not last long. People will imagine that all is lost; but the good God shall save all. It will be like a sign of the last judgement.** Paris shall be changed, also two or three other cities; God shall come to help; the good shall triumph when the return of the king shall be announced. This shall re-establish a peace and prosperity without example. Religion shall flourish again better than ever before. Paris shall be demolished and burnt in earnest, but not entirely. **Events shall transpire more terrible than what we have seen. However, there shall be a limit beyond which the destruction shall not go. A great triumph will be witnessed on the feast of our Lady.**

I believe that the Church of England will return to her ancient splendor.

Blessed Anna Maria Gianneti Taigi: (died 1837 A.D.) p. 197
God will ordain two punishments: One, in the form of wars, revolutions and other evils, will originate on earth; **the other will be sent from Heaven.** There shall come over all the earth an intense darkness lasting three days and three nights.[19] (...)
After the three days darkness, Saints Peter and Paul, having come down from heaven, will preach throughout the world and designate a new pope. A great light will flash from their bodies and will settle upon the cardinal, the future Pontiff. Then Christianity will spread throughout the world. Whole nations will join the Church shortly before the reign of Antichrist. These conversions will be amazing. There shall be innumerable conversions of heretics, who will return to the bosom of the Church; all will

---

[19] The specifics on the darkness afforded by this seer are already contained in *Our Revelationary Age...*' We herewith present new material from her prophecies.

203

note the edifying conduct of their lives, as well as that of all other Catholics. Russia, England, and China will come into the Church.[20]

Note: The reader may wish to mark the mention of two saints who are expected to come down from heaven. We shall see this type of evidence elsewhere as our study proceeds. The last sentence means that after the re-unification of the Christian Churches, the Russian Orthodox Church will be in harmony with the Roman Catholic Church. The Church of England will be no more, since the sovereign will no longer be the head of the church; finally, China will be evangelized.

Marie Lataste (died 1847 A.D.).
[She speaks in detail about the tribulations of Paris and then] Peace shall return to the world, because the Blessed Virgin Mary will breathe over the storms and quell them. Her name will be praised, blessed and exalted forever. Prisoners or captives shall recover their liberty; exiles shall return to their country, and the unfortunate or unhappy shall be restored to peace and happiness. Between the most august Mary and Her clients there will be a mutual exchange of prayers and graces, of love and affection. From the east to the west, from the north to the south, all shall proclaim the holy name of Mary; Mary conceived without original sin, Mary queen of heaven and earth. Amen."

Palma Maria Addolorata Matarelli d'Oria (died 1863 A.D.).
There will be an attempt of the sectaries to establish a republican government in France, Spain and Italy; a civil war will, in consequence, break out in those countries, accompanied by other dreadful punishments, as pestilence and famine, the massacre of priests, and also of some dignitaries of the church. Rome shall have to endure severe trials from the malice of wicked men. **But at the critical moment, when the rebellious Republicans shall attempt to take possession of the Holy City, they shall be suddenly arrested at the gates and forced to fly away in terror, crushed under the deadly blows of the exterminating angel, who, in behalf of the Israelites, destroyed 185,000 men of Sennacherib's army.** (...)[21]

---

[20] Her prophecy continues with specific events of WWIII.

[21] The portion which is excluded deals specifically with the Three Days Darkness.

Mother Alphonse Eppinger: (1867 A.D.) (p. 201).
Many priests have lost their fervor for the honor of God and the salvation of souls. Their hearts hang too much on the phantoms of this life. God will, by chastisements, cure them thereof and so thereby change them. In many religious houses the spirit of poverty and simplicity is forgotten. They look only for convenience, they carry a scandalous splendor to satisfy their pride, therefore must God, through a salutary remedy, restore the true religious spirit. It is indeed a sad thing to see religious houses desecrated, but it will be necessary in order to eradicate the pride and worldly luxuries and to bring all things back to simplicity.

After God has purified the world, faith and peace will return. Whole nations will adhere to the teaching of the Catholic Church.

The Ecstatic of Tours: (from prophecies made in 1872 and 1873).[22]
Before the war breaks out again, food will be scarce and expensive. There will be little work for the workers, and fathers will hear their children cry for food. **There will be earthquakes and signs in the sun. Towards the end darkness will cover the earth.**

When everyone believes that peace is assured, when everyone least expects it, the great happenings will begin. **Revolution will break out in Italy almost at the same time as in France. For some time, the Church will be without a Pope**. England, too, will have much to suffer. [She continues with the persecution of the clergy in France and specifically] (...) Many bishops and priests will be put to death. The Archbishop of Paris will be murdered. Many other priests, in Paris, will have their throats cut because they will not have time to find a hiding place. The wicked will be the masters for one year and a few months. (...) The French people will ask for the good King, he who was chosen by God. (...) He (the king) will ascend to the throne; he will free the Church and reassert the Pope's rights. **The Council will meet again after the victory**. (...)

A vision by Pope Pius X:
I saw (in a vision) one of my successors by name fleeing over the corpses of his brethren. He will flee to a place for a short respite where he is unknown, but he himself will die a cruel death.

---

[22] See also Culleton, op. cit. as well as Dupont, op. cit. among other sources.

Commentary

Neither Pius XI, nor Pius XII fit into this vision. Since Pope Pius XII's times there has been no Pope named Pius (either as a christened name or as an adopted one after ascension to the Papal throne), and after Pope Vojtyla (who was baptized Karol, and who chose as a Pope the name John Paul) there come the Popes on the St. Malachy list under '**gloria olivae**' and '**Petrus Romanus**'. Since Petrus Romanus must be excluded on the basis of name at least, and since all available prophecies indicate that 'gloria olivae', the Angelic Pastor will not die a cruel death amidst general persecution of the clergy, again we run out of plausible choices of Popes who could satisfy the above criterion of 'successor by name'.

Since the name *Pius*, as such, is not helpful in our search, we may consider that 'one of my successors by name' indicates something else: Pope Pius X, (**Ignis Ardens** in Saint Malachy's list), was born in Italy, on June 2, 1835, as Giuseppe Melchiorre Sarto. His father however, was born Jan Krawiec in Wilekopolska, Poland, and had emigrated to Italy, where he changed his name into Giovanni Battista Sarto. Sarto in Italian signifies simply a tailor (from the Latin sartor-ris). Krawiec in Polish means also a tailor, Jan corresponds to Giovanni.[23]

Mr. Jan Krawiec basically translated his name from Polish into its Italian equivalents. Since Giuseppe Melchiorre Sarto was born in Italy (and since at that time a tremendous effort was made to cover up the Polish background of the Pope for purely political reasons) the general public is not aware of the Polishness of Pius X. However, it could be that when Pius X spoke of 'one of my successors by name', perhaps he was referring to a characteristic common to both (such as nationality) rather than the baptismal or assumed Papal name, as such.

This is purely speculative on my part at this point, yet, considering the high probability that the present Pontiff will be contemporary to the eruption of an Italian civil war and possibly WWIII, the speculation is not too unlikely. Since there is ample evidence to make us suspect that the prelude of the war is already taking place in the Balkans, the present Pontiff is very much associated chronologically with the prophetic timetables. If my speculation concerning their common Polishness, hence the name, leads to the correct interpretation of Pope Pius X's vision, then the vision could supply us with

---

[23] See also Malachy Martin [1990].

additional information concerning the final days of the current Pontiff.

Again, such information is internally consistent with everything else we have been studying so far, because it is not at all unlikely, that in the event of a major war, which will ravage Italy, Rome, and the Vatican, the Pope may be forced to leave the city and change his headquarters.

Other prophecies consulted (several of which will be reproduced in this study) have indicated that a Pope will be forced to flee Rome and die while in exile. According to at least one of them, his destination will be Cologne. Since in Germany the Catholics are concentrated in the South and the Protestants in the North, Cologne has a very large Catholic population and the richest Catholic Church in Germany. In a sense, it is the stronghold of German Catholicism. It could be his natural choice for a refuge, if Germany becomes the preferred land of self-exile. Especially, in view of the current heightened tension between Protestants and Catholics in Germany and the prevailing schism within the Catholic Church of Germany exemplified by the teachings and works of Theologian/Psychologist Dr. Eugen Drewermann and his school of thought.[24]

Cologne, furthermore, started its career as Colonia Agrippina (a.k.a. Colonia Agrippinensis) during the Roman times, when the empire under the Antonines constructed the *limes* fortifications along the river Rhein to protect against invaders from beyond. Due to its unquestionable geographical and economic importance, Köln (Cologne) has been the theater of great battles and the object of much enemy fury through the ages. During WWII it suffered very much. Once again, in prophecies concerning the future war, Cologne is singled out for great ravage, massive killings and great destruction. Consequently, it is not at all farfetched to assume the possibility of the Pope being among the victims (of enemy action, for instance) while in Cologne. The great pope who will succeed him and reign over a unified Christianity will be the Papa Angelorum, the Gloria Olivae, the

---

[24] In fact, the R.C.C. does not allow his books to be published by Catholic Presses and many Catholic believers, incensed by some of his extreme positions have qualified him as 'the German Antichrist'. His supporters call him the New Luther.

Angelic Pastor.[25]

Last and not least, 'fleeing over the corpses of his brethren' is also very consistent with a large number of prophecies predicting the persecution of the Christian clergy, the more so, since Rome is destined to suffer more than the average European city during the coming tribulations. In all major previous wars, civil wars and revolutions, the clergy has fallen victim to persecution, military action, and the like. Yet, the enormity of the massacres prophesied for WWIII is quite suggestive of the vision of Pope Pius X. Never since the beginning of this century did a Pope have to flee over the bodies of his clergymen. This is an additional indication that the vision in question does not refer either to WWI or to WWII, but to a future conflict.

Theresa Neumann (September 6, 1936).
"The provocations have in these days attained their height. The furies of Hell rage now. The chastisement of God is inevitable. Every future petition to help them, to spare them, displeases Me. If you petition Me for the conversion of dying sinners in the last hour, I will hear you. No! do not petition Me to prevent this chastisement. Until now victims (many of whom existed in many parishes) have offered their merits to expiate for the crimes of mankind, which held back the wrath of God, but now their expiations are not enough and the chastisement is now certain and unpreventable. It will happen suddenly. Fortunate are those who already are in their graves. I have warned them and have postponed, as I did with Sodom, but Sodom would not listen to Me, nor do the people listen to Me nowadays, nor heed My warnings, therefore they will incur the sad experience of My wrath which they deserve.

New York Laywoman (given before 1943 A.D.).
'God wants a new world. This war is the judgment of nations. Rome will be invaded. **A German ruler will be converted and an English one assassinated.** Another Englishman once great now small will become a member of the Church and will be all powerful. There will be much suffering before this war ends and it will end as a religious war with terrible persecution everywhere. **Thereafter will be a crusade which will be**

---

[25] or, as Peter Bander [1973] suggested, a person of the Order of St. Benedict, known as the Olivetans. Yet these two versions are not mutually exclusive and exhaustive; he can very well be the Pope of Peace **and at the same time** he may be coming from the Order of the Olivetans.

victorious under Mary's banner.

Brother John of the Cleft Rock (given in 1340).
(...) The White Eagle by order of the Archangel Michael, will drive the crescent from Europe where none but Christians will remain - he himself will rule from Constantinople. An era of peace and prosperity will begin for the world. There will no longer be Protestants or Schismatics: the Lamb will reign and the bliss of the human race will begin. **Happy will they be who have escaped the perils of that terrible time, for they can taste of its fruit through the reign of the Holy Ghost and the sanctification of mankind, which can be accomplished only after the defeat of the Black Eagle.**

Recent Message given by Lord Jesus Christ to Georgette Faniel, of Montreal, Canada: My hands are nailed to the cross by My consecrated souls, My priests.

The Blessed Virgin to the Italian Priest Father Gobbi, on January 1, 1985: With extraordinary signs which I am giving in every part of the world, through My messages and through My so frequent apparitions, I am pointing out to everyone the approaching of the Great Day of the Lord.

SPECIFIC PROPHECIES ON THE FUTURE OF ISRAEL

Venerable Magdalene Porzat (died 1850).
(...) Mary comes from Heaven. She comes accompanied by a legion of angels. (...) After this, Mary, all powerful, shall change all men into good wheat. All shall be good. (...) **The Jews who have refused to receive Jesus Christ in His humiliation will acknowledge Him at the glorious arrival of Mary.** (...) She comes to announce the end of a deluge of evils. (...)

Venerable Anne Catherine Emmerich (1774-1824): (...) The Jews shall return to Palestine and become Christians towards the end of the world. (...)

Père Lamy (died in 1931 A.D., the current prophecy was created about 1929 A.D.):
(...) The Jews are scattered all over the world, but they will not be abandoned. God never forsakes his own. (...)

209

REVIEW OF THE MOST SALIENT POINTS

a)   The prophecies indicate a major chastisement from above to coincide with major civil wars and a war between faiths.

b)   There are several suggestions of a major ecumenical council following the end of the war and the re-unification of the Christian Churches.

c)   The properties of the Most Holy Virgin Mary as the Panaghia, the Queen of Angels and the Great Mediatrix of Graces will become most apparent during our future Tribulations. Such overwhelming evidence will entice many Protestants to abandon their erroneous views as to Her importance and re-consider several other ones. Thus the re-unification will be facilitated by the overwhelming evidence of the grace and power of the Most Holy Virgin.

d)   The Great Monarch will reign from Constantinople. The Muslims will be driven completely out of Europe. This will occur with the explicit assistance of the Archangel Michael. This is yet another reference to the Archangel. We shall review his prophesied role later on.

CHAPTER EIGHT

HARMONIZING THE PROPHECIES REGARDING THE FUTURE OF CHRISTIANITY AND ISRAEL THE MAINLY ORTHODOX EVIDENCE

(...) But in context of lessons taught by the Gulf crisis, it is not Saddam's miscalculations that matter but the timing of his challenge. He saw the aftermath of the Cold War as the most suitable moment for implementing his aggressive schemes. (...) Challenging the West, Saddam decided to test its capabilities in the new situation. (...) **The Baghdad dictator was just the first of totalitarian regime potentates to probe the superpowers' strength in the new situation, and his defeat is hardly going to teach to others a lesson, particularly because he managed to retain both his power and his life.** [Emphasis added]. Vladimir Nosenko[1]

Introduction

Although most of the evidence in this chapter comes from the Orthodox East, we will occasionally insert Catholic prophecies covering the same phenomena, so that the reader may have another opportunity to appreciate the prophetic consistency across denominations. The Holy Spirit treats democratically the Saints of East and West. As the Holy Virgin repeatedly remarked in Her recent apparitions, it is we that have created the divisions in this world. The format of presentation of the material is as follows: first the English translation will be presented, followed by commentary and suggested interpretation of the preceding paragraphs. The Greek Originals are collected in a separate Appendix, and will appear in exactly the same

---

[1] from his article entitled 'Iraq's Aggression against Kuwait in the Context of North-South Relations', [*Mediterranean Quarterly*, Spring 1992].

sequence as the translations in this chapter. Occasionally, portions of prophetic texts will be highlighted to assist us in their easier retrieval later on.

THE EVIDENCE

1)   St. Methodius of Patara ("Αγιος Μεθόδιος, 4th century A.D.)²
(...) and the seed (offspring) of Ishmael will come out of the desert... and ahead of them there will go four plagues against the earth, calamities and loss and destruction and depopulation, and it is not out of Divine love towards them that God will give them power to take control over Christian lands, but in order to punish the Christians for their disrespect for His laws.

(...) The blond nation will have control over the Seven-Hilled city for the course of five or six months; (...) There will be leaders in the East; following them will rise another, independent, one and following him another wolf very wild, ... and the nations that are located in the North will be moved into action with great speed and fierce anger and they will be organized into four groups; one will spend the winter in Ephesus, the second one in Melagia; the third in Pergamum and the fourth in Bythinia... then the nations that are situated in the southern corner will be roused into action and the Great Philip with an army composed of peoples speaking 18 different languages will get together in the Seventh-Hilled City and will begin a war such as one has never happened before; and they will be very swift in invading both the thoroughfares and the narrow streets of the Seventh-Hilled city and the killing of the people will flow like a river, and the sea will turn turbid and darkened by the blood till the bottom of the abyss.

At that time the ox will cry out and the Xirolophos will wail; and then the horses will stand still and a voice from heaven will cry out: let us stand still, let us stand still, peace be unto you! there has been enough revenge against

---

² Some authors place him in the iv. century of our era, others in the vi. Some locate him in Patara of Asia Minor, others in Olympus of Asia Minor. He had travelled extensively and was active over a geographical area that encompassed both locations. Sotiropoulos [1974], believes his death occurred about 310 A.D. and considers him to be the Bishop of Patara in Lycia of Asia Minor. His work, wherefrom the above prophecies are excerpted, is entitled Χρησμοί καί Προφητεΐαι διά τό Μέλλον τοῦ Κόσμου (Oracular Responses and Prophecies for the Future of the World).

the disobedient and those who did not want to listen. *Now, depart to the right-hand areas of the Seven-Hilled city and there you will find a man who is standing on two columns in very sober mood; (he will be bright in appearance, just, charitable, dressed modestly, severe in appearance but peace loving in character) he will have a sign: a corn in his right foot; and a voice from the Angel will be heard, make him your king!*

And they will give a sword to his right hand and they will say to him: take courage, oh John, and be strong and be victorious over your enemies; and taking in his hands the sword indicated by the Angel he will beat the sons of Ishmael and the dark-skinned ones and every infidel nation. And the sons of Ishmael he will divide into three groups: one third he will kill by the sword, one third he will baptize and the rest he will bring under submission in the East. **And upon his return from his expeditions and battles the treasures of the earth will be opened and everyone will become rich and nobody will be a poor man, and the earth will give its fruits 100-fold; and all weapons of war will be converted into ploughs and scythes; and he will rule for a period of thirty five years.**

2)   St. Tarasius (Ἅγιος Ταράσιος):[3]
(...) Following that, a great internecine war will begin and the entire infidel nation will be destroyed; and then will rise the Holy King whose name begins with an I and ends with a Sigma.[4]

---

[3]   St. Tarasius was born in Constantinople of noble parents, and became famous as a statesman who commanded a high religious learning. Although a layman, he had the mandate of the people and of the religious hierarchy to be elected to the Patriarchal throne of Constantinople in 784 A.D., having ascended in the course of a single week through the various ecclesiastical ranks necessary for his promotion (namely, reader, priest and bishop).   He convened the 7th Ecumenical Council for the restoration of the icons in 787 A.D. and died in 806 A.D.

[4]   This is consistent with my thesis that King Juan Carlos I de Borbón is the prophesied king.   Let us review what we already know about his name and its Greek language equivalents:
Juan, John, is in Greek Ἰωάννης which begins with an I and ends with a Sigma. In capital letters this is more obvious, ΙΩΑΝΝΗΣ.   On the other hand, Carlos, Charles, Karol, in Greek is spelled Κάρολος, (ΚΑΡΟΛΟΣ) in capital letters. 'K' in the Greek numeral system corresponds also to the number 20.

3) Leo VI, Emperor of the East (Leo the Philosopher, Λέων ὁ Σοφός):[5]

With regards to the legendary, poor and chosen king, who is well known and yet unknown, who lives at the edge of the geographical area of the Byzantine empire.[6] The true king, whom people have chased from his abode... will be revealed at the time when the end of the Ishmaelites approaches... **It will be on a Friday, in the third hour of the morning when he will be revealed[7] ... He, who is to be revealed, will be identified by means of celestial signs.** *While he is sleeping, he will hear a voice and see an Angel who will appear like a royal servant dressed in white; the Angel will take him by the hand and will tell him: you, who are sleeping, get up... Jesus Christ will be with you. It is your calling to lead a chosen people; and the Angel will add: you, who have been concealed, do not hide yourself any longer, many are asking for you... and furthermore, the Angel will give him plaques of stone upon which there are etched two commands; punish the evil doers and rule justly over your defeated enemies;*

And you should punish impiety and utterly consume with fire those who engage in acts of Sodomy; furthermore, the bad priests you should chase from the altar and you should restitute the worthy priests. And the King will have signs to be recognized by. The nail of his big toe on his right foot has a corn... on his shoulders he bears two red crosses... the name of the King is not revealed among the nations... the Lord will lay His hand upon the head of the King... In those days, the humans will become distressed and will turn

---

[5] Leo VI ruled from 886 to 912 A.D. He was called Leo the Wise in contrast to his father Basil I, the founder of the Macedonian dynasty, a man of limited education. Leo VI has been famous for a few other prophecies of his, especially one foretelling the Moslem conquest of Byzantium almost six centuries ahead of its occurrence. Shortly before the Fall of the City, there was found in a cloister of Constantinople a tablet ascribed to him, presenting the paired succession of the names of the Emperors and their Patriarchs till the end of the empire. Most of the prophecies though, are compiled from various sources and now are known as Prophecies of Leo.

[6] This is obviously trying to identify the geographical area wherefrom the King will come. We do not know exactly at what year this prophecy was written.

[7] In the time-measuring scheme of the New Testament, the third hour of the day would correspond to the period from 6.00 a.m. to 9.00 a.m.; the sixth hour of the day would go from 9.00 a.m. to 12.00 midday and so on.

*their faces towards the earth and they will put dirt on their heads and will cry with loud voice to the Lord God, the God of Heaven and earth, **and God will listen to their supplications and He will send them his Archangel, in the form of a human being who will come in the islands.** And the Archangel will find the holy one of God who is not seen or suspected by anybody... who is concealed to the eyes of the world and inconspicuous, but who is known to God and also to himself; he is descended from royalty and from dukes and he is a saintly person... God will make him revealed and he will be presented to the people and will be anointed with chrism (holy oil) in his old age...*

And this is how the king will be revealed to the people: there will be a star which will appear for the duration of three days and in the third hour of the night of the eve of the holiday of the Mother of the Most High, the star will be seen in the middle of the city. And this star is not one of the planets but it will be like the one which made its appearance during the salvation-bringing birth of Jesus. *And a herald will be crying out aloud in these three days calling and revealing the hoped-for king. Then, the citizens of the city seeing and hearing the thunderous voice will be amazed. And with joy and fear will come out and they will say that they ignore the identity of the hoped-for king. While all are watching and extensively and fervently praying 'Lord have Mercy' and beating their foreheads on the ground and putting dirt on their heads, and wailing and crying bitter tears for the coming sorrow, their prayers will be heard by God. God will receive favorably their supplication and with a well-disposed eye He will look down upon the inhabitants of the earth;* **and it is for the sake of the then remaining Elect that the chosen one will be made known.**

In the sky, at that time a nebulous (hazy) firmament will be visible and something circular resembling the image of the sun which will seemingly be of a size corresponding to a circle circumscribed on a threshing floor by six oxen. A cross will be hanging underneath it, and at the left side of the purple-colored cross, an extended arc such as the one given to our forefathers in eternal testament; *and since nobody will know the identity of the hoped-for person, the arc will be broken at its southern part, as it becomes decomposed in the firmament and this way the exact location of the true King will be shown. Then, the nations, having given praise to God, will rush to the area indicated by the edge of the arc; and having received the precious and elderly royal man with lit candles and palm tree branches, with singing and pomp they will bring him into the Great Zion... And an invisible herald with a thunderous voice calling from heaven* will address the people with the following words: Is this man agreeable to you? And everybody will be filled with fear and terror and ecstacy because of the thunderous voice from above. And beating their chest with wailing and tears, raising their arms towards heaven they will say: Yes, Lord, because You have given him to us, he is agreeable to us. And having bowed in submission before him, they will bring him into the Great Zion. And the King, having prayed to God in front of the gates, they will be opened up... And those who were there will run away in great terror; the people having prayed to God will receive the King and they will bring him to an elevated spot and proclaim him their King... And in this manner they will reach the palace in night time and the signs in the heavens will fade away. The King will be guided by two Angels in the guise of officials dressed in white; and they will whisper into his ears instructions concerning his future activities.

4)   Additional Oracles collected by Emperor Leo the Philosopher

Sovereignty
Woe to you city of the Seven Hills when the twentieth
element is being saluted and praised on your walls.
At that moment the fall and corruption of your strong leaders
will have finally arrived,
those who judge without justice;
of your leader who has scythe-like fingers
which scythe is the scythe of desolation
and a blasphemy before the Most High.

Piety
The already dead and not manifested one
many know him, although nobody sees him;
He will rise up, as if from a wine-revelry
and will receive the scepter of the kingdom.
For a column-shaped phenomenon having been seen in the heavens
an invisible herald will shout thunderously thrice:
Make haste and go to the western parts of the Seven-Hilled city
and you will find a praying man, who is dear to me;
Bring him to the royal palace,
he wears a helmet, is soft-spoken, calm, noble-minded,
he has a very sharp knowledge of the future.
Thus, you, Seven-Hilled city will achieve sovereignty once again.

You, who have been the courtyard of Byzas and the home of Constantine,

216

Rome, Babylon and another, new, Zion,
in six centuries minus about twenty years you will become powerful again.
You will amass the gold of the nations as if it were the dust of the earth.
And you will be the leader of all the surrounding powers.
But a blond nation, with fire-red hair
will turn to ashes and completely destroy your power.
You will appear again as if you had never began.
Till the moment that the finger of God will be visible at dawn
and will strike two fingers with the hand
the fingers having edges like the hot currents emanating from a furnace
and will take revenge over the seed of the fathers.
And from all around your children will arrive
in a centripetal fashion, from the periphery to the center
disembarking from the ships to administer justice
you will become renewed and renovated again
and your power will be greater than in the past.
Because you will become the house of the Glory of God
and those who will be near, will fall on their knees and ask forgiveness.

5)   Additional Byzantine Era Prophecies:[8]

... the Almighty God will bend His arc and give an aim to His pure anger. And the city will shake and will rise to the heights as if it were an apple spinning around. And having fallen back swiftly the waters will cover and conceal it and this way it will be sent to the terrible and boundless sea of the abyss. So definitive will be the submersion of the city, that after its fall only the column of the forum will be visible beyond the surface of the sea, and only because the column possesses the precious nails used in our Lord's crucifixion. This column only will be left behind, so that, when the ships arrive to tie their ropes around it, the sailors can bewail and lament that Babylon.

---

[8] These were excerpted from the collection of A. D. Delimpassis's book *Terrible and Wonderful Coming Events*. N. Sotiropoulos in *The Coming Sharp Two-Edged Sword* provides some of the same material while expanding on other manuscripts of the Byzantine era. It is my belief that the following one refers to the destruction of Constantinople through submersion in a future time, well beyond the events of WWIII. The event of its ultimate submersion would most likely coincide with the detailed events around the general time of the Antichrist, as they can be studied in the Book of Revelation.

6)   Ieronymous Agathangelos (1279 A.D.)[9]

Oh, Agathangelos, servant of the Lord, add the following prophecy to those by other prophets, observe carefully the visions of Ezekiel, of Isaiah, and realize what parts are missing from chapters 38 and 39 of Ezekiel, that they may become completed, for these events will happen at the very same time; following this, add this complete prophecy to the one by the son of Zebedee and compare your apocalypse with the ones by the aforementioned prophets; what they saw and said and wrote about for the benefit of the Hebrews; therefore, you too, do the same for the sake of the Christian peoples, whom He purchased with His own blood, so that the new ordering of (all these prophecies) opens your eyes and instructs you to the effect that you entertain no more doubts concerning the future.

Commentary

The very introduction of the prophecy of Agathangelos assists us in the temporal placing of his predictions. We are told right from the start, that Ezekiel's chaps. 38 & 39 are supplemented and completed by the prophecy, which also refers to the same events as those covered by certain prophecies of Isaiah and the son of Zebedee (i.e. St. John the Divine, and the Book of the Revelation by extension). Isaiah has many prophecies and we are not told which ones are the most relevant. However, in *Our Revelationary Age...*, I cover in detail which ones I believe to relate to our times (including those about signs in the heavens), while additional ones have been identified and appear in various chapters of this study.

---

[9] Ieronymous Agathangelos lived in the 13th century A.D. He was born in Rhodes and became a monk, spending 51 years in a cenobium. When he was 79 years old, according to his own account, he was in Messina of Sicily when a Sunday morning he saw a most spectacular vision which specifically covered the following events:

a)   the fall of Constantinople;
b)   the liberation of the Greek Nation from the Ottoman Empire;
c)   how Europe would evolve after 1453 A.D.;
d)   The Lutheran Reformation;
e)   Napoleon's rise to power and detailed references to his fatal invasion of Russia;
f)   the dismemberment of the Austrian Empire, and the fall of the German Kaiser;
g)   the change of political regime in Russia;
h)   the defeat and dismemberment of Germany after WWII; and finally,
i)   WWIII.

Also, this is our first hint that the Hebrew Prophets have been entrusted with the task of forewarning the Jews for the perilous times ahead, while Christian prophets are entrusted with the analogous duty to forewarn the Christians for the same perilous times. This would further imply that both Hebrews and Christians will face the same external enemies.

Read, oh son of Man, the Divine decision and judgement against the sin of this people, and know exactly, that the sin of such ungrateful people is shouting before the throne of God, and for this reason, God is anxious to punish them.

Commentary
This is a bitter prophecy against the Byzantine Empire. Since Agathangelos is an Orthodox Greek monk, it is improper for us to assume that he would be assigned to task of predicting the punishment of other peoples whose ingratitude also offended God, especially since we have ample evidence that God selects co-religionists of His target audience to bring the appropriate messages to them. Furthermore, since the prophecy was written in 1279 A.D. and the Byzantine Empire completely collapsed with the Fall of Constantinople in 1453 A.D., the target audience for this paragraph is not very hard to identify, especially in view of what follows.

A Constantine initiated and a Constantine will lose the Byzantine Kingdom of the East; son of man, begin counting from the first Constantine till the 12 occurrence of the same name, and you shall find out the number in which this will come to pass. God has decided and the confirmed and determined Divine Will shall remain irremovable. It will be completed during the fourth century (after the year 1000), in the course of the fifty-second to the fifty-third year, when the huge kingdom will fall in the hands of the Saracens; the houses will become corrupted, the holy churches will become profaned, and the faithful will become subject to persecution till the 1800s most definitely; all these are according to the Divine Will, so that the people realizes the weight of His omnipotent hand and repents and rushes back to Him, and afterwards the people becomes prosperous and welcome. As it happened with the Israelites who were subjected to Nebuchadrezzar, the same will occur with this people, who will become subjected to the impious sons of Agar till the appointed time, and they will remain captive under their yoke until about four hundred years have been completed.

Commentary
The above paragraph is self-explanatory. Constantine the Great founded the

Byzantine empire, Constantine Palaeologus was its last emperor.[10] He was killed while defending the city in 1453 A.D. Also, one will find most interesting the comparison of Jews and Greeks, as peoples under the protection of the Most High, but who become punished in the same way and fall under similar conditions when they fall from Grace. This theme is recurrent in the prophecies, as we have noticed already.[11]

Also, the prediction that it will take about four centuries before liberation from the sons of Agar is most fitting. The Greek War of Independence began in 1821 and through the 1800s and the beginning of the 1900s most of the European portions of the Byzantine empire became liberated in a long series of battles by Greeks and other Christian populations in the Peninsula of Haemus. *Sons of Agar*, let us be reminded, is a generic term used most frequently in the prophecies to signify Islamic enemies of the Orthodox Christians. The Turks are not sons of Agar (a term referring to the Arabs), but by being Muslim and by controlling many lands previously controlled by Arabs, the Ottoman empire was fused in the eyes of the Europeans with the Arabs and Islam in general. We should not allow such nomenclature to confuse us. Let us remember that the Turks were holding Palestine and Jerusalem till the end of WWI, and in many prophecies of more recent vintage we hear the expression 'the Turks', which may or may not be limited to the Turks only.

For all practical purposes, since there will be a great alliance of Islamic armies including Turks and Arabs in the next war, such fine distinctions in the nomenclature of very old prophecies are rather inconsequential for our purposes of interpretation.

---

[10] Depending on whether we count as Constantine XI, Constantine Lascaris, titular Byzantine Emperor, who moved the empire to Nicaea during the Fourth Crusade's control of Constantinople, then the last emperor would be Constantine XII, Paleologus. However, in many History books he appears as Constantine XI. These latter authors treat the empire from Nicaea as not a direct continuation of the Byzantine line, proper.

[11] In fact, numerous Christian prophecies researched for this study insist that the only reason the Turks have been successful in the past is not because God favors them; on the contrary, He uses them as a way of punishing the ungrateful Christians. Many parallelisms also are drawn between the Assyrians and the Turks as peoples selected by God as a means of bringing both Jews and Christians back into a life of holiness and obeisance to the Divine Will.

The terrible age approaches the golden number related to '10'. Afterwards, honey and milk will flow everywhere, the anxieties and troubles will come to an end, and for fifty full years peace will reign upon the world; the truth will triumph, and the heavens will rejoice with true glory; the Orthodox Faith will be elevated and it will expand from East to West and will be glorified. The barbarians will shake and tremble and will depart in haste leaving behind the metropolis of the world. God will then be glorified and the humans will see the works of His omnipotence. This is how it should be and this is how it will be, amen.

The monosyllabic golden number dilutes the confines (or, decomposes the limits); peace will become manifest upon the earth; the destruction of the offspring of Agar will ensue; following that, will come the triumph of the Apostolic Church. The end of sorrows is promised to commence in 55 years; on the seventh (day) there will be no more exiles, no more wretched people. And following that, after you returned to the nests of your forefathers, I will lead you to self-sufficiency.

Commentary
I have great difficulty with the meaning of terms such as 'golden number related to ten', or the 'monosyllabic golden number'. Obviously, they refer to very specific dates of our future. Avoiding dangerous conjectures, let us continue with the interpretation of the balance of these two paragraphs.

Again, we are told of a period of peace extending to 50-55 years, a most consistent number across many prophecies. The barbarians departing in haste from the metropolis of the world, I interpret to mean the great battle in Constantinople, where the Barbarians will be defeated by Christian armies.[12] The triumph of the Apostolic Church is a reference to the re-unification of the Christians (in the Eighth Ecumenical Council) under the Papa Angelorum, and the spreading of Christian missionaries to the four corners of the world. (If the above interpretation is the appropriate one, it would be in full consistence and agreement with the remaining body of our prophetic evidence. Last and not least, once everybody is established in their traditional lands and territories which lawfully belonged to them in the past, the Lord God will shower His mercies upon them so that they will be

---

[12] We cannot exclude, however, that it may refer to Jerusalem, being the holiest city for both Jews and Christians. We know that Jerusalem will be liberated, hence the barbarians will depart from it also, as they will depart from Constantinople.

deprived of nothing, becoming self-sufficient in all things. (This also is a most remarkable prediction re-iterated many times across prophecies).

As a final comment, one finds interesting the mention of honey and milk which will flow everywhere. Is it a metaphorical term of peace and plenty or a direct allusion to events associated with the creation or visual appearance of milk and honey upon the earth?

But you, son of man, do not be afraid to return anew to the Divine Grace, for, you will become more glorious than you were before, and under the command of this worldly power which will be eventually demolished at some future time, God again is going to conquer and submit countless new nations and most of the original ones.

Oh, Russia, come on, wake up from your sleep! Behold, your most technically advanced military instruments are filling the air with melodies! Oh, sister of mine, go on, join your voice to mine and defend and advocate the eternal truth emanating from Him; because it was in you that the sign of such a luminous glory was kept alive.

Commentary

It is my conviction that these two paragraphs are meant for Orthodox audiences mainly and in particular the Greeks and the Russians. First of all, this predicts the reconstruction of the Byzantine Empire (which will become 'more glorious than before') and a great evangelizing of new nations and re-evangelizing of old original Christian peoples who became lukewarm in their faith. Also it predicts its ultimate demolition at some future point in time! This, again is most consistent with other prophecies (some of which we touched upon already in either study).[13]

Russia will have its most technically advanced military instruments fill the air with melodies! What is this supposed to mean? Are the Slavic victors of Constantinople going to provide the high tech equipment decisive for the military victory and its aftermath? Or does it mean that the same

---

[13] W. Bousset had compiled an extensive body of prophetic evidence (both Jewish and Christian) speaking of the future demise of the new Byzantine Empire. He was dealing specifically with the Antichrist times and the majority of the material presented in The Antichrist Legend corroborates fully the previous statement in Agathangelos's prophecies.

sophisticated military equipment can be easily converted into civilian uses during its peace time utilization? For example, could the micro-wave activated weapons become centers of information dissemination at a massive scale later on? This would be quite possible, considering the advanced military technology achieved during the Soviet era, although I will opt for the first alternative as the meaning of the prophecy.

Oh sister of mine, (namely, you Orthodox land, who have taken your faith from me, Byzantium), you will become the beacon of the Christian faith and the spearhead of the evangelizing effort. **For, it was in you that the purity of the true Christian faith was kept alive.**

I am overwhelmed with the power of this last sentence. The Almighty God Himself is coming to the defence of Russian Christianity by identifying His martyred Remnant in that land as the purest and most worthy Christians in the course of the 20th century!

The day will come that the world will finally admit that no Christian population in the course of this most criminal century in History has suffered more than the Russians. The true Christians to be found among the population of the former Soviet Union today are the purest of the Christians living anywhere in the world; they kept the commands of the early Church with the greatest zeal and determination. Their numbers are small but their place in the Church is unmatched. And although they are still struggling in a shaken society facing incredible odds and much opposition from within and without, they will emerge victorious in the end.

I wish to make a few additional comments at this point: How come the Russian military equipment is praised so profusely and the frequently technologically superior one produced by the capitalist West is passed over in silence?

a)   Let us remember that Agathangelos was an Orthodox Greek Monk, he deals with the war and its consequences around Greece, Byzantium, Europe, Russia, Israel and the Middle East. This was the focus of his prophecies. Since America had not yet been discovered, the Holy Spirit did not wish to confuse the reader of Agathangelos by introducing material that the people would have great difficulty understanding and placing in the proper perspective. Furthermore, as we already know, God has assigned American seers with the task of predicting specific events concerning the USA.

b)	We are also reminded that failure to mention somebody in a specific place does not preclude the overall importance of that missing link in the entire scheme of things. We should not fall in the trap of certain zealous Catholic 'interpreters' who have pronounced that the Greeks will collaborate with the Turks in the coming war!...

c)	Russia is closer to Constantinople than the USA. In terms of logistics if nothing else, weapons from Russia can reach the straits and be used in battle faster, cheaper and more effectively.

I would like to insert at this juncture some dynastic considerations which will allow us to better understand how and why the next emperor from Byzantium will be agreeable also to the Russians.

In *Our Revelationary Age...*, as well as throughout the present study we re-iterate that King Juan Carlos I de Borbón y Borbón is the Great Monarch. His son Felipe, the Prince of Asturias, is the Great Philip who will fight with a multi-ethnic army in Constantinople. King Juan Carlos and other members of his family will excel in the military encounters of WWIII, 'going from victory to victory'.[14]

Let us retrace the history of a few royal marriages. King Juan Carlos I is married to Queen Sophia, the oldest child of King Paul and Queen Frederika of the Hellenes. Queen Sophia, her brother King Constantine of the Hellenes (living currently in London), their sister Princess Irene and their uncle, Prince Philip, the Duke of Edinburgh, as members of the Greek royal family, all descend from George I (born Danish Prince Christian Glucksburg) and Olga Romanovna, Grand Duchess of Russia, daughter of Grand Duke Constantine, brother of Czar Alexander I. Her father renounced his rights to the throne for the benefit of his brother Nicholas I (1825-1855).

---

[14] The reader may wish to re-examine the prophecies appearing in the first part of this chapter, for which no specific commentary was provided. In conjunction with the rest of this study they make manifest the personage of the King of the prophecies, the timing of his election as the Field Marshall, his military exploits in the Holy Land and the Eastern Mediterranean, etc. Also, the description of the time, the hour of the day and the nature of the phenomena in the sky, as plain enough to identify, once the deepest darkness of the Three Days Darkness has left, the comet in the skies, with a rounded nucleus, a purple color, of a diameter that renders it impressive in size, and, most importantly, the sign of the Cross.

Since the Bolsheviks assassinated the inner Romanov family and most of their relatives who were unable to leave the country on time, the only Romanovs remaining today have been those living outside the former USSR. It is quite conceivable that the Russians will not object at all to a Romanov-related prince of Europe ruling from Byzantium, the more so, since he and his relatives will have been so instrumental in the victories of WWIII.

Consequently, when Catholic prophecies speak of the Great Monarch and his family ruling from Constantinople, this is not inconsistent with what the Greek prophets are saying, now that we know the identity of the Great Monarch. Nor are all other prophecies speaking of exiled kings retrieving their thrones with the assistance of the Great Monarch irrelevant! We must keep such considerations always present in mind if we are to fully appreciate the many details concerning the future career of Constantinople as the new seat of empire.

Finally, as an obiter dictum, let us review a certain prophecy that always re-emerges in the popular press (although I have never encountered its origin in any of the prophetic sources I have investigated). It deals with a prediction that when a King Constantine and a Queen Sophia are again reigning, Constantinople will be liberated from the Turks. The saying was that Constantine and Sophia were the last sovereigns of the Byzantine Empire. Such explanation is false because it is historically unfounded.

The great Greek Historian Constantine Paparrigopoulos[15] provides the historical background information to clear the above issue.[16]

---

[15] Ἱστορία τοῦ Ἑλληνικοῦ Ἔθνους, (History of the Greek Nation), vol. 7, page 74.

[16] The Greek text has as follows: "ὁ Κωνσταντῖνος χηρεύσας τὸ δεύτερον τῷ 1442 εἶχε πέμψει μετὰ πενταετίαν τὸν πιστὸν αὐτοῦ φίλον καὶ ὑπουργὸν Γεώργιον Φραντζῆν εἰς Κωνσταντινούπολιν, ἵνα ἐκεῖθεν φροντίσῃ πρός τοῖς ἄλλοις περὶ νέου γάμου μετὰ τινος τῶν ἡγεμονίδων τῆς Τραπεζοῦντος ἤ τῆς Γοτθίας."

And later on, on page 81 of the same volume, he continues:

"Ὁ Κωνσταντῖνος (...) ἐπιστρέψαντος τοῦ Φραντζῆ ἐξ Ἰβηρίας κατὰ σεπτέμβριον, συνωμολόγησε τὸν γάμον αὐτοῦ μετὰ τῆς θυγατρός τοῦ βασιλέως τῆς χώρας ἐκείνης διὰ τοῦ συγχρόνως προσελθόντος πρέσβεως τοῦ βασιλέως τούτου, καὶ ἔπειτα δι᾽ ὅλου τοῦ χειμῶνος δὲν ἔπαυσε βουλευόμενος μετὰ τοῦ φίλου ἐκείνου καὶ ὑπουργοῦ του περί τε διαφόρων ἄλλων αὐτοῦ ἀποστολῶν καὶ ἰδίως περὶ τῆς εἰς τὴν Ἰβηρίαν μεταβάσε-

In a few words, Emperor Constantine Palaeologus planned to enter into a new marriage with a princess of Georgia, and for this purpose he sent his faithful Frantzis, who wrote down the chronicle of those events for posterity. We are not given the name of this princess, who, anyway, never came to Constantinople because her fiancé had been killed in the defense of the city. Furthermore, although Constantine XI (or XII) Palaeologus had been married and became a widower twice before, neither of his former wives was named Sophia. The first was Princess Magdalena, a niece of Carlo Tocco, who changed her name into Theodora upon her marriage with Constantine in March of 1428. She died two years later, without issue. The second wife was Catherine, daughter of Dorino Gattilusi (married in 1441) who died one year later, again without issue.

My feeling is that the prophecy on Sophia and Constantine and the re-taking of Constantinople must not include a constraint that Sophia and Constantine will be married to each other. When Constantinople falls to the Christians both Sophia and Constantine will be present but as sister and brother (Sophia Queen of Spain, and Constantine, King of the Hellenes).

However, there is another historical analogy which will be replicated when Constantinople becomes a Christian city once more. This involves a Sophia and a John, as a married couple this time. After the fall of Constantinople in 1453 A.D., and following a series of adventures and tribulations, a Byzantine Princess, who was a **niece** of Constantine XI (XII) Palaeologus, Zoe - (rechristened **Sophia**) Palaeologa, married Ivan III the Great, who ruled as Grand Prince of Muskovy between 1462 and 1505 A.D.[17]

ὡς αὐτοῦ κατὰ τὸ προσεχὲς ἔαρ ἵνα κομίσῃ ἐκεῖθεν τὴν νέαν βασίλισσαν...

For a detailed coverage in English of the same general events and details, derived from the same original historical sources, the interested reader may consult Sir Steven Runciman, [1987, pp. 49-55].

[17] After the Tatar Yoke was formally ended a few years after their marriage, her husband, who had by now adopted the Byzantine two-headed eagle as the new seal of state, and who saw through such an imperial marriage the 'translatio imperii' from Constantinople to Moscow, the 'third Rome', would introduce himself as follows: *I, Ioann, by the Grace of God, Sovereign (Gosudar) of all Rus, and grand Prince of Vladimir and of Moscow and of Novgorod and of Pskov and of Tver and of Yugria and of Viatka and of Perm and of Bolgary and of others.* Of course, this Ioann, (Ivan, John, Juan, ᾽Ιωάννης) was a member of the dynasty of Rurik, which

Thus, the Byzantine Princess Sophia married a Muscovite Grand Prince of the line of Rurik, named John. The current royal couple of Spain, namely, the Great Monarch of the Prophecies, King Juan Carlos I and his wife Sophia, are fully satisfying this prophetic constraint. Let us now continue with Agathangelos.

You (plural) consider it a good idea to draw up peace treaties but you are laboring in vain. I introduce a brief suspension of hostilities, (a brief truce) and I do not think about a true peace. Mars is threatening with a terrible destruction, the people will think that the end of the world will arrive soon.

Oh vain city! Rome, you have definitely been dyed with human blood; your kings were pouring rivers of blood emanating from saintly martyrdom, and the faithful of Christ, like sacrificial animals, ran in flocks to the slaughterhouse. Where is now your piety? Where is your zeal? God has abandoned you, Christ is rejecting you, and the Devil will conquer you; Devil is proud like yourself and a liar. You have become his conquest, his daughter and his concubine. For these reasons, you, lascivious one, you will be turned completely into a whore, the East will humiliate you, you will become its captive and an infernal subjected monster; your purple will be torn by your captors, the tiara will be thrown underfoot because you have concealed the eternal truth and you have painted it with lies; you have despised My holiness which I have founded in the East, you turned yourself into a tavern and a den of robbers, you introduced innovations in the faith of the people and you have impoverished My church; yes, yes, upon your walls stone will not remain upon a stone and you will become desolate like the holy city of David; however, the East will shine upon you, while you will become tested by fire and you will become a cornerstone; the East will humiliate your proud neck; you will come to worship along with the conqueror My altar which will be in Byzantium, Amen, Amen. A ring of hard iron will pass through your nostrils and your unholy lip will drip fatal poison; oh viper, you, seven-headed hydra, turret of Babylon, the eternal One will defeat you and put you to death.

The impious school of the Devil, which appears holy to the eyes of men, behold, it will disappear completely; then a most bright constitution of the Divine Providence will shine in the world. And lo, and behold, the triangular stone which was cast away by the builders became the head of the angle. Poor ones! raise the name of the Lord your God, sing to the great king of the

---

ended with the offspring of Ivan the Terrible to be succeeded by the Romanovs.

ages, give Him glory , oh come, come, pious race: also you, the inventors of the distorted heresies, come and join your own hymns to the Lord, for, He is benevolent, for, His mercy lives through the ages. Amen. And lo, a huge crowd of a heavenly army brought the great dragon and tied him up with terrible ties and threw him in the Tartarus of the furnace of fire.

Commentary
The prophecy speaks in no uncertain terms about the future of Rome and passes a severe judgement on its activities in the last 2000 years. First an allusion is made to its past, as the Roman Empire of old that persecuted Christians, later on as the 'only true church of Jesus Christ' with its history of violent evangelizing of the Americas, the Holy Inquisition, the wars of the Reformation, etc. Catholic seers and prophets have said similar things about the Vatican, the Jesuits and the various innovations produced by the Papacy over the Orthodox Faith of the Apostolic times.

ON THE FATE OF ROME AND
THE ROMAN CATHOLIC CHURCH OF TODAY,
FROM THE MOUTHS OF CATHOLIC PROPHETS

7)   **Saint John Bosco (Don Bosco) (1815-1888):** (Italian from Piedmont, Founder of the Salesian Order, canonized in 1934).

Introductory note
(Don Bosco prophesied about many events of WWIII, such as the detailed fate of Paris. Below we shall give only an excerpt on the fate of the Catholic Church and the city of Rome in particular):

(...) Ah, but you, Italy, land of blessings! Who has steeped you in desolation? Blame not your enemies, but rather your friends. Can you not hear your children asking for the bread of faith and find only those who smash it to pieces? What shall I do? I shall strike the shepherds, I shall disperse the flock, until those sitting on the throne of Moses search for good pastures and the flock listens attentively and is fed.

Over the flock and over the shepherds My hand will weigh heavy. Famine, pestilence and war will be such that mothers will have to cry on account of the blood of their sons and of their martyrs dead in a hostile country.

And to you, Rome, what will happen? Ungrateful Rome, effeminate Rome, proud Rome! You have reached such a height that you search no further.

You admire nothing else in your Sovereign except luxury, forgetting that you and your glory stands upon Golgotha. Now he is old, defenseless, and despoiled; and yet at his word, the word of one who was in bondage, the whole world trembles.

Rome! to you I will come four times!
The first time, I shall strike your lands and the inhabitants thereof.
The second time, I shall bring the massacre and the slaughter even to your very walls, And will you not yet open your eyes?'
I shall come a third time and I shall beat down to the ground your defenses and the defenders, and at the command of the Father, the reign of terror, of dreadful fear, and of desolation shall enter into your city.
But My wise men have now fled and My law is even now trampled under foot. Therefore I will make a fourth visit. Woe to you if My law shall still be considered as empty words. There will be deceit and falsehood amongst both the learned and the ignorant. Your blood and that of your children will wash away your stains upon God's law. War, pestilence, famine are the rods to scourge men's pride and wickedness. O wealthy men, where is your glory now, your estates, your palaces? They are the rubble on the highways and byways.

And you priests, why have you not run to 'cry between the vestibule and the Altar,' begging God to end these scourges? Why have you not, with the shield of faith, gone upon the housetops, into the homes, along the highways and byways, into every accessible corner to carry the seed of My word? Know you not that this is the terrible two-edged sword that cuts down my enemies and that breaks the Anger of God and of men?
These things must come one after another. They are inexorable.
Things are happening too slowly.

But the August Queen of Heaven is present.
The power of the Lord is in His hands. He scatters His enemies as a cloud. The Venerable Old Man attires himself in all his ancient raiment. There will come again a violent hurricane.

Iniquity is consummated. Sin will have its end. And before two full moons of the month of the flowers will have run their course, the rainbow of peace will rise above the earth.
The Great Minister will see the bride of his King arrayed in festive fashion.

Throughout the world the sun will appear so luminous that the likes of

which never has been seen since the tongues of fire descended on the Cenacle[18] until this day, nor will such a sun ever be seen again until the very last of days.

(...)

The cities, towns, and villages were thinly populated. **The land had been leveled down as if by a hurricane, by a tempest, and a hail storm. People went from one to another saying in tones of great emotion: 'there is a God in Israel.'**

From the beginning of the exile (of the Pope from the Vatican) until the singing of the 'Te Deum' the sun rose in the East two hundred times. The time that passed for the fulfilling of those things corresponds to four hundred risings of the sun. (...)

Commentary

The above prophecy suggests that the Greek prophets are neither unfair nor biased when they speak about the future of the current Roman Catholic Church. After the Papa Angelorum takes over, things will be different. The Greek prophet Agathangelos, for instance, predicts the physical destruction of Rome and the movement of the center of power to Constantinople, yet, he lets us know that 'Rome' will become the new cornerstone: καὶ χρηματίσεις λίθος ἀκρογωνιαῖος. This, I believe, is the allusion to the Angelic Pastor, the Papa Angelorum, whom the prophecies indicate as an Italian, of possibly royal descent, whose name begins with an R; Don Bosco also calls him the Venerable Old Man of Lazio.[19]

8)   **Abbot Merlin Joachim (Joachim de Fiore) (1130-1202):** (Italian mystic, who among his various prophecies adds the following information on the Papa Angelorum):

(...) A remarkable Pope will be seated on the pontifical throne, under the special protection of the angels. Holy and full of gentleness, he shall undo all wrong, he shall recover the states of the Church, and reunite the exiled temporal powers. He shall be revered by all people, and shall recover the

---

[18] Cenacle originally meant the room where Lord Jesus and His disciples ate the last supper. Here it is referring to the descent of the Holy Ghost upon the Disciples and the Virgin Mary, i.e., during their gathering of the Pentecost.

[19] Lazio is Latium, the territory of Italy around Rome.

kingdom of Jerusalem. As the only Pastor he shall reunite the Eastern to the Western Church, and thus one only faith will be in vigor. The sanctity of this beneficent Pontiff will be so great that the highest potentates shall bow down before his presence. This holy man shall crush the arrogance of religious schism and heresy. All men will return to the primitive Church, and there shall be one only pastor, one law, one master - humble, modest and fearing God. The true God of the Jews, our Lord Jesus Christ, will make everything prosper beyond all human hope, because God alone can and will pour down on the wounds of humanity the oily balm of sweetness.

The heavens proclaim the glory of God, and the faithful are in joy and happiness, because the Lord has vouchsafed to be merciful to them. He shall invite His elect to the banquet of the Lamb, where melodious canticles and harmonious concerts will be heard.

The power of this Pontiff's holiness will be so great as to be able to check the fury and impetuosity of threatening waves. **Mountains shall be lowered before him, the sea shall be dried up, the dead shall be raised**, the churches shall be re-opened and altars erected.

It should be known that there will be two heads, one in the East and the other in the West. This Pope shall break the weapons and scatter the fighting hordes. He will be the joy of God's elect. This angelic Pope will preach the gospel in every country. Through his zeal and solicitude the Greek Church shall be forever reunited to the Catholic Church.

Before, however, being firmly and solidly established in the Holy See, there will be innumerable wars and violent conflicts during which the sacred throne shall be shaken. But through the favor of Divine clemency, moved by the prayers of the faithful, everything will succeed so well that they shall be able to sing hymns of thanksgiving to the glory of the Lord.

This holy Pope shall be both pastor and reformer. Through him the East and West shall be in everlasting concord. The city of Babylon shall then be the head and guide of the world.[20] Rome, weakened in temporal power, shall forever preserve her spiritual dominion, and shall enjoy great peace. During these happy days the Angelic Pope shall be able to address to Heaven prayers full of sweetness. The dispersed nation shall also enjoy tranquility.

---

[20] (My note: Obviously Babylon in Mesopotamia is not implied here).

Six and a half years after this time the Pope will render his soul to God. The end of his days shall arrive in an arid province, situated between a river and a lake near the mountains.

*At the beginning, in order to obtain these happy results, having need of a powerful temporal assistance, this holy Pontiff will ask the cooperation of the generous Monarch of France. At that time a handsome monarch, a scion of King Pepin, will come as a pilgrim to witness the splendor of this glorious pontiff, **whose name shall begin with R.** A temporal throne becoming vacant, the Pope shall place on it this king whose assistance he shall ask.*

*(...) **When a monster shall appear to thee in the sky,** thou shalt find a ready escape towards the east, and after nine years thou shalt render thy soul to God.*

A man of remarkable sanctity will be his successor in the Pontifical chair. Through him God will work so many prodigies that all men shall revere him, and no person will dare to oppose his precepts. He shall not allow the clergy to have many benefices. He will induce them to live by the tithes and offerings of the faithful. He shall interdict pomp in dress, and all immorality in dances and songs. He will preach the gospel in person, and exhort all honest ladies to appear in public without any ornament of gold or precious stones. After having occupied the Holy See for a long period of time he shall happily return to the Lord.

His three immediate successors shall be men of exemplary holiness. One after the other will be models of virtue, and shall work miracles, confirming the teaching of their predecessors. Under their government the Church shall spread, and these Popes shall be called the Angelic Pastors.

9)   John of Vatiguero: (13th century):
(excerpts specific to the Pope only):

(...) Spoliation, devastation and pillage of that most famous city, which is the capitol and mistress of the whole kingdom of France, will take place when the Church and world will be grievously troubled: The Pope will change his residence; the Church will not be defended for the duration of 25 months, and more, because during all this time there will be no Pope, no Emperor of Rome and no ruler in France. Afterwards a young captive prince shall recover the crown of the Lilies and shall extend his dominion over all the universe. Once established he shall destroy the Sons of Brutus and their Isle

so that their memory shall pass into everlasting forgetfulness.

After many tribulations a Pope will be elected out of those who escaped persecution. He, by his sanctity, will reform the clergy and the whole world will venerate them for their virtue and perfection. He will travel barefoot and be devoid of fear. Almost all unbelievers and the Jews will be converted and there will be one law, one faith, one baptism, one life. All people will love one another and peace will last a long time.

10)   Father Laurence Ricci: (d. 1775)
(...) At a gathering of men noted for piety and wisdom, he (the Great Monarch) will, with the aid of the Pope, introduce new rules, and ban the spirit of confusion. Everywhere there will be one fold and one shepherd.

11)   Excerpts from a prophecy said to be Ancient Irish:[21]
(...) [The prophecy speaks of a terrible war which **shall come out of Asia and shall require the aid of every occidental on earth to put down.** (...) France restores order in England after her own recovery from a violent revolution. The close of the war finds a Celt in the Chair of Peter. He is the most perfect of all the popes - chosen miraculously amidst chaos. An angel in human form, he shall be called "Papa Angelorum". **This Celt is not an Irish Celt but one born in Galicia, and the only Celt to occupy Peter's throne.** [Emphasis added]. (...)

Commentary
The above prophecy identifies the Papa as coming from *Galicia*. Galicia is a generic toponym associated with the Gauls (Celts, Galatae); there was one in the East, a Galicia near the area wherefrom Papa Karol Vojtyla comes, but he is a Slav of Poland and not identified as a Celt by anybody so far, nor is he to be mistaken with the Papa Angelorum, considering all the information already available to us. There exists another Galicia in North-Western Spain. The Celts of Ireland emanate from the Celtiberos, the Celts of the Iberian Peninsula. However, the prophecy explicitly says that the Papa Angelorum will not be an Irish Celt. Considering that the Celts were spread all over Europe (from Iberia to the Ukraine and, mixed with the Greeks they reached even into Asia, where they established the Galatia (Gallograecia) in Asia Minor), we must look for other territories where such a Celt, mentioned in the ancient prophecy, will come from. Among the territories of the Italian

---

[21] Culleton, [op. cit. pp. 234-235].

Peninsula invaded and inhabited by Celts we can count also the Gallia Cisalpina (North Italy), the Gallia Cispadana (on this side of the Po river with respect to the city of Rome), and the Gallia Transpadana (on the other side of the Po, with respect to the location of Rome). And although the Celts, as noted above, were spread all over Europe, these toponyms in Italy seem to corroborate other prophecies on the origin of Papa Angelorum, as we shall find out soon.

Let us now return to Greek prophecies which corroborate the Catholic ones:

12)   A prophecy by St. Neilos the Myrrh-Gusher:[22]
(He lived in the village of Saint Peter in Peloponnesus and died in 1592 A.D.[23] The excerpt given below applies to the events of our own times):

"... *During that time the eighth and last Ecumenic Synod will take place, which will pacify the contentions of the Heretics, it will separate the wheat from the chaff, and the right doctrine from the false doctrine, and for the short length of fifty years there will be peace upon the earth. Afterwards they will turn again towards evil and they will go to their perdition*".[24]

13)   Excerpts from the visions of General John Makriyannis:[25]
excerpt a) p. 197-198:
(...) *During my nightly vision I saw a great light and the glory of our Lord God and His kingdom, something I am unable to describe to you, readers; between God the Father and Jesus Christ a cross appeared; Christ took the cross in His hand and immediately a person holding a great trumpet came forth; he put the trumpet in his mouth and started blowing first at his left side then at his right, and immediate two horsemen bearing flags moved forward*

---

[22] *Myrrh-Gusher* is an epithet of a saint from whose grave myrrh has been issuing forth. A famous example of a Myrrh-Gusher Saint is the Great-Martyr Demetrius, the Patron Saint of Salonica.

[23] To the best of my knowledge, his work has not been published to date; our information came via the book by Sotiropoulos (see bibliography).

[24] Elsewhere in his prophecies St. Neilos mentioned that after 1913 A.D. there remain about 79 years for the materialization of the predicted evils.

[25] All following material derives from Makriyannis's book entitled 'Visions and Wonders', '*Ὁράματα καὶ Θάματα*', 1983 edition.

and the cross moved along with them. Behind them followed armies and troops. Then I saw a sea covered with ships great and grand bearing diverse flags, the entire sea was covered by their numbers and they moved in front of me in the vision; then I saw myriads upon myriads of troops, black, red, etc.

While they were marching forward for a prolonged period of time, **something like a fog suddenly appears with a great amount of smoke and a great river full of blood;** after these images had passed by, (I saw) characters of the Turkish alphabet; first appeared the Sultan's monogram symbol and the letters followed. After them I see our Greek alphabet's characters. They created the words: **The end is at hand.** Then many numerals appear. And again, I can read the sentence **"The Kingdom comes to an end"**. After that the vision faded and I felt exhausted (...).

excerpt b) p. 198:
(...) Some time ago I saw a vision regarding Turkey: I saw in a dream that a man dressed in a Bishop's official ceremonial attire gave me two Turkish documents and said to me: "Give these documents to Spyridon and ask him to hand them over to Turkey; these are the old contracts made with Turkey, now I have drawn up new ones. (...)

excerpt c) p. 201:
(...) While I was sitting on my bed awake, suddenly I see in a vision the arrival of our Lord, the whole room became immersed in light; at the right hand side of our Lord was Christ and the Theotokos and all the saints following, each one in his proper order; a trumpet bearer appears and begins to blow all around for quite a long time three times; then I began seeing the characters of the Turkish alphabet with the Sultan's monogram and following that a multitude of troops dressed in red, as well as other types of clothes, infantry and horsemen and all equipment for warfare followed in many carriages; this procession lasted a long time; but they were approaching as if in a shadow and at a very slow pace and the whole territory became covered by them, as if drowned under their weight. Then a few men, dressed in white where added to another small number and march against that great multitude of troops. And the Virgin Theotokos with a bright cross in Her hand and the saints following Her and two horsemen with shiny flags behind, they move in front of that huge torrent of humanity. And the multitudes were unable to see each other. They were crushing and smashing each other. (...)

excerpt d) p. 205-206:
(...) Then the Lord God spoke and said: and the entire family of the Western nations should abandon their idea and their demands at the expense of Orthodoxy. This is a new edifice, it is My wish and the wish of those within My Kingdom that they (the Greeks) will receive again their glory of the past; I was the One Who took that glory away from them, I Am the One Who gives it back to them; no nation among you should ever raise that claim again, not even, not even Russia, herself; whoever raises such a claim will have to face My wrath, not only he, himself, but also all those who may wish to run to his assistance; this realm will be the domain of My Only-Begotten Son, this will become My domain also, and herewith I appoint as My deputy the man named after John the Baptist, and I bequeath the realm to him and his offspring and the offspring of his offspring through the ages. This is My wish and this is My pleasure.

You, king John, you are faithful to Me and to My kingdom, let your issue follow your own example; you and your progeny are going to move your residence into the Palace of Constantine, and nowhere else. (...)

Commentary

The above vision of General Makriyannis continues with very detailed instructions given to King John on how to begin with the construction of Christian Churches. The instructions include the future location of the churches and the name of the Saints they will be dedicated to. Also instructions are given to the King to be just and generous and charitable to the widows and the orphans.

King John is urged not to waste any time rebuilding the churches, one of which (along with all other pertinent structures for a Bishopric) will be erected in *'the country of your birth'*. (Πέφτον, ἄλλη οἰκία μου εἰς τὴν πατρίδα τῆς γεννήσεώς σου, ἐπισκοπὴ καὶ τ᾽ἄλλα πλησίον της). This is particularly interesting, since several cities in Greece besides Constantinople are explicitly mentioned in the divine instructions as locales to receive several of the temples to be erected by King John. But here we also have a distinction being made in the vision indicating, once more, that King John will have been born in a country other than the one in which he will establish his empire by the Grace of God. Considering that King Juan Carlos I de Borbón y Borbón was born in exile in Rome, it is very remarkable that Makriyannis guided by the Spirit makes allusion to the fact that the 'country of his birth' has to be distinguished from Spain, France, Mainland Greece and Constantinople.

Another item of importance is the explicit mention of Russia in the vision. In this case, we have a Divine Interdiction against Russia's potential raising of any objection regarding the new empire from Constantinople. That King John will reign from Constantinople becomes obvious by the command to move his residence and that of his offspring into the 'Palace of Constantine'.

General John Makriyannis was a revolutionary hero, a man of action and also of great piety. But he was almost illiterate; he taught himself how to read and write while fighting on the mountains of Greece during the War of Independence. His books are written in the language of a middle-19th century Greek peasant. He spoke no foreign languages, obviously, and had no access to learned books even in Greek. And yet, through his mouth and through his simple pen we receive a testimony that agrees so remarkably with hundreds of other prophets spread over the ages and the globe. This is one of the manifestations of the glory of the Spirit.

A few additional remarks may be helpful with regards to General Makriyannis's visions: He saw the future in images presented to him by the Holy Ones. In the images, the trumpet and the trumpet blower are symbols for the commencement of wars. The huge fleet he sees is reminiscent of so many other prophecies speaking of the greatest fleet the world has ever seen fighting around Constantinople. He tells us that two small armies join forces against a huge one of their enemies, while the Virgin Mary Theotokos, the Champion and Leader in Battle, is assisting them. By means of imagery Makriyannis informs us that the enemy troops will be reduced further by their own internecine strife. All prophecies predict a very fierce war to rage among the Muslim allies of yesterday, which will further enable the army under the Russians and the one under the command of the Great Monarch to achieve their final victories and expedite the end of the war.

14)   Augustin Bader's Prophecy:[26]

"In one of his astrological prognostications, a common form of political pamphlet, Paracelsus repeated predictions which the furrier, Augustin Bader of Augsburg, had made in his Anabaptist prophecy for the same year):
All secular and ecclesiastical authorities would be destroyed, the Turks would reach the Rhine, and an empire uniting Christians, Jews, Turks and pagans would be established to end all empires.

---

[26] Quoted in Henry M. Pachter's [1951, pp. 104-105].

<u>Commentary</u>
This appears to refer to the time when the people of Israel, liberated from the Muslim invaders, as well as those Muslims who will have adopted Christianity, join in an empire under the Great Monarch and his offspring. I find no inconsistency in this prophecy and its application to the period of peace following WWIII.

I believe the following prophecy is in a class by itself for the wealth of information it affords us. Therefore it is presented below out of chronological sequence:

15) Anonymous (1053 A.D.)[27]

1. *Great European War.*
2. *Defeat of Germany, destruction of Russia and Austria.*
3. *Defeat of the Sons of Agar by the Greeks.*
4. *Reinforcement offered to the Sons of Agar by Western nations and defeat of the Greeks by the Sons of Agar.*
5. *Slaughter of Orthodox populations.*
6. *Furthermore, great anxiety among Orthodox populations.*
7. *Invasion of foreign troops through the Adriatic sea; Woe to the inhabitants of the Earth; Hades is ready.*
8. *For a moment the Son of Agar appears to be great.*
9. *New European War.*
10. *Union of Orthodox Populations with Germany.*
11. *Defeat of the French by the Germans.*
12. *Revolution in India and its separation from England.*
13. *England to the Saxons only.*
14. *Victory of Orthodox peoples and general slaughter of the sons of Agar by the Orthodox.*
15. *Anxiety in the world.*
16. *General despair upon the earth.*
17. *Battle of seven nations in Constantinople. Three days- and three nights-long slaughter. Victory of the greatest nation against the six nations.*
18. *Alliance of six nations against the seventh nation, three days- and three nights-long slaughter.*
19. *Cessation of the war through the intervention of an angel and delivery*

---

[27] The original manuscript is preserved in the library of the Monastery of Koutloumoussiou, in Mount Athos.

of the city to the Greeks.

20. *Deferring of the Latins to the error-free faith of the Orthodox.*
21. *The Orthodox Faith will expand from the East to the West.*
22. *Fear and Terror of the Barbarians under the True Faith.*
23. *Cessation of Papism and establishment of a single Patriarch for the entire European Continent.*
24. *The end of sorrows will arrive in 55 years; on the seventh (day) nobody will remain any longer wretched, nor exiled; the exile will return in the arms of the rejoicing Mother. This is how it is going to happen and this is how we wish it come to pass. Amen, Amen, Amen. I am the Alpha and the Omega. The First and the Last. In the end, there will be only one flock and one shepherd coming from the true orthodox faith. Let it happen this way. Amen, Amen, Amen. (Written by a servant of Jesus, our true God).*

Commentary

The above prophecy, in its parsimonious and spartan choice of words succeeds in detailing all major events of the 20th century as they affected and will affect the fortunes of the Christian populations of Europe. By extension, we receive valuable insights for many other issues of great import. I will venture an interpretation to the individual verses, preceded by historical commentary.

1. **Great European War** is quite clearly WWI, considering the next item on the chronological list.

2. **Defeat of Germany** (followed by the collapse of the Hohenzollern regime and the abdication of the Kaiser), **destruction of Russia** (brought about by violent change of regime by the Bolsheviks), **and of Austria** (the collapse of the Austro-Hungarian Empire, the loss of imperial lands).

3. **The defeat of the sons of Agar by the Greeks** is the initially victorious campaign of the Greeks in Asia Minor, immediately following WWI. This defeat refers to the period following the victory over the central powers and their ally, the Ottoman empire, during WWI.

4. **Reinforcement of the Agarini by Western nations and defeat of the Greeks by the sons of Agar**. This refers to the newly created political situation in Turkey after the revolution of Kemal Atatürk, the

abolition of the Ottoman Empire, the abrogation of its former treaties, the striking of separate deals with France and England, the signing of new political and economic treaties, and generally the turning of the tables on the Greek ally and its expeditionary forces in Asia Minor. This culminated in the events leading to the Asia Minor Catastrophe.[28]

5. **Slaughter of Orthodox populations.** This must be understood as a fairly generic prophecy that applies to several peoples and distinct nations at the same time. First of all, once Atatürk consolidated his position, he began slaughtering the Greek civilian populations of Asia Minor and Eastern Thrace. He resumed the slaughtering of the Armenians who were still remaining in Asia Minor. These events transpired around 1922 A.D. At the same time, the peoples of the Russian empire (predominantly Orthodox populations also, like the Greeks and the Armenians) are not faring too well under the atheist communist regime which moved into the Kremlin. This was the time that the Bolsheviks declared a wholesale war against the Church.

Some background material will help clarify these points. Following the Bolshevik attempt to power, a civil war erupted in Russia. In the course of this civil war the food production in the Western parts came to a halt, and the grain districts in the East could not suffice for all the needs. To make matters worse, a drought came upon the empire in 1920-1921. This resulted in an unprecedented famine lasting from the summer of 1921 to the summer of 1922. The saintly Patriarch Tikhon appealed to the heads of the Christian Churches outside Russia to come to the rescue of his people.

Collections for the starving were also taken in every church, on the initiative of the Church, which had established a national ecclesiastical committee for this purpose. The government, hating such competition, ordered the committee disbanded and took all the collections to be administered by the government-run Famine Relief Committee.

On February 19, 1922, Patriarch Tikhon appealed to the parochial

---

[28] *Our Revelationary Age...* provides a detailed analysis of those events, some of which were predicted in the Book of Revelation, as well.

councils to offer all items of value still to be found within the churches for the alleviation of hunger, explicitly excepting all those items necessary for the religious needs of the church, namely, for the Holy Eucharist and the other sacraments. The government insisted that all the sacramental objects must be handed over, as well. The Patriarch refused to part with the most indispensable items for the needs of the Church services. To cut a long story short, the government exploited the resistance of the Church and began a campaign of propaganda, disinformation and misrepresentation of the facts in order to brand the Church as an inhuman institution insensitive to human suffering. The Patriarch was arrested on May 10, 1922. Under the above pretense of unwillingness to sanction the confiscation of all valuable Church property, thousands of clergymen lost their lives. Only for the period between 1921-1923, we have information of the 'liquidation' of 2,691 married priests, 1,962 monks, and 3,447 nuns, for whom personal data had been available. The number of lay persons who remained loyal to the Patriarch and perished as a result, remains unknown to this day.[29]

The only point I wish to make with this historical overview is that the persecution and slaughter of Orthodox Greeks and Armenians coincided with the beginning of the holocaust of the Orthodox populations of the Russian empire, now under the grip of the Bolsheviks. In this sense, it is interesting to note item 6 on our prophetic list.

6. **Furthermore, great anxiety among Orthodox populations.** Because, again, this was only the preamble and the beginning of more persecutions and sufferings to come in the 1930s. By then

---

[29] This was the brave new world which turned John Reed and Armand Hammer millionaires over a short period of time. In 1995 the Yale University Press announced the publication of *The Secret World of American Communism* and *Stalin's Letters to Molotov, 1925-1936*. These documents have great revelations to offer. For instance, how Armand Hammer helped launder money for the Soviet Government and in the process received valuable Russian treasures for his 'art gallery' in New York City that had been stolen from churches and private collections. Ditto, for the glamorized Journalist John Reed, the founder of the US Communist Party, who was paid by the Bolsheviks the non-trivial amount of 1 million US dollars (at 1920s prices) for his truth promoting services... (See also, Roger Kimball, The Wall Street Journal, April 11, 1995, p. A3).

Stalin was well established and the campaigns to eradicate even the name of God had been inserted as part and parcel of the 5-year-plan.[30]

7.   **Invasion of foreign troops through the Adriatic sea; Woe to the inhabitants of the Earth; Hades is ready.** This, I believe, brings us up to the preparations for WWII. The invasion from the Adriatic is referring to the attempt by Italian Dictator Benito Mussolini to establish a puppet state in Albania, as part and parcel of his empire-building schemes. 'Woe to the inhabitants of the earth', indeed, because these events usher WWII.

8.   **For a moment the Son of Agar appears to be great.** I believe that this sentence refers to the sudden ascension to political power and clout of the Arab nations, owners of the oil so important for the war effort of the Western democracies. Here the Son of Agar applies to the Arabs proper, considering that Turkey remained neutral in WWII.

9.   **New European War.** 1939 - 1945 A.D.

10.   **Union of Orthodox Populations with Germany.** I believe the alliance of Rumania with Germany is referred to, here. The Orthodox populations in the remainder of the Peninsula of Haemus were not, strictly speaking, united with Germany, although they became occupied. One may wish to consider here the Ukrainians and other Eastern Slavic groups who saw in Hitler's invasion their great chance to break the yoke of Communism. Assessing that a German victory would eliminate Stalin and his regime from power they preferred to side with the Germans when they invaded their lands rather than perpetuate their slavery under the Soviets. This is not the place to debate the pros and cons of those issues (which, by the way, have

---

[30] The Orthodox populations of the former Russian empire began to breath again as Christians only when Hitler invaded the USSR and Stalin realized how indispensable was the cooperation of the Church for winning the war. Not only did he allow the churches to be opened again, but even the czarist flags were permitted to fly whenever the Russians charged in battle. The history of the Russian Church under the Soviet Regime is a most fascinating subject and many are the books covering that period. Many more will become available now that freedom of information is established in the lands of the former USSR.

not yet been given the attention they deserve by Western analysts). But I find it remarkable that the anonymous prophet almost 900 years ago could be so specific on the fate of the Orthodox populations of Eastern and Southern Europe, during WWII.

11. **Defeat of the French by the Germans.** This again refers to the invasion of France by Germany and the occupation of half its territory by Nazi forces, while the rest of the country was under the Vichy Government, which was 'very tolerant' of the status quo in Paris. This prophecy reaches to 1944 with the Normandy invasion and the re-capture of France by allied troops and French partisan forces.

12. **Revolution in India and its separation from England.** India achieved its independence in 1947.

13. **England to the Saxons only.** Here we should include many historical events following India's independence and stretching to our proximate future. We should begin with the events which brought about the dissolution of the British Empire, especially the wars of independence in several of the former colonies, a process completed several years after the Revolution of India. (For instance Pakistan became independent in 1950 and several African colonies and protectorates followed suit, such as Nasser's coup and the nationalization of the Suez Canal). The prophecy in this sentence refers to future events also, because this tiny sentence, 'England to the Saxons only', marks a long period which began in 1945 and will end with the events of WWIII, proper.

'England', as we know it, is a term used frequently and inappropriately as synonymous with the British Isles. But the Angles (whence Anglia, England) were a Germanic people like the Saxons and the Jutes. The indigenous peoples had originated in France, (the Gaulic Celts) who had crossed the Channel about 400 B.C. They were the Britons who were romanized by the time of the German invasions. The Picts in the North, (the area of Scotland) received that name because they painted their body for a purpose: with their pictorially emphasized outer appearance they scared their Roman enemies, who called them Picti.

After the invasions from Germany the local Celts retreated into

Cornwall (and became the Cornish) and Wales (becoming the Welsh). The Welsh and Breton languages came from the Brythonic Celtic tongue which is related to Gaulish. Ireland was occupied by Iberian Celts, primarily, before the invasion by Englishmen. Although the French area of Brittany (Bretagne) would be associated with the homeland of the original Celts who settled in the British Isles, William the Conqueror was a Norman. A Norman was a left-over on French soil of the Norse Men, namely men of Germanic and Scandinavian origin, not Celts. These considerations become useful when studying the prophecies of the Irish, the Scots and the Welsh (especially those written in their own languages) to the effect that one day their lands will become liberated from the English and they, the indigenous populations, will become eventually again the owners of their ancestral lands.[31] It is precisely for such reasons that I believe that 'England to the Saxons only' will materialize in the course of WWIII and its aftermath.

Last and not least, since the dissolution of the British Empire, there is a great number of Muslim Pakistanis who settled in Britain under the immigration provisions of the British Commonwealth of Nations. Those Muslims are a source of political and civilian tension and things in the proximate future can only get worse. Since at the end of WWIII there will remain no Muslim living on European soil (as per several prophecies) *England to the Saxons only* assumes yet another, this time ethnological and religious dimension.

14. **Victory of Orthodox peoples and general slaughter of the sons of Agar by the Orthodox.** This is a part of the prophecy that also awaits materialization, and hence becomes of greater relevance for the purposes of our study. Item (14) is consistent with everything else treated in this book concerning the great conflict to arise between the lands of Islam, on the one hand, and the lands of Christianity and Israel on the other. Although the entire prophecy seems to have a slant towards the fate of the Orthodox populations and Christians by extension (since it was written in Greek, obviously by a Greek, although an anonymous one), one cannot exclude, on this basis only, other relevant considerations, such as the fate of the

---

[31] See for instance, M. E. Griffiths [1937], several prophecies by Irish Saints, and numerous English sources.

Jews and their alliance with the lands of Christianity. We shall not expand any further upon paragraph (14), but when the additional data are collected and analyzed and the internal consistencies established, we shall return to it again.

15. **Anxiety in the world.** We may notice here the reference to the **world**, i.e., the anxiety will envelope the entire global population rather than Christians specifically or more narrowly defined the Orthodox populations only. This discrepancy in the terminology is not fortuitous. Consequently, this is implying the generalization of the conflict and the many evils it will bring along, which will be encompassing the globe. But also, this connects very tightly to the next sentence:

16. **General despair upon the earth.** Again, the term *earth* is being selected to convey the essence of the universality of the despair (which, furthermore, is **general**). It is my belief that the general despair upon the earth is the anticipation of the catastrophes that will be heaped upon the belligerent humanity by the approaching visitor from outer space and its consequences, along with other God-sent catastrophes.

17. **Battle of seven nations in Constantinople. Three days- and three nights-long slaughter. Victory of the greatest nation against the six nations.** We are informed of a great battle in Constantinople in the course of the war, which temporally is being placed after the 'general despair', i.e., after the comet's effects. On the other hand, paragraph 14 above, indicates that the beginning of the war will precede the despair, and will involve Orthodox peoples fighting victoriously against Muslim armies, at least till then. The specific belligerent nations are not identified but we know their number. Also, I wish to draw the reader's attention to a potential linguistic trap in the present case: the Greek terms μεγαλυτέρου κράτους can be translated as the greatest of the states, the greatest of the powers, the biggest state, the most populous state. We cannot be perfectly certain what the prophet intended, the best version must be derived from the overall context. Also,

18. **Alliance of six nations against the seventh nation, slaughter lasting three days- and three nights-long.** All we can say by the joint analysis of paragraphs 17 and 18 is that the nations that were

245

originally being beaten will regroup. Yet, we still do not know the composition of this alliance, nor who will be the victor of this last battle. Such information will become available by means of the simultaneous analysis of other prophecies relating to the same period and the same general events. Maybe the battle will be terminated before a final victor is identified, by the events following in the next paragraph:

19.   **Cessation of the war through the intervention of an angel and delivery of the city to the Greeks.** This is in full agreement with the rest of the prophetic texts of our study. Notice the intervention of an angel. It will be the hand of God that will put an end to the conflict, through the occurrence of extraordinary events. (Could this last mentioned battle in Constantinople be between the forces of the Christian coalition on who is the legitimate conqueror of Constantinople? I am willing to speculate that there will be a disagreement on who is the lawful owner thereof. Therefore, the Angel's intervention will frustrate the further unnecessary spilling of brotherly blood, once God's chosen ruler has been manifested to the people). The Catholic prophecies are consistent with the Orthodox sources when dealing with the workings of the intervention of this agent from above. Both Catholics and Orthodox speak explicitly of Archangel Michael. Archangel Michael is also watching over Israel!

Hence, the angel not mentioned by the anonymous prophet may refer to St. Michael. Now, many Catholic prophecies speak of the Great Monarch establishing his empire with capital in Constantinople. The Great Monarch has been identified as Juan Carlos I de Borbón; His brother-in-law is King Constantine of the Hellenes; consequently, it becomes easy to see how this prophecy can be consistent with the Catholic prophecies, when analyzed properly. Note that the King of Spain is a Catholic and the brother of Queen Sophia, Constantine of the Hellenes, is an Orthodox. The city will be delivered to the Greeks, proper, via King Constantine (and his sons), and Queen Sophia (and her son, Prince Felipe), along and the other members of both royal families. The Hellenic Royal family will be re-established in Greece, while King Juan Carlos will lead the **empire**, not the **kingdom**, from Constantinople.

20.   **Deferring of the Latins to the error-free faith of the Orthodox.** This is a rather 'tricky' sentence that might raise a few eyebrows,

therefore it needs a much lengthier analysis: Many Catholic prophecies speak of the victory of the 'true Catholic Faith', while the Orthodox prophecies, although they agree on everything else, predict a victory of the 'true Orthodox faith'. Is there any serious contradiction present that would render the rest of the prophetic texts questionable? Hardly. Both Catholic seers and Orthodox seers are correct and both say the truth. Let us see why:

When Catholics prophets and prophetesses predict victory of the true Catholic faith they do not mean the present-state-of-affairs Roman Catholic Church, which, in the words of many Catholics (both prophets and commoners) is in a sorry state.[32]

True Catholic Faith is not synonymous with the RCC, as the terms 'the true Orthodox Faith' is not to be understood always as a tautology to the Orthodox Church, as a religious organization. Both Catholic and Orthodox seers speak of a great Ecumenical Council of the church to take place within this same time frame of wars and tribulations. A few Catholic 'interpreters of prophecies', have jumped to the remarkable conclusion that only Catholic priesthood will partake of the deliberations of such a council. In such a case, of course, the council could not be called 'Ecumenical'. Those interpreters (who apparently speak no foreign languages and never entered an Orthodox church in their entire life or read anything authored by an Orthodox writer), reached this sweeping conclusion based exclusively on Catholic seers, most of whom were concentrating their prophetic predictions on Catholic lands and left the Orthodox ones out of explicit, detailed, consideration.

So, when we speak of the future Council, **it is bound to be Ecumenical, which in the jargon of the Greek prophecies has nothing to do with the current term of 'ecumenism' but rather indicates a council incorporating all Christians (i.e., all Christian denominations).** In this Council, (which in the Greek prophecies is correctly identified as the 8th Ecumenical Council), only the worthy clergymen will be present. Since the evil priests will be already dead, or otherwise excluded, (as several Catholic Prophecies also

---

[32] Pope John Paul II, while on a trip to Germany in the 1980s categorically stated that the Roman Church cannot be reformed in its current state.

have indicated), the good remaining priests, being persons of great holiness and good will, shall be able to bring their differences and complaints out in the open, debate them fully in the best theological tradition and smooth out all their differences. Both Churches recite a Credo/Symbol of Faith that believes in one, Holy, Catholic, and Apostolic Church.

Since all the errors associated with individual theological positions will be clarified and those found to be heretical and erroneous will be eventually abandoned, there will come **a true re-unification of the Christian Churches**. There will be no differences between Orthodox and Catholics then; everybody was an Orthodox and a Catholic during the Apostolic age, and also there were no splinter groups of Catholicism **Protesting against Rome**. Therefore, the Western Church will also be so purified and will return to its pristine condition; consequently, the Protestants will have nothing more to protest against. Therefore, they will return to the one Holy Catholic and Apostolic Church of their own free will.

This Holy Catholic and Apostolic Church is not going to be Roman Catholic, but rather Catholic in the sense of Universal, (which, after all, is the etymology of the Greek word 'Catholic').

Finally, let us take a moment and contemplate the exact chronological sequencing in the prophecy of the Anonymous author. The paragraph we just finished is obviously the one referring to the calling of the Ecumenical Council no. 8, namely, it follows the **cessation of the war through the intervention of the angel,** and precedes the paragraph of **the evangelizing of non-Christians after the re-unification of the Christian Churches.**

21.   **The Orthodox Faith will expand from the East to the West.**
Again, the Orthodox Faith, not the Orthodox Church. This will be the true Christian faith, (true=orthodox in Greek), the one and only Christian faith re-formulated after the Eighth Ecumenical Council, which will bring the religion to the beliefs and precepts of the Apostolic Age, and which will now be preached in all nations. Being raised in the Orthodox church, I have to say, however, without a trace of chauvinism, that since the Orthodox Church has kept the religion of the Apostolic times most faithfully, it will have to make the least number of concessions in the Ecumenical Council. Professor

Nikita Struve, the editor of the Viestnik has summarized the Orthodox position on this issue succinctly:[33]

The Orthodox Church (and those most closely associated with it among the Pre-Chalcedonean Council churches) can look with confidence into the 21st century: They have not added superfluous and extraneous material (like the R.C.C. has done over the centuries) nor subtracted valuable truths (like the Protestant Churches since the Reformation, when they began eliminating so much substantive matter and introduce innovations over the faith of the apostolic times).

Hence, it does not take a world-class genius to realize that a Church that has not brought into its theology the Papal infallibility dogma, the Jesuits, and the capital punishment against heretics, alleged witches and wealthy Jews, has in final analysis much fewer things to apologize and make reparations for. Other Christians never felt compelled to protest against Orthodoxy and branch out into eight thousand different versions of the ultimate truth as spoken by Lord Jesus Christ.

22. **Fear and Terror of the Barbarians under the True Faith.** This paragraph is consistent with Catholic and Orthodox predictors of the spread of Christianity after the defeat of the enemies of the Western alliance.

23. **Cessation of the Institution of Papism and establishment of one Patriarch for the entire continent of Europe.** The Papa Angelorum, the prophesied Catholic Pope who will be the leader of the Western Church at that time, is the self-same Papa Angelorum through whose solicitation the various Christian Churches will be united and he will preside over the Eighth Ecumenical Council. The Catholic seers speak of four holy men appointed by him, who will become very busy after the war with their apostolic efforts. The Papa Angelorum will introduce innovations such as the elimination of the Jesuits. He will be a Pope quite distinct in theory and practice from those who gave rise to the term Papism. He will delegate power for the governance of the Christian continents. This Holy Man, whom the

---

[33] *The Viestnik*, no. 171, I-II - 1995, pp. 3-4.

Greeks foresee as the Patriarch of the entire continent of Europe, is destined to be one of the four holy men assisting the 'Papa Angelorum' mentioned in the Catholic prophecies. The three other Holy Men will oversee the religious affairs of the other Continents. What is their nationality, name and specific title, has not become known to me from the prophetic sources researched so far for this study. I am confident, however, that everything will be as it ought to be, in full agreement with the will of God, and this should be more than enough for us, Christians, regardless of Denomination.

Needless to say, the Papa Angelorum is going to introduce a different institutional structure for the Western Churches. It is specifically this regeneration of the Roman Catholic Church that will convince all Orthodox to join and all Protestants to stop protesting, for, there will be nothing left to protest against! When prophecies speak so explicitly that 'Protestantism will cease' they do not mean that all Protestants will be slaughtered or forced to submission to the See of Rome in its current form. Only the ignorant and the 'self-appointed interpreters' of ill will and personal agendas can reach such ludicrous conclusions. Fyodor Dostoyevsky, the genial Russian writer and Mystic had already foreseen this beautiful moment in the life of Christianity more than a century ago. His analysis on the future of Protestantism is still a classic that touches upon pure prophecy.[34]

24.   **The end of sorrows will arrive in 55 years; on the seventh (day) nobody will remain any longer wretched, nor exiled; the exile will return in the arms of the rejoicing Mother. This is how it is going to happen and this is how we wish it come to pass. Amen, Amen, Amen. I am the Alpha and the Omega (...).** The informational content of this last paragraph is rich, indeed: First of all, the closing remarks that 'I am the Alpha and the Omega', clearly denote that it is Lord Jesus Christ Himself delivering this prophecy to us, and this is the reason why the man who penned it decided to remain anonymous. Although all genuine prophecies are possible only through the Holy Spirit and only by means of Divine Revelation,

---

[34] See in particular *'The Brothers Karamazov'*, (especially, the award-winning new translation by Richard Pevear and Larissa Volokhonsky, Vintage Books, 1991), as well as N. O. Losskii, [1994, chap. 7, and passim], among other sources.

in this case, we have Lord Jesus Christ Himself sealing the text of the prophecy.

Secondly, all exiles and persecuted men will return to the arms of the rejoicing Mother (the Church). It will be done in a way fully satisfying our highest expectations ('this is how we wish it come to pass').

Finally, we are also offered a time frame: In 55 years (from the end of the last major war, namely from 1945 more or less plus 55 years). If so, then we get yet another piece of information denoting the end of the tribulations and of WWIII, namely around the year 2000 A.D., with a few additional years to complete the process.

From a Byzantine Prophecy (studied in detail in the chapter entitled The Signs Before the End(s) the following excerpt mentions also the fate of bad clergymen following the peace of WWIII):

(After the selection of the new secular leader is effected through the intercession of angels), "the secular rulers and the priests who had offended God with their lack of piety will be forced to escape in the badly-lit, cold, and inhospitable corners of the world. The remainder will give praise to God and will live in peace."[35] (Of course, under 'priests' one must here include those of other religions, as well; for instance many militant fundamentalist Muslim mullahs who have been instrumental in fanning the fires of hatred over the years. After all, it is also the mullahs who will be bringing about WWIII, in the first place.

From an excerpt from the prophecies compiled by the Emperor Leo the Philosopher:
(While describing the characteristics of the Great Monarch and the special role he will assume after the celestial phenomena, among other things, the following instructions are given to him by the Angels:) "furthermore (he is expected to) chase the bad priests from the holy of holies of the churches,

---

[35] "(...) Πολλοὶ δὲ ἀσεβέστατοι ἄρχοντες καὶ ἱερεῖς "ἀποδράσουσιν εἰς τοὺς φεγγώδεις σελασφόρους καὶ ψυχροὺς δι᾽ αὐτοὺς τόπους καὶ στραγγαλιώδεις τῆς οἰκουμένης". Οἱ δὲ λοιποὶ πάντες δοξάσαντες τὸν Θεὸν ἠρεμήσουσιν."

while on the other hand he will be restoring the worthy and pious ones".[36]

It is no secret that the evils of the age will befall the Christian populations for their apostasy from the word of God, their lukewarm faith and their many sins. It is not laypersons only that the prophecies are addressing, but the clergy as well. Clergymen of **all Christian denominations** are explicitly mentioned. The good clergy, furthermore, do not have to wait for the invasions and the Three Days Darkness and their aftermath to begin feeling persecuted and harassed. Their tribulations have already started. The true men of God are the prime target of the Devil and his armies in our days.

Let us now cover prophetic material on Protestantism and the Protestant churches, in greater detail.

THE FUTURE FORTUNES OF THE HOUSE OF BRANDENBURG AND GERMANY BY EXTENSION

About 1300 A.D., Abbot Hermann from the Cistercian Cloister of Lehnin prepared a manuscript in Latin, which in 100 verses predicted all major political and religious events in Germany. Specifically, the Reformation, under what conditions the Reformation would be established in the land, and so on and so forth, culminating with the time when the fold will receive its Shepherd and Germany her King, and a blessed era of peace and happiness would follow.[37] In summary, the Lehnin Prophecy predicts that

---

[36] ὡσαύτως καὶ τοὺς κακοὺς ἱερεῖς ἐκ τοῦ ἱεροῦ ἐκδιῶξαι καὶ τοὺς ἀξίους εἰς τὸ δεῖον ἀποκαταστεῖσαι.

[37] The entire Latin text can be found in M. Kemmerich [1921, pp. 173-193], who also supplies a German translation and a lengthy historical commentary establishing what portion of the prophetic pronouncements had already materialized during his lifetime. The prophecy proved remarkably accurate. I feel that the last 10 verses await materialization, not only the last five as believed by Dr. Kemmerich who wrote his study in the beginning of this century (and confused the era of peace to begin after WWI with the prophesied one after WWIII. Dr. Kemmerich did not live long enough to see WWII coming, hence he did not have the benefit of so many additional years of accumulated experience and hindsight.

M. Kemmerich has been one of the most thorough researchers I had the privilege of studying in the course of this study. He was alert enough to notice that the antiquity of the source of Lehnin's prophecy and the inability to historically identify

Protestantism will disappear from Germany when a new King becomes established after a war.[38]

ON PROTESTANTISM AND LUTHER

Henry James Forman, [1936, pp. 122-123] relates how in Nüremberg, a famed astrologer by the name of Cardan, or Cardanus, who had boldly and correctly predicted death by hanging for the Archbishop of St. Andrews, published a book in 1543 A.D. containing 67 horoscopes of noted men of all times. With regards to Martin Luther, who was alive at that time, Cardanus reported:

"Incredible is the vast number of followers which this doctrine has in a brief space achieved. Already the world is on fire with the wild struggle over this madness, which, owing to the position of Mars, must ultimately break up of itself. Countless are the heads which desire to reign in it and if nothing else could convince us of its futility, then at least the number of its diverse interpretations must convince us, since the truth is but one and all the numerous aspects must be errors. Nevertheless, the Sun and Saturn in the position of their future great conjunction indicate both the strength and the long duration of this heresy."

ST. HILDEGARD OF BINGEN ON PROTESTANTISM

Among the many visions of this German prophetess, who, even as a child 'saw future things as if they were present', was the coming of Protestantism. She began writing down her prophecies ca. 1138 A.D., namely a few

---

Abbot Hermann could be used as an excuse to discredit the text. However, the proof of the prophecy is in its predictive ability. Considering that we have successfully dealt with 'anonymous' prophets before, we should feel encouraged to proceed without being intimidated by our intellectual enemies. Furthermore, by supplementing such material by numerous other sources for which **we happen to know** the personage of the prophets, potential discreditors will become dissuaded. Last and not least, most of the prophecy of Lehnin is already History and first class history, at that.

[38] Let us be reminded of yet another mention of the Eighth Ecumenical Council that will be convened at the end of WWIII: In the prophecies made by the 'Ecstatic of Tours' in 1872 and 1873 (treated in a separate chapter), we were told that *The Council will meet again after the victory.*

hundred years ahead of time.[39]

FROM THE PROPHECIES OF IERONYMOUS AGATHANGELOS[40]

The following is new material of the long prophecy introduced earlier in this chapter. It concerns the rise of Luther, the Protestant movement and the ultimate return of Germany to the true faith of the Apostolic era. Let us remember that the entire prophecy of Agathangelos was written in 1279 A.D., in other words much before the Reformation.

But, you Germany, be informed that one of your sons of the same blood turns against you, casts away in abhorrence the Latin dogma and becomes the Head of the Heretics. I see your friends dispossessed, introducing so many novel heresies as there are shades on the wings of the white swan. I see the religious holidays pushed aside, the faith crippled and limping, your Church without a leader, like a tiny vessel without a rudder and a captain, and your faith without (spiritual) foundations. Terrible is the corpse, oh God! But you, son of man, you do have reason to feel amazed, because it is precisely from this very heretical Germany, and through her doings that the truth and the veritable worship of the Orthodox faith will be extolled at some future time. It is precisely Germany which, more than any other race, will support most firmly the Apostolic truth. The Eastern dogma will shine through Germany.

Commentary
One must find rather intriguing his comparing the variety of the novel heresies with the wings of a swan: while Jan Hus, the Czech scholar and university lecturer, condemned for heresy by the Council of Constance was dying at the stake in 1415 A.D., he uttered the following prophetic wordplay: *You may burn a goose today, but soon a swan will arise whom you shall be*

---

[39] St. Hildegard has been a very prolific writer. Her prophecies continue way beyond the end of WWIII and the era of peace of the Great Monarch. She has written many predictions of military events and natural catastrophes which will coincide with the Antichrist times, as well. For this reason, it is possible that some of her prophecies have been erroneously attributed to the wrong time period. Since there are many books available with her prophecies we shall not replicate their text here, for reasons of space and time. We shall only cover only a few sentences from various prophecies of hers as they seem to tie up most intrinsically with the specific subjects covered in our study.

[40] See also Neilos Sotiropoulos, [op. cit. pp. 95-96].

unable to burn. ('Hus' is the word for a goose in Czech). This swan was Luther who admitted deriving much of his inspiration from the writings of Jan Hus, written more than a 100 years earlier. Agathangelos, on the other hand, might only have wished to speak of the nearly eight thousand different sub-groups which sprang out of the Reformation eventually.

We also cannot fail to notice that Agathangelos's assessment of the overall consequences of the Reformation is rather sober. He predicts that a German once again (or a number of Germans) will do much for returning the true faith back to its ancient purity. This could be a reference to the Papa Angelorum who (besides Italian) may also have German blood in his veins. Or, it may be a reference to the Great Monarch, considering that King Juan Carlos I and his offspring issue also from Charlemagne, the Great Emperor of the Holy Roman Empire of the German Nation of old. A certain prophecy even suggests that a grave man will come from Aquisgranum (Aachen).[41]

Agathangelos looks upon this man with great delight, for, he will support the Apostolic faith. Since the Orthodox Church have kept intact the teaching of the Apostolic Faith it is natural for an Orthodox prophet to associate such event with the *truth and the veritable worship of the Orthodox faith.* Consequently, if the German renovator applies to Papa Angelorum, he will be accepted by everybody as the ideal Church leader, because his efforts of purifying the Church of all its errors will bring it back to the true faith, namely orthodoxy.

We may also find very intriguing a short sentence injected into a purely religious string of text: *'Terrible is the corpse, oh God!'.* This could indicate the great carnage of WWIII, losses through plagues and other causes, which, all taken together, would inflict a horrendous depopulation upon Germany, a theme present in many other prophecies either by German Catholics, or by other European Catholics.

---

[41] Both the family of the Great Monarch and the Greek royal family have additional blood ties with German royal houses. Consequently, both King Juan Carlos I and Prince Felipe can be understood and accepted as emanating from Germany, also, Prince Felipe more so than his father, considering the German ties from both parents. However, the reference may be to a purely religious figure and not a political one.

A definitive set of events culminating to the ceasing of Protestantism, however, will be directly connected with the role of the Most Blessed Virgin Mary Theotokos. And the reasons are obvious enough: The Most Blessed Virgin will interfere directly in our affairs during the war as She is now interfering through apparitions, admonitions, advice and miracles. The overwhelming evidence of Her grace will not continue being ignored, unnoticed and discounted by Protestant clergymen who are unwilling to reconsider their intellectual positions (and risk market share) in view of such overwhelming evidence. But the Protestant faithful will not fail noticing the presence and the power and the grace emanating from the First among the Saints.

Having experienced first hand the powers of Her direct intervention, it will be impossible for the Protestants alive at that time to continue disregarding hard evidence in order to prop up their erroneous dogmatic positions in Her regard. Considering that 'facts are obstinate things', either the sum total of Orthodox plus Catholics who persist in the veneration of the Holy Virgin with great devotion are gullible morons, or the Protestant are merely misguided in their theorizing with regards to Her. (A 'superstition' that persists in the past 2000 years among the majority of the Christians without sign of abating surely deserves a second look and a more methodical scrutiny. This subject being of tremendous vital importance to our personal future, a separate chapter will be dedicated to its coverage.

A few final remarks:
The Eastern Church recognizes only seven councils so far, as truly ecumenical. Several subsequent councils within the Roman Catholic Church have not been accepted as 'ecumenical' by either the Orthodox or the Protestant churches, for that matter, therefore, it is no matter of wonder that they are not counted as such, by the prophets, either. Therefore, so far we can count as 'ecumenical' only those in which all Christian churches then in existence participated. Their findings are binding. Other innovations either by the Vatican or the Reformation are not acceptable to the Eastern Churches. The prophesied Eighth Ecumenical Council, therefore, is going to be an event of tremendous importance for all Christians. Since, theologically speaking, the Orthodox and the Catholics are not departing very much from each other, their prophets are correct when they speak of the triumph of either the 'Catholic Church', 'Orthodoxy', or 'The true Church'. These semantic discrepancies will melt and disappear in the atmosphere of good-will, reconciliation and true Christian spirit which will prevail in the 8th Ecumenical Council. The Papa Angelorum, although a Western European

by origin, and while preserving a Roman title, will have his theology anchored in the teachings of the Apostolic Fathers and the Tradition. These are precisely most closely associated with the Eastern Churches. Consequently, the Papa Angelorum will be both a Catholic and an Orthodox, at the same time.

REVIEW OF THE MOST SALIENT POINTS

a)   The predominantly Eastern sources of prophetic evidence treated in this chapter allow us to accept with greater confidence data from elsewhere. Great consistency obtains, while additional details are offered to improve upon our overall understanding and help us complete the picture.

b)   We have many new data corroborating the evidence supplied in *Our Revelationary Age...* Accordingly, Juan Carlos I de Borbón y Borbón, King of Spain **is** the Great Monarch of the Prophecies.

c)   Russia will be very instrumental in the victory in WWIII against the Turkic populations in particular. The Great Monarch and the allied nations under his command will fight the Arabs and their Muslim allies. (There is no special mention of the USA in Byzantine era prophecies for the reason that America was not discovered yet. The prophets had to use periphrastic terms, such as the Sibylline reference to 'a King of Rome and the leaders of the West'; or speak in general terms under the King of the Romans and the Greeks, where 'Romans' includes not only Western European Christians but also American Christians of Western European origin.

d)   The Re-unification of the Christian churches will be effected in the Eighth Ecumenical Council.

e)   Those who will survive the perils of the age are promised a most blissful existence.

CHAPTER NINE

PROPHECIES ON THE CHRISTIAN RELIGION

> *and to wait for His Son from heaven, whom He raised from the dead, that is Jesus, who is going to deliver us from the wrath to come.* (1 Thes. 1:10).

> *Of the times and seasons, brethren, you need not, that we should write to you; for yourselves know perfectly, that the day of the lord shall so come, as a thief in the night. For when they shall say, peace and security, then shall sudden destruction come upon them, as the pains upon her that is with child and they shall not escape.* (1 Thes. 5:1-3).

Introduction
In this short chapter we shall primarily present prophetic evidence covering the fate of the Christian churches in general during the coming great tribulations. Once again, we take the liberty of emphasizing certain passages of the original texts.

From a message given by Lord Jesus Christ at Heede, Germany:[1]
This generation deserves to be annihilated, but I desire to show Myself as merciful. Great and terrible things are being prepared. That which is about to happen will be terrible, like nothing ever seen since the beginning of the world.[2]

From a private revelation given by Lord Jesus Christ to Julka, one of the children associated with the Medjugorje apparitions of the Most Blessed Virgin Mary:
(...) As you have seen, so it will be. I shall come quickly and in splendor. All My creatures who survive the great tribulation, will see Me.

---

[1] published in "Charlas de Actualidad", S.a.r. Ediciones ERSA, Madrid, Spain, in 1955.

[2] Quoted also in Al. Hebert's, *The Three Days Darkness*, p. 11.

No one will then be able to say that I do not exist, because I shall be near the earth; and all the creatures of the earth will hear My Voice. They will see Me present then, and, for a second time at the Final Judgment.

Old Italian Prophecy (date unknown):
When the White Pope and the Black Pope shall die during the same night, then there will dawn upon the Christian nations the Great White Day.[3] Woe unto the City of Philosophers, woe unto Lombardy for thy towers of joy shall be broken down; all the tyrants shall be put out of God's church, and there shall occur a general conversion to the faith of Christ under the Great Lion.

Venerable Anne Catherine Emmerich (1774-1824 A.D.):[4]
(From the very voluminous accounts of her visions, the following excerpts are taken):

I wish the time were here when the Pope dressed in red will reign. I see the Apostles, not those of the past, but the apostles of the last times, and it seems to me, the Pope is among them.
I was likewise told, if I remember right, that he (Satan) will be unchained for a time fifty or sixty years before the year of Christ 2000.

---

[3] This may indicate that the Pope and the head of the Jesuits will die in the same night.

[4] She was known in her day as "the Seer of Dülmen", had many visions and messages from her guardian angel as well as from Lord Jesus Christ and the Virgin Mary. For more than a dozen years she subsisted on water and the Holy Eucharist only, (a feat also shared by certain Orthodox saints and hermits). She bore the stigmata of Lord Jesus Christ. Her body when exhumed was found to be free of corruption and odor, (another common feature shared by saintly men and women elsewhere). Her visions were not accepted by the Vatican for a long time. She was officially rehabilitated by the R.C.C. in the Spring of 1989 A.D.

As Kenneth L. Woodward [1990], shows, much of what was originally attributed to Emmerich has been the 'conscious elaboration of an overwrought Romantic poet', Clemens Brentano (1778-1842), who held numerous conversations with her and wrote down the content thereof, with much embellishment of his own, as was later found out. After much research, however, the relatively few pieces of paper that could be safely attributed to her own words were accepted by the Church which removed the original ban against her cause for beatification.

259

A pale faced man floated slowly over the earth and, loosening the cloths, which wrapped his sword, he threw them on sleeping cities, which were bound by them. This figure also dropped pestilence on Russia, Italy, and Spain. A red noose lay around Berlin, and from there it came to Westphalia. Now the man's sword was naked, bands red as blood hung from its hilt and blood trickled from it on Westphalia. (...)

(...) I saw how baleful would be the consequences of this false church. I saw it increase in size; heretics of every kind came into the city of Rome. The local clergy grew lukewarm, and I saw a great darkness... Then the vision seemed to extend on every side. (...) I saw many churches close down; great miseries everywhere, wars and bloodshed. (...) Once more I saw that the Church of Peter was undermined by a plan evolved by the secret sect, while storms were damaging it. (...) I saw a Pope who was at once gentle, but very firm... I saw a great renewal, and the Church rose high in the sky.

(...) I saw a strange church being built against every rule. No angels were supervising the building operations. In that church, nothing came from high above... There was only division and chaos. (...) I saw again the strange big church that was being built there (in Rome). There was nothing holy in it. I saw this just as I saw a movement led by Ecclesiastics to which contributed angels, saints and other Christians. (...)

(...) I see the Holy Father in great anguish. He lives in a palace other than before and he admits only a limited number of friends near him. (...) I see that the false church of darkness is making progress, and I see the dreadful influence it has on people. The Holy Father and the Church are verily in so great distress that one must implore God day and night. (...)

(...) I saw deplorable things; they were gambling, drinking, and talking in church; they were also courting women. All sorts of abominations were perpetrated there. Priests allowed everything and said Mass with much irreverence. I saw that few of them were still godly, and only a few had sound views on things. (...)

(...) As we were going through Rome (...) we finally reached the Pope. He was sitting in the dark and slept in a large arm-chair. (...) The ecclesiastics in the inner circle looked insincere and lacking in zeal; I did not like them. I told the Pope and the bishops who are to be appointed soon, I told him also that he must not leave Rome. If he did so, it would be chaos. He thought that the evil was inevitable and that he should leave in order to save many things beside himself. He was very much inclined to leave Rome, and he was insistently urged to do so. The Pope is still attached to the things of this earth in many ways. The Church is completely isolated and as if completely deserted. It seems that everyone is running away. Everywhere I see great misery, hatred, treason, rancor, confusion, and an utter blindness.

(...) Among the strangest things that I saw, were long processions of bishops. Their thoughts and utterances were made known to me through images issuing from their mouths. Their faults towards religion were shown by external deformities. A few had only a body, with a dark cloud of fog instead of a head. Others had only a head, their bodies and hearts were like thick vapors. Some were lame; others were paralytics; others were asleep or staggering. (...)

(...) Then, I saw that everything that pertained to Protestantism was gradually gaining the upper hand, and the Catholic faith fell into complete decadence. Most priests were lured by the glittering but false knowledge of your school-teachers, and they all contributed to the work of destruction. In those days, Faith will fall very low, and it will be preserved in some places only, in a few cottages and in a few families which God has protected from disasters and wars.

(...) I had another vision of the great tribulation. It seems to me that a concession was demanded from the clergy which could not be granted. I saw many older priests, especially one, who wept bitterly. A few younger ones were also weeping. But others, and the lukewarm among them, readily did what was demanded. It was as if people were splitting into two camps. (...)

(...) I saw that many pastors allowed themselves to be taken up with ideas that were dangerous to the Church. They were building a great, strange, and extravagant Church. Everyone was to be admitted in it in order to be united and have equal rights: Evangelicals, Catholics, sects of every description. Such was to be the new Church... But God had other designs.[5]

---

[5] It is my belief that this last paragraph may apply to Ecumenism, an idea the Orthodox Churches have been opposed to.

<u>Additional Commentary</u>
Venerable Emmerich provides a most extensive testimony on the internal problems facing the Roman Catholic Church today. The interested reader may wish to consult more detailed sources of her prophecies. An additional item of great interest to our study is that she saw in a vision **the Blessed Virgin ascend on the Church and spread Her mantle over it.** Furthermore, in her vision dated January 27, 1822, Emmerich reports: *I saw a new Pope who will be very strict. He will estrange from him the cold and lukewarm bishops. He is not a Roman, but he is Italian. He comes from a place which is not very far from Rome, and I think he comes from a devout family of royal blood. But there must still be for a while much fighting and unrest.* This, I believe, refers to the Papa Angelorum, who has been also called the Venerable Old man of Lazio.

St. Senanus:[6]
(...) The clergy of the holy church will be addicted to pride and injustice; the advantages they will aim at shall be possession of worldly substance. (...) All will rush into iniquity against the will of the Son of the Blessed Virgin Mary. The earth will not produce its fruits for the race of people to whom I allude; (...) Dreadful plagues will come upon all the race of Adam.(...)

St. Columbkille:[7]
(...) The clergy shall be led into error by the misinterpretation of their readings; the relics of the saints will be considered powerless, every race of mankind will become wicked! (...)

Nicholas of Flue (1417-1487):[8]

---

[6] He died ca. 544 A.D. He was an Irish abbot, founder of monasteries. His prophecies have covered more events and we shall see him again in a different chapter covering prophecies on England.

[7] St. Columba (Colum-cille) of Iona, abbot, born at Gartan, Donegal, ca. 521 A.D., He died in the church before Matins in 597 A.D.

[8] Nicholas of Flue, hermit and Patron Saint of Switzerland, born at Flueli (Unterwalden) canonized in 1947. In 1467, after years of prayer and the experience of visions and revelations, with his wife's consent he abandoned his positions and his family (10 children born to their marriage) and became a hermit near Strasbourg. He spent his subsequent years in saintly contemplation, advising religious and lay visitors; he later became instrumental in the lasting political

The Church will be punished because the majority of Her members - high and low- will become so perverted.

Sister Marianne Gaultier (died 1804):
(...) Before the great combat the wicked shall be masters. They will perpetrate all the evils in their power, but not as much as they desire, because they shall not have the time. Good and faithful Catholics, less in number, shall be on the point of being annihilated, **but a stroke from Heaven will save them**.

O power of God! O power of God! All the wicked shall perish, and also many good men. O, how frightful shall these calamities be! The churches shall be closed, but only for the space of twenty-four hours. Religious women, being terrified, shall be on the point of abandoning the convent, but they shall remain. At this time such extraordinary events shall take place that the most incredulous will be forced to say, 'the finger of God is there'. O power of God! **There shall be a terrible night, during which no one shall be able to sleep. These trials shall not last long, because no person could endure them**. When all shall appear lost, all will be saved. It is then that dispatches shall arrive, announcing good news, when the *Te Deum* shall be sung, in a manner in which it has never been heard before. It is then that the Prince shall reign, whom people will seek, that before did not esteem him. At that time the triumph of religion will be so great that no one has ever seen the equal. All injustices will be repaired, civil laws will be formed in harmony with the laws of God and of the Church. The instruction given to children will be most Christian; pious guilds for workmen shall be reestablished; the triumph of the Church and of France shall be most glorious.

Bishop George Michael Wittman (died 1833):
'Woe is me! The Passion of Jesus will be renewed in the most dolorous manner in the Church and in her Supreme Head. In all parts of the world there will be wars and revolutions and much blood will be spilled. Distress, disasters and poverty will everywhere be great, since pestilential maladies, scarcity, and other misfortunes will follow one another.

Violent hands will be laid on the Supreme Head of the Catholic Church;

---

achievement of Swiss national unity. He was also reputed of never needing food or drink.

bishops and priests will be persecuted, and schisms will be provoked, and confusion will reign amid all classes. Times will come, so pre-eminently bad, that it will seem as if the enemies of Christ and of His Holy Church, which He founded with His blood, were about to triumph over her. But the priesthood will remain firm and resolute, and good people will adhere faithfully to that body. A general separation will be made. **The wheat shall be winnowed, and the floor swept. Secret societies will work great ruin, and exercise a marvelous monetary power, and through that many will be blinded, and infected with most horrible errors; however, all this shall avail naught.** Christ says, He who is not with Me is against Me, and he who gathereth not with Me, scattereth. Scandals will be but too rife, and woe to those by whom they come! Although the tempests will be terrible, and will turn many in their passage, nevertheless they cannot shake the rock whereon Christ has founded His Church: "Portae inferi non prevalebunt."[9] The faithful sheep will gather together, and in unions of prayer will offer potent resistance to the enemies of the Catholic Church. Yes, yes, the flock will become small. Many of you will see those sad times and days which will bring such evil in their train; but I shall not behold them. A marvelous thing will occur, but then hell will rise in opposition against it, and terrible agitation will ensue. Great confusion will reign amid princes and nations. The incredulity of the present day is preparing those horrid evils."

Cardinal La Roque (ca. 1837):
A regeneration of Faith will appear in Asia through a descendant of Mohammed. Three nations will appear on the ocean with mighty fleets. In that time the Great Monarch will be in Europe. Devastating storms and earthquakes will frighten the inhabitants of Switzerland and remind them of their frailty. **Plagues amongst humans and beasts will accompany the earthquakes.** The sickle of death will harvest in Prussia, in palaces as well as in the houses of the poor, many will flee to England but to no avail, for even there death will overtake them. In 1938 will appear the Great Comet which will foreshadow these calamities.[10]

---

[9] The gates of Hades will not prevail over it.

[10] This 'great comet' was identified by many as a specially impressive aurora borealis visible almost throughout Europe during January of 1938. As far as foreshadowing calamities, the year 1938 was fateful enough in terms of preparations for WWII.

Blessed Gaspare del Bufalo (1786-1837):[11]
Besides foretelling the 'destruction of impenitent persecutors of the Church during the three days darkness', he added that 'he who outlives the darkness and fear of the three days will seem to him as if he were alone on earth, because of the fact that the world will be covered everywhere with carcasses'.

Blessed Maria Taigi:[12]
(...) (Before the Three Days of Darkness) religious shall be persecuted, priests shall be massacred, the churches shall be closed, but only for a short time; the Holy Father shall be obliged to abandon Rome'.

Sister Rose Asdenti of Taggia (1847):
A great revolution will spread over all of Europe and peace will not be restored until the white flower has taken possession of the throne of France.[13] Not only religious communities, but also good lay Catholics shall have their property confiscated. Many of the nobility shall be cast into prison. A lawless democratic spirit of disorder shall reign supreme throughout all Europe. There will be a general overthrow. (...) **The persecution in Italy is to begin by the suppression of the Jesuits; they shall be called back again; then a third time they will be suppressed and never more be revived.** During a frightful storm against the Church, all religious orders will be abolished except two, namely, the Capuchins and the Dominicans, together with the Hospitaliers, who shall receive the pious pilgrims, who, in great numbers, shall go to visit and venerate the many martyrs in Italy, killed during the impeding persecution. (...)

Father Bernard Maria Clausi of the Order of Friars Minor (he died in 1849 A.D.):

---

[11] He worked very effectively in reversing the wave of secularization following the Napoleonic conquest of Italy. He trained young clergy to become missionaries and founded charitable institutions in Rome where he succumbed to the cholera epidemic. Miracles associated with him were reported during his lifetime and after his death.

[12] Only the portion of her prophecies relevant to the subject of this chapter will be presented below.

[13] She refers to the fleur de lis, the white lily, symbol of the Bourbons of France and also of the Spanish Royal Family.

"Before the triumph of the Church comes, God will first take vengeance on the wicked, especially against the Godless. It will be a new Judgment, the like has never been before and it will be universal. It will be so terrible that those who outlive it will imagine that they are the only ones spared. All people will then be good and contrite. This judgment will come suddenly and be of short duration. Then comes the triumph of the holy Church and the reign of brotherly love. Happy, indeed, they who live to see those blessed days. However, before that, evil will have made such progress that it will look like all the devils of Hell were let loose on earth, so terrible will be the persecution of the wicked against the just, who will have to suffer true martyrdom."

Abbess Maria Steiner (died 1862 A.D.):
I see the Lord as he will be scourging the world, and chastising it in a fearful manner so that few men and women will remain. The monks will have to leave their monasteries, and the nuns will be driven from their convents, especially in Italy. (...) Unless people obtain pardon through their prayers, the time will come when they will see the sword and death, and Rome will be without a shepherd. The Lord showed me how beautiful the world will be after the awful chastisement. The people will be like the Christians of the primitive Church.

Mother Alphonse Eppinger (1867):
Many priests have lost their fervor for the honor of God and the salvation of souls. Their hearts hang too much on the phantoms of this life. God will, by chastisements, cure them thereof and so thereby change them. In many religious houses the spirit of poverty and simplicity is forgotten. They look only for convenience, they carry a scandalous splendor to satisfy their pride, therefore must God, through a salutary remedy, restore the true religious spirit. It is indeed a sad thing to see religious houses desecrated, but it will be necessary in order to eradicate pride and worldly luxuries and to bring all things back to simplicity. (...)[14]

---

[14] In a book entitled *La Médiacratie*, published in France by Flammarion, the author François-Henri de Virieu, a Journalist by trade, was expressing similar concerns. Analysing the attempts by the R.C.C. to re-establish a temporal power through the Mass Media (whence the title of the book) he identified the counter-productive consequences (from a theological point of view) of such attempts. "One does not announce the Gospel of the poor through the means of the rich", says he, echoing many of the prophetic verdicts against the contemporary Church.

The Ecstatic of Tours (from prophecies made in 1872 and 1873):
(...) There will be earthquakes and signs in the sun. Towards the end darkness will cover the earth. When everyone believes that peace is assured, when everyone least expects it, the great happenings will begin. Revolution will break out in Italy almost at the same time as in France. For some time, the Church will be without a Pope. England, too, will have much to suffer. [She continues with the persecution of clergy in France and specifically]: Many bishops and priests will be put to death. The Archbishop of Paris will be murdered. (...) He (the king) will ascend to the throne; he will free the Church and reassert the Pope's rights. **The Council will meet again after the victory.** (...)

Cardinal Pie of Poitiers: (died 1880 A.D.)
At no time in the history of the world have we seen such universal rebellion against God as today. All grasp weapons against Him. Never has man dissolved so entirely every covenant with God and been so completely against Him. *'Go away from us, leave us;'* that is what modern nations say. *'We don't want a God we will do all against Him and do all without Him.'* That is what the modern nations, with France in the lead, do. *'The State must be anti-cleric, atheistic, purely worldly.'* And God takes them at their word and leaves them to their defiance and self will, until they, in their madness, tear one another to pieces and cover Europe with blood and ruin. Then God will come again, though armed; then will all see that He is the Lord of the world, created by Him, out of which they tried to expel Him."

St. John (Don) Bosco (1815-1888):[15]
Now Heaven's voice is addressed to the Shepherd of shepherds. You are not in conference with your advisors. The enemy of the good does not stand idle one moment. He studies and practices all his arts against you. He will sow discord amongst your consultors; He will raise up enemies amongst My children. The powers of the world will belch forth fire, and they would that the words be suffocated in the throats of the custodians of My law. That will not happen. They will do harm - harm to themselves. You must hurry. If you cannot untie the knots, cut them. If you find yourself hard pressed do not give up but continue until the head of the hydra of error

---

[15] We met him in the previous chapter, while analyzing his predictions on Italy. Now we shall study a vision of his detailing the career of the Angelic Pope.

is cut off. This stroke will make the world and Hell beneath it tremble, but the world will be safe and all the good will rejoice. Keep your consultors always with you, even if only two. Wherever you go, continue to bring to an end the work entrusted to you. The days fly by, your years will reach the destined number; **but the great Queen will ever be your help, and as in times past so in the future She will always be the exceeding great fortress of the Church.**

It was a dark night. Men could no longer tell which way to take in order to return to their homes. Of a sudden there appeared in the heavens a very bright light that illuminated the steps of the travelers as though it were midday. At that moment there was seen a host of men and women, of young and old, of nuns, monks and priests with the Holy Father at the head. They were going out from the Vatican and were arranging themselves in line for a procession.

Then there came a furious storm which clouded that light somewhat and made it appear that light and darkness were engaged in battle. In the meantime they arrived at a little square covered with dead and wounded, some of whom cried aloud and asked for help.

Very many were dropping out of the line of procession. After having walked for a time that would correspond to two hundred rising of the sun they all realized that they were no longer in Rome. Struck with fear they all ran to the Holy Father to defend him personally and to attend his wants. Instantly two angels were seen carrying a banner, going they presented it to the Holy Father and said: 'Receive the banner of He Who fights and scatters the strongest armies of the world. Your enemies are dispersed. Your children with tears and sighs beg you to return.'

Looking at the banner one could see written on one side, **'Queen conceived without sin'**; and on the other side, **'Help of Christians'**.

The Holy Father joyfully took the banner, but looking closely at the small number of those who remained with him, he became very sad.

The two angels added: 'Go, quickly to console your children. Write your brothers dispersed throughout the world that there must be a reform in the morals of men. That cannot be obtained except by distributing to the people the bread of the Divine Word. Catechize the children. Preach the detaching of the heart from the things that are of the earth. 'The time has come,' concluded the two angels, 'when the poor shall evangelize the people. Vocations will come from among those working with the spade, the axe, and the hammer to the end that they fulfill the words of David: God has raised up the poor from the land in order to place them on the thrones of the princes of His people.'

Having heard that the Holy Father began the march. The farther he went the greater did the procession behind increase. When finally he set foot in the Holy City, he wept bitter tears for the distress in which he found the people and the large number now missing. As he entered St. Peter's he intoned the *Te Deum* to which a choir of angels replied singing: *Glory to God in the highest and on earth peace to men of good will.* With the ending of the hymn there came an end to the thick darkness and the sun shone with a brightness all its own. (...)

Père Lamy (died 1931, the current prophecy was created during WWI, and the portion given below is referring to the aftermath of WWIII):

(...) When peace has been established in the world many things will be changed. (...) The manufacture of airplanes, the exploitation of mines, iron works, all this will diminish. There will be no more of these great factories where morality suffers and dies. Workers will be obliged to go back to the land. Work on the land will receive a great impetus. (...) Industry will be reduced to smaller proportions and it will remain so. But still old workmen will insist on dying in the towns.

When peace has been restored to the world, it will be necessary to re-evangelize it, and that will be the work of a whole generation. (...) There will be many difficulties. (...) The state of the early Christians will come back again; but there will be few men on the earth then! And there will be another magnificent revival of Orders and Congregations.

Countess Francesca de Billiante (died 1935):
(...) **God will shame the professors of theology with whom he is displeased due to their pride.** He will elevate to sainthood the ignorant Brother Konrad and the unknown Brother Jordan Lai. Likewise God will cause Don Bosco to be canonized.[16] (...) I see yellow and red warriors

---

[16] This took place in 1934 A.D., as mentioned earlier, namely, several years after the above prophecy became public.

marching against Europe and Europe will be covered by a yellow fog. The cattle in the fields will die from this yellow fog. **The nations, who have risen against Christ will be destroyed by flames.** Famine will annihilate those who remain, so that Europe will be too large. In those days there will be many saints. Then the Sons of St. Francis and St. Dominic will pass through the world and lead it back to Christ. Then the Holy Father will gather the remnant in an open field under the Cross. The hooked cross will be branded on the forehead of the criminals. (...)

The Blessed Virgin: (during Her Garabandal apparitions): *Many Cardinals, many Bishops and many Priests are on the road to perdition and are taking many souls with them. Less and less importance is being given to the Eucharist.*[17]

St. Cosmas the Aetolean (1714-1779):[18]

no. 56:   A time will come that the harmony that exists today between the people and the clergy will exist no more.

no. 57   The clergymen will become the worst and the most impious of all people.

<u>A few observations from the world around us</u>

<u>From Nikolai Zernov's *Three Russian Prophets*</u>[19]
The antireligious legislation in the USSR, instituted from 1929 A.D. onwards, allowed to the faithful only one avenue for religious expression, namely the freedom to celebrate Mass in the churches. All other forms of religious activity, educational, cultural, social welfare, all these were forbidden. From an Atheist's point of view, since God does not exist, worshiping Him is the most useless and harmless of all human activities. And for this reason a

---

[17] See also, *'Pittsburgh Center for Peace' Special Edition II*, Winter 1993, p. 8).

[18] Here we include prophecies of St. Cosmas explicitly on the relationship of laypersons and the clergy. His sentences are terse and it is impossible to conclude whether the prophecies given here apply to our own times or the next great apostasy of Christianity, which will usher in the Antichrist. For this reason it is left with the reader to decide whether the prophecies do, indeed, refer to our proximate future or to the later era.

[19] [Moscow, 1995, p. 191], my translation.

godless government tolerated the Holy Eucharist. On the other hand, from a Christian's point of view, the Holy Eucharist is the most important component of his human existence; to the extent that the center of divine worship in the Russian Church is the Divine Liturgy, namely the medicine offered by God Himself for our sins and vices, this continuity of the ability to participate in the Divine Liturgy was destined to have far-reaching positive consequences for Russian Christianity.

Some recent German statistics
In 1992 the German periodical Der Spiegel published a broad survey of the religious beliefs of West Germans primarily, (considering that religious persecution in the East would have made the comparisons with East Germans not very informative). The results of the survey (especially when contrasted to a similar one of 1967) were sobering. 'West Germany has become a heathen nation with a few Christian leftovers' concluded Der Spiegel. Only 22% believe in a Virgin birth, only 38% believe in the Omnipotence of God and only 56% believe in the existence of God. All statistics exhibited a marked drop from their 1967 percentages. In summary, it appears that only 25% of the Germans consider themselves Christians and only 10% are regular churchgoers.

And as a post scriptum: Not too long ago, the British writer H. G. Wells (1866-1946), proposed the abandoning of the Christian Scriptures for the benefit of a new 'Bible' which would be composed of excerpts from the work of the following poets: William Shakespeare, Percy Shelley, Thomas Jefferson, Abraham Lincoln and Karl Marx! Now, it so happens that some of the poets on his list did not know they were poets, and some of the others were poets and quotable persons precisely because they were deeply spiritual people and derived their inspiration from those very forces which Mr. Wells wanted to discard.

One cannot fail to notice another peculiarity: All the candidates for inclusion in the New Bible came from the English speaking world, including to a certain extent Karl Marx (who spent several years in English exile and died there). The remarkable thing is that there has been a book authored by Leon Stover,[20] where some of the theories by Wells are propounded in detail; in this ideal world, needless to say, Christianity is destroyed for the

---

[20] *The Prophetic Soul: A Reading of H.G. Wells's Things to Come...*, McFarland & Company, Inc., Jefferson, North Carolina and London.

benefit of a new godless technocracy where individual freedom does not exist, and God is replaced by the divinized state.

REVIEW OF THE MOST SALIENT POINTS

a) The Three Days Darkness events are inextricably connected with the prophecies on the fortunes of the Christian Church.

b) We have seen references to the Ecumenical Council following the victory in WWIII, as well as the present state of Christianity with secret sects, secret societies and much inner disorder.

c) 'When everyone believes that peace is assured', says the prophet, the great happenings of chastisement and horror will commence. Time and again the prophets suggest that our current fervent 'peace securing' endeavors in the Balkans and elsewhere are short-lived and futile at best.

d) The beginning of our tribulations has its roots in a godless 19th century. It is interesting to note that several prophets have already identified the secularism of the 'age of scientific discovery' in France and elsewhere as the beginning of sorrows.

CHAPTER TEN

ON THE GREAT MEDIATRIX OF GRACES AND HER ROLE IN THE EVENTS OF THE AGE

The walls erected to separate the various Christian denominations are not high enough to reach Heaven.
Philaret Moskovskii, Orthodox Hierarch.[1]

Introduction
At the very beginning of this study the target audience was identified as educated laypersons who assume full responsibility for their destiny and wish to make the right use of their spiritual freedom. This chapter primarily addresses the members of the Protestant Churches. Due to some unfortunate revisions since the Reformation, this branch of Christianity has been deprived of a close relationship with the Most Holy Virgin and Her many Graces towards mankind. I would urge, therefore, the reader to carefully consider and scrutinize the evidence provided herewith before reaching any premature conclusions or discarding any evidence and/or facts presented here.

This chapter's purpose is primarily to provide information not otherwise available to the Western Christian public. As the adage goes, *knowledge is power.* Right now we are going through a very traumatic period; we shall draw strength and perseverance from the knowledge that the Most Blessed Virgin, in Her infinite love for the human race is at our side and She will use Her great powers to guide and protect us through the perils and disasters of the age.

The Roman Catholic Church, so far, has not been able to break the vicious circle of holier-than-thou *"we are the Only True Church of Jesus Christ"*, kind of message. For such a message to be more palatable to the Catholic layman, a conspiracy of silence has been imposed by its various popular presses upon anything that deals with the realities of Orthodoxy. The motto seems to be, if it is positive, ignore it. Unless it can be made to look inferior

---

[1] Quoted in Nikolai O. Losskii, [1994, p. 215].

don't bother to print it at all.

Having vilified for decades unending the martyred Christians of Russia and vicinity as heathens who are unworthy of religious self-determination because 'they collaborated with the KGB', the official organs of the R.C.C. and the majority of their popular presses have passed in silence anything that has to do with the religious realities in the other lands of Orthodoxy. Since the latter churches cannot be accused for collaborating with the KGB, the smart thing would be to pretend they do not exist or they are frozen in suspended animation in the ages of ages.

One must assume that the Orthodox communities themselves bear some of the blame for such a state of affairs because they do not react vigorously enough when such consternation-causing attitudes become manifest.[2] The final outcome of such practices is that the general public in the West, and in the USA in particular, have a most distorted view of Orthodoxy, its historical importance and its theological positions. Again, the overall neglect of historical education in our schools is to blame for such a vacuum which has been invariably filled by many a creative theory propounded by vested interest groups.

A self-instruction course appears to be the best bet for the interested Protestant reader and it promises rich rewards. He will have ample opportunity to realize that the Most Holy Virgin has been extremely active in the affairs of the faithful in the course of the last 2000 years. This is a historically established fact, chronicled by many publications in many lands and in many languages and also during the ages following the Reformation, most definitely.

Despite the impression projected by various Catholic presses, that the Virgin Mary deigns to appear only to Catholics, the truth is quite different. She has

---

[2] And if they do, they address usually their own crowd, which does not need such elucidation, in the first place. I spoke earlier of tribalism. Nothing is sadder to behold in a country boasting all kinds of freedoms than the so-called religious presses fiercely opposing any book that might contradict their official positions (and cut into the profit margin of the books they currently carry). It is one thing to uphold ideological purity and safeguard the most sacred Biblical truths and quite another to try to extract monopolistic profits from a captive market that is jealously kept from trying out a competitive product.

made Her presence felt in all lands where Christian populations exhibit towards Her a profound veneration, and where they receive Her with open minds and open hearts. This would include not only the lands where Orthodoxy is professed by the majority of the population, but also countries where Christians remain a minority, such as the Copts of Egypt and the Orthodox enclaves in the Middle East.

Last and not least, the Orthodox Communities in the USA have had several opportunities to experience Her presence and concern in the recent past. As an example, some were connected with the miraculous healings associated with Her myrrh-gushing icon of Portaitissa, a copy of an original miraculous icon kept at the Iveron Monastery in Aghion Oros (Μονή Ἰβήρων).[3]

The faithful everywhere attribute such heightened activity of apparitions, myrrh-gushing miracles, healings and other such occurrences to the seriousness of the times and the severity of our human condition. *It has been observed that in the history of the Church such miracles have occurred in times of great tribulation; we saw this in the Apostolic times, and more recently, in Russia, where the Church has suffered cruel persecution for 70 years. The miracles strengthen the faithful and prepare them to endure trials. The appearance of the myrrh-gushing icon in our time may well signify a period of further great trials for the Russian Orthodox Church and, at the same time, offer consolation that the Mother of God will be a Protectress of*

---

[3] The Most Holy Virgin's icon has healed not only Orthodox Christians who travelled to the churches where it was being exhibited over the years, but also Catholics and Protestants who were present. The myrrh-gushing ceases during the Holy Week. It stops on Holy Monday and resumes on the Midnight service of the Resurrection. This phenomenon has been observed by thousands of Christians across Canada and the USA where the icon has been shown, and many also experience the spiritual healing that begins with compunction and repentance and consolation at the same time. Similar phenomena have been reported with many other icons of the Blessed Virgin in the Orthodox World today, continuing a centuries-long tradition in the Eastern Churches.

(The adjective *Portaitissa* for this particular icon derives from the Greek word for a gate, the portal of the monastery on Mt. Athos where the Virgin requested a chapel to be built, housing her original, Byzantine era, icon, which reached the monastery in a most miraculous way).

the faithful.[4]

Analogous phenomena have been observed by millions of persons in the Coptic community of Zeitoun, in the vicinity of Cairo, where the Most Holy Virgin appeared moving on the roof of the Coptic Church over a period of months. During these apparitions, which were also witnessed by many thousands who travelled from everywhere to Zeitoun for the occasion, many miraculous healings have been registered.[5] The Zeitoun visits occurred during a period of heightened persecutions against the Coptic community of Egypt by militant Muslims. Her apparitions strengthened the faith and perseverance of the Copts in their times of trial.

As we can see most clearly from the accumulated evidence the world over, the Most Holy Virgin has been particularly active during this century and the frequency of Her apparitions seems to increase exponentially as we approach to the end of this decade. Her messages are of a most urgent nature and Her detailed predictions concerning our proximate future are literally indispensable for our survival and salvation.

ADDRESSING SOME DISTORTED VIEWS
AND MISREPRESENTATIONS
CONCERNING THE RELIGIOSITY OF RUSSIA

A few historical details will be clarified below, that will enable the Western reader to better assess the validity and plausibility of certain claims by the militant religious presses. These clarifications are very important if we are to properly understand and evaluate the message of the prophets concerning the relative standing of various Christian countries in the eyes of God now and in the future.

It is my conviction that the great hoopla among certain authors to the effect that the Vatican must bring Christianity to Russia since its own Orthodox clergy is unworthy of that task (having collaborated with the KGB, etc.) is a

---

[4] Excerpted from a relevant publication of the Russian Orthodox Cathedral of St. John the Baptist, in Washington D.C., in the year 1986.

[5] The images of the Virgin were photographed and appeared in newsreels and other publications and have been repeated in various TV programs.

very thinly veiled argument.[6] One must suspect that in the absence of a KGB-connection a different argument would have been concocted in its place by such authors, some of whom have never outgrown their militant Jesuit past. Let us go back to the times of the Crimean War, for instance, when Holy Russia had a very pious Czar, and furthermore no trace of an atheist KGB was infesting the land. Then we can better appreciate the ulterior motivation of such authors.

The Czar of that period was interested in protecting the Orthodox Churches operating in the Holy Land against Ottoman abuses and in allowing the unobstructed and free pilgrimage to Jerusalem by Christians from everywhere. The Western powers had many reasons to fear the political ascendancy of Russia. This was particularly true of the British who were concerned about the Suez Canal and an eventual penetration of the Czarist Empire in the vicinity of their Indian subcontinent. They exploited the situation and made it the bone of contention that initiated the Crimean War.

Fiodor Dostoyevsky, reminiscing on the events of that period recorded his impressions in the *Writer's Diary* in 1877: *Here we are not speaking about any prelate whatsoever, but of the Pope himself, who, in the Vatican gatherings with loud voice and great joy spoke of the 'Turkish victories' and foresaw a 'terrible future' for Russia (in the outcome of that war). This old man, who already has one foot in the grave (and who furthermore is the Head of Christianity) does not feel any shame when he claims urbi et orbi that 'it is with joy that he listens every time to the news of Russian defeats'.*[7]

The Crimean War lasted from 1853 to 1856, and the Pope in question was Pius IX (1846-1878, born Giovanni Maria Mastai-Ferretti). What is most amazing, however, is that at that very time, the destiny of the Vatican and

---

[6] An ardent proponent of the 'unworthiness'-theory is the former Vatican insider Malachi Martin, [1990].

[7] Quoted in N. O. Losskii, [1994, p. 215].

Whether the 'Russian defeats' were a matter that should delight any Catholic or any European is an issue covered in all thorough historical accounts of the Crimean War and its consequences in the 19th but also the 20th century. Whether the Russians truly 'lost' that war has been fully answered by Solzhenitsyn in *The Russian Question in the End of the 20th century*, originally published in Russian by Novii Mir in Moscow, 1994, reprinted by the Viestnik, no. 169, I-II 1994.

of the territories under its jurisdiction were hanging from a thread in the ferment of the Italian Nationalist movement of the time; the Pope had more immediate problems in his own backyard with Count Cavour and Victor Emmanuel of Piedmont to be concerned with.

One has reasons to suspect that the antipathy of the Vatican towards Russia was not born during the Atheism of the Soviet era or the Crimean War, but reaches far deeper into time, quite possibly to the year 988 A.D., and most definitely to the decades immediately following the fall of Constantinople in 1453 A.D. If the above sounds like a far-fetched and undeserved suspicion, I invite the readers to come with a more plausible theory explaining the evidence presented below.

THE CHRONICLE OF THE PECULIAR FATE OF THE INSTRUCTIONS GIVEN TO THE POPES BY THE MOST HOLY VIRGIN ON BEHALF OF RUSSIA

As the reader may know, the Virgin Mary appeared to three Portuguese children at Fátima, in 1917 A.D. Through the children, She gave several instructions to the faithful, promised to protect Portugal from a socialist takeover as well as the ravages of WWII, performed a number of miracles witnessed by thousands, and handed down a number of most specific prophecies and relevant instructions to the Pope. Most of the prophecies have already materialized, except for the famous Third Secret, which is zealously guarded by the Vatican to this day, with questionable effectiveness as we shall soon see. The testimony on the fate of the Marian instructions to the Pope on behalf of Russia are already in the public domain and many are detailed below.

The Most Holy Virgin was aware of the great disasters that would befall Russia in the aftermath of WWI. Her concern was to frustrate a communist takeover. That would have been possible through a concerted action of the Christian brethren of the Russians in the West, and specific demands to this end were addressed by the Most Holy Virgin to the Pope. In Her words:

The war (WWI) is going to end. But if people do not stop offending God, another and worse one will begin in the reign of Pius XI. When you shall see a night illuminated by an unknown light, know that this is the great sign that God gives you that He is going to punish the world for its many crimes by means of war, hunger and persecution of the Church and the Holy Father.[8]

(...) To prevent this, I shall come to ask for the consecration of Russia to my Immaculate Heart and the Communion of Reparation on the five first Saturdays. If my requests are granted, Russia will be converted and there will be peace. If not, she will scatter her errors throughout the world provoking wars and great persecution of the Church. The good will be martyred and the Holy Father will have much to suffer and several entire nations will be annihilated...

(...) But in the end, my Immaculate Heart will triumph, the Holy Father will consecrate Russia to me, Russia will be converted, and a certain period of peace will be granted to the world.

According to the explicit requests of the Virgin Mary, the Pope was to consecrate Russia. He had to do it **collegially with all his bishops.** In a vision of our Lord Jesus Christ to Sister Lucia (the only survivor of the three children of Fátima) in 1929 A.D., the message was most categorical: The holy father must consecrate Russia will ALL the Bishops of the world, because '*I want my entire Church to know that this favor (concerning Russia) was obtained through the Immaculate Heart of My Mother so that it may extend this devotion of the first Five Saturdays later on and put the devotion to this Immaculate Heart beside the devotion of My Sacred Heart'.*[9]

What exactly happened, however, is quite different. No action was taken by a Pope even after the message by Lord Jesus Christ of 1929 was communicated to them. And yet, Sister Lucia (who is known as *Maria das*

---

[8] As we noted earlier, (referring to prophecies by Cardinal LaRoque, 1837 A.D.) this event occurred around January 25, 1938. Many believed it applied to a new comet, the scientists associated it with a visually heightened aurora borealis. It was visible through most of Europe. (Incidentally, King Juan Carlos I de Borbón y Borbón was born on January 5, 1938).

[9] If I understand that correctly, the Lord Jesus Christ wished to make the salvation of Russia a personal gift to His Mother upon Her requestr. This a) indicates the love and interest of the Most Holy Virgin vis-à-vis Russia, specifically and b) it corroborates once again a very cherished belief in the Orthodox lands that the Holy Virgin requests and receives a great number of specific graces from God, on account of the Christians. She is considered by every Orthodox Christian the Intercessor par excellence.

Dores, Mary of the Sorrows, after taking the veil), has been most categorical on the true message of the Virgin: *"What Our Lady wants is that the Pope and all the bishops in the world shall consecrate Russia to her Immaculate Heart on one special day. If this is done, She will convert Russia and there will be peace. If it is not done, the errors of Russia will spread through every country in the world"*.

After many tergiversations and delays, finally in 1942, Pope Pius XII consecrated **the world**, not Russia, to the Immaculate Heart. During the 25th anniversary of the apparition, on May 13, 1942, Pius XII sent a telegram to the pilgrims of Fátima, adding his prayers to theirs. However, **he did not even mention Russia**, but used a rather round-about way to refer to *"the peoples separated from us by error and by schism, especially the one which professes a singular devotion for you, the one in which there is not a single house which did not display your venerated icon, today perhaps hidden and put away for better days."*

Obviously, this was deemed inadequate by the Holy Ones, as the history of WWII and the history of the post-WWII era makes manifest. On May 13, 1982, the anniversary of the Fátima apparitions, all Catholic bishops were invited by Pope John Paul II (in writing) to meet him at Fátima for the festivities. Only a small number joined him physically while another small number paralleled the celebrations in their home parishes. In 1984, Pope John Paul II mailed a letter to his bishops inviting them 'in union with him to make the consecration to the Immaculate Heart of Mary'. Certain Catholic apologists already declare urbi et orbi that the papal initiative bore miraculous fruits already (arguing that it was precisely this action by John Paul II which destroyed Communism in Russia!...). Such self-appointed saviors go a step further with their effrontery. Enters Jean Whalen:

On March 25, 1984, Pope John Paul II requested the original statue of Our Lady from Fátima be flown to the Vatican. At that time, he again offered a Consecration to the Immaculate Heart of Mary in much the same manner as in 1982 - however, with one important difference: This time, he had written to every Bishop in the world, in advance, requesting each to privately join with him on that day in the same Consecration. Again, "Russia" is not spoken but referred to in a veiled way. As you know, it was shortly after that Gorbachev instituted Glasnost and certain new freedoms of religion began to open up in Russia and its other States. Now there are Cardinals, Bishops and priests actually located in all Russia and its Republics. (sic).

(...) Most Mariologists believe that the 1984 consecration, although not totally enacted in the manner requested, has brought about 1) the downfall of Communism in Russia and 2) new-found religious freedom! However, the conversion of Russia has not yet taken place. (...) Certain Marian scholars and Mariologists believe the 1984 Consecration was "accepted" - that the conversion is coming. Other scholars believe the conversion will come only after the world's Bishops will finally agree to join publicly with the Pope enacting a Consecration and the word "Russia" spoken. (...).[10]

However, the seers, visionaries and receivers of private revelations in general, deny the efficacy of the above measures and insist that **the consecration was not properly done and will have to be repeated at some time in the future...**

The triumphalisms of the apologists are not only misplaced, but in direct contradiction to the specific instructions of the Most Blessed Virgin, Who in subsequent apparitions the world over redresses some of those wrongs. Specifically, in Her messages to the US visionary Estela Ruiz on October 31, 1992, She said also the following: **I have begun My plan for the conversion of all communist countries, especially Russia, which has been the foundation of this evil. I again tell you that it is through the conversion of Russia that the world will see the triumph of My Immaculate Heart.** These words of the Most Blessed Virgin testify to the fact that She, Herself, is the instrument of the conversion of Russia. Furthermore, the Blessed Virgin in a subsequent apparition predicted the following: **The Holy Father will consecrate Russia to me, but it will be late."**

Now, the apologists jumped up once more with the verdict: *It was not the Pope's fault. The fault appears to lie with the faithful having taken so long to respond to Our Lady's call.*

The Fátima messages have had a most adventurous career so far:
a)   they were originally ignored, and their authenticity denied;
b)   once accepted, their instructions were not obeyed;
c)   they were not made public in their totality as was expected as per the Holy Virgin's instructions. The treatment of The Third Secret in particular is most eloquent concerning the modus operandi of the

---

[10] See also, the Catholic Publication Queen of Peace, Special Edition II, p. 4.

d)   Vatican information brokers;
d)   they were manipulated by the R.C.C. for propaganda purposes. (Vide, their claims on how instrumental they have been for Russia's freedom);
e)   Last and not least, the very words of the Holy Virgin have been stretched on the Procrustean beds of Catholic propaganda and still confuse the Catholics to this day.

For instance, when the Theotokos said that **The Holy Father will consecrate Russia to me, but it will be late,** She did not mean John Paul II, or the famous year 1984 with its mockery of an attempt to a consecration.[11]   This verdict of the Virgin Mary, (in conjunction with everything else the prophecies tell us about the future) is reserved for the period following WWIII.   The Holy Father She is referring to is the Papa Angelorum, the consecration will be most likely during the Eighth Ecumenical Council and 'it will be late' in the sense that the WWIII will not have been avoided, and the current over-cautious and reluctant Catholic Bishops who cannot bring themselves to even pronounce the word "Russia", great promoters of the Holy Catholic and Apostolic Church that they are, will have missed the Boat of Peter.   It will be too late for **them**, not for Russia.

ON THE ADVENTUROUS CAREER
OF THE THIRD SECRET OF FÁTIMA

The content of the prophecy of the Most Blessed Virgin generally referred to as 'The Third Secret' was written by Sister Maria das Dores and mailed to the Vatican to be read by the Pope <u>at any time after 1960</u>. Catholics the world over were extremely interested in the message of the secret and were pressing the Vatican for the promulgation of its text. The following bits and pieces of information surfacing in regards to that secret emanate from various Catholic sources and contain information in the public domain.

According to Dr.Joaquin Alonso, C.M.F.:
The Third Secret was kept in the archives of the Sacred Congregation during

---

[11]   Again, the apologists hastened to inform us that "it will be late" actually translates that already 60+ millions of citizens of the USSR have perished. Of course, this is merely water under the bridge, what can one do?   But now Christians, rejoice, the Cardinals are already in Russia and 'all its Republics' and salvation is at the gate!

282

the remaining years of Pope Pius XII's pontificate. Pope Pius XII died on October 9, 1958, having never read the third secret.

According to Cardinal Ottaviani and Msgr. Loris Capovilla:
The secret was delivered to the new pope, John XXIII still sealed in August 1959. He read it but he decided to leave it to his successor's concern, since it did not pertain to his times. No official statement was ever released by that Pope in reference to The Third Secret.

According to Cardinal Ottaviani:
Yes, the secret is important; it is important for the Holy Father for whom it was destined. It was addressed to him. And if the one to whom it was addressed has decided not to declare 'now is the moment to make it known to the world' we should be content with the fact that in his wisdom he wished it to remain a secret.

Pope Paul VI expressed his views on The Third Secret in a legalistic and convoluted jargon completely devoid of informational content. This was in 1967. Many other highly placed Vatican officials, challenged by the public to comment on The Third Secret, supplied tergiversations, equivocations, evasions, subterfuges and platitudes.

Yet, there are also 'renegades' within the Catholic fold: For one, a highly reputable, and most unbiased Catholic Chronicler of the Fátima story, William Thomas Walsh,[12] already exasperated by the Papal consecration of the 'world' instead of 'Russia' in 1942, informs us with respect to The Third Secret that *'nothing has been divulged except that it means woe to some and joy to others.'*

Another one, the late Fr. Joaquin Alonso (whom we met earlier) had the following comments: *In the period which precedes the great Triumph of the Immaculate Heart of Mary, terrible things will occur, and these are the object of the third part of the secret. What things? If 'in Portugal the dogmas of the faith will always be preserved...' it can be deduced with all clarity that in other parts of the Church these dogmas will be obscured or even lost. It is quite possible that the message not only speaks of 'a crisis of faith' in the Church during this period, but also, like the Secret of La Salette, that it makes concrete references to internal strife among Catholics and to the deficiencies*

---

[12] [1947, p. 211 and elsewhere]

of priests and religious. It is also possible that it may imply deficiencies even among the upper ranks of the hierarchy.[13]

The above historical overview of the Fátima messages is by no way complete and exhaustive. But we hope it will help to set the record straight and enable the reader of our study to better appreciate the prophetic evidence. In a previous chapter we introduced material from the prophecies at La Salette. That message, uttered in 1846, was covering the time from that apparition, through the entire 20th century, down to the era of the Antichrist and up until the end of times. The Theotokos spoke most explicitly about the fate of those lands of Christianity which have abandoned the ways of the Gospel. Her theme, that the Christians will be subjected to a terrible impending punishment for having abandoned the Christian way of life, is a recurrent one in Her subsequent apparitions. But so is also the instruction on how we can divert, diffuse and diminish the terrible punishment with the proper individual conduct. Let us now study Her more recent messages to us.

<u>A short coverage of the Garabandal apparitions:</u>[14]
In the remote village of San Sebastian de Garabandal, in N.W. Spain, about two thousand apparitions of the Virgin Mary to four girls have been reported in the period from 1961 to 1965.[15] All four described the Virgin Mary as a young woman attired in a white dress with a blue mantle and a brown Scapular on Her right arm. Her face was oval-shaped with a fine nose. The girls claimed that *no other woman looks like Her or sounds like her.*

The assorted skeptics of this world would discount such description as the fancy of four little children in a remote Spanish village. They will counter that the girls have seen pictures of the Virgin Mary before (possibly in churches, shrines and in the popular and religious literature) and in all likelihood they had such images imprinted on their subconscious mind.

---

[13] *Queen of Peace*, Winter 1993, p. 5.

[14] This is not the place to expand on the Garabandal story. There exists a number of dependable Catholic sources which provide plentiful material to the interested reader. One could add the organizations whose only reason of existence is the study and promulgation of the Garabandal data.

[15] The visionaries were Conchita Gonzalez age 12; Jacinta Gonzalez age 12; Mari Cruz Gonzalez age 11 and Mari-Loli Mazon age 12.

Therefore, when they began describing the facial characteristics of the Virgin Mary, they were practically quoting from memory.

The skeptics may also pinpoint that different alleged seers and visionaries would describe the exterior appearance of the Virgin Mary quite differently, and have, indeed, done so in the past. It is true that the Virgin Mary has been documented as appearing under many colors of apparel of varying degrees of luxury and splendor. However, rather than considering such discrepancies as evidence of inconsistency in reporting (hence, of untruthful stating of facts by the seers), we ought to consider them as yet another proof of the powers of God. The apparel of the Virgin Mary, for one thing, seems to be appropriate for the occasion of the apparition and the tenor of Her message.

On the issue of the variation of the apparel and overall appearance we have the following reports from other sources:

1) General Makriyannis, the Greek freedom-fighter and mystic (whom we met earlier) had related in detail the varying apparel of the Virgin Mary in the numerous visions of Hers he was blessed with over a period of many years.[16]

2) The anonymous author of the Russian spiritual Classic 'The Way of the Pilgrim...' relates at a certain point to a well-educated Russian Christian interlocutor of his how his (by then deceased) spiritual father, a very holy man, appeared in his dream and gave him specific instructions on how to study most effectively the book entitled Philocalia. In the dream, the deceased monk even took a piece of coal from the hearth and made marginal marks on specific pages of the book, while he was addressing the Pilgrim. When the Pilgrim woke up in the following morning he was amazed to find his copy of the Philocalia lying on a different spot of the room from

---

[16] He also reported how the Virgin Mary and Her Saints 'operated' on his wife. Mrs. Makriyannis was in terrible pain, suffering from what appears to have been (considering the description and the terminology used) a breast cancer which had already spread throughout her body. ['Ορἀματα καί Θἀματα, (Visions and Wonders), passim]. Makriyannis' s description of the operation matches very closely that of a similar intervention on behalf of a young woman in Zeitoun, the Coptic community we met earlier in this chapter. The Theotokos is reported of having operated and removed a breast cancer from a young lady, without living any scar or any other operation-related wound on the body.

where he had left it the night before, and the pages mentioned by his spiritual father were marked exactly as in the dream.

While relating this mystery, the Pilgrim took the book out of his knapsack and showed it to his interlocutor, who, after examining the marked pages, proceeded with the following interpretation:
This is a spiritual mystery and I will explain it to you. When the spirits need a physical form in which to appear before a living person, they create a visible body for themselves out of ethers and then return it to the atmosphere when they no longer need it. Because the elements of the atmosphere from which the body is made have elasticity - that is, they can expand and contract - the soul, when it is clothed with these elements, has the ability to perform different actions, including writing.[17]

This interpretation may help explain some of the 'technology' features of our Saints' interference with the physical Universe, so that they bring about their miraculous healing, perform operations without surgical instruments, leave an indelible mark on stones and rocks, and effect cures and other feats. If the spirits can take what they need for the specific occasion from the world around them, what would inhibit them from selecting the appropriate color from the spectrum to clothe themselves accordingly and properly match the specific occasion?[18]

---

[17] *The Way of the Pilgrim...*, pp. 44-45. (The author is anonymous, the version I have used has been translated by Helen Bacovcin).

[18] A miraculous event, analogous to the earlier one related by the Pilgrim, is reported by Abbé Curicque, on his chronicle of the *Appearance of the Blessed André Bobola at Vilna*. Bobola appeared to Father Korzeniecki, a Dominican monk at Vilna (Wilna, Vilnius, the capital of Lithuania) one night in 1819 and prophesied about future events covering Poland, his country. Bobola stood in the middle of the monk's cell and addressed him as follows:
Here am I, Father Korzeniecki. Open your window and you will behold things you have never seen. The Dominican monk opened the window of his cell and to his surprise, instead of the expected view of the monastery's garden, he saw a huge plain expanding as far as the eyes could see. *The plain before you is the territory of Pinsk. (...)* Father Korzeniecki saw that the plain was covered with the bodies of troops, Russian, Turkish, English, Austrians, Prussians, almost from all the nations of the world. The battle was raging. André Bobola continued: *When the war you have been watching gives way to peace, then Poland shall be restored and I shall be recognized as its chief patron. For our holy religion will then be free there.*

Other older apparitions by the Theotokos with foot imprint and other signs left behind, would include the very old **Pochaev apparition**, summarized below.

Although the territory of Pochaev has changed hands repeatedly over the centuries and many Christians today, if they know anything about Pochaev at all, they tend to associate it more readily with the Ukraine, the Pochaev apparitions and miracles are much older, dating from a time when this entire region was yet but an empty, uninhabited land. Around 1340 A.D. two solitary monks and a shepherd saw the Virgin Mary, enveloped by fire, standing on the top of the mountain in Pochaev. The imprint of Her right foot was left for ever on the rock where She stood during the apparition; (in later centuries this very spot became a locus of pilgrimage and veneration to the Pochaevskaya Lavra, a religious compound erected around that spot). In 1559 A.D., about a century after Constantinople had fallen to the Turks, the Greek Metropolitan Neophytos visited the region of Volinia, bringing along a cherished icon of the Virgin Mary, of Byzantine origin. He was offered protection and warm hospitality by a local family for a number of years, and, in appreciation, he presented them with his valuable icon. After many tribulations and changes of fortune, the icon was finally bequeathed to the religious compound of Pochaev. Hundreds of miracles have been associated with that icon, the most celebrated being, of course, the defeat of the Turks in 1675 A.D. The footprint of the Virgin Mary, surrounded by works of art, can be seen by every pilgrim visiting that holy place today. Understandably, the Virgin of Pochaev is considered one of the most important and venerated religious treasures of Russia, also.[19]

The list of apparitions of this nature, accompanied by miraculous events and

---

Further, to convince the monk that this vision was not a hallucination of his, St. Bobola, before vanishing from sight, left the imprint of his hand on the monk's table. When Father Korzeniecki woke up the following morning, the imprint was there.

This event is doubly important for our study: a) it corroborates similar phenomena reported by Christians elsewhere, on the extraordinary abilities of blessed spirits and b) it provides a most relevant prophecy for our times. Such a variety of troops was never seen before in the plains of Pinsk. They refer to WWIII as is proposed in greater detail in *Our Revelationary Age...*

[19] For more details on this account see also *Chudotvornie ikoni...*, (Miracle-working Icons of the Mother of God), vol ii., pp. 582-586.

the creation of water fountains endowed with healing power can be expanded with those in Lourdes (France), several in Russia, in Constantinople, and those which have occurred (or may be occurring at this very moment) elsewhere.[20]

In the Garabandal apparitions the Virgin Mary is asked to kiss objects and She does so. In other apparitions She is handing out specific objects to Her faithful. General Makriyannis's personal accounts of Her visitations and the conversations he held with Her and other Saints of Her retinue provide a most remarkable testimony on what feats the Holy Ones are willing to perform on account of their favorite mortals. And *The Way of the Pilgrim...* bears testimony of a miraculous healing on the instigation of the Pilgrim's dead spiritual father, who conveys to him in the course of a dream life-saving information not otherwise available.

So far, the claim of the four girls at Garabandal that the Virgin Mary even kissed objects given to Her is entirely consistent with accumulated evidence from previous sources including many non-Catholic ones.

NOTES ON THE VISUAL FEATURES OF THE THEOTOKOS

As we noted earlier, the four girls at Garabandal categorically reported that 'no other woman looks like Her or sounds like Her'. Again, the skeptic may attempt to discount such claim as the exaggerations of impressionable children confined in a limited environment: in a remote mountain village, where life is hard and women age prematurely, a face, which our society might discard as inadequate for a career in high fashion, may still look quite youthful and pretty. Other reviewers of the evidence may feel that such enthusiastic, liberal praise-heaping is a concealed self-serving attempt by kids who like to look important: the more attractive and exalted the object of their visions, the more important they become, by sheer association.

Yet, for those who believe in the powers of the Most Blessed Virgin and Her Graces to the human race these reports do not raise any eyebrows. They are in the same vein with hundreds of others accumulated over the centuries in many lands of Christendom. Such reports, furthermore, began during Her

---

[20] An excellent book in English on the miraculous springs of the Holy Virgin is William J. Walsh, [1904]. The book covers Catholic lands primarily and provides a rich supplement to similar reports from Eastern Orthodox countries.

own life time.

Almost two thousand years ago, a most sophisticated eyewitness wrote such a report. Dionysius Areopagites was (as his name indicates) a Justice in the Supreme Court of Ancient Athens, the Areos Pagos (the Hill of Mars, located opposite the Acropolis). The most important affairs of the state where decided by the Areos Pagos.[21] This Dionysius was present when St. Paul preached to the Athenians on the 'unknown God'. Dionysius was among the initial audience that adopted Christianity and became the great friend and disciple of the Apostle of the Gentiles.[22]

---

[21] There are several conflicting views on why the Hill was named after Ares, Mars, the god of War. One proposes that since Mars was associated with bloodshed, and since the Court at Areos Pagos was specifically involved in cases of bloodshed, war, and murder, the title was appropriate. The Court of Justice at Areos Pagos was such an old institution that nobody knew when it was first established. The cream of the Athenian society were elected to serve there. The appointment was for life; however, if any justice was even seen sitting in a tavern or occasionally using foul language, he would be automatically expelled from the Court and held henceforth in the greatest disgrace. The judges of the Areos Pagos were specializing in the cases of murders, immoral behavior, impiety and idleness, the 'mother of all vices'. They watched over the laws, the public treasury, the upholding of the religious rites and the proper celebration of the holy mysteries. Pericles, who sought admission to that select body but was denied it, avenged himself when he came to power by allowing persons of questionable moral standards to be admitted to that egregious group. And although during the Athenian decadence era following the death of Pericles and the defeat in the Peloponnesian War, many institutions suffered in prestige and virtue, including the Areos Pagos, the Court, as an institution, survived for long centuries afterwards as the foremost judicial establishment of Athens.

[22] It is reported in the Eastern Tradition that Dionysius Areopagites was on a visit in Egypt during the Crucifixion. Observing the great inexplicable darkness which enveloped the world when the spirit left Him, Dionysius is reported of saying: Ἢ τὸ πᾶν ἀπόλλυται ἢ Θεὸς πάσχει (either the universe is coming to an end, or a God is suffering). Dionysius became the Patron Saint of Athens, and according to certain sources he might have been the same Dionysius who had gone to France to evangelize the Galls, where he died a martyr's death. Others believe that later authors confused three different men called Dionysius and fused them into one, the St. Denis of France. We must keep in mind that Dionysius Areopagites was a contemporary of St. Paul and of the Virgin Mary, and St. Denis, patron saint of France, according to Gallic Tradition, lived in the 3rd century of our era.

The Ancient Tradition of the Eastern Church has preserved the following letter addressed by St. Dionysius to St. Paul, following the former's journey to Jerusalem with the explicit purpose of meeting the mother of Jesus Christ:

My Leader and Superior, I offer testimony before God, that except from God Himself there is nobody in the entire world who is filled to such degree with Divine power and grace. No human being can imagine through his own mental power what I have seen, or conceive and understand it not only through his spiritual eyes but also through the corporeal ones. I confess before God: when John, who shines among the apostles like the sun shines in the skies, led me before the Most Holy Virgin, I experienced emotions that I cannot express. Before me shone a kind of divine radiance. It lit up my spirit; I experienced the fragrances from undescribable perfumes and became overfilled with such ecstasy that neither my weak body nor my spirit could endure those signs and elements of eternal bliss and heavenly glory. In the presence of Her Grace my heart and spirit failed me. And if I did not have always present in my mind your strong exhortation, I would have believed Her to be truly a Divinity. It is impossible for me to even imagine a greater happiness than the one experienced in that place.[23]

Such testimony originating in the first century of our era supports fully the later ones, such as that of Garabandal and subsequent ones, scattered through the globe. I trust the reader will accept the admissibility of the above testimony on the following grounds:

a)   Dionysius was as sophisticated a thinker and observer as one could find in his age. When he uses superlatives and humbly laments his paucity of language and poverty of expression, one must assume that even the Greek language was not rich enough to capture the intensity of the experience of one of the most educated and bright citizens of Athens in the first century;

b)   He was an eyewitness. He saw Her in the flesh, (while subsequent visionaries might be reproached of relating a vision only...). In fact, he travelled to Jerusalem with only one purpose: to make the

---

[23]   See also, Царица небесная, спаси землю русскую - (Сказания о чудотворних иконах богоматери и о Ея милостях роду человеческому), *On the Miracle-working Icons...*, vol. I, p. 3 and p. 71, my translation.

personal acquaintance of the mother of his God. For him, as well as for St. Paul, the Virgin Mary was the closest they ever came to know the human nature in Lord Jesus Christ. For them She was the consolation for never having seen the Savior in the flesh. It is widely believed by the Eastern Church that the reason why the Virgin Mary lived to about 70 years of age was not because She needed any additional years to earn Heaven, but only in order to inspire and comfort the early Christians who so strongly desired a glimpse of the Lord. In other words, the Divine plan was that She remain long on this earth for the benefit of mankind. Observed and described by eyewitnesses contemporaries, having Her likeness recorded by saints/iconographers, all these were but the beginnings of Her many graces and mercies for the benefit of the human race.

These eyewitnesses' reports which are a part of the Tradition of the Church describe the Virgin Mary very much the way our contemporaries - visionaries have described Her. Long oval face, dark eyebrows, straight hair, straight nose, great beauty, a woman without Her equal in this world.

c)   Dionysius was an eyewitness detailing his impressions to another eyewitness. He lived in a less skeptic era (if this qualifier could ever apply to the first century A.D...) and his report did not meet with the incredulity of an inimical audience. Consequently, his testimony was preserved verbatim by the Christian community which lacked the opportunity of a personal interview with the Virgin Mary, and treated such documents as a surrogate for the experience itself.

d)   Dionysius was a citizen beyond reproach and had no reason in the world to associate himself with any untruthful statement. Nor had he any reason to impress anybody, especially St. Paul, the recipient of the letter, who had already met with the Virgin Mary and conversed with Her repeatedly in the past. Other contemporaries were no less enthusiastic: In a letter addressed to the Evangelist John from the Golden Antioch, the head of the local Christians, Ignatius, speaks of the great desire of the Antiochian Christians to visit the Virgin Mary. *Trustworthy reports have reached us that in the person of Mary, the Mother of Jesus, thanks to Her great holiness, the human substance seems fused with the angelic one...*[24]

In conclusion, during the past 2000 years, beginning with reports by Her contemporaries, and followed by a great number of most fortunate individuals who saw Her, the Virgin Mary has been described in a most consistent fashion. The testimonies from Garabandal (as well as the later ones from Medjugorje and elsewhere) belong to the same population of truthful and legitimate reports.

In other words, there is no ground to suspect the veracity of reports appearing during the past few years in the various Roman Catholic publications regarding the Theotokos. These reports are fully corroborated by similar reports from different nationalities and time periods. The only objection a non-Catholic reader may have is that they are projected as being **the only** apparitions of the Virgin. There is a shroud of silence on all Her other activities in the world, and one cannot always assume this is only due to ignorance.

The most impressive casualty of the fallacious reasoning developed by the Reformation was the rejection of the veneration of the Most Holy Theotokos. Since they insist in treating Her as someone very secondary (on the basis of misinterpretations of biblical passages), why should She impose Her presence upon them? Christianity is the religion of freedom par excellence. Jesus Christ never imposed Himself on us. If we are going to be His, it will be out of our own free will. The same must be said for His Mother.

The following statistics will elucidate the point I am trying to make: Professor William A. Christian (a Garabandal aficionado in his own words) reports that apparitions by Saints have occurred in large numbers during our century. Only in Italy, for instance, they amount in the hundreds, over the period since 1930 A.D. However, on the Spanish cases he writes that: *Apparitions documented for Spain fall into two categories. The first is the kind common in the twentieth century - one or more divine figures who appear to one or more seers "in the flesh" as it were. They usually speak, sometimes touch the seers; often they walk with them and show them things; and sometimes they leave sacred objects for the seers. These are apparitions proper. Those I know about in Spain occurred mainly in two periods: from around 1400 to about 1525 and from 1900 to the present.*

---

[24] [ibid. p. 71].

Apparently because of the activities of the Inquisition, only a handful of cases occurred in the years between 1525 and 1900. [Emphasis added].[25] Could it be possible, then, that the denial by the Protestants to recognize both the infinite care of the Virgin Mary for the human race **and** Her great powers to bring mercy and grace to this world have in effect slammed the door in their faces? Or, that the Protestants who searched fervently on their own account and were granted such a grace quietly abandoned their original Protestant views and joined the throngs of those who do not deride such events, but rather accept them like manna from Heaven?

Our self-proclaimed enlightened age ought to invest more effort in separating the wheat from the chaff regarding matters of so vital importance. We retain detective companies to generate intelligence for our corporate needs while neglecting the need for spiritual intelligence. Why should it be less vital or urgent to invest in information when our salvation and survival is at stake? Furthermore, most of such intelligence is offered free of charge by a legion of holy men and women. In conclusion, the fact that certain groups of Christians have no apparitions of the Virgin to report is due exclusively to their own denial rather than to Her inability and unwillingness to extend Her graces to them.

This chapter's main reason of existence was dual:

a)   to add credence to the claims by Roman Catholics as to contemporary apparitions of the Most Holy Virgin by supplying a small, well diversified sample of similar evidence from other sources. Therefore, since the evidence is, basically, universal within that portion of the Christian world that never stopped venerating the Virgin or trust in Her extraordinary powers of intercession, there is no reason for the Protestants to discard the evidence as a ploy of the RCC at the expense of gullible persons. Their loss is great as it is, the least thing they can now afford is to fail to heed Her messages concerning **the immediate future and our available options**.

b)   to prepare mentally the reader of this study for the remarkable revelations of the prophecies on behalf of post-WWIII Russia. We

---

[25] [op. cit. p. 8]. Spain, let the reader be reminded was the very last country to abolish the Inquisition around 1900 A.D.

had to re-construct the History of Russia in each and every chapter in order to be able to fully understand and appreciate what our global future has in store. The great concern of the Most Holy Virgin on behalf of Russia beginning with Fátima in 1917 (a little before the Communist take-over) and continuing to this very day through many apparitions and graces should provide us with food for thought.

Having researched many hundreds of prophecies for the two studies, I reached the conclusion that the prophetic evidence on the USA is rather sparse. There are very few written prophecies by well known seers in the literature; most of the evidence comes from the 20th century and the most detailed information comes from private revelations to US faithful by either our Lord Jesus Christ or His Most Holy Mother. We cannot afford to discard data points in general, and particularly the ones coming from the Highest sources. Whether the revelations are genuine or simply the work of fast operators can be decided upon in a professional manner with the assistance of the rest of the evidence at hand. It is true that the subject of apparitions and miracles has been abused (like so many other issues involving religion) and utmost caution and circumspection is a sine-qua-non. I can only speak of my own research and I can say that whatever I have researched in Catholic publications so far falls in two categories:

a)   the data are admissible but the interpretation is flawed;
b)   the data are admissible and the interpretation appears plausible;

There is no evidence suggesting that the data are inadmissible. The Roman Catholics may have occasionally caused consternation to the rest of us, Christians, with some of their initiatives, but fabricating evidence on the Most Holy Virgin is not one of them. They may have kept some of the texts unjustifiably secret, or they may have edited some portions from other prophecies to reduce or strengthen the prophets' punch. Or, they may have 'improved' upon the original wording to promote the R.C.C. as the savior of Christianity. And again, not **all** Catholics have acted in this way.

We must understand that many prophecies of our proximate future predict dire days not only for the world in general but also for the RCC in particular. Some of these texts do not appear in their entirety on each and every book published by Catholics, especially by the authors who wish to tell us that we have to bend to the commands of the Vatican. This is one of the reasons why a study on prophecies requires a voluminous bibliography and must depend upon well-diversified sources. One must search patiently to put all the pieces of the puzzle together, and at times the text of a single prophecy in its totality must be collected and collated from three or four different sources, or contrasted with alternative books covering the same material.

But this task is feasible, because there are many marvelous Catholic authors who have created veritable jewels of scholarship in the best Christian tradition. They do not accept everything at face value either, and with painstaking efforts, years of travelling and hundreds of interviews they put together the evidence, which is so indispensable for us today.

REVIEW OF THE MOST SALIENT POINTS

a)   The messages of the Most Holy Virgin at La Salette, Fátima, Garabandal and Medjugorje are most relevant and of the utmost importance concerning our immediate future. They should be studied with great reverence and the utmost attention ought to be paid to them. Our very life and salvation depends on them.

b)   The Most Holy Virgin's **role** in the events soon to occur is a pivotal one. The body of the prophetic evidence (from other sources) speaks of Her direct assistance and the powers of Her intercession. In this chapter we provided a small sample of historical evidence to indicate the power of that intercession in the past and the avenues of Her assistance through the ages. All prophecies predict that the veneration of the Virgin Mary after WWIII will reach unprecedented levels. I believe that Nostradamus has also touched upon this very issue and below we shall see exactly how.

Post scripta on the Virgin's Past and Future Roles

Post scriptum 1: The material presented below identifies a prophecy by Nostradamus on the great future role of the Holy Theotokos.

Century X: Quatrain 96:
Religion du nom des mers vaincra,
Contre la secte fils Adaluncatif,
Secte obstinée deplorée craindra
Des deux blessez par Aleph & Aleph.

Verbatim translation:
A religion called after the name of the seas will be victorious against the sect

which is an offspring of 'Adaluncatif'. This obstinate and deplorable sect will become fearful at the sight of those two wounded by Aleph and Aleph.

Suggested interpretation:
The version of the Anagram for Adaluncatif which I believe to be the correct one would be *An du Califat*, namely, the year the caliphate was established.[26] Therefore, 'Califat' came to signify the ascendancy of Islamic secular power besides the religious one, considering the bellicose nature of the first Caliph, Abu Bakr. Nostradamus speaks of a 'sect' which will be the son of the year of the Caliphate. In other words he does not speak generally of Islam but specifically of the sect which will be associated basically with the Sunni version of Islam, propounded by Abu Bakr. Ali, on the other hand, the son-in-law of Mohammed, who became Caliph years later, was assassinated, and is venerated as a saint, became the Head of the Shia' sect of Islam. Except the Iranians who are predominantly Shi'ites, the bulk of Islam from Mauritania to Indonesia are Sunni Muslims. In other words, Nostradamus even tells us that the religion of the name of the seas will be victorious predominantly over the Sunni sect (to which belong Arabs, Iraqis and Turkic peoples, namely the major belligerent nationalities against Israel and Europe!...)

In Latin, *mare-maris* is the word for the sea. In the plural, it is *maria*, which looks very much like Maria. In Greek, the female name Πελαγία is already a name associated with the Virgin Mary. Πελαγία comes from the Greek word for a body of water smaller than a sea and even smaller than an ocean: Ionion Pelagos, vs. Mediterranean Sea, vs. Atlantic Ocean.[27]

Nostradamus further suggests that the obstinate sect will be fearful of the defeat of two men wounded by mysterious personalities whose name begins with an Alpha (a Latin A) (*Aleph* is the original Phoenician phonetic symbol which is also the first character in the Hebrew system, and which became the first letter of the Greek Alphabet as well). Aleph originally designated the

---

[26] Califat, or Khalifat in French, is known as Caliphate, or Kaliphate, in English. Since all these are transliterations from an Arabic original, such diversity of spellings is easily explainable. The term Kalifa (Kalifah, Khalifah) means a Successor and was a title given to the Successors to Mohammed upon his death on June 8, 632 A.D.

[27] (The English 'archipelago' derives from τό πέλαγος, ἀρχιπέλαγος, a name given to the Aegean Sea).

head of an ox, and in its ancient written form it resembled a stylized ox-head.

From this point on, my interpretation may be somewhat speculative: If the defeat of the Sunni Muslims is the one predicted to occur in WWIII through Christian armies (with the special assistance of the Virgin Mary), who could then be these Aleph and Aleph? We have already proven that the prophesied Great Monarch is Juan Carlos I, King of Spain. In both studies we spoke of the 'Great Philip' of Greek prophecies corresponding most likely to Felipe de Borbón, Prince of Asturias. However, the full names of both men expected to play such an important military role in the future are respectively:

- Juan Carlos **Alfonso** Victor María de Borbón y Borbón;
- Felipe Juan Pablo **Alfonso** de Todos los Santos Borbón Sondeburg Glucksburg, Prince of Asturias.

The Great Monarch is named in the prophecies numerous times under John (and its variations) as well as under Charles (and its variations). It would appear that Nostradamus now refers to him by his third baptismal name, down the list. Alfonso XIII was the grandfather of the current King of Spain and the great-grandfather of the Prince of Asturias. The fact that both have Alfonso among their names (honoring their ancestor Alfonso XIII) at least does not contradict, prima facie, the hypothesis that they are the ones Nostradamus is indicating.

On the other hand, we know it for a fact that the victorious Western coalition will be composed of two separate armies. One under the Slavs, the other under the Borbones. It could be possible, therefore, that Aleph and Aleph could correspond to the commanders in chief of these two armies: one being a member of the Borbón dynasty, the other, for instance an Aleksandr, being a Russian. (I have no access to such details from the Russian side of relevant prophecies. This does not mean that it could not happen in such a way, however).

Regardless of what the identities of Aleph and Aleph prove to be, however, we can consider the above quatrain as yet another proof of the future great veneration to be given to the Blessed Virgin after the defeat of the Muslims in WWIII, and it appears that Nostradamus echoes many other prophets on the role of the Holy Virgin even during the war (which will be fought under Her banner).

Additional evidence on the great mercies of the Holy Virgin during this most difficult period for mankind can be found in the other treasure chest of prophecies available to us: in *Les Prophecies de Merlin*, (prophecy **CCLXIX**), which makes explicit mention of events generated directly by the Almighty that are going to be so terrible 'as to give the impression that the end of the world has come' it is revealed that the tears and the supplications of the Most Holy Virgin on the one hand, and Her direct instructions to us on how to mend our ways and atone, on the other, will earn us divine mercy, saving many lives and salvaging many souls.[28]

Post scriptum 2: The Great Mediatrix of Graces, and the Russian Church in the last 1000 Years

Ever since Her apparitions at Fátima, the Theotokos has been very vocal of Her concern about the fate of Russia's Christians. Let us try to place Her interest into historical and theological perspective so that persons of good will learn to not only set the historical record straight but also study in a real life situation the marvelous and many ways She manifests Her interest in the affairs of an entire nation.

Regardless of the West's distorted impressions on this subject, Russia was, is, and always will be a spiritual country. The term 'Holy Russia' was not a hollow expression of a chauvinist race, it signified a modus vivendi, a way of being. As I have been repeatedly stressing in this study it was the Russians themselves who toppled Communism and attempted coups d' état in the USSR. Whether they were closet Christians among the Party members, dissident churchgoers and common folk among the Biespartiinie (namely non-Communist Party members), it was definitely they and not the Jesuits of the Vatican, the staunch Turkish allies of the USA or the crisis-resolution-oriented shuttle diplomacy of former US policians who effected the changes.

Considering that the Eastern Slavs know better their daily realities and their history than the Christians of the West, they have every reason to feel aggravated by those who now try to lecture them on any moral and religious

---

[28] Rennes, Bibliothèque Municipale. *(...) Li Tout Puissant fera semblant de finer le monde. Mes elle se metra a genous devant lui et dira, Biaus fius, souffres vous que ils amenderont lor vies. Et il se souffrera et dira, (...).* Lucy Allen Paton, [op. cit. v. 1, p. 305].

subject under the sun. The Russians, ever since they adopted Orthodox Christianity from Byzantium (988 A.D.), have been presented by emperors and Patriarchs alike with some of the most precious icons of the Virgin Mary till then in the possession of the Byzantines. Monasteries, patrician families and other sources added further to the Russian repository by way of gifts and bequests.

Later on, to this imported stock the Russians added their own artistic masterpieces.[29] Many such icons of the Virgin Mary have been associated with events most vital for the life of the Russian people, beginning with Kievan Rus' up to our own times. Such events included even the selection of specific locations where shrines and churches (and later on entire cities) would be built. The relevant instructions of the Virgin Mary would be expressed in various forms, frequently by appearing to a powerful, pious, ruler in a dream and proposing Her ideas concerning their future.

One will not fail to notice a very remarkable parallel at this point. During Greek antiquity the Oracle of Delphi was instrumental in selecting the location where new colonies would be founded by citizens from the mainland. For this reason Delphic Apollo was celebrated and worshipped as 'The Founder' by the Greeks of Magna Grecia (Sicily and Southern Italy).

During the Christian era the Virgin Mary has assumed the function of the Founder, beside so many others. Consequently, it was through Her input (communicated through visions) that many cities were founded, not to mention the monasteries, churches and other religious establishments. This is documented in many lands, both in the Orthodox East and the Catholic West.

Concerning the founding of Russian cities in particular, the most remarkable thing is that their creation, exclusively at Her instigation, occurred during a period when the Kievan Rus State was powerful, did not suffer from external enemies, and hence perceived no immediate need to expand beyond its borders. Yet, in the following centuries under the Tatar Yoke, those far-away towns and communities, which had already been built at the periphery of the Kievan Rus' State became the nucleus for the new Russia which

---

[29] I fully share the proposition advanced repeatedly in the literature that the greatest artistic contributions of Russia lie in her iconography and her religious architecture.

emerged and grew in the wake of the ravages wrought by the Tatar invasions. So, in a way, the Virgin Mary has contributed to the founding of the State of Muskovy in a most unique fashion.[30]

In numerous occasions, (to make Her specific instructions more convincing to the doubting Thomases) She predicted events which materialized shortly afterwards, miraculously healed persons who were abandoned by the medical science and also accompanied the message by external phenomena, such as the springing forth of fountains of healing water. Such measures, besides increasing the effectiveness of Her insistence in the short run, left behind indelible marks on the landscape for the edification of subsequent generations.

The antiquity of the Saints's intervention in the affairs of the local faithful has not been lost to the Russians. Many written reports account for the details of hundreds of such events. Beginning with the oldest chronicle available, the *Povest' Vremennikh Liet* it is reported that when St. Andrew the Apostle travelled beyond the Black Sea to evangelize the lands situated north of it, one day he showed a location to his disciples on the river Dniepr and said: *Do you see these mountains? On them one day will shine the grace of the Lord, a great city will be built and God will erect many churches.* This future city was Kiev, and St. Andrew became the Patron Saint of Russia, also.

In conclusion, one must seriously doubt the motivation of all those saviors who rose at the 12th hour to redeem Russia from its heathen ignorance, its godlessness and its theologically inferior positions. All these attempts to evangelize persons who have already proven their ethical superiority, their religious perseverance and their theological sophistication cannot be always ascribed to brotherly love and motivations beyond reproach, considering the technology used in many occasions and the blatant use of money to open doors and buy preferential treatment with public officials. In the eyes of better informed observers, they rather resemble attempts by monopolistically competitive firms to penetrate a new market and compete for market share in an environment of overall economic and social stress. The men of God

---

[30] Very specific historical accounts on the manifold city-founding functions of the Virgin Mary on behalf of Russia are also included in *On the Miracle Working Icons...*, introduced earlier. This publication is actually a reprinting of much older books from the library of the Colomna Convent, following the liberalization of press and religion in Russia.

have gone to the export business, basically. Russia is weakened, bleeding and vulnerable. If they can capitalize on a few market inefficiencies, so to say, they could get a temporary advantage for a couple of years or so. In the eyes of those who have already converted the religion of Jesus Christ into a Service Industry in the Entertainment Sector of the Economy, going Multinational is perceived as **the** strategy for long-term survival.

Under the circumstances, is it a matter of wonder that the Mother of God, as we saw earlier, has finally decided to step in Herself and take full command of the task of the miraculous rebirth of Russia?

Post scriptum 3: A few personal observations and experiences on the issue of contemporary realities

According to the legend from the Soviet Gulag *somewhere in the heart of the Taiga, not too far from the Ocean, many inmates in a moment of utmost despair cut off their own hands with the axe to free themselves from a labor so inhuman. Afterwards, they concealed the severed limbs in a cargo of Siberian lumber destined for the export market in the hope that so pathetic a message would alert the Occident. In order to give each other courage, the prisoners of the Gulag were repeating this story 'like an eternal dream of supreme justice dreamt by every condemned person.*

Of course, the Occident had more pressing needs at the time to pay any attention to the cut-of hands of the Taiga. Misunderstanding of Communism continued in the post-WWII world. Averell W. Harriman, who in the mean time had served as the US Ambassador to Moscow, in a January 1982 television interview commemorating the 100th anniversary of Franklin D. Roosevelt's birth made the following revelation: *Roosevelt never understood Communism. He viewed it as a sort of extension of the New Deal.*[31]

In the years between 1983-1985 I was working at the University of Houston, Department of Economics, on my doctoral dissertation on the Economics of the Construction Sector of the USSR. This was initially designed to be a project making part of a major study financed by the USA taxpayer and several private US foundations to collect and analyse material through

---

[31] J.-F. Revel, [1985, pp. 219-220], who comments that *perhaps the veteran diplomat should have noticed this when he was in a position to do something about it.*

interviews with recent Soviet emigrés living in the USA. (These were predominantly Soviet Jews who were allowed under the provision of the Jackson-Vanik Amendent to emigrate and a large number thereof came to the USA).[32] From my interviews with many knowledgeable professionals who had worked in the Soviet Construction in various capacities, plus my independent study from samizdat and other publication sources it became apparent that in the 1980s, Gorbachev's Glasnost' and Perestroika propaganda not-withstanding, at least twenty percent of the labor force used in Construction was recruited from the Gulag inmates. In other words, the Gulag had not died with the De-Stalinization. It was very much alive and well and was fed regularly by Soviet citizens convicted predominantly on 'economic crimes'.

Such Gulag conscripts, who more often than not were highly trained and professionally qualified technical personnel, were deliberately prosecuted and eventually condemned in order to be converted into slave-labor working for a pittance in territories no volunteers would like to go, no matter what the pay and the fringe benefits. This was designed to keep the cost of the prestigious Construction projects low for the bosses in the Kremlin.

The process of identifying 'criminals' was fairly straightforward: for a construction project that would require a few thousand additional professionals somewhere in Siberia, the KGB was receiving special directives from the relevant ministry and its associates. It was handing down the figures to the legal system, that such and such a body count is needed between now and, say, x months down the future. The judges would then begin to 'hear cases of economic crimes', which the KGB had no difficulty 'identifying' among enterprise managers, civil and construction engineers, procurement specialists and the like. Sooner or later everybody in the USSR was forced to commit 'economic crimes', in a desperate effort to fulfill an unrealistic and inhuman production plan.

The plans were designed to be unfulfillable on purpose, in order to facilitate the mass-production of such 'economic criminals', that could be mobilized in Siberia and elsewhere when the Gosplan dictated so. In other words,

---

[32]   The Jackson-Vanik Amendment of the United States - U.S.S.R Trade Agreeent of 1972, was an attempt to link trade to emigration. For a detailed treatment, the interested reader may consult John H. Jackson's *Legal Problems of International Economic Relations...*, West Publishing Co., 1977.

they were removed from their current positions where their services were obviously needed and shipped into the 'Taiga' were their services were needed even more and the wages could be drastically curtailed. That quintessential cheap fodder of the Gulag, indispensable for the 'Construction of Socialism', had not legal recourse to speak of, because the Gosplan was the Law of the Land, and wrecking the Gosplan was a serious crime. Furthermore, who was really the law-maker in the USSR at that time?...

As soon as the new quota of needed 'law-breakers' was handed down to the courts by the KGB, the courts produced the necessary number of condemned 'criminals' in a matter of weeks, essentially as fast as they could fake the hearing of cases and delivering justice, the Soviet way.

Since such facts (only too well known to every Soviet citizen) were an anathema to the US apologists of Communism, I met with violent resistance by the head of my doctoral committee when I put them on paper. I was not supposed to 'print such things' because 'they were just hearsay, by disgruntled émigrés, who obviously hate the USSR, that is why they emigrated in the first place'...[33]

I was further told repeatedly and most categorically that it is most un-academic and unprofessional to print something that was not corroborated by the Pravda and the Izvestia, which represented a different point of view, and their views had an equal right to appear on my dissertation. In other words, their testimony was at least as reliable as my data from the interviews and the Russian émigré presses. (Since the official Communist Party line claimed that the Gulag had died with the De-Stalinization, the chairman of my dissertation and his friends hoped to fully 'dilute the equity' of my findings, so to say, by forcing me to give equal weight to contradictory 'evidence' from more official sources...). I was branded as 'Anti-Sovietic'

---

[33] The population of respondents for the entire Soviet Interview Project, in other words, for whose identification and responses many millions of US taxpayer money had already been spent, suddenly became unreliable sycophants with axes to grind and unprintable verdicts. Needless to say, the S.I.P. managers continued collecting unperturbed data from such unreliable sources for years afterwards and finally produced their learned volumes based on such shaky evidence. One must assume that whatever they did not like in the data they removed it as unreliable and immoderate.

and immoderate, and laughed at for 'wanting to go alone against the whole world'.

The impasse went on for long months and was finally resolved by one of the Lord's peculiar ways: A French journalist stationed in Moscow, Patrick Meney, was conducting personal interviews with Soviet former inmates of the Gulag and was collecting a wealth of information analogous to mine (although his respondents came from all sides and not only from Construction). He also was successful (under great personal risk) in whisking out of the USSR the text of the Penal Code of the Soviet Ministry of the Interior; upon his return to France he wrote a documentary book appropriately entitled *Les Mains Coupées de la Taiga* (the Severed Hands of the Taiga), making the connection of the 1980s realities with those of the Stalinist era.

Both his text and the articles of the Penal Code corroborated in the nth power with all the tees crossed and all the iotas dotted everything I was saying in my study that the Sovietological establishment around my chairman found so offensive and unacceptable. My deus ex machina could have not possibly chosen a more fitting title for the chronicling of the long martyrdom of the Russian people. *Les Mains Coupées de la Taiga* earned for Patrick Meney the most prestigious award for French Journalism (the Prix Albert Londres), and the gratitude of millions.

I submitted a copy of the Penal Code to my Dissertation Chairman through the Dean of the School of Social Science who was also a Professor of Economics (and who was the only person, to his eternal credit, refusing to be co-opted by the 'politically powerful' Sovietologist in the department). The dissertation was signed within 3 days. These remarkable happenings of US academia took place in Ano Domini 1985.

The majority of the US Sovietological establishement was taken by surprise by the unexpected (to them) collapse of the system they worked so hard to praise and support.[34]   There was a fury of literary activity to either

---

[34] The majority, not the totality. There exists a small group of Sovietologists in this country whose work withstood the test of time and has earned them the respect of the Dissident Intellectuals expelled from the USSR, as well as of the Emigré community here and in Europe. These are truly knowledgeable persons and professionally proficient ones who have been working outside the mainstream

exonerate oneself for past predictions that never materialized or jump on the bandwaggon of the 'new wave' around the metamorphosed Leninist Gorbachev who would save Communism from its internal contradictions.[35] In one of those debates in the US media I had the pleasure of reading Mr. Vladimir K. Bukovsky's assessment in an editorial submitted to the *Commentary*, November 1988.[36] *(...) Yes, indeed, these Sovietologists have a skeleton in their filing cabinets. Unlike real scientists, they would rather be "moderate" than correct, and so they invented a lot of "reasons" why the testimony of émigrés should be ignored. We were, they said, "reactionary" and "biased"; and our views represented at best, only a tiny minority. (...) Thanks to the efforts of these people, whose arrogance was matched only by their ignorance, we émigrés were virtually ostracized, banned from the public debate, silenced in the media.*[37] *(...) How many scholars were forced to sacrifice the truth in order to be accepted in academic circles as "moderates," or in order to get their works published by prestigious presses? How many of those (particularly in the émigré community) seeking grants and tenure were forced to lie in order to survive professionally? What we have here are not the honest errors of some misled scholars but the acts of a mafia establishing its authority and protecting its interests. And yet, at the end of the day, all the sophisticated books and learned articles of the Sovietological mafia have been exposed for what they are - a pile of trash. (...). When we émigré intellectuals were living in the Soviet Union we were sent to jails and lunatic asylums for demanding glasnost' (...) now Moscow itself has confirmed word for word what we have been saying for a good*

Sovietological establishment and rarely, if ever, appeared in the former's Journals. The reader may have had occasions to listen to their views in the Robert McNeal and Jim Lehrer News Hour, which appears to have functioned as a much more dependable quality control mechanism vis-à-vis our Academia and our Professional Journals.

[35] Who has been all along a true Sovietologist and who not can be easily established by a perusal of their past positions, analysis and predictions. There is nothing safer than a post mortem examination on intellectual progeny.

[36] Anybody who asserts to possess any knowledge of contemporary Russia worth having, should already know who Mr. Bukovsky is, therefore an introduction is superfluous here.

[37] Mr. Bukovsky refers to all émigrés from the USSR and not exclusively those of the last Emigration.

twenty-five years. (...)

In subsequent correspondence with Mr. Bukovsky, where I related to him some of the highlights of my personal experiences, his assessment was quite chilling: *I cannot pretend to be very surprised by your story, in fact, I hear similar stories almost once a week.*

On December 4, the Eastern Churches celebrate St. John of Damascus, a luminary of the Christian faith and scholarship, highly honored by Catholics also who included him among their Doctors of the Church. St. John lived in Damascus when that portion of the Byzantine empire had fallen to the Muslim Arabs. Unjustly accused for treachery against the local Caliph, St. John was brought to trial and his hand was severed by a scimitar, according to Islamic Law. To the amazement of all present, St. John retrieved the severed hand and attached it to his wrist. The hand was fully restored and St. John of Damascus was allowed to continue his most productive career as a Theologian.

Those who take their Christian responsibilities seriously should never lose sight of the severed hand of St. John of Damascus and should abstain from joining in the self-promotion and triumphalist claims by a multitude of special interest groups in the West competing on who is going to get the highest credit for bringing about the collapse of Communism in Russia. Most of those claims are ludicrous, pathetic, with no basis in hard facts, and, at best, highly obfuscated and self-serving.

Let us abstain from adding affront to injury. A dispassionate analysis of contemporary politics and recent history makes more and more clear that the liberation came from within and from Above; it did not come from without. There are completely different agents at work here. Amidst the economic and social dislocations, the insecurities and the poverty, the pressures and stresses from within and without, they gradually restore Russia to its lost wholeness and heal the broken organism of a Church abandoned and betrayed by its current assorted 'saviors'. It will eventually be through the power and the grace of the Holy Virgin that the conversion of Russia's scattered and lost sheep back to the Christian fold will be completed and the severed hands of the Taiga will find their fitting place in History.

CHAPTER ELEVEN

ADDITIONAL PROPHETIC EVIDENCE ON INDIVIDUAL COUNTRIES: RUSSIA, USA, JAPAN AND CHINA, GERMANY AND AUSTRIA, TURKEY

But the fight for our planet, physical and spiritual, a fight of cosmic proportions, is not a vague matter of the future; it has already started. The forces of Evil have begun their decisive offensive. You can feel their pressure, yet your screens and publications are full of prescribed smiles and raised glasses. What is the joy about? Aleksandr Solzhenitsyn.[1]

There is no doubt that Western politicians are strongly interested in a Russian weakness and they consider as desirable its splitting-up over time (such a stubborn urge has been hammered upon the Russian audience of the American Radio 'Liberty' for quite a time now). But I maintain with conviction: these politicians do not have an adequate visualization of the long term perspectives into the 21st century. In that century there will appear situations when all of Europe plus the USA oh! how they will need Russia as an ally! Aleksandr Solzhenitsyn.[2]

Either the 21st century will be a spiritual one or it will not be at all. André Malraux.[3]

---

[1] Quoted by Charles Colson, [1989, p. 55].

[2] *"The Russian Problem" in the end of the 20th century* , reprinted in the Viestnik, no. 169, I-II - 1994, p 264, (my translation).

[3] French intellectual and statesman, (1901-1976). During his lifetime 18% of the Frenchmen were practicing Catholics. Today they are only 6%, and as François-Henri de Virieu, of *La Mediacratie* mused, if Malraux were alive today, he would be

Introduction
Russia features most prominently in the predictions of our near future. The testimony of the prophets with regards to its future role is in direct contradiction to many of the 'theories' and 'interpretations' proposed in the contemporary literature by instant experts. To economize time and space we shall abstain from dealing with these issues here, since several thereof have been already covered in my previous study. Yet, the fact remains, that few areas of learning have been subjected to such a fervent manipulation or such an outright neglect during most of this century as the historical realities of Russia. The reasons for such phenomena are many and various and would deserve an entire study of their own.

But let us touch upon some of the most obvious and blatant sources of the current predicament. It all began with the overall neglect of historical education in our schools. The words of a New York City school teacher who, in the mid 1980s explained the pointlessness of teaching history by saying that *our children don't think they have anything to learn from dead people* succinctly summarize the attitude imbedded in our culture.[4]

The Soviet Union was the architect of Atheistic Communism and the archenemy of the United States for more than 40 years. The Russians, in particular, were viewed as the driving force behind the "evil empire" and were painted in the darkest colors by the uninformed Westerners who saw in them only Atheists, brutal, undereducated beasts, KGB collaborators and World Peace-destabilizers. Neither our intellectual elites nor our political leaders nor our Sovietological establishment seemed to realize, or want to admit, that the Russians bore the worst punishment for the creation, expansion, and sustenance of the Soviet Empire, and were victimized above and beyond any other nationality of the former USSR.

They were the primary feeding stock of the Gulag, they built the industrial projects, infra-structure and economic production units that brought the Central Asian Republics out of their centuries-long slumber into the 20th century, they manned the armies sent to fight in God-forsaken places for the ego and the glory and the self-aggrandizement of a handful of under-educated party bosses, they launched the satellites and the space-crafts

---

surprised on how frequently he is being quoted and how infrequently followed.

[4] Quoted by L. H. Lapham, [1988, p. 149].

while the Party was getting all the glory and their own names were shrouded in mysterious generalities and blurring adjectives. They were required to finance the empire through long hours of work and longer hours in the queues for consumer goods, while at the same time they were forbidden even the privilege of foreign travel and tourism, (even in the unlikely event enough income could be left over to pay for the tickets...). As for domestic travel, an internal passport system and the ubiquitous KGB made certain that unless you travel strictly on business (with all necessary papers proving so), or you go to the predestined location of your yearly vacation break, you could get into very serious trouble...

In the end, in a moment of grandeur's folly matched only by his supreme ignorance and his stupidity, Mr. Brezhnev proposed the re-direction of the Russian rivers through the Central Asian deserts, in order to bring irrigation to the Turanians and improve their economic performance, while destroying the productivity and the climate of the Russian lands, and at the same time unleashing global environmental catastrophes. What other people, identified as the 'driving force' behind an empire has ever been asked to give so much while receiving so little in return?

The above concerns were expressed by the émigré community and the samizdat publications for decades. Most of our information brokers propounded different views to the US taxpayer. The intellectual vacuum could be easily filled, at low cost to the average perpetrator, with all kinds of theories, views, and expert opinions. Generic information brokers did not allow themselves to fall behind. A US journal whose target audience are the relatively affluent members of the American bourgeoisie educated them in the following manner on the issue of Antiques for Imperial Russia: *Basking in a Medieval Mongolian twilight, which only broke into Augustan dawn at the end of the seventeenth century, Russia's dusk of development was inhabited by a tall people of Turkish Byzantine and Oriental backgrounds.*[5] Therefore, when Solzhenitsyn complains that *the word Russia, has become soiled and tattered through careless use*, one could not agree more.

One must realize, however, that the Lord of History may have different views and opinions on peoples and nations, including Russia, and He makes

---

[5] *Architectural Digest*, August 1981. Its author, Sir Humphry Wakefield of Mallet in London, apparently 'lectures and writes on antique furniture and its allied art forms'.

those views public through His prophets. Furthermore, Russia, as a historical entity clearly delineated, precedes the creation of many modern states (such as the USA and Italy) by several centuries. Over that period of time many prophetic pronouncements dealing with the future of the world in general and of Russia in particular began accumulating in the land, either endogenously produced or imported from other lands of Christendom and the Holy Land.

Also, Russia, thanks to its Orthodoxy, is blessed with a plethora of prophetic information to start with, for the reasons we already introduced in the beginning of this study: they do not only have the Bible but also the Tradition and they have been collecting prophetic evidence (like the rest of the Orthodox and all of the Catholics) over the centuries of the Christian era.

Therefore, the prophetic testimony on Russia is expected to be much richer and more detailed, if for no other reasons, surely from a mere time-series accumulation perspective. While for instance, the prophetic testimony on the USA is much more limited; most of the endogenous prophetic evidence, furthermore, dates from the 19th and the 20th century. In Russia it begins with the evangelizing of the inhabitants along the river Dnieper during the Apostolic times, when Russia as a politically and cultural entity did not even exist, nor did its name. Since Russia's future is of vital interest to all Christians and Jews, we need to know more true facts about its past, and it pays to introduce some of the lessons of Contemporary History worth learning, even with a delay.

WHO BROUGHT ABOUT THE END OF SOVIET COMMUNISM?

Communism eventually collapsed when the Poles, the Baltic peoples, the Georgians, Armenians, Ukrainians and Russians, the Balkan Slavs and the East Germans decided to take a more active part in the shaping of their national destinies. It was **not** defeated by our military interventions, nor by the exploits of our 'staunch allies', the Turks, the Pakistanis, or the Egyptians.

Such realizations should not only increase our respect towards the democratic forces alive today among the Eastern Slavs but it should also sober us to the prospects on what will happen to us all when all that sophisticated hardware left in the hands of Turkey, Afghanistan, Pakistan, etc. is turned the other direction. Our experience in Iran and Iraq, for that matter, militates against complacency and historical amnesia. While the

Shah was in power, the USA could not have imagined a more staunch ally than Iran in all of Asia. It took a few weeks for the best friend to become the worst of all enemies. Those who think such a thing would never happen with Turkey and other allies from the Muslim world are just fooling themselves.

The CIA is trying to repurchase in the black market the sophisticated equipment given to the Afghan rebels free of charge. They are willing to pay top dollar to get back what they gave away. To put it charitably, the US taxpayer is punished twice for the same crime of the political short-sightedness, the historical dilettantism and the cheap military solutions of the late 1970s and the early 1980s. To make matters worse, the CIA is not that effective in this shopping spree, either. Having tasted the potency of the equipment, the warriors of Allah are not that eager to part with the hardware. Money they can get from the drug trafficking that is flourishing in their Golden Crescent. The income stream generated therefrom is an ever-replenishing one, since poppies are a renewable resource!

Parting with a stinger missile, however, is a more serious economic decision. You cannot plant a stinger missile and increase production the way you do with poppies. In the absence of domestic know-how that can render the production of hardware a quasi regenerative resource, arms trafficking does not respond strictly to the forces of the market place and money is not necessarily everything. Furthermore, religious fanaticism is a force stronger than money, anyway.

It is an irony of History that one day we will have reasons to be thankful to the military industrial complex of the former USSR and its reproductive capabilities. In the hands of an intelligent, well-educated, patriotic and creative people, military hardware is a renewable commodity that can be re-generated domestically; so, the Russians can be counted upon to produce the weapons necessary for defending themselves in the course of WWIII and countering the consequences of our diplomatic failures **(as well as theirs...)** the world over.

THE RELIGION OF THE RUSSIAN PEOPLE

Communism was not introduced in Russia by the faithful of the Eastern Orthodox Church. It was fomented by godless Russian intellectuals imbued with the cynicism and 'enlightenment' of the scientific revolution of the 19th century. Their idols were such imported species as the British Charles

Darwin, the German Karl Marx, and the French Claude-Henri de Saint Simon and Charles Fourier. To this group, which practically denied the most quintessential features of 'Russian'-ness, namely, its spirituality, were attached many Russian Jews, who were openly espousing atheism.[6]

The leaders of the Soviet Union, therefore, were not that Russian after all, either in character, or Weltanschauung or even name. Let us not forget that the Bolshevik leaders rose to power under pseudonyms! From Vladimir Ilich Oulianov (Lenin), to Iossif Vissarionovich Dzougashvili (Stalin), to Grigori Yefseyevich Radomylski (Zinoviev), to Lev Davidovich Bronstein (Trotsky), to Viacheslav Mikhailovich Skriabin (Molotov), to Lev Borissovich Rozenfeld (Kamenev) and so forth...

Those intellectual Russian Christians who did not perish in the firing squads or the Gulag right away were forced to emigration by the government of the Soviet Union as early as 1922. No less than 120 university professors, intellectuals and public figures were ousted in one stroke merely for not espousing the Marxist ideology. The *band of pseudonyms* took over, and with the commercial and technological injections from Europe and the United States they erected the Soviet military machinery against which we had to recruit so many a "staunch" ally after WWII in Africa, Central and South America, the Middle East, the Philippines and many other corners of the world.

As a final remark to wrap up the history of failures and missed opportunities with regards to the Soviet Union, before we proceed with the prophetic evidence on behalf of Russia's future:

It is not to the credit of our "staunch" allies but to a citizen of the Evil Empire, the Russian Colonel Oleg Penkovsky, that the Cuban Missile Crisis was diffused without bloodshed. Penkovsky had to pay with torture and a traitor's execution for his willingness to fight the evil empire from within. And what do we have to compare with Penkovsky? Aldrich Ames and company?

---

[6] Of course, one might argue that being a Jew **and** an Atheist is a contradiction in terms. I am willing to speculate that those Jews who were so instrumental in bringing Communism to Russia (Trotsky, Zinoviev, and company) would not be the pride of their race, either, nor would they have the eternal gratitude of the Soviet Jews who were born and trained into an atheist culture that instills fear in the heart and trepidation before the morrow.

THE PROPHETIC EVIDENCE ON RUSSIA
REGARDING WWIII

<u>Anne Catherine Emmerich</u>: (1774-1824 A.D.; the following prophecies dated 1820-1821 A.D.)
I saw the various regions of the earth. My Guide, (Jesus) named Europe, and pointing to a small and sandy region, He uttered these remarkable words: 'Here is Prussia, the enemy.' Then He showed me another place, to the north, and He said: 'This is Moskva, the land of Moscow, bringing many evils.'

<u>Commentary</u>
This prophecy does **not** apply so much to WWIII but I begin with it to clarify certain misunderstandings spread in the popular literature. There are several mentions of the evils emanating either from Moscow, or speaking (such as in the apparition of the Holy Virgin, at Garabandal, for instance) of Communism being a great force to be reckoned with in the future.

But let us consider the following:

a)   Anne Catherine Emmerich had this vision in the early 1800s;
b)   in the Fátima apparitions of the Holy Virgin when the Catholics were exhorted to pray for Russia, Communism had not taken over Russia yet; and
c)   when the Lady Theotokos spoke in Garabandal of Spain in the 1960s of Communism again as being an evil future force she did **not** specify Russia. Today the most probable threat of Communism will come from mainland China. The left-overs of Communists in Europe (either former USSR or Eastern Europe or anywhere else for that matter) pale in comparison to the Eastern threat, although they will be most instrumental in the prophesied internal dissensions and civil wars which will break out in many European countries, such as Italy, France, and Spain, explicitly referred to by many prophecies.

Consequently, my interpretation of prophecies referring to Russia will not follow the line advanced in many Catholic and Protestant authors producing their learned volumes for the mass-circulation presses. Some of the reasons became apparent in *Our Revelationary Age*.... But there exist additional ones:

Primarily, I enjoy 'the home advantage' in a sense: being a Greek Orthodox by choice, and having become familiarized academically with the history of Russia, the history of Communism, the history of the Russian Church in the past 1000 years, and other related matters, I am able to submit whatever is written with regards to the former USSR to greater degree of scrutiny and quality control procedures than the average person who believes all information reaching him comes from honest, hardworking people who desire to promote the truth, only the truth and nothing but the truth.

Secondly, there exists no paucity of information within Russia today regarding the truth. As the Gospel teaches us, *search for the truth and the truth will make you free*. Furthermore, the truth of the past and the present will allow us to better understand the truth about the future, and more specifically the prophecies about the future, the main object of enquiry in this study. Hence the pursuit of truth will considerably enhance the benefit we may be able to derive from an interpretation of prophecies dealing with the future of the world.

Thirdly, those who pontificate so liberally at the expense of Russia, almost never speak Russian, are ignorant of its History and quite possibly at some point in time they ascribed to the 'better red than dead'- school of thought. Now, that the Soviet threat has disappeared, they came out of the bunker and began delivering cheap sermons to the Russians on subjects ranging from their acceptable posture vis-à-vis the Balkan crisis, to the war in Chechnya, to the effective way of protecting 20 million Russian nationals stranded in hostile former Soviet Republics, to their concerns about the fermentation in their borders, to their superstitious hangovers exemplified by attitudes such as the veneration and devotion to their Czaricza Nebesnaya (the Queen of Heaven), etc. etc. etc. But as José Ortega y Gasset would have said, they are disqualifiable and disqualified by their very contexture in engaging in such activities and in pronouncing a premature death sentence on a people destined by Providence for a major heroic role during WWIII, and a happier life in the century to come.

In view of the above, the intimation by Lord Jesus Christ to Emmerich that Moscow will bring many evils was foreshadowing the Communist take-over by secular powers and the destruction of the Russian Empire by the 'band of pseudonyms' in the late 1910s. The Lord Jesus Christ was referring to His faithful Russian Orthodox Christians who were persecuted and martyred by the warlords of Kremlin, that 'Synagogue of Satan' in the words of Father Sergii Bulgakov, a Russian exile and champion of Russian Orthodoxy, himself. The warlords of Kremlin brought many evils with the acquiescence of secular and ecclesiastic powers in the West. And a few of those self-same Catholic refuters of Russia in a lucid moment confess that many a Kremlin boss were favored with a papal audience during the Cold War era...

Further material from the visions of Anne Catherine Emmerich:
Very bad times will come when non-Catholics will lead many people astray. A great confusion will result. I saw the battle also. The enemies were far more numerous, but the small army of the faithful cut down whole rows. During the battle the Blessed Virgin stood on a hill, wearing a suit of armor. It was a terrible war. At the end, only a few fighters for the just cause survived, but the victory was theirs.

It never occurred to Catholic writer Dupont, [1973], that the above passage may refer to **non-Christian** armies fighting against the **faithful**. Non-Catholics is not synonymous to Russian! The Muslims, or the Communist Chinese, or the Shintoist Japanese, or the Animists, or the Jews, or the Orthodox, or the Southern Baptists, or the Godless are among those many who also qualify as non-Catholics. But most importantly, when the Blessed Virgin stands on a hill wearing a suit of armor, we have every reason to believe (thanks to our knowledge of analogous events from history) that Her grace is defending Christians against Muslims. The Virgin Mary has been assisting Russian armies as well into military victories for the last one thousand years. The Greeks call Her their 'Champion and Leader in Battle' for the same reason![7]

It remains a source of wonder and amazement for me, how can any one reading the above passage from Emmerich reach the remarkable conclusion that Russia is implied here. Furthermore, Emmerich's words are 'I saw the battle also'. She did not specify which battle and she may have used the term 'battle' as a synonym for an armed conflict that was prolonged, desperate and very bloody. With so little information available in the text it

---

[7] The Most Blessed Virgin Mary has been the well established 'Champion in Battle' for the Orthodox peoples throughout their history in wars against Muslim forces. Consequently, it would be much more appropriate to connect the above vision, where She wears a suit of armor, as a major war between faiths, the numerous Muslims on the one hand and the victorious, though smaller forces of the Christian armies on the other. After all, such a version is consistent with the voluminous testimony from the History of the peoples of Orthodoxy, including the 'heathen' Russians and their numerous battles against Mongols, Tatars and Turks in centuries past.

takes something other than genius to conclude that a very specific battle to be fought in Westphalia is predicted, considering that during WWIII battles will be fought on all continents and on all major oceans and for a duration of 3.5 - 4 years, give and take.[8]

From a 16th century manuscript of Greek prophecies:
Text
(...) After these events, the blond nations from the East and the West will be troubled; the sons of Agar will get together and wage a war and one blond nation will defeat them completely. The sons of Agar will fall like the stalks of wheat. An enormous fleet will gather against them and they shall converge in the Seven-Hilled city (Constantinople). There, the war will be fought on land and sea; and they will enter into the Seven-Hilled City via Kontoskalion (Contoscalion) and they will utterly crush the Ishmaelite.[9]

---

[8] The same author, [op. cit., pp. 14-15], makes additional remarkable revelations on the subject of Russia: "St. Methodius was one of the earliest prophets of the Christian era to foresee the victory of Communism. He did not name Communism, but correlations with other prophecies will make this clear. Many other prophecies say that the victory of Communism will seem so certain that they, the Communists, will throw up their caps and shout about their triumph. At that very moment a cosmic phenomenon will take place, and help the designs of the future King's small army (it is only later that his army will grow to be very large). This most Christian prince will reduce the Communists to a rabble".

He fails to supply evidence on which other specific prophecies we ought to correlate with St. Methodius's dictum. If that writer had been any less biased and prejudiced, he would have read the text of St. Methodius with more profit for himself and his readers. Since St. Methodius was Greek (and wrote in Greek), this author probably would have read him in some form of translation, for, I detected no Greek text mentioned in his bibliography. Even so, it is rather risqué to claim that St. Methodius was 'foreseeing the victory of Communism', which he did not even bother to mention even periphrastically, or give us any hint on the identity of this evil prophesied by him.

In chapter eight, dealing predominantly with Greek prophecies of WWIII we had an opportunity to see what St. Methodius really said. As far as its 'correlation with other prophecies' is concerned, the readers can judge for themselves.

[9] Καὶ μετὰ ταῦτα ταραχθήσονται τὰ ξανθὰ γένη ἐξ ἀνατολῶν καί δυσμῶν· καί συναχθήσονται ᾽Αγαρηνοὶ καὶ συνάψουσι πόλεμον, καί τό ξανθὸν γένος τροπώσει αὐτούς, καὶ ὡς στάχυες πεσοῦνται, καί στόλος μυρμηκόστολος κινηθήσεται

Interpretation

'The blond nations from East and West will be troubled' can be understood without danger of misinterpretation as pertaining to Christian populations of Europe (or emanating from Europe, as the case can be made for many US citizens today), and the USA. The Greeks of that era made a general distinction of the northern nations vs. the Arabs and the Turks, (their southern and eastern enemies) who are dark skinned, or at least dark haired. The victors will enter the old city of Byzantium through Kontoskalion (Contoscalion). The Constantinople mentioned in the Byzantine era prophets was contained within the walls and was built on the original seven hills within those walls, particularly the ones built by emperor Theodosius II. It spilled over the other side of the Golden Horn, but it did not expand on the Asian side of the Sea of Marmara. There were other cities arleady established there and they were treated as distinct entities, with their own names.

By contrast, today's Istanbul spills over on the side of Asiatic Turkey. The Byzantine era Constantinople could be accessed by several ports on the Golden Horn and more importantly through the Sea of Marmara. Kontoskalion was one of them. In fact, as far as the old city of Constantinople is concerned, Kontoskalion (Contoscalion), which was the name of a harbor and the adjacent gate in the walls of the city, can be found on period maps and historical accounts.[10]

Consequently, we are even told by the prophets exactly where the army will disembark! Namely, in a port which is upon the Sea of Marmara, positioned almost halfway between the two extremes of the side of the triangle corresponding to the old Constantinople, enclosed within the walls of Theodosius II. The entirety of this side is washed by the Sea of Marmara. Looking at the geography of the area and the relative width of the sea lanes from the Dardanelles all the way through the Bosphorus to the Black Sea, Kontoskalion (Contoscalion) is a most plausible choice, because the sea at

---

κατ᾽ αὐτῶν καὶ συναχθήσονται ἐν τῇ ᾽Επταλόφῳ, καί γενήσεται πόλεμος μέγας διά ξηρᾶς καί θαλάσσης· καὶ διὰ τοῦ Κοντοσκαλίου εἰσέλθωσιν εἰς τὴν ᾽Επτάλοφον καί συντρίψουσιν τόν ᾽Ισμαηλίτην. (Sotiropoulos, [1974, pp. 86-87]).

[10] See, for instance Sir Steven Runciman, [1987, p. 88], and J. Ch. Kiomourdjian, [1992, pp. 21-22] for detailed reports and corresponding maps. After the fall to the Turks, the Contoscalion gate was renamed Kum-Kapi.

that location affords much greater freedom of movement to a fleet.

From the prophecies of Leo the Philosopher:[11]
Translation of the text
In the end times of the reign of the Ishmaelites, Agarenes, Saracens etc. the human race will be troubled by kinds of war not seen before. Then, the blond nation, will make an expedition against many, using in the warfare its many war machines. In the Seven-Hilled Constantinople the occupation of the Agarenes will end "when the 20th element is being saluted on its walls". (PG 107, 1141).

Interpretation
In *Our Revelationary Age...* we established the identity of the victor of WWIII, as Juan Carlos I de Borbón, King of Spain, using a large set of prophetic material completely unrelated to the material employed in the current study. When the Byzantines spoke of "the 20th element as being saluted on its walls", they make an allusion to the name of Juan Carlos, which in Greek is Karolos, begins with a K. In the numbering system of the Greeks it corresponds to 20. The name of the exiled King Constantine of the Hellenes (Konstantinos), also begins with a K, hence, he could also be saluted on the walls!

In a different chapter we explained how Queen Sophia of Spain (and her children) have Romanov blood in their veins. (This was through the 1867 marriage of Grand Duchess Olga of Russia to the founder of the Greek royal dynasty, George I of the Hellenes, son of King Christian IX of Denmark). Crown Prince Constantine, one of the seven children born to that marriage, later King Constantine I, is a direct ancestor of King Constantine II of the Hellenes, Queen Sophia of Spain, and their sister Princess Irene. Therefore, all of them could satisfy a prophetic constraint of a 'Russian Czar' reigning

---

[11] Ἀνωνύμου Παράφρασις τῶν τοῦ Βασιλέως Λέοντος τοῦ Σοφοῦ Χρησμῶν, πγ 107, 1141. The Byzantine Emperor Leo the Philosopher reigned 886-889 A.D. His texts foretold the Moslem conquest of Constantinople of 1453 A.D. Shortly before the fall of the City a tablet was found in a cloister, attributed to Leo, which contained the correct succession of the names of all the Byzantine emperors and Patriarchs for the next 600 years. Every name had its own space on the tablet. The last one was empty, showing that Constantine was to be the last emperor. Constantine Paleologus was killed by the Turks during the assault on the City. We shall have more to say on Leo the Philosopher's prophecies in another chapter, where we shall also study a more detailed version of the one given here.

from Constantinople.[12]

The blond nation, making an expedition against many, using in the warfare its many war machines, **could,** once again, be a reference to Russia. The term 'blond nation' relating to Russia appears frequently in old Greek and Byzantine era prophecies. But since the evidence is still inconclusive, we shall search further.

Prophecy of St. Andrew the Fool-For-Christ:[13]
Translation
This city which is sitting above many nations will become unassailable by the nations; because the mother of God has protected it under the aegis of Her own wings; and by Her intercessions it will be preserved; There is talk that the Agarenes will enter the city and will kill by the sword many multitudes; however, I say that the blond nation will enter the city, as well; **this blond nation's name begins with the 17th letter among the 24 ones of the Greek alphabet** [emphasis added]; so, the blond nation will enter into the city and the bodies of the sinners will be strewn upon the earth; woe to the sinners and what will befall on them through the two offsprings who have swords like the wind and the sharp scythe, as when it cuts down the wheat in the summer. (...) Because, in the last times, the Lord God will raise a King who was born in poverty and whose ways will be just, and through his charity he will be liked by everybody; he will put an end to all wars; the poor men he will make rich, and the peace upon the earth will be reminiscent of the times of Noah, when the men did not engage in warfare. The people will be extremely wealthy in those days, and in peace and in

---

[12] I did not have the opportunity to study such prophecies first hand. Through my general reading, however, I became aware that several existed in Russia for a long time speaking of their capturing Constantinople and ruling therefrom. It must be said with all frankness that besides the Greeks nobody felt so painfully the loss of Constantinople as did the Orthodox Russians. Their literature is imbued with the dream of its recapture. Also, their history attests to the fact that no other Christian nations has fought as many wars against the Ottomans as the Russians have.

[13] This St. Andrew apparently lived between 450-515 A.D. Yet, A. D. Delimpasis, author of *Terrible and Wonderful Coming Events*, has moved him to the period between 880 and 936 A.D. I do not know which of the two is correct. The title Fool-for-Christ is given to a person who has renounced the logic of the world to be an example of Christ to others. There are several Orthodox saints (in various countries) who were known during their lifetime as Fools-for-Christs.

profound serenity they will engage in eating and drinking, in getting married and giving their relatives to marriage, living without pressure and enjoying the things of the earth without cares; and since there will be no war upon the earth, they will cut down their swords and convert them into various agricultural implements and tools.

And later he will turn towards the East and he will humble the sons of Agar; because the Lord will become very angry for their blasphemy against our Lord Jesus Christ and for the Sodomitic lewdness they are engaging in; and many among them will receive the Holy Baptism and will become agreeable and will be honored by that pious king; the remainder among the sons of Agar he will destroy by fire and violent death. During those times the entire earth will be restored; the lands of the Adriatic, will be part of the Roman empire and Egypt will become an ally. And the king will put his hand on the nations that are all around; and he will pacify the blond nations and those who hate him he will defeat in battle; he will be king for thirty two years. For the length of twelve years he will not impose any taxes and contributions. He will raise the altars which were destroyed and he will erect holy churches. There will be no lawsuits in those days because nobody will become defendant and nobody will become plaintiff; before him all earth will shrink in terror and the fear will convince the sons of men to behave prudently. And he will exterminate all lawless lords.

<u>Commentary</u>
Let us begin with a historical overview: The patron Saint of Constantinople was the Most Blessed Panaghia. Many have been the historically marked instances of Her miraculous protection of the City during wars and sieges. Western readers may not realize the impressive number of wars and battles and expeditions the Byzantines had to fight in order to protect the empire from a multitude of enemies in the course of 11 centuries. Consequently, many have been the instances when only Divine Assistance could turn the overwhelming odds in favor of a numerically negligible defending force. Once Divine Assistance was removed, the City fell. But even then, it took the Ottoman armies made up of 80,000 regulars assisted by hordes of irregulars, plus the greatest artillely force till that time, plus a huge armada, several days of continuous fighting to break the opposition of 7,000

Constantinople defenders.[14]

The truly future part of the prophecy begins therefore with the words *however I say that the...* Once again we hear of the **blond nation**, but now we are also told that its name begins with the 17th letter of the Greek alphabet. This letter is ρ, P (the Latin sound of 'r').[15] Russia is spelled Ρωσσία in Greek and begins with a P. But so, the reader may argue, does Romania, although not a 'blond nation' per se, and a very small country

---

[14] Even before the City fell, there was a torrent of prophecies predicting its capture but also its recovery at some distant future. One of them, immortalized in a popular song included the following text: *God willed it so that the City by taken by the Turks; however, all sacred objects from the churches must be shipped without delay to the lands of Christianity in Western Europe, so that they do not become profaned by the enemy. As soon as the Queen of Heaven heard the verdict, She became troubled and Her icons began shedding copious tears. Please stop, oh Lady, Queen of ours, do not cry, do not shed Your tears. After many years and seasons, all these will become Yours, once again!*

[15] The reader may feel bewildered and nonplused to hear that 'r' is the seventeenth letter in the Greek Alphabet, having just read that K = 20 and corresponds to Karolos and Konstantinos. However, the issue becomes clarified once we distinguish the letters in their application as letters in the alphabet vs. their use as numerals in the ancient Greek numbering system. The reader may remember that the Greek mathematical system used letters as figures and numerals (with limited success as one can imagine. Consequently, although Algebra was a Greek invention, it waited for the Arabic numbering system (itself an evolution from an Indian one) before it could develop further.

Let us see what these distinctions imply:

$\alpha, \beta, \gamma, \delta, \epsilon, \zeta, \eta, \theta, \iota, \kappa, \lambda, \mu, \nu, \xi, o, \pi, \rho, \sigma, \tau, \upsilon, \phi, \chi, \psi, \omega$, correspond to the 24 letters of the Greek alphabet.

On the other hand, in terms of mathematical value,
$\alpha = 1; \beta = 2; \gamma = 3; \delta = 4; \epsilon = 5; \sigma\tau = 6; \zeta = 7;...\iota = 10; \iota\alpha = 11; \kappa = 20; \kappa\beta = 22; ... \pi = 80, \rho = 100; ... \omega = 800$. A few additional symbols that connote numbers do not correspond any longer to letters of the Greek alphabet currently in use. In any event, we have shown that ρ is the seventeenth letter of the alphabet, while it corresponds to 100 in the old Greek numbering system, which had no symbol for 0 and was unable to count beyond 10,000, unless it were to use multiples of that number (myriad, two myriads, etc.).

compared with Russia, but still a Christian one that could fight against Islam. So, let us continue with our search. For one thing, the previous prophecy informs us about the great king of victory and peace, which is consistent with everything else we know about that personage.

The Tombstone Prophecy:
(The following prophecy was carved on the tombstone of Constantine the Great in the year 339 A.D. It was supplying only a portion of the letters in each word, but if the words were to be filled up correctly, the entire prophecy could be read as a smoothly flowing poem. It was deciphered by Patriarch Gennadios in 1440 A.D., namely, only 13 years preceding the fall of Constantinople).

<u>Translation</u>
The first day of the Indictus[16] the kingdom of Ishmael, whose name is Moameth (Mohammed) will defeat the race of the Palaeologus; it will conquer the Seven-Hilled city; it will make it his capital; it will conquer many nations and will devastate the islands even those located in the Black Sea. On the eight day of the Indictus (Mohammed) will conquer our neighbors along the Danube. On the ninth day of the Indictus he will take over the Peloponnesus and then he will prepare a campaign against the North. On the tenth day of the Indictus he will overthrow the Dalmatians, he will come back for a short while, and subsequently he will prepare a great war against the Dalmatians where he will suffer a few defeats; and the multitudes and nations from the West will engage in war against the kingdom of Ishmael by land and sea and they will defeat Ishmael. Afterwards, Ishmael's offspring will reign once again for a short period. **But the blond nation along with its allies will utterly defeat the entire Ishmael,** [emphasis added] will take the Seven-Hilled city and will receive all prerogatives and rights associated with it.[17] Then, they will raise an internecine strife, very fierce, till the fifth

---

[16] *Indiction* or *Indictus* (from the Latin Indictio) was a 15-year-cycle used as a temporal unit by the Church. Nowadays, the first of Indictus corresponds to the first of September, which denotes the beginning of the ecclesiastical year in the Orthodox Church. In the poem on the tombstone the time-measurement can be taken as an approximation of time periods which elapsed between events, but primarily it was meant to show the chronological sequencing of the events in the order of their materialization.

[17] Considering the strategically located city of Constantinople, such prerogatives are dealing with the rights of passage, navigation, etc.

hour (of the day). And a loud voice will be heard shouting thrice: cease and desist in trepidation, make haste and go to search in the territories located at the right hand and there you will find a man who is valiant, admirable and robust; you will proclaim him your ruler, because he is dear to Me, and having accepted him you are fulfilling My wish.

Commentary
The totality of the data already at our disposal (combined with the Byzantine era prophecies in a previous chapter, and data from my previous study) indicate that the victor par excellence against the Turkic armies will be the Russians. The Great Monarch will fight and conquer other Islamic nations, such as the Arab coalition. Once the two Christian armies converge in Byzantium it appears that there will be a conflict on who will get what spoils of the war, including Constantinople. The conflict will be resolved through Divine intervention and the appointment of the Great Monarch as the legitimate ruler from new Byzantium with the blessings from Above.

The Apocalypse of Daniel:[18]
(I took the liberty of emphasizing certain passages for easier retrieval. Since only the most relevant excerpts from the prophecy are given here, the interested reader may wish to consult Dr. Zervos's text for the rest of the text, in the source given below).

According to the God-spoken word which says: *When you hear of wars and rumors of wars, **nation will fight against nation, and kingdom against kingdom, earthquakes, plagues and deviations of stars.*** Then the bush which restrains the sons of Hagar will dry up. And three sons of Hagar will go forth into great Babylonia... And Ishmael will come down the region of the land of swift passage. And he will establish his camp in **Chalcedon across from Byzantium.** And the other one will come to **Antioch, Cilicia,** and **Iberian Anatolia**, the **Thrakysan** country and **Smyrna** and as far as the **Seven-Hilled city.** And he will spill Roman blood. And another will come to the region of Persia and the **Galilean** country the **Armenian border**, and the city of **Trebizond.** And he will come to the region of the **land of the Meropes.** And he will massacre male children from two and three years old

---

[18] It was written in Greek, in Constantinople around the year 800 AD. I had no access to the original manuscripts. The English translation given above is a reproduction of the text's translation prepared by G.T. Zervos, as it appears in the *Old Testament Pseudepigrapha*, vol. 1, pp. 763-767, published by Doubleday.

and younger. And he will consume them by the sword. And the third one will come down the regions of the north and **Mesiaspolis** and **Synopolis**, and **Zalichos**, the regions of **Chrysiapetra**, and the well-lit valley and **Bithynia**, and of **Daphnousia**, **Chrysioupolis** and **Damoulion** and as far as the Seven-Hilled city.

And therefore all these (will) slaughter an infinite multitude of Romans from two and three years old and younger. And they will gather together toward the sea. And in their ships (will be) a myriad myriads. (...) Woe, woe then. How will the orthodox faith of the Christians and the invincible power of the honorable and life-giving cross be overcome?

But hear, brethren, that because of their iniquity God forbears. And the first will set up his couch across from Byzantium. And he will strike and they will be stricken. And then the rulers of the Romans blaspheme, saying, *Woe, woe, neither in heaven do we have a king nor on the earth*. And with this word the Lord will incline his mercy toward the Romans and toward their revenge and will repay justice to his enemies. **And there will be a great sound from heaven and a fearful earthquake and a voice from the angel from heaven.** And the Lord will incline his head and will set his fury against the sons of Hagar and upon the implacable race of Ishmael. And the Lord will lift up the cowardice of the Romans and put it into the hearts of Ishmael, and the courage of the Ishmaelites into the hearts of the Romans. And the Lord will raise up a king of the Romans, who people say is dead and useful for nothing, who people think died many years before. The Lord is reserving this man in the outer country of Persia.[19] This is his name: that which begins with the letter K of the alphabet. And this man is coming to the Seven-Hilled city toward the evening.[20] And he will prepare for his enemies. And on Saturday morning as the sun rises, he will engage in a great war with the nation and the sons of Hagar, both he and the two small boys. And the rulers of the Romans will gather together in Byzantium. **Then even the priests of the Romans and the bishops and abbots who are found will bear weapons of war.**

---

[19] In a different manuscript there was written in the inner country of the Persian and Syrian nations.

[20] The manuscript M mentions that *this man's entrance will occur on a Friday*. This detail will prove valuable to us, later on.

... And Ishmael and the sons of Hagar will be butchered to the end. And there will be war and great bloodshed such as has not been since the foundation of the world. The blood will be mixed in the sea one and a half miles. And in the streets of the Seven-Hilled city horses will be submerged, drowning in blood. And from that nation and from Ishmael there will remain only three tents of men. And the sons of Ishmael will serve the Romans to the end and will serve the chief donkey drivers of the Seven-Hilled city for thirty years. (...) And the Roman race will desire to see a trace of Ishmael and will not find it. And then the prophetic word will be fulfilled that says: *How will one pursue a thousand and two remove myriads unless the Lord God rejected them and the Lord gave them over?* And the king of the Romans will subdue every enemy and adversary (...) There will be one empire. And there will be great peace. ... And all the islands and the mountains will be inhabited. ... And his reign will be for 36 years. And his two small boys will be taken up in peace after 33 years.

And after him there will arise from the north another king. And working great impurities and many injustices he will also work great iniquities. ... Woe, woe then to the Christian race. Woe to those who are pregnant. And the praises of God also will cease. **And the Lord God will call fire from heaven and will consume them**. And after him a foul and alien woman will reign in the Seven-hilled city. (...).

... Woe, to you, the Christian race. Again there will be an inroad of nations, again fear among the Romans again slaughters and disturbances for the Roman nation. ... And therefore woe to you, wretched Babylon (Constantinople) the mother of cities, because God will incline his wrath which emits fire. ...

And another great scepter will arise from Judaea. (...)
(The prophecy continues with the career of the Antichrist...).

Commentary
In view of our analysis, the predictions given above do not present a mystery any longer, since the WWIII will be a coalition of Muslims, emanating from Assyria (Iraq), Turkey, other Arab nations and other Muslim lands. The wording of the *Apocalypse of Daniel* corroborates this thesis fully, because the nationality of the armies and their points of departure are in consistence with events prophesied elsewhere to occur during the WWIII. Most of the geographical localities correspond to cities in Turkey presented under their original Greek names during the Byzantine empire centuries.

The land of the Meropes, we believe to have identified as the Island groups in Southern Aegean, namely the Dodecanese, the Cyclades and possibly their vicinity, Crete, and the Greek portion of Cyprus, namely, Greek Territory.[21]   The sons of Hagar, was a term given by Greek Christians to both the Arabs and the Turks, as we saw already.

There are several elements in this prophecy that deserve a more detailed explanation. Let us begin with *and the Lord will lift up the cowardice of the Romans and put it into the hearts of Ishmael, and the courage of the Ishmaelites into the hearts of the Romans*. I will 'translate' it as follows: The Muslim religion has the remarkable feature of Kismet (Fate, Destiny). This implies the fatalism so endemic to Muslim peoples. This fatalism works both ways: in periods of prolonged peace it can lull the human spirit into a dejected inactivity that can also lead to economic decay; on the other hand, in the case of war it can be harnessed as an incentive and a motivator par excellence.   So, the Kismet has much to do with the manifested performance of Islam in all human economic and technological activities except war.[22]

In the case of war, which basically always has elements of a Ji'had, (namely a 'holy war' against the 'Infidels', who refuse to adopt Islam) the Muslims can be easily persuaded that they cannot loose; if they win and manage to survive, they shall inherit both the wealth of the defeated and the defeated themselves; therefore, they shall extract economic rent from their slaves for the duration of their earthly existence.   Therefore, war for them, as an economic activity, can generate both wealth and income. It was precisely this ability to extract economic rent from the non-Muslim nationalities of the Ottoman Empire that guaranteed its survival for so long. Islam has not succeeded to add much to the wealth of the nations. It has managed, however, to live on the wealth and the incomes of many nations that were more productive but not careful enough to safeguard their gains.[23]

---

[21] We studied earlier that the Royal Meropeia was part of the Cyclades before the destruction of Calliste and adjacent areas.

[22] War can be a major economic activity even when dressed in the veil of 'ideals' and 'holy duty'.

[23] Before the apologists of Islam express their opprobrium for such heretical economic reasoning I will present a characteristic example that I trust will suffice to make the point. It deals with the notorious 'Capitulations' between the European

Now, suppose that the Muslim warrior dies in battle, instead. Since he is fighting 'a holy war' allegedly condoned by Allah, he will die as a martyr of the faith and hence will be amply rewarded in Paradise. So, the warrior is brainwashed to believe that he cannot lose. One needs only to remember the Iranian 10-year-olds that the Ayatollah Khomeini launched against the Iraqi weapons in the 1980s. A key on a chain around their necks reminded them always of the gates of Heaven, because dying for the Ayatollah was equivalent to dying for God Himself...

So, basically, the heroism exhibited in battle derives from a distorted view of what constitutes in a statistical and economic sense the expected economic value of a military enterprise in the pay-off matrix called Ji'had. As long as the Muslim is led to the unquestionable belief that for him the 'ultima ratio' is a win-win economic activity, he will act heroically in the battle-field, especially when his economic options back home look very bleak. Having already lost in the economic competition game in the global economy he has not much to hope for. For Islam in our days, war has become a very low opportunity cost activity. A sense of uselessness and

---

Powers and the Ottoman Empire. The 'Capitulations' as the title suggests (deriving from capitula and not capitulation) referred to the articles of commercial and other agreements (identified by the chapter title and number), between the Kings and Capitalists of Europe, on the one hand, and the Sultan on the other. Accordingly, the Europeans were given the right to establish trading colonies in the Ottoman Empire and were bestowed a number of privileges, such as the right of being tried in their own courts rather than the Islamic ones. All those privileges were stipulated under the terms of reciprocity. Namely, that the Turks had exactly the same rights and privileges to establish trading colonies and engage in analogous activities in the ports and capitals of Europe. And if need be, the right to be tried by their own courts, and the like.
While the Europeans made full use of the stipulated agreements and grew in economic might and political influence within the Ottoman Empire, the Turks did not bother to establish commercial colonies and take any advantage of their parallel rights and privileges. Therefore, in the end they came to resent and hate the foreigners who enjoyed such blatant privileges like extraterritoriality and 'sapped the blood' of the Turk in his own land! The Turks never admitted their own economic inability to take care of their own trade, both domestic and foreign. The domestic traders who had no recourse to foreign laws, (such as Greeks, Armenians and Jews) were either massacred or expelled under Kemal's 'nationalist policies'. As for the blood-sucking foreigners, their status was repealed following the collapse of the Ottoman Empire.

despair will foment further heroism in battle, because in our days the battlefield becomes the ultimate card left to the disenfranchised, unemployed Muslim citizen of the Third World to play.

However, the Almighty will remove this kind of heroism from the heart of Ishmael, as we learn also from the Apocalypse of Daniel. This is an artificial heroism that can never lead to long run wealth accumulation and welfare for the nations, since it is always based on the calculus of a zero-sum-game. A new heroism will be instilled in the hearts of the Romans, the heroism that comes from the conviction that the Lord has not abandoned them. At this point let us heed the advice of Theodore Roosevelt, arguably the greatest US statesman, at least in the course of this century: *Prayer is our greatest weapon in these or any other times. Best we not send our boys across the sea to face the heathen hoards lest we have a nation at home one in prayer. If history teaches us nothing else, let us at least remember what the Byzantines learned, what the Crusaders learned, and what the French learned: you cannot face the dread terror of Islam in mere human strength. When the quietude of the desert has been stirred, let all Christian men and women turn to the sovereign Lord. Let all Christian men and women turn to Him in holy seasons of prayer.*[24]

Unfortunately, our laptop bombardiers are not only ignorant of the true underlying forces predicating the current Balkan crisis; they are also oblivious to the lessons of their country's history. And this is yet another reason why the predictions of the Apocalypse of Daniel, like so many others, cannot be averted any longer but are destined to materialize, instead. But let us turn to the text with additional commentary.

On the appointment of the Field Marshal through miraculous means: **And there will be a great sound from heaven and a fearful earthquake and a voice from the angel from heaven.** And the Lord will raise up a king of the Romans, who people say is dead and useful for nothing, who people think died many years before. This is his name: that which begins with the letter K of the alphabet. And this man is coming to the Seven-Hilled city toward the evening. And he will prepare for his enemies. And on Saturday morning as the sun rises, he will engage in a great war with the nation and

---

[24] Quoted in David L. Johnson, *Theodore Roosevelt: American Monarch* [1981, p. 193].

the sons of Hagar, both he and the two small boys.[25]

All of which is consistent with the idea of a great Christian alliance fighting in Constantinople, in fact, on the European side of the city, because the part of the city on the Asiatic side would have been called *Chalcedon* in the prophecy. *Romans*, in the jargon of the prophecy, is a generic term for Christians (peoples of the Roman empire who adopted christianity centuries ago). The name of the King of victory begins with a K! This is yet another suggestion of the Great Monarch's name, Karolos, Juan Carlos I.

An apparent contradiction seems to exist with the 'outer region of Persia' because all other prophecies indicate a European King, approaching from the West. However, this discrepancy may be due to interpolation in the meaning by copyists of the manuscript, not intended by the original author. I suspect that the original text was mentioning *Iberia* proper, and the copyists transcribed it into 'outer regions of Persia'. **Iberia**, was the official name, at the time the prophecy was written, of *Georgia*, on the East of the Black Sea, a country between **Colchis** in the west and **Albania** in the east (namely, the region between Caucasus and the Caspian Sea). This *Iberia* was conquered by the Roman legions under Pompey. In that sense, the geographical term *Iberia* could well be re-cast as the 'outer region of Persia', since the Persians had expanded their dominion on the Caucasus, and consequently Iberia constituted a border land to Persia at the time the prophecy was written.

On the other hand, there already existed another *Iberia* at the time the prophecy was written: that of the Iberian peninsula, (modern Spain and Portugal). The name Iberia (Hiberia) by which the Romans were referring to Spain in this latter case, is derived from the river Iberus (or Hiberus), the *Ebro* of modern Spain. It is plausible that the prophet referred to the Western Iberia, but his copyists mistook it for the Eastern Iberia, and then went on to expand the term to designate instead the 'outer region of Persia'.

However, in a different manuscript of the Apocalypse of Daniel instead of Persia it is written 'in the inner country of the Persian and Syrian nations'. Considering that the prophesied military activities of the Great Monarch will

---

[25] These refer to two specific blood relatives of King Juan Carlos I, and of course they will not be 'small'. Only in comparison with the Field Marshall himself, they will appear quite young.

bring him in the Middle East, that may be the correct version of the original text. (We already covered material speaking of the Holy Land, Syria, Damascus, Jaffa, etc.). Therefore, my feeling is that the second manuscript has the most plausible reference to his whereabouts at that critical time.

The text continues with the advent of the Antichrist which is to follow the string of events arleady treated. Again, this is most consistent with everything else covered in *Our Revelationary Age...*, and also with the sequence of events in the Revelation. Since the Antichrist will emanate from the tribe of Dan (a suggestion in many prophecies) and since the Antichrist will persecute the Christians, then, the entire Apocalypse of Daniel **does not apply to past historical occurrences** but to the future.

Let us review some of the details of the *Apocalypse of Daniel* in greater detail:

And this man is coming to the Seven-Hilled city toward the evening. (The manuscript M mentions that *this man's entrance will occur on a Friday*). And he will prepare for his enemies. And on Saturday morning as the sun rises, he will engage in a great war with the nation and the sons of Hagar, both he and the two small boys. And the rulers of the Romans will gather together in Byzantium. Then even the priests of the Romans and the bishops and abbots who are found will bear weapons of war.

As we had opportunity to notice while studying other Byzantine era prophecies (Leo the Philosopher, in particular), the Great Monarch will be identified miraculously in those prophecies also. *The true king, whom people have chased from his abode... he will be revealed at the time when the end of the Ishmaelites approaches... it will be on a Friday, in the third hour of the morning when he will be revealed.... He, who is to be revealed, will be indicated by means of celestial signs. (...)*

And again, *And this is how the king will be revealed to the people: there will be a star which will appear for the duration of three days and in the third hour of the night of the eve of the holiday of the Mother of the Most High, the star will be seen in the middle of the city. And this star is not one of the planets but it will be like the one which made its appearance during the salvation-bringing birth of Jesus. (...)*

I speculated then that since the comet and the earthquakes will happen in

Spring and during late March and early April in particular, the holiday mentioned here probably refers to the Day of the Life Giving Fountain, i.e., the Friday following Easter Sunday. The above paragraph from the Apocalypse of Daniel seems to corroborate this speculation.

What we also learn from the paragraph is that King Juan Carlos I and two blood relatives of his who shall be in age to bear weapons and fight are going to participate very decisively in the military events prophesied. (We already saw that the Great Philip will fight in Constantinople). It appears, however, that King Juan Carlos I will be fighting at a different front of the same war. For these details we need to go back to Nostradamus, for new material.

Century VI, Quatrain 85:
La grand cité de Tharse par Gaulois
Sera destruite, captifs tous à Turban:
Secours par mer, du grand Portugalois,
Premier d' esté, le jour du sacre Urban.

Translation:
The great city of Tarsus (the home town of St. Paul) will be destroyed by Frenchmen; all those who wear turbans (Muslims) will be taken captive; assistance will come from the sea through the Great Portuguese, this will happen in the first day of summer, the name day of St. Urban.

Interpretation:
As the great Portuguese (those who read my previous study) will easily identify as King Juan Carlos I, who was raised in Portuguese exile before he came to Spain to be educated for his future royal duties. French forces will destroy Tarsus and this is plausible, considering that the Great Monarch will be the leader of a great Christian coalition, including the French who will have re-instituted the monarchy and will have brought the Bourbons back to power. When will this happen? Nostradamus speaks of a day about May 25, this being the most widely accepted holiday for St. Urban in the Western Church. Could this happen the same year that the selection and ascension of the Great Monarch to the position of Field Marshal takes place? It is probable, although we cannot say for certain. His appointment as Supreme Commander will occur in April, and he may have had enough time to invade Turkish territories by mid-May. But again, this is only a speculation at this time.

Nostradamus gives us additional hints. We repeat below a most important quatrain already mentioned in the previous study:

Century VI, Quatrain 21:
Quand ceux du polle artique unis ensemble,
En Orient grand effrayeur & crainte,
Esleu nouveau soustenu le grand tremble
Rodes, Bisance de sang barbare tainte.

Translation:
When those of the arctic pole are united together, in the Orient great terror and fear. The newly elected one, having sustained the great earthquake, Rhodes and Byzantium will be stained with barbarian blood.

Interpretation:
Those of the Arctic Pole are the Russians and the North Americans of Canada and the USA. Their alliance in the future will bring terror to the 'Orient' (I believe this includes China as well as the Islamic coalition). The newly elected one (Field Marshal Juan Carlos I), having sustained the great earthquake (and the various disasters of the fateful April), will proceed in the battles. Rhodes and Byzantium will correspond, therefore, to the two major battlefields of the Christian Coalition. One fighting from the North (Russians and their European allies) in Constantinople, while (as it appears) King Juan Carlos himself will be fighting in the South. Rhodes will be one of his early targets, while Tarsus will be taken later by the French, apparently again under his command (the Great Portuguese).[26] Considering the geography of the area, this is most plausible. Consequently, the Western forces will move towards the Sea of Marmara.

Furthermore,

Century X, Quatrain 95:
Dans les Espagnes viendra Roy tres-puissant,
Par mer & terre subjugant or midy,
Ce mal sera, rabaissant le croissant,
Baisser les aesles à ceux du vendredy.

---

[26] In Greek prophecies the 'Great Portuguese' is always invariably and unanimously described as 'King of the Romans and the Greeks'.

Translation:
In the Spains will come a most-powerful King,
he will subjugate the south by land and sea,
The evil spoken of here refers to the fall of the crescent
and the dropping of the wings of those associated with Friday.

Suggested Interpretation:
The plural of the word Spain denotes the extensive area of command over the allied forces. It is an allusion to the times when the Habsburgs of Spain controlled a large part of Europe but it could also refer to the American countries that will be part of the Christian Army under the Great Monarch fighting the Muslims. Nostradamus lived while the Spaniards were busy colonizing the Americas. Consequently, since sizeable parts of the current USA were under Spanish influence or control when the USA did not exist as a political entity, this may have been his way of identifying a coalition spanning two continents.

Other Christian lands on the American Continent must be included here. (Remember the prophecy predicting that the war will come out of Asia and it **shall require the aid of every occidental on earth** to put down?)
One may add that it also refers to the present status of Juan Carlos I as the King of Spain, the metropolis of these Espagnes. The crescent is a symbol of Islam, and it appears in many national Muslim flags. Those associated with Friday are again easily identified as the Muslims, having adopted Friday as their religious holiday.

Century X, Quatrain 86:
Comme un gryphon viendra le Roy d' Europe
Accompagné de ceux d' Aquilon.
De rouges & blancs conduira grand troppe
Et iront contre le Roy de Babylon.

Translation:
Like a griffin will come the King of Europe, accompanied by those to the Northern Realms. He will lead a great troupe of soldiers dressed in white and red and they will go against the King of Babylon.

Interpretation:
A griffin is a fabulous animal, whose front half is like an eagle, his rear half like a lion, and is equipped with a long, serpentine tail. The blending of eagle and lion, both of which were highly regarded, points to the generally

beneficent character of such a being, and, therefore, it was consecrated by the Greeks to Apollo and Nemesis. Northern Realms are the USA, Canada, and Russia. This signifies the great military alliance of the future. The King of Europe, Juan Carlos I, will go against the Muslim enemy from Babylon. I may be reading too much in this quatrain, but I feel it offers yet another hint of the fact that the King of Europe and those around him will attack the Arabic side of the Islamic coalition while the Russians and those around them will attack the Turkic-Turanian side, in the Northern battlefields.

St. Thomas of Canterbury (à Becket) (1118-1170 A.D.): (Born in London of a Norman family).
A knight shall come from the West - he shall capture Milan, Lombardy, and the three crowns, and then sail to Famagoste and Cyprus and land at Jaffa and reach Christ's grave, where he will fight. War and wonders later shall befall till the people believe in Christ - towards the end of the world.[27]

From the prophecies of Edgar Cayce, the 'Sleeping Prophet' (1877-1945):[28]
One given in 1932: *'from Russia's religious development will come the greater hope of the world'*.

Brother Louis Rocco: (a Catholic seer, died 1840 A.D.).
(...) In Constantinople the cross will replace the half moon of Moslemism and Jerusalem will be the seat of a king. (...) The Slavs of the South will form a great Catholic empire and drive out of Europe the Turks, who will settle in Northern Africa and subsequently embrace the Catholic faith.

Commentary
This is our first mention of Slavs as being those who drive out of Europe the Turks. The rest of his prophecy will make sense a few chapters later when we collect all the data available and clear out all their superficial verbal inconsistencies. Also, what is meant by 'Catholic empire' or which particular 'Turks' will settle in North Africa, we have seen in several previously treated prophecies.

---

[27] This refers to the career of the Great Monarch. This prophecy fills some of the gaps of his military exploits for us.

[28] [1990, pp. 67-70].

Madame Yelena P. Blavatsky (ca. 1891 A.D):
When England ceases to carry the torch of democracy, out of Russia will come the greatest civilization the world has ever seen.

From the predictions of Mother Maria Skobtsova (1891-1945 A.D.), dated June 22, 1941 when the USSR was invaded by Hitler:[29]

"I have no fears for Russia. I know she will win. The day will come when we shall hear on the radio that the Soviet air force has destroyed Berlin. Then there will be a "Russian period" of history. Russia will stretch from the Arctic to the Indian Ocean. A great future awaits Russia. But what an ocean of blood."[30]

Interpretation
Obviously, a portion of the text already materialized with the outcome of WWII and the Soviet expansion during the Cold War Era. The stretching from the Arctic to the Indian Ocean, however, will happen after the Muslim defeat in WWIII. The rest of the text is in perfect internal consistence with all other prophecies regarding both the destructiveness of the war and the great future of the Christian coalition nations, and in particular the rebirth of Byzantium and of Holy Russia.

PROPHECIES ON THE USA

Relevant excerpt from a vision of **a woman from Phoenix Arizona**, dating from the 20th century:[31]

"A terrific wind seemed to blow from earth to heaven. It rent the blue sky as though it were a canvas. The opening was at first in the form of a cross. The wind kept up and blew back the four triangular flaps whose edges formed the cross and in this kite-shaped opening there appeared a happy

---

[29] See also Sergei Hackel, [1981 pp. 99-100].

[30] Some of the text was included in the previous study. The portion predicting that Russia will stretch from the Arctic to the Indian Ocean, however, is new material. Similar text has also been included in another unpublished manuscript of Mother Maria written in 1941, under the title *Razmyshleniia o sud'bakh Evropy i Azii*, (Meditation on the Destinies of Europe and Asia).

[31] Quoted in Culleton, op. cit. p. 231.

young mother with a child in her arm. That was in the south-west sky. The vision faded. Eleven months later after being warned to remember the vision described above "there opened to my view a scene beyond description. My only thought was that could it be reduced to canvas it would convert all men. Since that time it is no credit to me that I love God.

When intellectual Christianity will have suffered long enough it will find its heart, and the whole world will see it: then will come the peace of Christ. **This peace will come first to the United States.**

St. Hildegard of Bingen (1098-1179 A.D.):[32]
"The time is coming when princes and people will renounce the authority of the Pope. Individual countries will prefer their own Church rulers to the Pope. The German Empire will be divided. Church property will be secularized. Priests will preach their false doctrines undisturbed, resulting in 'Christians having doubts about their holy Catholic faith'.

Toward the end of the world, mankind will be purified through sufferings. This will be true especially of the clergy, who will be robbed of all property (...). When the clergy has adopted a simple manner of living, conditions will improve.

A powerful wind will rise in the North carrying heavy fog and the densest dust by divine command and it will fill their throats and eyes so they will cease their savagery and be stricken with a great fear. So after that there will be so few men left that seven women will fight for one man, that they will say to the man: 'marry me to take the disgrace from me,' for in those days it will be a disgrace for a woman to be without child, as it was by the Jews in the Old Testament.

Before the Comet comes, many nations, the good excepted, will be scoured with want and famine. The great nation in the ocean that is inhabited by people of different tribes and descent by an earthquake, storm and tidal

---

[32] She was a Benedictine nun and visionary born in Germany, who in 1136 A.D. began writing the content of her visions in a work entitled *Scivias* (sciens vias Domini, i.e., the one who knows the ways of the Lord). I feel that St. Hildegard's prophecies are most important among those specifically referring to our times, because they are sufficiently detailed to provide adequate information and facilitate the placing of the events in a temporal sequence.

waves will be devastated. It will be divided, and in great part submerged. That nation will also have many misfortunes at sea, and loose its colonies in the East through a Tiger and a Lion. The Comet by its tremendous pressure, will force much out of the ocean and flood many countries, causing much want and many plagues. All sea coast cities will be fearful and many of them will be destroyed by tidal waves, and most living creatures will be killed and even those who escape will die from a horrible disease. For in none of those cities does a person live according to the laws of God.

Peace will return to Europe when the white flower again takes possession of the throne of France. During this time of peace the people will be forbidden to carry weapons and iron will be used only for making agricultural implements and tools. Also during this period the soil will be very productive and many Jews, heathens and heretics will join the Church."[33]

<u>Commentary</u>
St. Hildegard, as noted above, lived in a period preceding Columbus and by extension the discovery of America. Since the United States as a nation was born ca. 600 years later, it is obvious that St. Hildegard needed to use periphrastic means to identify it.

Dupont (op. cit.) believed that the great nation in the ocean is Britain. I disagree with that version for a number of reasons:

a)   England, Britain, Anglia, Albio, Anglo-Saxons, Normans, Brittany, Gallia, etc. all these were terms already in use at the time of St. Hildegard and one must assume that she was fully aware of them, being a very learned person. She could have spoken directly of England and the British Isles by extension, if they were to be the case. Furthermore, Britain was not inhabited by a larger number of different tribes than any other continental European nation of that

---

[33] I have investigated the Latin text of the Scivias in J.P. Migne, but the explicit reference to a comet was not found. However, her prophecy **including the comet** was found in two separate compilations of prophecies by Catholics. I suspect that the entire text of the prophecy emanates from a different manuscript of St. Hildegard, which is also included in Scivias (but in a different section) or in a different manuscript of hers, altogether.

period, so 'different tribes and descent' was not per se a unique specifying characteristic for the British Isles.

b) We have researched several prophecies speaking of inundations befalling the British Isles. (As the reader may remember a poem attributed to Mother Shipton speaks of such phenomena as well, as do Anton Johanson, Joanna Southcott and others). Inundations are to be expected and will be widely felt. Consequently, this, by itself, does not signify that the above prophecy refers to the British Isles. Numerous other coastal areas will be inundated during the same time, such as in Italy, in the South of France, in parts of Greece, in India, and in other areas for which we have explicit reference already at our disposal.

c) Although Britain once ruled over an empire that was geographically most extended, (and upon which the sun did never set), the USA after WWII has expanded as a international empire by means of its military presence, its multinationals, and overall economic spheres of influence. I have reasons to believe that **loosing its colonies in the East through a Tiger and a Lion** refers to two distinct enemy groups, while the 'colonies' can be military bases (abandoned, taken over, expropriated, non-renewed, or destroyed, capital investment, joint ventures, MNCs, etc. Consider for instance the bases on Subic Bay in the Philippines after the last major Mt. Pinatubo eruption. We can expect similar problems with the US multinational corporation facilities, capital investments in the oil resources of Asia and the Middle East, pipeline networks, etc.

Since these are all located in the 'East' and are prime candidates for take-over or destruction in the eventuality of a war against China and the Islamic coalition, the prophecy makes a lot of sense in its USA-version. Military bases in many countries would be lost, oil-extraction and development installations (such as those in Nigeria, Algeria, and the one proposed for the Turkic Republics of the former USSR), and many such investments by US multinationals, could be lost for ever! Similar losses would occur in Singapore, Hong Kong, and many areas later falling to enemy hands.

However, there are additional reasons why we have reasons to believe that the prophecy refers to the USA:

338

- At the time the prophecy materializes, Great Britain will have no colonies in the East to lose, anyway. For one thing, Hong Kong is already by treaty being transferred over to China in a couple of years. Most of the colonies in the East have been lost at the end of WWII and nothing in the prophecy of St. Hildegard makes us believe that the time frame she refers to are the years following WWII.

- The prophetic testimony provided by a US seer, and contemporary of ours, Mr. Gordon Michael Scallion, which fits perfectly into the image generated by St. Hildegard. Mr. Scallion has been having a number of visions concerning the future of the USA. In the maps of the USA he saw in his visions, much of California will be submerged, and the Mississippi river will expand its bed so drastically that the Eastern United States will become separated from the central regions. In other words his predictions are most consistent with St. Hildegard's prophecy.[34]

- With our current level of knowledge on how precarious the fate of California will be in the event of massive earthquakes (to be further aggravated by the consequences of the gravitational pull of a comet, for instance) who is to doubt the eventuality of a partial submersion of the Western United States, when we have prophetic evidence that this will happen in many other parts of the world as well, at the same time?

- The remainder of St. Hildegard's prediction of the submersion of many coastal cities is corroborated not only by the tenets of geological science but also by a number of different prophetic sources (as we had the opportunity to find out in this study).

- There is still the issue of the prophesied 'misfortunes the great nation on the ocean will have at sea'. One cannot decide from the wording of the text whether such misfortunes refer to military ones (such as battles lost in naval-warfare), or the destruction of oil-producing equipment offshore on the oil-platforms due to sabotage, the natural calamities caused by the comet, enemy action, etc. etc. Since at the

---

[34] Similar predictions about geological upheavals in the USA have been made by other US seers. For instance, Rev. Paul Solomon, and Lori Adaile Toye. And let us not forget the rich evidence emanating from Edgar Cayce.

time of St. Hildegard oil platforms did not exist, let alone the jargon associated with them, she must have felt the need for periphrasis to describe the eventuality of such phenomena. My feeling is that since the comet will strike while the WWIII will be raging, 'misfortunes at sea' can be interpreted to signify both the military ones as well as those due to natural causes. One cannot exclude a priori the possibility of a sudden strike against US navy positions (against the various fleets away from home) such as the one inflicted upon Pearl Harbor in Hawaii during WWII.

In conclusion, bitter as the realization of such events may be, we have to brace for them and realize that in no way we are going to be excused from the bitter cup offered to the rest of humanity. It is still time to mitigate the consequences of the disasters ahead.

PROPHECIES ON CHINA

Fr. Freinademetz (20th century):
"All foreign missionaries shall soon be expelled from China. You will have to walk hundreds of miles before you can find a priest. Even then, your journey will often be fruitless. Some priests and some Catholics shall apostatize. A war shall break out once all foreign missionaries have been expelled. Then, some foreign powers shall occupy the whole of China and shall divide it into zones. One of the occupying powers will be pitiless, and very hard on the people. But during this period, nearly the whole of China shall turn to Christianity.

Commentary
This prophecy is straightforward, and it affords us a valuable hint on when the war will break out: once all foreign missionaries are expelled. The fact that most of China will turn to Christianity is consistent with very many other prophecies speaking of the spreading of Christian missionary activity following the victory in WWIII. We have no way of knowing which exactly will be the occupying powers and what will be their activity.

Anonymous Prophecy recorded in the course of the 20th century:[35]
(...) Now is it come to pass that the hearts of men and nations are hardened like flint upon the face of the earth. For this is the last hour of

---

[35] Referenced in Culleton, op. cit. pp. 233-234.

self-righteousness and of the hypocrite; when men of smug face and smooth tongue gather into their snares all the people of simple mind, to pour upon them the force of hatred and jealousy and lead them into slaughter.

Behold, the whole Earth is filled with turbulence and discontent. The rulers use their vast powers for greater domination and the struggling multitude uncoils itself like a serpent seeking its prey. They seize nations against their neighbors and waste their strength to break one another. The victors are too far spent to shout, and the defeated utterly despoiled (...) For the last half of the hour is wombed with the most terrible period of the Earth's history. (...) And it came to pass that when the last quarter of the last hour arrived **the yellow hordes in the place of the Rising Sun and the white hosts of the middle kingdom have joined hands... And behold, they pour out their terrifying wrath upon the inhabitants of the island kingdom which is swelled with victory and grown fat upon the commerce of sea and land.**

(...) Behold, saith the Lord: I will turn thee inside out, who in the folly of thine hypocrisy imagined a vain thing in thine heart. Thou art a harlot among the vain people of the earth. Thou hast lain in the beds of divers nations, and by charm and deceit, by beguilements thou hast brought under thy dominion the uttermost parts of the earth. But I shall make thee over... Thy seamen and thy pilots and all men of war that are within thee, with all thy company, shall fall into the heart of the sea. And I will break thee in pieces as thou hast broken many before thee. For the nations from the ends of the earth, and of the middle kingdom, which I have pitched against thy strength, are cruel beyond endurance whose might thou canst not overcome... Thou and thy companions shall be brought down to earth and it shall be a day of repentance. (...) On that day, when the day of thy repentance is full, when remorse hath broken thy heart, and thy cry is raised unto Me, I shall remember and send thee thy deliverer." [Emphasis added].

Commentary
Since the prophecy speaks of the 'most terrible period of the Earth's History' we may rest assured that it deals with our proximate future. *Middle Kingdom* is a very old term for China. It is clear that the prophecy does not refer neither to WWI nor to WWII for the introductory wording does not fit those experiences. The *place of the rising sun* most plausibly refers to Japan and its tremendous financial and commercial expansion in our times.

And yet, it could signify Mongolic tribes, North Koreans, and other East-Asians. The prophecy indicates that at some point during WWIII these Asian peoples will form a military alliance. The sentence *And behold, they pour out their terrifying wrath upon the inhabitants of the island kingdom which is swelled with victory and grown fat upon the commerce of sea and land,* deserves further scrutiny. There might be two island kingdoms that could fit very well in this description:

a)   Hong Kong (which, generally speaking, corresponds to the islands of Lantau and Hong Kong proper, a number of several minor ones, plus an expansion (New Territories) upon the mainland), or,

b)   Taiwan.

Both areas are inhabited by Chinese who detested Communism and rejected the economic policies of mainland China. Both of them are tremendously successful economically and financially. So, *swelled with victory* may mean in terms of GNP per capita and stature and prestige in the international economic and financial community rather than military victory, (a rather tenuous thought, considering the relevant populations involved). Both are detested by the Communists who still control political life in mainland China. Hong Kong in particular, which by virtue of treaties will have to revert to Communist China on July 1, 1997 A.D., is already bombarded with negative propaganda from the mainland and orders to cease and desist from its democratizing activities.

Hong Kong is a thorn in the eye of the Chinese Communists. With a population of 6 million people who are among the best educated and trained of the entire world, it produces already the equivalent of 1/5 of the Gross National Product of mainland China, whose population is ca. 1.2 billions. The former assurances by Deng Hsiao Ping that there will exist in the future one country with two economic systems is not taken seriously by anybody, any longer. In brief, Hong Kong could be 'the island kingdom swollen with victory' upon which the wrath of its ideological enemies (and/or economic competitors) will descend.

However, analogous statements can be made with regards to Taiwan. Taiwan is an independent country, with high standards of living and an up-to-date military force, yet, numerically it is a dwarf vis-à-vis the mainland. Taiwan is the other big thorn in the eye of the Chinese Communists and there are no a priori reasons to exclude an attack upon both Hong Kong **and** Taiwan, although Hong Kong 'legally' will revert to China in 1997.

It is a **mere speculation** on my part, but I feel that the prophecy applies to Hong Kong and not Taiwan, because of the hint of the *island kingdom which is swelled with victory and grown fat upon the commerce of sea and land*. Now, since Hong Kong is still a British Colony, the term *kingdom* is appropriate, since until 1997 the British Crown and Queen Elizabeth II are essentially the highest political authorities in Hong Kong. (The term kingdom would not have been an appropriate reference in the case of Taiwan).

But the most important hint is that it grew fat upon the commerce of sea **and** land. Since Taiwan is an island, it can grow fat only through sea and air trade, but not land-trade, and especially not with Communist China which is their best known enemy. But Hong Kong, as noted earlier, already territorially flows over into the land mass of mainland China (via the New Territories and Kowloon). Therefore, for all practical purposes, it engages in the commerce of sea **and** land. In fact, for long years before trade with mainland China was opened to the Western markets directly, many items produced in Communist China were exported first in Hong Kong (were they received the 'made in Hong Kong' stamp) before being re-exported into foreign markets under the guise of a presumably capitalist product from capitalist Hong Kong.

This kind of 'brokerage' of the embargoed Communist Chinese exports definitely assisted the Hong Kong economy in the years before the US-China rapprochement. Consequently we can say with certainty that indeed it grew fat upon the commerce of sea and land. Furthermore, the not-so-well publicized behind-the-scenes economic agreements between Western partners and Communist Chinese via Hong Kong could add further support to the above thesis.[36]

---

[36] The interested reader may wish to consult J. J. Tierney Jr. [1979], a book 'published in direct response to the decision by President Carter on December 15, 1978 to unilaterally terminate America's historical commitment to the Republic of China on Taiwan'. The book is an eye-opener on the ambiguous morality of our foreign policy making. A striking passage, of timeless value, written by Senator Barry Goldwater follows:

*"On the evening of December 15, President Carter delivered a short speech to the nation which history may well record as **ten minutes that lived in infamy**. In that address, the President - without prior consultation with the Congress - recognized a communist regime on the mainland of China which has one of the worst records*

So far, if my speculations are correct, we may assume that Communist China will invade and turn Hong Kong upside down regardless of its legal claims on it.

To complete our coverage of China, we may also include here a Mormon prophecy by Joseph Smith, who, while speaking of the future of the USA, specifically said that *there is a land beyond the Rocky Mountains that will be invaded by the Heathen Chinese unless great care and protection be given.* In the prophecies on the USA by a Phoenix, Arizona, seer the reader may remember the last sentence to the effect that the peace of Christ will come first to the USA.

This may imply a number of scenarios:

a)   The USA is invaded but pushes away the enemy and liberates its lands earlier than its European and Israeli allies liberate their own; or,

b)   there are domestic upheavals (like those also predicated for Europe) but in the USA domestic peace is established first; or

c)   domestic upheavals lead to an internal turmoil which further weakens our national vigilance; this in turn (like the European case) will be exploited by the Chinese who decide to invade the West Coast of the USA, desirous of controlling the Alaskan Oil Resources, among other things. (We may also suspect that since Islam and China will be partners in WWIII they may coordinate their attacks and their geographical targets for maximum effect).

This last scenario is not farfetched at all, at least not to a person who has studied the history of WWII, the blunders of Western diplomacy vis-à-vis the Soviet - type Communism, and the swiftness with which Western capitalists helped consolidate the power of Lenin, Stalin, ... Brezhnev, and were ready to do the same with Gorbachev. These blunders are being now replicated

---

on human rights in the history of the world. In that address, the president downgraded, humiliated, and victimized the Republic of China on Taiwan, one of this nation's most faithful and valuable allies. (...)" (p. 23). Mr. Carter, furthermore, chose a holiday period when the old Congress was out of session and the new Congress was not yet in, in order to announce his decision to terminate unilaterally and without cause the diplomatic relations and Mutual Defense Treaty with Taiwan.

in the case of the Mainland China - type Communism. We are essentially selling them the rope with which they will later try to hang us. Any observer of the current high-tech arms'- building frenzy of China, their resentment and enmity towards the West (expressed in no uncertain terms in their Party Congresses and whose text has leaked in the West and has already appeared in Der Spiegel), the psychological pressure they exert at the expense of Chinese students studying abroad, the diplomatic pressure they exert against their trading partners, all these are signs of the times and should be a matter of concern to all Americans.[37]

The more so, since the limited evidence at our disposal already indicates that China will aggressively pursue its interests at the expense of the USA in the future (without excluding Canada as their target, also). I cannot be more forceful on the basis of the prophetic evidence available to me. I can, however, be forceful on the basis of a historical analysis of our ambivalent stance vis-à-vis Communism, so far. The only consolation is that eventually China will be defeated.

ADDITIONAL PROPHECIES ON EUROPEAN LANDS, TURKEY AND ITS EASTERN CONNECTIONS

Introduction
As we had opportunity to establish already, prophecies on the ultimate destruction of the new Turkish Empire in the course of a fierce global conflict abound in the apocalyptic literature.[38] The sources are most

---

[37] Nicholas Eftimiades's book *Chinese Intelligence Operations*, [1994], would be an excellent starting point for the self-edification and enlightenment of all the readers who feel that something must be wrong with our great tolerance towards a land that has a huge Gulag, ruthlessly persecutes its dissidents, tries to dictate to us whom shall we give a visa to visit his alma-mater, and the like.

[38] Patrick Brogan, [1990, p. x], muses that 'Diplomatic incompetence remains one of the greatest dangers to the peace of the world". Covering the Armenian genocide with references also to the Greek one by the Turks in the 1920s he writes the following: "*The Armenian Holocaust has been the central national experience for all Armenians ever since, as the Jewish Holocaust is for the Jews. Unlike West Germany, Turkey has never admitted guilt and has never made the least reparation; in fact, it denies that the Holocaust ever happened. (...) There is a strong residuum of chauvinism in Turkey, and a great reluctance to admit error, even after 70 years. It must be added that at the time of the Holocaust, Armenians were actively helping*

remarkably diversified and cover time periods extending to Millennia. Ample evidence on Turkey has been already presented in *Our Revelationary Age....* Additional material will be introduced below, from new sources. We may wish to keep in mind that under the term 'Turk' or 'Saracen', the broader notion of Islamic warrior was implied by several authors.

ON GERMANY <u>AND</u> TURKEY
FROM THE PROPHECIES OF CHRISTIAN HEERING OF PROSSEN

<u>A Few Introductory Notes</u>
Christian Heering lived about the middle of the 18th century. Born in Postelwitz, by the Bohemian borders in 1710, the son of a fisherman, in 1746 A.D. he moved to Prossen, where his wife had inherited a small property. He had a sparse education; he could read but his writing skills

---

the enemy in the east, and the British were at the gates of the capital. Also, though countless Armenians were massacred by Turkish troops, and the Turkish army was responsible for the death of the others who were driven on foot through the mountains, Turkey's object was its own security, not genocide. There were no gas chambers." [ibid. p. 550].

With all due respect towards a superior journalist, I beg to disagree with Mr. Brogan's acquittal for the following reasons:

a)   under the excuse of one's own security we must also forgive Stalin's crimes, Hitler's crimes, Saddam Hussein's crimes and so on. National security has been for centuries a very thin veil for covering the most hideous crimes against humanity. At least, let us be fair in our assessment of the relative importance of peoples and their genocides.

b   There were no gas chambers in Turkey only because the Turks were a technologically primitive people during the 1920s; they had no access to Chemistry patents, had no I.G. Farben to implement mass-extinction technologies in their Konzlagers (Concentration Camps). Consequently, while the Nazis would cremate a body before retrieving the gold from one's teeth and other marketable resources from a cadaver, the soldiers of Kemal would tear a dead victim's belly open (in front of other live ones) to search of objects of value in the intestines, such as gold coins and jewelry, that the victim might have swallowed as a means of protection. If the Turks had facilities equal to the Konzlager of the Nazis they would not have driven on foot their victims all the way to Mesopotamia, to force them to die slowly by hunger, exposure and exhaustion.

346

were limited to the signing of his name. He earned his living as a fisherman by the river Elbe. Heering was a very religious person who raised his family in the Church. He related his prophecies to his spiritual father, Johann Gabriel Süsse, in 1759. Father Süsse, being trained as a Protestant Pastor was not supposed to believe in modern day prophecies; therefore he had a great difficulty dealing with the cognitive dissonance between the dogmas of his church on one hand and hard evidence on the other. The fisherman was able to even specify the total number of soldiers that would die in an upcoming battle. He did so repeatedly with a most impressive accuracy. Therefore, Father Süsse agonized and waited for another 12 years *to double check the veracity of the prophecies* before he would publish them.[39]

To cut a long title short, the question raised by pious Father Süsse was whether revelation is possible in our days and capable of predicting important events in the Church, the State, the fate of specific persons, etc. To his great credit, in this search for answers he also included in a German translation a famous older treatise by Jean Charliers, a.k.a. Gerson, entitled the *'Proof of all Spirits'*. Convinced of the superior quality of Heering's prophecies, Father Süsse finally published the text of 1759 without alterations, with only a few additional notes of his.[40]

---

[39] With a meticulousness characteristic of a German he chose the following title: *"Umständliche Nachricht von dem sogenanten Prossner Manne, Christian Heerings, eines Elb-Fischers und Innwohners zu Prossen bey Königstein, seit etliche zwanzig Jahren bekannt gewordene Voraussagugnen betreffend benebst einer Historisch-Theologischen Abhandlung der Causal-Frage: Ob es noch heut zu Tage neue Offenbarungen von wichtigen Revolutionen in der Kirche, im Statt, und von besonderen Schicksalen einzelner Personen gebe, and was von selbigen zu halten sey?....."*

[40] Some background information on Gerson might be of interest: Gerson was a recognized authority on the evaluation of Spirits. He interviewed Jeanne d' Arc, yet his testimony did not get included in the court proceedings against her, for the reason that Gerson belonged to the 'wrong political party'. Since the court judging and condemning Jeanne d'Arc were allied with the Burgundians and would not wish to see the future Charles VII claiming the crown, they completely discarded the favorable verdict of Jean Gerson with regards to Jeanne d'Arc. Gerson was already a recognized authority ever since the publication of his treatise *De Distinctione Verarum Visionum a Falsis*, ca 1400 A.D. At the Council of Constance, in 1415, where he was called to decide whether or not Bridget of Sweden's visions were authentic, he felt they were not and wrote another treatise, *De Probatione Spirituum*,

The following material is being extracted from Max Kemmerich [1921, chap. 5]. Most of Christian Heering's prophecies materialized within a short time thereafter, which made his prophecy of a Turkish invasion of particular interest to subsequent analysts and commentators. Besides events around the military career of Friedrich the Great and the various wars and rulers of the time, Heering prophesied a most important event which I believe relates to our own times. In a summary form it runs as follows:

"Fisher Heering speaks what the Lord God has ordered him to make public concerning the coming storm. All over the land penance must be preached in the churches and the alliance with the Southwest and the Southeast must be abandoned, then the Lord will bless the House of Saxony."(...) [41] "The Southeast and the Southwest will create an alliance against the North-West; the Southwest would be defeated; how four Heroes will stand together against the Southeast and the Southwest until the Southeast and the Southwest tie is broken." Heering added this statement: "(The Lord God showed to me) that the army that comes from the East, which if it were to be called by name would signify the Turk, would invade, in which case the war would move from the side to the North."

Father Süsse was careful enough to mark in the *Umständliche Nachricht...* that Heering insisted on the accuracy and veracity of his predictions and 'with tears in his eyes bade the Priest to promulgate with special forcefulness the invasion by the Turks that he saw in his vision". [42]

Kemmerich was a remarkably thorough and astute researcher of prophecies.

---

which set out the principles and procedures by which one would discern good spirits from evil ones in visions. It is this second treatise that Priest Süsse was referring to, when he published the prophecies of Christian Heering.

[41] "Es würde sich Süd-Ost und Süd-West mit einander wider Nord-West verbinden, Süd-West wäre gedemütiget worden, wie Vier Helden neben einander gegen Süd-Ost und Süd-West stünden, welche vier Helden so lange hinter und neben einander stehen würden, bis Süd-Ost und Süd-West von einander abliessen." Es setzte hinzu: **"Es wäre ihm endlich gezeiget worden, dass der aus Morgen, welcher ihm mit dem Namen wäre genennet worden, dass es der Türke sey, herangezogen wäre, worauf sich der Krieg seitwärts gegen Norden gezogen hätte."**

[42] [op. cit. p. 227, ft. 1].

He was puzzled by the fact that although most of the Herring prophecies materialized within the 18th century, such an attack by Turkey was not by far close to the details of the above prediction. Therefore, he was meticulous to note that only a broad interpretation would come close to the Turkish meddling in the Polish upheavals of 1768, when Marshall Michael Krasinski asked the Turks for assistance; however, the Polish senate asked for Russian assistance and the Turks were thereby defeated. But even that was not an accurate match, considering that Heering explicitly predicted that **"the Turks will be involved after a peace has been concluded"**, and that was definitely not the case of the Polish campaign. So, the question remains open, the more so, since as Kemmerich carefully reports, there was never any explicit and categorical statement by Heering that his prophecies ought to materialize soon. In fact, quite the contrary; in the specific Turkish prophecy Heering forcefully stated: "The Lord has not given me the specifics of the time and the hour relating to this issue".[43]

Let us review once again the introductory remark leading to the Turkish prophecy by Heering: It is implied that the House of Saxony must abandon any alliance with Southeast and Southwest in order to receive Divine blessings. Southwest I interpret to mean the Arab armies of North Africa invading Europe through the Western Mediterranean. Southeast, to indicate a Muslim alliance (of Arabs and Turkic populations) attacking from the sea and through the Peninsula of Haemus. The Northwest are France, possibly West Germany, the Benelux and the British Isles. So far, everything dovetails with numerous other prophecies of WWIII from different sources. Since East Germany (Saxony) is so repeatedly mentioned as a major belligerent nation during WWIII, the explicit instructions regarding the appropriate modus operandi for Saxony so that it re-gain divine favor are most interesting.

There are other prophecies which speak of the Turks reaching the Danube and the Rhine (besides those by Nostradamus and Paracelcus). So far they have reached the Danube repeatedly as conquerors, but the Rhine only as Gast-Arbeiter in West Germany's industries. Therefore, when Herring speaks of an invasion of the North by Turkey "from the side", I believe this is an event to materialize in our future, viz. WWIII.

Furthermore, the alliance of the Southeast and the Southwest will be broken

---

[43] "Zeit und Stunde hat mir der HErr hiervon nicht bestimmt."

at some point in time. This too, is most consistent with other prophecies, including those by Nostradamus and several Byzantine sources speaking of a fierce war breaking out among the Muslim allies of yesterday.

MORE ON TURKEY
FROM MAX KEMMERICH'S *PROPHEZEIUNGEN...*:

In Turkey there exists a most ancient prophecy according to which, the comet appearing in the beginning of the 20th century will harbinger the breakout of a world war. During the first part of the century, Turkey will be expelled almost entirely from Europe, during the last part of the century Turkey will fight again for domination of Europe in a war in which also the Yellow Race will participate.

Commentary
Previous researchers, including Dr. Kemmerich, saw in the *yellow race* and the beginning of the century the Japanese during the Russo-Japanese war of 1905 A.D. However, the Halley's comet had not appeared yet, nor was that war of any great importance in a global context.

Therefore, I submit that this prophecy has materialized in part only, the rationale being as follows:

1)   Halley's Comet appeared in 1910, essentially presaging the Balkan wars of 1912-1913 which reduced most drastically the   Ottoman empire's European holdings. Then came WWI, which lasted from 1914-1918. Although during the Balkan wars Turkey lost most of its remaining European possessions, during the WWI it lost also Constantinople and only after the end of WWI and thanks to special treaties with the victorious allies it was allowed to keep Eastern Thrace, its only current possession on European soil, which includes Constantinople.

2)   Throughout WWII (which involved a major participation of the yellow race with the Japanese as invaders) Turkey remained neutral.

3)   Before the end of the century the comet (namely Halley's) came again (1986). It is not clear that the prophecy's reference is to the Halley's comet of 1986 or to a different one, destined to appear before the end of the century but after 1986 (such as the comet so central to our study). The year 1986 marked the beginning of the

end for Communism in the Soviet Union and ushered in the new world disorder which will culminate in WWIII. We are told, however, that before the end of the century Turkey will fight once again for domination of Europe in a war in which the Yellow Race will participate. We do not know from the prophecies what role Japan will play in WWIII but it is certain that China will play a major aggressive role, because we have several references to China, already. Suffice it to say at this juncture that the 'West' will have to face both Islam and China as its enemies in WWIII. (We have only one piece of prophetic evidence that could be interpreted as a suggestion to a possible alliance between China and Japan during WWIII (the rising sun). The vision of a rousing *Pan-Mongolism* as the future threat to the Russian Christian Church and the Russian nation, as well as Europe, seems to conflict with a Japan version of the 'rising sun', at least in terms of linguistics. This Pan-Mongolism prophecy can already be found in the writings of the Russian religious philosophers of the 19th century.[44] Pan-Mongolism, broadly defined, would include the Chinese, **and** the Turanian Turks and other Tataro-Mongolic nationalities, including those of Inner Mongolia, which is already treated by the Communist Chinese as their 'province'.

While China has been invaded in centuries past by Mongols and Turanians, the Panmongolism-attack should not apply to Japan, prima facie, because they have never been invaded by the Mongols. In 1281 A.D. Kublai Khan, the Mongol conqueror and ruler of China, sent an invasion fleet of 1000 ships against Japan. At the most critical moment a devastating typhoon came to the defense of the Samurais. It utterly destroyed the fleet of the expeditionary forces. The Japanese believed that the gods had sent them this Divine Wind, the Kamikaze, to defend their homeland against invaders. Although the Japanese islands were ultimately invaded, the armies came from America and not from Mongolian or Turanian Asian lands. Consequently, on the basis of the etymological hints at our disposal, the plausibility of a future war between Japan and the West is further weakened. It would appear that Japan may prefer to remain neutral (in view of its dependance on Middle-Eastern oil, for instance, and in view of other national economic considerations). It seems unlikely

---

[44] Nikolai Berdyaev, [1968].

that it will send expeditionary forces against the Western alliance; on the other hand, we have no evidence whatsoever that it will side with the West. (Rather, I have no such evidence. And consequently, nothing more specific or caterogical can be said in this case).

In conclusion, the prophecy supplied by Kemmerich on the future war where the Yellow Race will also participate, may still exclude Japan while including Northern Korea. The *Yellow Race* can still be more than adequately represented by the Mainland Chinese, and the more than 6 millions Chinese of the Diaspora, which is based primarily in East Asian countries and to a lesser degree in the West (primarily the USA and Canada). A portion of those Chinese living outside the People's Republic of China could be co-opted in one form or another in a future conflict initiated by the Mainland.

ON GERMANY AND AUSTRIA

From the Catholic Seer Brother Louis Rocco (died 1840)
(...) Vienna will be hated by all nations, suffer great devastation and become a waste place. A venerable monarchy will collapse after many battles, but its ruling dynasty will be preserved. The kings and lords of Germany will abdicate. The king of Prussia will suffer particularly. The German sections of Austria will join Germany, so also will the commercial cities of Belgium and Switzerland. A Catholic descendant of a German imperial house will rule a united Germany with peace, prosperity and great power, for God will be with this sovereign. (...)

(...) The reign of the Great Ruler may be compared with that of Caesar Augustus who became Emperor after his victory over his enemies, thereby giving peace to the world, also with the reign of Emperor Constantine the Great, who was sent by God, after severe persecutions, to deliver both the Church and State. By his victories on water and land he brought the Roman Empire under subjection, which he then ruled in peace. (...) The Great Monarch will have the special help of God and will be unconquerable. (...)

REVIEW OF THE MOST SALIENT POINTS

a)   In this chapter we evaluated additional prophetic evidence on the future of specific countries and primarily the major participants of WWIII.

b)	The new evidence adds more texture and details in the huge tapestry we are putting together, while strengthening the underlying fabric. It becomes manifest, and beyond the shadow of doubt that no country will be spared its share of troubles and tribulations, although some countries may suffer more than others or be rewarded more than others according to their standing in the eyes of the Lord.

c)	The prophecies predict the re-birth of the Byzantine empire under the Great Monarch and his offspring. The emperor from Constantinople will be a King of the Romans (Western Europeans) and the Greeks. He will be acceptable to the Russians also.

d)	Whether they are identified under the terms Aquilon, the blond nation, one of those of the Arctic Pole, those whose name commences with an R, etc. etc., the Russians are destined for an overall performance in direct contradiction to that currently propounded by many popular religious presses engaged in prophecy interpretation. We hope that the evidence supplied in this study will put an end to the prevailing confusion and redirect the attention and concern of the Western observer to the real source of our military troubles.

e)	The Great Monarch will be appointed the Field Marshal of the great Christian coalition of Europeans and Americans. The prophecies indicate that he will fight in the Mediterranean, the Holy Land and Southern-Eastern Mediterranean, moving north-east. The Russians and their Slavic allies will be fighting around the Black Sea and they will come down towards Constantinople where they shall fight victoriously. (In my previous study I show that French and Italian troops will invade Albania and Greece (which will already have been invaded by Turkey) by way of the Adriatic and the Ionian Sea. The war will be over before those troops have an opportunity to reach Constantinople). A massive Western naval power will also converge in Constantinople, which will witness a tremendous battle, unprecedented in its history.

f)	Communist China will be one of the aggressors during WWIII. We have no dependable evidence that Japan will side with China against the West. In fact, we have no evidence showing unequivocally and clearly that Japan will turn against the West altogether, either alone, or as a part of an Asiatic coalition. The future troubles of Japan appear to emanate primarily from geological sources, particularly through earthquakes and submersions, namely, through the same forces which will destroy so much of the rest of the world. Considering the paucity of data on Japan (and my linguistic ignorance and inability to evaluate potentially contradictory information from other sources), I have to conclude that this appears to be the most likely scenario currently available to us.

SUMMARY AND CONCLUSIONS

Democratic civilization is the first in history to blame itself because another power is working to destroy it. Jean-François Revel.[1]

<u>Summary of the Salient Points</u>
A comet will approach our planet before the year 2000 A.D. At the geological level, we shall experience a replay of the Exodus events and the destruction of Thera. At the personal and spiritual levels (depending on whether we are Jews or Christians) we shall experience the emotions of the Passover and the Passion of the Lord Jesus Christ, respectively. All those who in the eyes of the Lord are *children of Light*, regardless of race, color or creed, will be under the protection of the Angels during the Three Days Darkness. A most powerful emotional and spiritual experience will complete the purification process and prepare them for the life beyond the horrors of the age.

Since the Jews and the Christians have received more, from them more is expected in return, vis-à-vis all other peoples and races who have not yet experienced Divine Revelation in so rich a manifestation and so continuous a flow. In other words, the prophets indicate that greater leniency will be exhibited to those who never knew the Word of God, vs. those who know and prefer to ignore.

It appears certain that the events accompanying the Eminent Day of the Lord will take several days to work themselves out and will occur in late March and early April, since they will coincide with the general period of the Jewish Passover and the Christian Holy Week and Easter Week. The Darkness is expected to commence at sunrise or shortly thereafter. The Remnant of Lord Jesus Christ will share both in His suffering during the darkness but also in the unspeakable joy and the spiritual elation of His resurrection. The prophecies analyzed in this study do not give us exact information regarding the specific year of the Comet. However, by simultaneously solving all pieces of available evidence for the most likely date, the internal consistency observed and the mutual corroboration of

---

[1] *How Democracies Perish*, p. 7.

many independent prophecies allow us to formulate a few speculations with relative confidence:

The most probable year appears to be 1998, primarily because the religious calendar of all Christian denominations allow them to celebrate Easter within April. Also that year guarantees that the Holiday of the Life Giving Fountain will also occur in April. The Lord Jesus Christ in the Epistle of Sunday most categorically identifies April. All other pieces either agree or at least do not exhibit evidence of disagreement with this date. Nostradamus provides evidence corroborating a 'Spring' timing of the events. His very celebrated quatrain giving July of 1999, (the only one where Nostradamus gives a specific date) either relates to the return of the fateful comet from perihelion, or to a different celestial phenomenon appearing while WWIII is still raging.

In any event, we expect other signs and wonders in the heavens and other events on this planet to precede the Darkness and/or to be contemporaneous with the geological upheavals. Specifically, Israel will have been invaded already when the volcanic explosions in the Mediterranean commence on a massive scale and when the world-wide earthquakes begin. Also, European lands will be at war at that time. It appears that the Russians will already be at war against the Turks by April of 1998. Therefore, once Gog and Magog begin their attack westward, we turn our eyes to the heavens and to the bottomless pits upon this planet. There are a few additional hints scattered through the prophecies that are worth keeping in mind, as time progresses, for the temporal fine-tuning they afford us. For instance, when all foreign missionaries are expelled from Communist China; when *the conflagration of the dockyards of the English and/or the burning of the Treasury where gold is deposited*, have already began; when Civil Wars have began at least in Italy and France. All these are events that may all have commenced before the year 1998 A.D.

There is nothing in the prophecies excluding volcanic eruptions and other geological upheavals preceding the events associated with the Comet and the Darkness. Such events, currently isolated and sporadic in their nature, are expected to increase in frequency and severity as time goes by. However, in terms of their destructiveness and geographic comprehensiveness, the upheavals elicited by the events around the Three Days Darkness cannot be confused with anything preceding them.

We are told by the Spirit that during the Three Days Darkness a great war will be fought between the Angels of Light under the Command of the

Archangel Michael and the Virgin Mary on the one hand, and the Angels of Darkness under the command of Belial on the other. During the Darkness, the devil will be allowed to harvest many of his followers and devotees, who will perish in terror and despair, unprotected by the Holy Ones.

The Chosen are exhorted to spend the horrible hours in fervent and continuous prayer, because prayer is the only weapon against the evil spirits that mortal men have at their disposal. The demons will not attack and torment those who are already theirs. Rather, they will make the last ditch effort to recruit the marginal faithful and harvest those who had the potentiality of being saved, but failed to take the necessary steps in a timely fashion. It is against such eventuality that the Holy Ones have been exhorting us with specific advice, admonition and detailed 'battle orders', beginning with the Hebrew Prophets and the Greek Sibyls.

The chastisement will emanate from the Hand of the Almighty and will be universal. It purports to purify and cleanse the earth from its iniquity, *because the disorders and the crimes of men have pierced the vault of heaven.* No race and nation will be spared. No individual country, no matter what its contribution to civilization and the degree of purity among its Chosen, will avoid losing a sizeable portion of its population to the demons and/or the natural agents of the catastrophes. The percentages will differ from land to land according to the overall standing of its Elect and their percentage participation in the total population, but also according to the degree of preparedness of the Elect to help themselves and take all necessary precautions to avoid the worst.

God helps those who help themselves. We must not tempt God by failing to do what is within our power. After having done all we can, we turn with our prayers to the Lord and His Angels to afford us the protection we are unable to generate ourselves. It is expected that a number of the Elect will subsequently die in the war. However, their final destination will be the Heavenly Kingdom, and from what the prophecies indicate, their numbers will be overall much, much smaller vis-à-vis those who will perish in the Darkness. When everything will be finished and peace will dawn on the world, we expect that the earth's population will be about 1/3 of its current level.

The major groups of the events composing the chastisement and leading to the Terrible Day of the Lord can be organized into: volcanic eruptions; hurricanes; firebrands; tidal waves; inundations; submersions; earthquakes;

destruction of cities and crops; boiling fresh and sea waters at the vicinity of submerged volcanoes; death of fishes and animals and reduction of food-stuffs; famine; diseases; epidemics.

A tremendously rich reward awaits the survivors of the Darkness and WWIII. The earth will be blessed with great fecundity (among other things through the enrichment of the soil resulting from massive volcanic activities). The persons addicted to vice, crime and Godlessness will have died and Satan will be confined for long decades up till the Antichrist's times. Never before in written History have the survivors of a major disaster and a world conflict of horrendous proportions been given an inheritance so rich in earthly terms and so gratifying to spirit and soul. While the experience of the Three Days Darkness is identified in all prophecies as the most horrendous in written History, the era that follows will be most blissful, as to wipe out the tears from all eyes.

The Holy Ones have provided us with a most detailed road-map of our Apocalyptic future and have offered us the most specific instructions on how to cease and desist from activities fatal to body and soul, so that we can share in the rewards of the new century and the world to come. Consequently, we have no excuse, after being enlightened with so much Grace, to ignore it and pretend we did not know. We cannot invoke the extenuating circumstances of the tragic Greek hero, emotionally tormented for sins committed in ignorance, or not committed at all. We are fully responsible for the use we chose to make of all the intimations from Heaven pouring down on us in the course of millennia. *He who hath ears to hear, let him hear*. The Lord Jesus Christ has already preempted our potential excuses with His parable of Lazarus and the rich man (Luke 16:19-31). He suspected that even if one were to rise from the dead and personally deliver the salutary message to those whose heart is hardened, still they would not be convinced.

We live in an age that is proud of its technological achievements. We talk matter-of-factly of the electronic Information Super-Highway and the marvelous vistas and possibilities it has opened to us. What do we plan to do with respect to the Information Hyper-Awesome Celestial-Way that connects us directly to the Throne of the Almighty from Whom every good and perfect gift derives? Shall we shake our heads and dismiss the evidence as poetic hyperboles and irrelevant literary constructions by dead Theologians and Historians? Or, shall we, instead, after the initial shock is mastered, arise from the lethargy of 'the business as usual' - self-delusion and effectively use the limited remaining time for a complete overhaul of our life? Or, shall we turn, instead, to the Sirens of the majority opinion, which have identified more pressing vital concerns for our undivided attention?

In conclusion, we must be alert, in fervent prayer and in complete mobilization of body, spirit and soul if we are to survive the Devil, **and** the 'Turk' (and his Chinese allies) **and** the Comet.

ON HOMO ECONOMICUS

It is by now obvious that we go through a tremendous Paradigm Shift in human history. The Remnant can be somehow compared to Biblical Job who had great riches and a happy family life. He lost everything within a few days, including his health. His faith and submission to God brought him eventually rewards that more than compensated for his material and emotional losses. The Remnant will go through an ordeal similar to Job's. They will lose most of what they have accumulated during this century, but, if they persevere and make it through they will be compensated in a manner analogous to Job. Let us draw inspiration and encouragement from the Book of Job while we cope on a daily basis with the challenges and the strains that lie ahead.

One immediate consequence of the major Paradigm Shift is the wholesale obliteration of the status quo. An obvious example of things that will change is our job description, provided we are blessed enough to count among the Remnant. Catastrophism, in other words, does not operate only on the geological level and the Earth's polarity. It does not only submerge lands and gives birth to new ones. It does not only modify the bed of rivers and the height of mountains and volcanoes. Catastrophism will operate even more visibly on the human level. We shall shed erroneous beliefs of yesteryear, we shall restitute old, forgotten values, we shall eliminate professions that have proven outdated, obsolete and even detrimental to society, we shall re-construct and modify those professions which will prove vital and valuable in the future. No profession and no area of human aptitude will remain unaffected. If military weapons can be turned into agricultural implements and the demobilized veterans can join the civilian economy, one must expect similar evolution for the clergy of the post-reunification Christian churches and the political elites of our contemporary democracies.

The post WWIII society, with its enormous needs for re-construction activities will have no place for fancy job descriptions, parasitical groups and transfer-payments' recipients with nothing to offer in return. For one thing, the prophecies tell us that the Great Monarch will not collect any taxes for a number of years. No taxes, no central governmental financing system, no transfer payments. The survivors will become the owners of the means of production and the responsibility for their sustenance will revert to them and to their labor. They will be expected to support their own family members that are too old or too young to provide for themselves. Considering how close we are to the materialization of these events, there is no time left for tergiversations and delays. We have been given the necessary knowledge, we must begin to act **now** to prepare the way for a successful conversion of the old system into the new. To use economic jargon, the re-tooling must begin now, for the machine to begin production tomorrow.

A last historical analogy: According to calculations by the Historians, the Black Death which devastated Asia and Europe in the 14th century of our era, killed ca. 24 million people in Europe alone, about one fourth of the Continent's entire population. The survivors inherited the wealth, and the value of their labor skyrocketed in view of the huge aggregate demand generated by wealthy heirs and the relative scarcity of labor to satisfy that demand in the short run. That was the first great impetus in European history for switching to labor-saving production technologies. If this can happen with only 1/4 of the population being eliminated, what could be the labor shortage and its consequences when 2/3 of the population are eliminated?

The corollary is obvious enough: The new century will need every pair of working hands that are available. But since our technical know how will not be destroyed or eliminated in the catastrophes (nor should it be, by any means) we must begin by directing the education of our youth towards the technologies that are truly transferable into the next century. The prophets predict a great exodus from the cities and a massive return to the land. It may be that, in analogy to our contemporary electronic cottage industries, we may witness a great advance in the electronically connected small communities around farms and other units in the extraction industries such as mining and wood processing.

ON HOMO POLITICUS

In the Platonic dialogue entitled *Protagoras*, the Sophist is asked who possesses "the science of politics". He replies with a myth. *When Zeus distributed professional specialties to the human race he did not create a specialist politician but evenly distributed political knowledge and made it common to all. And in fact, when the Athenians needed to discuss the building of temples or ships in their political assembly they would turn to architects and ship-builders for expert opinion. But when general political discussions were held, the word of each citizen weighed the same.*

Never before was the advice of Sophist Protagoras more relevant than today. With so much discussion about peace being 'enforced in the world', and the USA troops being dispatched to the four corners of the earth (frequently for questionable objectives), let us turn to the verdicts of the prophets and Protagoras's suggestions to us. When covering the Byzantine era prophecies, we encountered the following: *You consider it a good idea to draw up peace treaties but you are laboring in vain. I introduce a brief truce, and I do not think about a true peace. Mars is threatening with a terrible destruction, the people will think that the end of the world will arrive soon.*

Words like these ought to remove the wind from the sails of all those who embark on 'enforcing' peace around the world, especially at the expense of Christian populations for the benefit of their Islamic foes. The *unnecessary wars in Europe,* predicated for our proximate future, although unavoidable at this stage, need not be so bloody and so prolonged and so internecine among the natural allies of the lands of Judeo-Christianity as to afford them only a Pyrrhic victory in the end.

To frustrate a Pyrrhic victory, however, a massive mobilization of public opinion would be necessary. In *Antigone*, there is a famous passage where the chorus begins with enumerating the many reasons making Man the most marvelous and wonderful and terrible creature that walks upon the Earth. Among them is the ἀστυνόμος ὀργά, "astynomos orga.[2]

---

[2] These two small words have given a lot of trouble to non-Greek translators of Sophocles as the representative sample given below would suggest:
a)   and *aptitudes of civic life*; (in two translations)
b)   *griefs to give laws to nations;*
c)   *the lore of ruling a town.*
d)   *he builds the State to his mood.* The winner is (e): *Ten Greek Plays in Contemporary Translations*, p. 90. Houghton Mifflin Co., Boston, 1957. The translator Shaemas O'Sheel, came the closest to the spirit of Sophocles, as well as the etymology of the Greek.

The "astynomos orga", verbally translates as the longing for, impulse, passion for deliberating and instituting legislation. It suggests an impetus, an emotional need to participate in a responsible manner in the political activity and the law-making process. It is the urge for direct participation in the decisions which shape men's future in a democracy. As Professor Cornelius Castoriades recently reminded his Greek audience while lecturing on a similar issue,[3] the ancient Attican peasant would go on foot 25 km (one way) in order to deliberate in the Athenian Assembly. The seaman from Piraeus would do likewise to exercise the rights and the privileges of a citizen aware of his freedom and his responsibilities.

While several of the advantages of the Athenian-style participatory democracy are lost to us in our complicated and populous modern societies, the prophets urge us to resuscitate this marvelous gift given to man, unparalleled in the animal kingdom: the astynomos orga, which derives from the freedom with which God the Creator has endowed us.

The *astynomos orga* must be resuscitated, harnessed, and made manifest in our lives from now on. Whether we are taking care of personal preparations for the terrible events ahead, whether we are expressing our opinion on where should the cream of our youth be dispatched to fight wars, and/or question the legitimacy of national policies on life and death, whether we decide to follow the example and advice of our current pastor or religious advisor or to reconsider our doctrinal positions, it is no longer time to sit quietly by the wayside and relegate all vital political, social and spiritual decisions for our future to third parties on a carte blanche basis. The main concern of our lives from now on should be how to achieve salvation and survival. The intimation of the prophets can provide us with a starting point and the proper guidance for such a personal search. Everything else should become subordinate to these two objectives.

ON HOMO RELIGIOSUS

Let us begin by completely regenerating our inner world. An endogenous purification will render an exogenous one unnecessary. We avert the anger of the Lord by complying with His Laws. A life lived according to the Will of God, a life of prayer, penance, confession, honoring the day of the Lord,

---

[3] [1990, the lecture was entitled *The Problem of Democracy Today*, pp. 111-132].

strictly observing the fasts, along with all additional acts of reparation required by each of us individually, will help us defeat the evil within, will purify us and render us worthy of the great Mercies from Above in the days to come. We, as merely human, do not possess the power to combat the evil spirits. Yet, the power rests with us to render ourselves attractive and acceptable places of habitation of the Holy Spirit. When the Kingdom of Heaven reigns inside, the Angels of the Lord will protect the outside also, against the angels of Belial, or any other evil, wrath, danger, and necessity.

God will help those who help themselves. We must take all precautionary measures at our disposal to reduce the impact of the natural events to life and limb. If we can evacuate entire coastal areas at the approach of a hurricane on short warning, should we do anything less when the Big One is expected? The Holy Ones are preparing us for the events through a thousand mouths speaking in many languages and dialects, through men and women from all walks of life, degrees of education, or social standing. As we can see, the Holy Ones never tire of forewarning us; never tire of guiding those who have eyes to see, ears to hear and minds to understand. (We also have the Hubble Telescope and other high-tech devices which can be re-calibrated to look for different wonders in the skies and track down the comet and the other celestial phenomena intimated by the prophets, thus affording us the maximum available advance notice. Ditto, for Meteorologists, Volcanologists and other experts with valuable knowledge to impart and life-saving advice to offer).

The prophecies have delivered us our future with all the tees crossed and all the iotas dotted. Would they be so explicit and categorical in their details if the designs of the Almighty were not intent on enhancing our chances of survival and salvation? **God does not play dice with the Universe, especially not with a planet housing a species for whose benefit He had His Son given to the Cross.** We intimated at the very beginning of this study that when evil increases in the world so does Divine Grace. An Omniscient God knows the difficulties the Remnant will face while trying to cope simultaneously with the Devil, WWIII, and the Comet. For this reason, He has given us an enormous wealth of advance notice and specific instructions to guide us through. This advance notice, needless to say, is addressed also to the political elites of many countries whose burden will be more onerous than ever in the years immediately following.

The Politicians' share in the mobilization burden. When the proverbial Seven Lean Years eventually came upon the land of Egypt, the warehouses were full and there was excess grain for the export trade with neighboring lands, which, by being deprived of dream interpreters such as Joseph or rulers as provident as his Pharaoh, were experiencing serious food shortages. If a ruler can take such drastic measures on the basis of a dream only, what should the contemporary rulers do in the presence of evidence so diversified, overwhelming and categorical?

Perhaps, they could begin by advising their citizens to begin accumulating buffer stocks in view of the crop failures to be wrought by volcanic eruptions, hurricanes, volcanic ejecta upon crops and other such eventualities. One must expect also the world temperatures to drop for a year or two after the massive volcanic eruptions by analogy to the year without summer we studied earlier. This could also lead to unsatisfactory crops and further shortages down the road. The individual citizen, on the other hand, should take every conceivable step within his power to provide for his own needs. Persuading the citizen to act in this way may be the hardest part of the politicians' dilemma, given the current political parameters.

One of the great victories of the devil in the course of this century has been his persuading so many millions that the State is basically a Santa Claus of unlimited resources and responsibilities and that they all are entitled to lengthy wish-lists for its never-ending Providence.   This entitlement psychosis, exacerbated by the inflated expectations fanned by domestic and foreign demagogues, will increase the strains and stresses exerted upon the state in the years ahead in view of the overwhelming consequences of massive global catastrophes. These will only be further aggravated by the demands of fighting a global war. One cannot exclude, a priori, civil unrest and armed conflicts when the State fails to 'fulfill its obligations' and the populace rises and asserts with violent means its 'natural rights' and the recoupment of all 'social gains' washed away in the presence of shortages, rampant inflation and the other cataclysms of the age. In the process, the world population will be further trimmed down and *blood will flow in the streets* as the prophets predict.

And while the shepherd in a church has to worry about the closet Atheists only, the political leader has to explicitly take into consideration all the citizenry, including the Atheists. The Atheists are triple jeopardy in the given case because:

a) They do not believe in the prophets and in the imminence of the

Seven Lean Cows. Hence they are unwilling to contribute towards the buffer stocks and other contingency plans.

b) An Atheist, by definition negates Divine Providence. Hence he expects nothing from Above and directs all his demands, requests, petitions and exigencies to the Santa-Claus-State from whose bag all good things are supposed to emanate. If he also happens to be conditioned to expecting entitlements and government transfers, his exigencies become more imperative and his demands more urgent. Hence, if the state fails to deliver or chooses not to, our fellow citizen may take the law in his hands and start breaking into grocery markets and neighborhood kitchens.

c) An Atheist does not believe in Afterlife and cherishes the one he now has as the only possible one, to be preserved at any cost. It is not fortuitous that the greatest 'pacifists' in our century have been Atheists, for whom the motto seems to be 'peace at any price'. The great peace rallies organized by the KGB in the Western Democracies during the Cold War Era could not boast too many Churchgoers among their regular participants. Motivated by the erroneous belief that absence of war is synonymous to longevity, these kinds of people will resist any military mobilization in the future, as well, and create additional problems for the political leadership.

Preparing the country for the troubles ahead should become a matter of the utmost priority for the rulers. A little bit of panic today will have a very salutary effect later on, much like a vaccination against a lethal epidemic which temporarily causes fever and pain and discomfort and frequently has to be imposed and administered under government decree to minimize the risk of non-compliance. The consolation is that all Godless the world over will disappear in the Three Days Darkness and they will not impose additional burdens on an over-extended Remnant which will still have to fight the last decisive battles of WWIII.

The above deliberations make rather manifest the stress that will be imposed upon society in the years to come, when the state in all probability, will fall short of expectations for reasons too obvious to detail here. We are already entering a period of heightened social unrest and disaffection, the world over. The prophets predict that WWIII will follow in the wake of civil wars in many countries of Europe. In fact, it will be once again the inherent internal weaknesses of liberal democracies and their openness (to practically everything) that will wet the appetite of Islam to try the reconquest of Europe at a low opportunity cost, so to say: Inherit the achievements of liberal democracy and capitalism and be made the lord of their prime real estate, while enslaving the decadent Infidels who were unwilling to safeguard and defend their freedoms. Ditto, for the expansionary plans of an economically strengthened, militarily well-equipped mainland China, which has the competitive advantage of the largest army in the world.

THE PROBLEM WITH DEMOCRACY TODAY

Jean-François Revel's *How Democracies Perish* was written during the Cold War Era and addressed primarily the Soviet and Chinese Totalitarianisms. In a chapter entitled 'A Willing Victim', Revel analyzed the *humility with which democracy is not only consenting to its own obliteration but is contriving to legitimize its deadliest enemy's victory.* After the collapse of the USSR, the Western Democracies continue to be vulnerable to other forms of Totalitarianism and most amenable to all forms of manipulations, ideological warfare and disinformation or sheer economic calculus by those with the 'deep pockets' and their recruited armies of intellectual apologists in Academia, the Lobbying Firms, and the Mass Media.

We now have to deal with Chinese Totalitarianism and Islamic Fundamentalism. The enemy may have shifted ideological focus, geographical location, and social agenda. But the weakness of democracies to deal with these problems has not been dealt with and Revel's analysis, mutatis mutandis, is still applicable and his messages valid and urgent. He cautions us that the retrospective knowledge of the truth by the democracies cannot repair the damage caused by years of ignorance.

The prophet Brother Louis Rocco (whom we met in a previous chapter) predicted that the Great Monarch, the victor of WWIII, will 'uproot all Republics', will re-establish exiled kings in their kingdoms and will be compared by History to Caesar Augustus and Constantine the Great. From all the great warriors of History, why should he compare King Juan Carlos I de Borbón to those two empire builders, specifically? I feel that besides the reasons already advanced by him, there are a few additional similarities worth noting:

a)   Both Octavian and Constantine led their men to battle in person. This earned the respect and confidence and loyalty of their soldiers. (Octavian's sickly constitution was never used as a pretext for absence from a battle). This was a tremendous boost for the morale of their legions, who were willing to fight and die for such leaders.

b)   They were pious men, revering the signs and omens from Above: Octavian was a pagan and Constantine might have remained more or less a pagan (despite his mother) at least till the eve of the encounter on the Milvian Bridge.[4] However, both were aware of the power of Deity to shape human history and both were extremely sensitive to divine messages expressed in Omens. In the case of Constantine, most Christians have already read of his seeing a luminous cross in the sky accompanied by the message *in hoc signo vincas* (be victorious in this symbol). However, less well known is a seemingly irrelevant event that preceded the sea-battle of Actium, (the Milvian Bridge-equivalent in Octavian's military and political career). In the night preceding the naval engagement of September 2, 31 B.C., Octavian went out from his tent to observe the movements of Marc Antony's forces. He encountered a man leading a donkey. Replying to Octavian's questions of who he was and what was he doing there at such hour, the stranger said that his name was Nicon, that of his donkey was Nicandros and that they were both coming over to Octavian's side. Both Nicon and Nicandros, however, are etymologically deriving from *víκη*, the Greek word for victory, a detail not lost to Octavian.[5]

c)   As the Actium victory was signaling the end of the Roman republic (and Octavian now became Caius Julius Caesar Augustus, instead), so the prophets tell us that the Great Monarch will uproot all republics. Similarly, Constantinus Augustus, graduated to Constantine the Great after his victory over Maxentius on 312 A.D. and now the empire had but one ruler only.

---

[4] At least this is the theory propounded by his detractors who accused him as an opportunist and a hypocrite in adopting a symbol of Christianity for his armies. One might argue that a hypocrite and an opportunist is by nature unwilling to commit himself so completely to an extraneous emotional force and he would most probably vacillate on the eve of his decisive encounter and forget about the sign in the skies completely.

[5] After his triumphal victory at Actium, Octavian ordered a marvelous sculpture depicting Nicon and his Nicandros. This statue was later moved to Constantinople where it was finally destroyed by the Crusaders of the Fourth Crusade.

These instances testify to the fact that the Lord of History not only interferes in human events but He strengthens the side He favors, in advance, with signs and omens. (The History of the world has hundreds of additional instances of advance notice on the eve of decisive wars and battles to add to the above testimony). He has given us ample evidence in advance that He favors our side in battle. May this be our source of motivation par excellence when 'the quietude of the desert has been stirred'.

Dear Reader: I thank you for drinking the bitter cup you have been offered to the very end. But having done so, like the potentates of old, who developed immunity to lethal doses of poison by drinking smaller ones more frequently, you are in a position to countenance more successfully the tougher days ahead. And if I were allowed to advance one last speculation, I would say that by exhibiting so receptive an attitude so far, your eyes are not blind, you ears are not deaf and your heart is not hardened. May the Grace of the Lord continue to provide you with salutary discernment and life-giving guidance now and forever. Amen.

SELECTED BIBLIOGRAPHY

Bibles and Reference Books Consulted

Analytical Greek New Testament, (Edited by Kurt Aland, Matthew Black, Carlo M. Martini, Bruce M. Metzger and Allen Wikgren), Baker Book House, Grand Rapids, Michigan, 1981.

The Comparative Study Bible, A parallel Bible presenting the New International Version, New American Standard Version, Amplified Bible, and King James Version, The Zondervan Corp. Grand Rapids, MI, 1984.

De Santos Otero, A. Los Evangelios Apócrifos, Edición crítica y bilingue, 6a Edición, Biblioteca de Autores Cristianos, de la Editorial Católica, S.A., Madrid, Spain, 1988.

Библия, (The Bible) Книги священного писания ветхого и нового завета - канонические. (В русском переходе с параллельными местами, Библейское Общества), UBS-EPF-8319-10M-043.

Библия, (The Bible) Книги священного писания ветхого и нового завета. В русском переходе с параллельными местами. (Перепечатано с издания Московской Патриархии). Российское Библейское Общество, Москва, 1993.

The Greek New Testament, United Bible Societies, 3rd Edition, (printed in West Germany), 1975.

The Harper Concise Atlas of the Bible, (Edited by J. B. Pritchard), Harper Collins Publishers, Times Books, Great Britain, 1991.

Τά Ἱερά Γράμματα Μεταφρασθέντα ἐκ τῶν Θείων Ἀρχετύπων, Βιβλική Ἑταιρία, Athens, Greece, UBS-EPF-1981-12M-053.

Holy Bible, (Catholic Family Edition), Confraternity Edition, John J. Crawley and Co. Inc., Washington, D.C., 1953.

Holy Bible, La Sagrada Biblia, (traducida de la vulgata latina al español, por Felix Torres Amat), Edicomunicación, SA., Barcelona, Spain, 1987.

Ἡ Ἁγία Γραφή, Ἀδελφότης Θεολόγων Ἡ Ζωή, 12th edition, Athens, Greece, 1991.

Novum Testamentum Graece - Pocketbook edition of the New Testament in Greek, 25th edition, by Nestle, Erwin and Aland, Kurt, United Bible Societies, London, England, (Printed in Germany) 1973.

The NIV Triglot Old Testament, Zondervan Publishing House, Grand Rapids, MI, 1981.

Septuaginta (The Old Testament according to the 70), Deutsche Bibelgesellschaft, Stuttgart, 1979.

The Septuagint with Apocrypha: Greek and English, Sir Lancelot C.L. Brenton, Zondervan Publishing House, Grand Rapids, Michigan, 1981.

The Greek New Testament, edited by: Kurt Aland, Matthew Black, Carlo M. Martini, Bruce M. Metzger and Allen Wikgren, (Third Edition), United Bible Societies, West Germany, 1975.

BOOKS

Alexander, Paul J.: The Oracle of Baalbek - The Tiburtine Sibyl in Greek Dress, Dumbarton Oaks Center for Byzantine Studies, Trustees for Harvard University, Washington, D.C., 1967.

Allen, Paul Marshall: Vladimir Soloviev, Russian Mystic, First Edition, Steinerbooks, Blauvelt, N.Y., 1978.

Bacovcin, Helen (translator): The Way of a Pilgrim and The Pilgrim Continues His Way, (anonymous author), Image Books, Doubleday, New York, N.Y., 1978.

Bailey, M.E., Clube S.V.M., and Napier W.M.: The Origin of Comets, Pergamon Press, Oxford, England, 1990.

Bander, Peter: Introduction and Commentary to The Prophecies of St. Malachy, TAN Books and Publishers, Inc., Rockford, Ill. 1973.

Berdyaev, Nicolas: Leontiev, Academic International/orbis academicus, Orono, Maine, 1968.

Bernal, Martin: Black Athena, vol. II, (The Archaeological and Documentary Evidence), Rutgers University Press, New Brunswick, N.J., 1993.

Besançon, Alain: Русское прошлое и советское настоящее, First Russian Edition by Overseas Publications Interchange, Ltd., London,

England, 1984.

Bevan, Edwyn: Sibyls and Seers: A Survey of Some Ancient Theories of Revelation and Inspiration, (originally published by George Allen & Unwin Ltd., London, 1928), Norwood Editions, 1977.

Bloch, R. Howard: God's Plagiarist: Being an Account of the Fabulous Industry and Irregular Commerce of the Abbé Migne, The University of Chicago Press, Chicago, IL 1994.

Bousset, Wilhelm: Die Antichrist Legende, (originally published by Hutchinson and Company, London, U.K., 1896; English Translation by A.H. Keane 'The Antichrist Legend') AMS Press, Inc., New York, N. Y., 1985).

Brogan, Patrick: The Fighting Never Stopped: A Comprehensive Guide to World Conflict Since 1945, Vintage Books, New York, N. Y., 1990.

Brianchianinov, Ign. Θαύματα καί Σημεῖα, (Miracles and Signs), (Greek Translation by Meletios Kalamaras, Metropolitan of Nicopolis, 3rd Edition), Preveza, Greece, 1991.

Burn, A.R. & Mary: The Living Past of Greece, Icon Editions (HarperCollins), New York, N.Y. 1980.

Butterfield, Fox: China: Alive in the Bitter Sea, Bantam Books, New York, N.Y., (Bantam Books Edition of 1983).

Carter, Mary Ellen: Edgar Cayce Modern Prophet, (under the editorship of Hugh Lynn Cayce), Gramercy Books, New Jersey, 1990, (reprint of works originally published 1967-1989).

Cartwright F. F. in collab. with Biddiss M.D.: Disease and History, Dorset Press, New York, N.Y., 1972.

Carusi, Andrea and Valsecchi Giovanni B., Editors: Dynamics of Comets: Their Origin and Evolution, (Proceedings of the 83rd Colloquium of the International Astronomical Union, held in Rome, June 1984), D. Reidel Publishing Company, Dordrecht, Holland, 1985.

Castoriades, Cornelius: Οἱ ὁμιλίες στήν Ἑλλάδα, (Lectures delivered in Greece) Ὕψιλον/Βιβλία, Athens, Greece, 1990.

Chapman, Clark R. and Morrison David: Cosmic Catastrophes, Plenum Press, New York, N.Y., 1989.

Charlesworth, James H., Editor: The Old Testament Pseudepigrapha, vol. i, Doubleday & Co., Inc., Garden City, N.Y., 1983.

Charlesworth, James H., Editor: The Old Testament Pseudepigrapha, vol. ii, Doubleday & Co., Inc., Garden City, N.Y., 1985.

Cheetham, Erika: The Prophecies of Nostradamus, Wideview/Perigee Books, N.Y., 1975.

Choate, Pat: Agents of Influence - How Japan Manipulates America's Political and Economic System, A Touchstone Book, New York, N.Y., 1990.

Choniates, Nicetas: 'O City of Byzantium', The Annals, (translated by Harry J. Magoulias), Wayne State University Press, Detroit, MI., 1984.

Christian, William A. Jr.: Apparitions in Late Medieval and Renaissance Spain, Princeton University Press, Princeton, N.J., 1981.

Clarkson, J. D.: A History of Russia, Second Edition, Random House, New York, N.Y., 1969.

Colson, Charles: Against the Night: Living in the New Dark Ages, with Ellen Santilli Vaughn, Servant Books, Ann Arbor Michigan, 1989.

Crouch, Dora P.: Water Management in Ancient Greek Cities, Oxford University Press, New York, N.Y., 1993.

Culleton, R. Gerald (Rev.): The Prophets and Our Times, (third Edition), TAN Books and Publishers, Inc., Rockford, Ill., 1974.

Davidson, Gustav: A Dictionary of Angels Including the Fallen Angels, The Free Press, New York, N.Y., 1971.

Davies, John Keith: Cosmic Impact, St. Martin's Press, New York, N.Y., 1986.

Delimpasis, A. D. (Δελίμπασης, A. Δ.): Φοβερά καί Θαυμαστά Ἐρχόμενα Γεγονότα, (Terrible and Wonderful Coming Events), Athens, Greece, 1986.

Delsemme, A. H., Editor: Comets, Asteroids, Meteorites - interrelations, evolution and origins, The University of Toledo Press, Toledo, Ohio, 1977.

de Diesbach, Ghislain: Secrets of the Gotha - Private lives of the Royal Families of Europe, translated from the French by Margaret Crosland,

Barnes & Noble Books, New York, N.Y., 1993.

de Voragine, Jacobus: The Golden Legend, (translated and adapted from the Latin by Granger Ryan and Helmut Ripperger), Arno Press/New York Times, New York, N.Y., 1969.

Dupont, Yves: Catholic Prophecy: The Coming Chastisement, Tan Books and Publishers, Inc., Rockford, Illinois, 1973.

Durant, Will: The Story of Civilization, vol. i, "Our Oriental Heritage", Simon and Schuster, New York, N.Y., 1954.

-- The Story of Civilization, vol. ii, "The Life of Greece", Simon and Schuster, New York, N.Y., 1966.

-- The Story of Civilization, vol. iii, "Caesar and Christ", Simon and Schuster, New York, N.Y., 1944, 1972.

Eftimiades, Nicholas: Chinese Intelligence Operations, Naval Institute Press, Annapolis, Maryland, 1994.

Eisenman, Robert H. & Wise, Michael: The Dead Sea Scrolls Uncovered, Barnes & Noble Books, New York, N.Y., 1992.

Emmerson, Richard Kenneth: Antichrist in the Middle Ages, The University of Washington Press, Seattle, WA., 1981.

Flaste, Richard, Noble Holcomb, Sullivan Walter, and Wilford John Noble: The New York Times Guide to the Return of Halley's Comet, Times Books, New York, N.Y. 1985.

de Fontbrune, Jean-Charles: Nostradamus - Countdown to Apocalypse & Into the Twenty-First Century, (translated by Alexis Lykiard), Cresset, 1992.

Forman, Henry James: The Story of Prophecy in the Life of Mankind, from Early Times to the Present Day, Farrar & Rinehart, Inc., New York, N. Y., 1936.

Geffcken, Johannes: Die Oracula Sibyllina, (im Auftrage der Kirchenväter-Commission der Königlichen Preussischen Akademie der Wissenschaften), J.C. HINRICHS'sche BUCHHANDLUNG, Leipzig, 1902.

Gorainov Irina (Горайнов Ирина): Ὁ Ἅγιος Σεραφείμ τοῦ Σάρωφ, (Saint Seraphim of Sarov), Greek Translation by Pitsa K. Skouteri, 8th Edition,

TINOS, Athens, Greece, 1991.

Goritschewa, Tatiana: Die Kraft der ohnmächtigen, (Greek translation by Evi Voulgaraki, under the title Ἡ Ἀθέατη Πλευρά τῆς Ῥωσσίας, Series no. 33, AKRITAS Publishers, Nea Smyrni, Athens, Greece, 1989.

Grant, George: The Blood of the Moon - The Roots of the Middle East Crisis, Wolgemuth & Hyatt, Publishers, Inc., Brentwood, Tennessee, 1991.

Griffiths, Margaret Enid: Early Vaticination in Welsh - with English Parallels, University of Wales, Cardiff, Wales, 1937.

Hackel, Sergei: Pearl of Great Price - The Life of Mother Maria Skobtsova 1891-1945, St. Vladimir's Seminary Press, Crestwood, N.Y., 1981.

Hall, Angus & King, Francis: Mysteries of Prediction, Bloomsbury Books, London, U.K., 1991.

Hartmann, William K. & Miller Ron: The History of the Earth: An Illustrated Chronicle of an Evolving Planet, Workman Publishing, New York, N.Y., 1991.

Hebert, Albert J. S.M. The Three Days Darkness, Signs of the Times, Sterling, Va., yopu.

Heist, William W.: The Fifteen Signs Before Doomsday, Michigan State College Press, East Lansing, MI, 1952.

Herodotus: The Histories, (translated by Aubrey de Selincourt) Penguin Books, Revised Edition, 17th printing, Middlesex, England, 1987.

Hildegard of Bingen: Book of Divine Works, edited by Matthew Fox, Bear & Co. Santa Fe, N.M., 1987.

Hildegard of Bingen: Scivias, (translated by Columba Hart and Jane Bishop), The Classics of Western Spirituality, Paulist Press, Mahwah, N.J., 1990.

Hildegard of Bingen (Sanctae Hildegardis abbatissae): Opera Omnia - De Operatione Dei, in Patrologiae Cursus Completus, Series Latina, vol. 197 col. 739-1038, in J.P. Migne (Editor), 1855.

House, Francis: Millennium of Faith: Christianity in Russia 988 - 1988 A.D., St. Vladimir's Seminary Press, Crestwood, N.Y., 1988.

Hroch, Miroslav and Skybová Anna: Ecclesia Militans: The Inquisition, (Translated from the German by Janet Fraser), 2nd English Language Printing, Dorset Press, 1990.

Huysmans, J.-K.: Là-Haut ou Notre-Dame de la Salette, Casterman, Belgium, 1965.

Johanson, Anton: Visions of Anton Johanson, the Seer from the Norwegian Finnmark, (an English translation by Nathaniel Carlson of the original book on Johanson written by A. Gustafson and published in Sweden in 1918).

Kalamaras, Meletios (Metropolitan of Nicopolis): Τί εἶναι ὁ Χριστός; (What exactly is Christ?), 4th Edition, The Nicopolis Bishopric Publishing House, Preveza, Greece, 1991.

Kantiotis, Augustinus, (Καντιώτης, Αὐγουστῖνος) Metropolitan of Phlorina: Ὁ Ἅγιος Κοσμᾶς ὁ Αἰτωλός, Ὀρθόδοξος Ἱεραποστολική Ἀδελφότης Ὁ Σταυρός, 15th Edition, Athens, Greece, 1992.

Kaiser, Daniel H. and Marker Gary, Editors: Reinterpreting Russian History: Readings, 860-1860s, Oxford University Press, New York, N.Y., 1994.

Karpodini-Dimitriadi, E.: The Greek Islands: A traveller's guide to all the Greek Islands, (translated by Alexandra Doumas), Ekdotike Athenon, S.A., Athens, Greece, 1995.

Kemmerich, Max: Prophezeiungen - Alter Aberglaube oder neue Wahrheit?, (Prophecies, old Superstition or New Truth?), Albert Langen Verlag, München, Germany, 1921.

Kiomourdjian, J. Ch. (Κιομουρτζιὰν, Ιερεμία Τσελεμπὶ): Ὀδοιπορικὸ στήν Πόλη, (A Traveller's Guide through Constantinople) (Greek Translation and Historical Commentary by Soula Bozi), Publishers Τροχαλία, Athens, Greece, 1992.

Kirk, G.S. & Raven, J.E.: The Presocratic Philosophers, Cambridge University Press, U.K., U.S.A., 1957.

Komarov E., and Komarova I.: Патриарх, Ellis Luck, Moscow, Russia, 1994.

Kronk, Gary W.: Comets: A Descriptive Catalog, Enslow Publishers, Inc., Hillside, N.J., 1984.

375

Lanczkowski, Günter, Altägyptischer Prophetismus, vol. 4 of the Series Ägyptologische Abhandlungen, Otto Harrassowitz, Wiesbaden, 1960.

Lapham, Lewis H.: Money and Class in America: Notes and Observations on our Civil Religion, Weidenfeld & Nicolson, New York, N.Y. 1988.

Lemprière, John: Lemprière's Classical Dictionary of Proper Names mentioned in Ancient Authors, 3rd Edition, Routledge & Kegan Paul, London and New York, 1987.

Leong, Albert (Editor): The Millennium: Christianity and Russia 988-1988, St. Vladimir's Seminary Press, Crestwood, N.Y., 1990.

Leoni, Edgar: Nostradamus and His Prophecies, Bell Publishing Company, New York, N.Y., 1982.

Levi, Peter: Atlas of the Greek World, An Equinox Book, published by Facts on File, Inc. New York, N.Y., 1984, printing of 1989.

Lewis, Bernard: Race and Slavery in the Middle East: An Historical Enquiry, Oxford University Press, New York, N.Y., 1990.

Lewis, C. S.: The Screwtape Letters, The Macmillan Company, New York, N.Y., 1961.

Lleget, Marius: El enigma del quinto planeta, Libroexprés, Barcelona, España, 1988.

Losskii, N. O.: Бог и мировое зло - Достоевский и его христианское миропонимание, Республика, Moscow, Russia, 1994.

Martin, Malachy: The Keys of This Blood, Simon and Schuster, New York, N.Y., 1990.

McNeill, William H.: Plagues and Peoples, Anchor Books - Doubleday, New York, N.Y., 1989.

Makriyannis, John: The Memoirs of General Makriyannis 1797-1864, (Edited and translated by H. A. Lidderdale), Oxford University Press, London, U.K., 1966.

Makriyannis John, (General) (Στρατηγοῦ Μακρυγιάννη): Ὁράματα καί Θάματα, (Visions and Wonders), (introduction, text and notes by Angelos Papakostas), Educational Foundation of the National Bank of Greece,

Athens, Greece, 1983.

Meney, Patrick: Les mains coupées de la Taiga, (The severed Hands of the Taiga), La Table Ronde, Paris, France, 1984.

Metallinos, George D., Archpriest (Μεταλλινός, Γεώργιος Δ. Πρωτοπρεσβίτερος): Τουρκοκρατία - Οἱ "Ελληνες στήν 'Οθωμανική Αὐτοκρατορία, (The Turkish Yoke: the Greeks in the Ottoman Empire) σειρά Αἶπος, no. 3, 2nd edition, AKRITAS Publishers, Nea Smyrni, Athens, Greece, 1989.

Meyendorff, John Th. (Протоиерей Иоанн Ф. Мейендорф) Византия и Московская Русь, Russian Edition by YMCA-Press, Paris, France, 1990. (Originally Published as 'Byzantium and Muskovy') by Cambridge University Press, 1981).

Monk Isaac ('Ιερομόναχος 'Ισαάκ): 'Εμφανίσεις καί Θαύματα τῆς Παναγίας, (Apparitions and Miracles of the Panaghia), 2nd edition, Paracletos Monastery, Oropos, Attica, 1991.

Monk Seraphim ('Ιερομόναχος Σεραφείμ): Χαρίσματα καί Χαρισματοῦχοι, (Charisma and Those Who Have Received it), vol. 1, 5th Edition, Paracletos Monastery, Oropos, Attica, 1991.

Moore, Patrick: Comets, Charles Scribner's Sons, New York, N.Y. 1976.

Mosher, Steven W.: Broken Earth: The Rural Chinese, The Free Press, New York, N.Y., 1983.

Mother Shipton's : Prophecy published in Mercurius Propheticus, or 'A Collection of some old Predictions' printed in the Yeere M.DC.XLIII. (available in microfilm, Government Publications, England, 1600s).

Nahm, Milton C.: Selections from Early Greek Philosophy, 4rth Edition, Meredith Publishing Co., New York, N.Y., 1964.

Nostradamus, Michael: Les vrayes centuries de Maistre Michel Nostradamus, Paris, 1649 (reedited in September of 1940 by the Editions Utiles, Geneva, Switzerland).

Otto, Helen Tzima: Our Revelationary Age, the Prophecies for WWIII and the Year 2000, The Verenikia Press, Houston, Texas, 1994.

Pachter, Henry M.: Magic into Science - The Story of Paracelsus, Henry

Schuman, New York, N.Y., 1951.

Packard, Jerrold M.: The Queen and Her Court, Charles Scribner's Sons, New York, N.Y., 1981.

Paparrigopoulos, Constantine (Παπαρρηγόπουλος, Κωνσταντῖνος): ᾿Ιστορία τοῦ ῾Ελληνικοῦ ῎Εθνους, (History of the Greek Nation), vols. i - vii, Charalampos Bouras Publisher, Athens, Greece, 1885.

Parke, H.W.: Sibyls and Sibylline Prophecy in Classical Antiquity, (Edited by B.C. McGing), Routledge, London, U.K., 1988.

Parry, J. J. : Vita Merlini of Geoffrey of Monmouth, (English Translation plus commentary published by the University of Illinois Studies in Language and Literature), Urbana, IL, 1925.

Pascal, Pierre: The Religion of the Russian People, (La religion du peuple russe) (translated by Rowan Williams), St. Vladimir's Seminary Press, Crestwood, N.Y., 1976.

Paton, Lucy Allen: Les Prophecies de Merlin, vols. i & ii, The Modern Language Association of America/Oxford University Press, New York and London, 1926.

Payne, Robert: The History of Islam, Barnes & Noble Books, New York, N. Y., 1992.

Pei, Mario: The Story of Language, Revised Edition, A Mentor Book published by the New American Library, New York. N.Y., 1966.

le Pelletier, Anatole: Les Oracles de Michel de Nostredame, tome ii, Slatkine Reprints, Geneva, Switzerland, 1969.

Petroff, Elizabeth Alvilda: Medieval Women's Visionary Literature, Oxford University Press, New York, N.Y., 1986.

Puaux, René: Δυστυχισμένη Βόρειος ῎Ηπειρος, (Unhappy North Epirus), (translation from the French by A. Ach. Lazarou, Introduction and Commentary by Ach. G. Lazarou; (original title: La malheureuse Épire), ᾿Εκδόσεις Τροχαλία, Athens, Greece, y.o.p.u.

The Prophecy of Humphrey Tindal Vicar of Wellenger, shewing the Downfall of the Clergy...." London, England, printed for I.M., 1643, (available in microfilm. Government Publications, England, 1600s).

378

Raspail, Jean: The Camp of the Saints, (originally published as Le Camp des Saints, translated by Norman Shapiro), The Institute for Western Values, Inc., Alexandria, VA., 1975.

Revel, Jean-François: How Democracies Perish, (English translation by William Byron of Comment les démocraties finissent), Perennial Library, Harper & Row, New York, N.Y., 1985.

Runciman, Steven: The Fall of Constantinople 1453, Cambridge University Press, Cambridge, UK., a 1987 reprint.

Sagan, Carl and Druyan Ann: Comet, Random House, New York, N.Y., 1985.

Santos, D.: El enigma del fin cósmico de la tierra, Libroexprés, Barcelona, España, 1989.

Свято-Троицкий Ново-Голутвин женский монастырь г. Коломна (Editors): Царица небесная, спаси землю русскую - (Сказания о чудотворних иконах богоматери и о Ея милостях роду человеческому), (On the Miracle-working Icons of the Mother of God and on Her Favors towards the Human Race) (vols. i and ii), Kolomna, Russia, Christmas of 1993.

Sellner, Edward C.: Wisdom of the Celtic Saints, Ave Maria Press, Notre Dame, Indiana, 1993.

Seymour, Percy: The Scientific Basis of Astrology: Tuning to the Music of the Planets, St. Martin's Press, New York, N.Y., 1992.

Shalamov, Varlam: Kolyma Tales, (translated by John Glad) Penguin Books, England, U.K. 1994.

Skinner, Brian J. & Porter, Stephen C.: The Dynamic Earth: an introduction to physical geology, John Wiley & Sons, New York, N.Y. 1989.

Solzhenitsyn, Aleksandr Isaevich: Rebuilding Russia - Reflections and Tentative Proposals, (translated and annotated by Alexis Klimoff), Farrar, Straus and Giroux, New York, N.Y., 1991.

Solzhenitsyn, Aleksandr Isaevich: «"Русский Вопрос» к концу xx века» (The 'Russian Question' in the end of the 20th century), reprinted from Novii Mir in Le Messager (Viestnik), no. 169, I-II - 1994, pp. 193-274.

Solovyov Vlad., and Klepikova Elena: Boris Yeltsin: A Political Biography, (translated by David Gurevich in collaboration with the authors), G. P. Putnam's Sons, New York, N.Y., 1992.

Soren David & James Jamie: Kourion: The Search for a Lost Roman City, Anchor Press, (Doubleday), New York, N.Y., 1988.

Sotiropoulos, Neilos (Σωτηρόπουλος Νεῖλος, Ἱερομόναχος): Ἡ Ἐρχομένη Ὀξεία καί Δίστομος Ῥομφαία, (The Coming Sharp, Two-edged Sword), 6th Edition, 1974, Athens, Greece.

Stavrianos, L. S.: Lifelines From Our Past: a New World History, Pantheon Books, New York, N.Y. 1989.

Strabo: The Geography of Strabo volumes i to viii, (with an English Translation by Horace Leonard Jones Ph.D., LL.D.), Harvard University Press, Cambridge Massachusetts, 1944.

Struve, Nikita: Православие и культура, Христианское издательство, Moscow, Russia, 1992.

Taylor, Rupert: The Political Prophecy in England, The Columbia University Press, New York, N. Y. 1911.

Tierney, J.J. Jr. (Editor): About Face: The China Decision and its Consequences, Arlington House Publishers, New Rochelle, N.Y., 1979.

Trento, Susan B.: The Power House: Robert Keith Gray and the Selling of Access and Influence in Washington, St. Martin's Press, New York, N.Y., 1992.

Truell, Peter & Gurwin, Larry: False Profits: The Inside Story of BCCI, the World's Most Corrupt Financial Empire, Houghton Mifflin Company, New York, N.Y., 1992.

Velikovsky, Immanuel: Worlds in Collision, Doubleday & Company, Inc., Garden City, New York, 1950.

Vielhauer, Inge: Das Leben des Zauberers Merlin, (Geoffrey von Monmouth Vita Merlini, erstmalig in deutscher Übertragung mit anderen Überlieferungen), Castrum Peregrini Presse, 2nd Edition, Amsterdam, The Netherlands, 1964.

Walsh, William J.: The Apparitions and Shrines of Heaven's Bright Queen

In Legend, Poetry and History, v. i, Carey-Stafford Company, New York, New Orleans, 1904.

Walsh, William Thomas: Our Lady of Fátima, The Macmillan Company, New York, N.Y., 1947.

Whipple, Fred L. (assisted by Daniel W.E. Green): The Mystery of Comets, Smithsonian Institution Press, Washington, D.C., 1985.

Wood, Robert Muir: Earthquakes and Volcanoes - Causes, Effects & Predictions, Weidenfeld & Nicolson, New York, N. Y., 1987.

Woodward, Kenneth L.: Making Saints - How the Catholic Church Determines Who Becomes a Saint, Who Doesn't and Why, Simon and Schuster, New York, N.Y., 1990.

Wunderlich, Hans Georg: The Secret of Crete, (originally published in German under the title Wohin der Stier Europa trug, (Whereto did the bull carry Europa?), Macmillan Publishing Co., Inc., New York, N.Y., 1974.

Yeltsin, Boris: The Struggle for Russia, (translated by Catherine A. Fitzpatrick), Belka Publishing Company, New York, Toronto, London, 1994.

Yeomans Donald K.: Comets - A Chronological History of Observation, Science, Myth, and Folklore, Wiley Science Editions, U.S.A. 1991.

Zelinsky, Vladimir (Зелинский, Владимир): Приходящие в Церковь (Ceux qui viennent vers l'eglise), La Presse Libre, Paris, France, 1982.

Zernov, Nikolai, M. (Зернов, Николай М.): Три Русских Пророка - Хомяков, Достоевский, Соловьев, (Three Russian Prophets: Khomiakov, Dostoyevsky, Solovyov), (перебод ц английского Ю. М. Табака), Московский рабочий, Moscow, Russia, 1995.

APPENDIX ONE

DEFENDING THE ANCIENTS' BELIEFS REGARDING THE PORTENTS IN THE SKY BY MEANS OF HISTORICAL REFERENCES

A few historical notes, a mere sample from the body of 'Coincidental' apparitions of comets during major military conflicts will be given below. The readers are invited to draw their own conclusions.

The comet of 480 B.C. (observed in Greece, described as a horn shaped comet (ceratias): Persian Invasion of Greece; battles of Artemisium, and Thermopylae (in August). Destruction of Athens, looting and burning of the Acropolis temples. Themistocles achieves a victory at Salamis (in September). The Carthaginian Hamilcar Barca defeated by Gelo of Syracuse.

The comet of 373-372 B.C. (Winter, Greece): Great earthquake and tidal wave at Achaea. War between Spartans and Thebans. Spartans defeated at Leuctra by Epaminondas. (371).

The comet of 87 B.C. (Summer. Observed in China and Italy, and apparently being Halley's comet). The ruthless Roman General Sulla invades Greece and subjugates Athens. He spreads destruction everywhere and plunders an immense number of Greek works of art. Mithridatic war continues.

The comet of 32 B.C. (February, observed and recorded by the Chinese): Octavian declares war against Cleopatra. On September 2, 31, he utterly defeats Antony and Cleopatra at Actium. This marks the beginning of the Roman Principate, with Octavian now the unquestionable ruler of the Roman Empire.

From Byzantine History:

In the *'Annals...'* which deals with the Byzantine era, Nicetas (Nikitas) Choniates reports the following:

'During these days a comet appeared in the heavens, a portent of future calamities which clearly pointed to Emperor Andronicus I. Now the fiery mass appeared to be stretched out, portraying a serpent's sinuous shape, and now it contracted into coils; at other times, opening up into a yawning chasm as though it were about to swallow from above everything below, thirsting after human blood, it struck terror into those who gazed at it. It continued on its course that day and through the next night, and then it vanished.[1]

And another report on a different historical period by the same Byzantine author:

'At this time, the following omens made their appearance in the sky: stars showed forth in the daytime, the air was turbulent, certain phenomena called halos appeared around the sun, and the light it cast was no longer bright and luminous but pale'.[2]

Choniates, (1150-1213), born Nicetas Acominatus (in Chonae, whence Choniates) was a consummate statesman, historian and theologian. Today he is considered among the most brilliant medieval Greek historiographers. He is the author of a 21-volume History of the Times, and our best source of the Fourth Crusade, besides his theological treatises. We can hardly call him an ignorant and superstitious man.

On more modern phenomena:

The comet which appeared on the European skies presaging the campaign of Napoleon Buonaparte's grande armée against Russia (1812) was not immortalized only in Lev Tolstoi's *War and Peace*. Several astronomical accounts and reports of the time gave ample description of that *great comet of 1911*.

---

[1] This Andronicus I (1183-1185 A.D.) was a sorry kind of an Emperor, indeed. Brilliant and cruel, a peculiar mixture of genius and supreme evil, he managed to favorably impress only Edward Gibbon, who in his overall rather remarkable coverage of the Byzantine Empire showered Andronicus with superlatives!... Yet, none among the Greek Historians shared the Gibbonian view on this matter as in so many others involving Byzantium. Andronicus I died a cruel death, literally by installments, in the hands of an enraged mob. See also Con. Paparrigopoulos [op. cit.], vol. 6, pp. 221-257.

[2] This occurred on September 4, 1187, in the middle of a great military conflict, the first major war between Christians and Turks. See also Con. Paparrigopoulos, *History of the Greek Nation*, vol. 5, pp. 505-511.

On a more contemporary level:

Comet Kohoutek of 1973 A.D. This most widely publicized comet of all time was discovered by Dr. Lubosh Kohoutek on **March 7, 1973**, while he was searching the skies for asteroids. Like all comets, it was named after its discoverer and was classified as 1973 XII Kohoutek). The first fuzzy view of what turned out to be a new comet was taken while the comet was 370,000,000 miles away from the earth. At that time it was 10,000 times fainter than the faintest naked eye object. It reached perihelion on **December 28, 1973**. It is estimated to possess a ten miles diameter and it is not expected to return for another 75,000 years, according to the astronomers.

On October 6, 1973, Anwar El Sadat sent his troops across the Suez Canal. Since El Sadat had cried wolf several times in the past but nothing had happened, the Israelis were busy celebrating the Day of Atonement, Yom Kippur, when the invasion began. The Yom Kippur war might have passed relatively unnoticed, but the oil-embargo that it helped bring into life, and all the dislocations that ensued in the world economy may forever be a reminder that comets **also in our own lifetime** can be a harbinger of war, evil and suffering.

In *'Our Revelationary Age...'* adequate space is consecrated to making all the necessary connections between **Halley's Comet of 1986** and the Chernobyl explosion; Chernobyl was the final straw for the Soviet Proletariat (which decided that it is far better to be active today rather than radio-active tomorrow); Chernobyl marked the beginning of the end of the Soviet Empire and the ushering of the New World Disorder.

Donald K. Yeomans, [1991], supplies in an appendix the list of comets that have been observed with the naked eye from 1059 B.C. up to the year 1700 A.D. He connected many of them with military events and included that information in his appendix. I juxtaposed his list with several chronological lists at my disposal and I was able to fill many of the empty spots on his list with military events from Greek and Roman History. I am sure that a professional Historian could fill more of the remaining empty entries, if not all of them with similar military information from other countries and parts of the world. Strange as it may seem, there appears to be some kind of correlation between the apparition of major comets and unpleasant events on this planet.

If we persist in discounting such correlations as potential evidence of the non-observable underlying causal links, we are rendering ourselves a great disservice. There may be a reason, still unknown to us, why such phenomena tend to appear together. The fact is that we are still unable to come up with a plausible and scientifically satisfactory explanation. While searching for the missing links, let us continue, therefore, the labor of the ancients: mark the connections, collect the data documenting them, increase the databank, and hope and pray that someday we may know.[3]

---

[3] The study of the heavens for the potential messages they may hold for our future is not limited to cometary appearances. The conjunction of certain planets and other periodic stellar configurations are believed to have their own meaning and messages. At times, these messages cannot be understood and appreciated right away, as the following historical case would indicate:

On September 16, 1186 A.D., the Persian astrologer and Poet Anwari observed in the sign of Libra the conjunction of five bodies: Sun, Moon, Mars, Jupiter and Saturn. His mathematical calculations indicated that this conjunction was a foreboding of great evil, 'a great storm'. He made his fears public, but nothing happened and people started ridiculing the astrologer. As it was discovered years later, on that specific night of September 16, 1186, a boy was born in Mongolia, and according to legend he came into the world holding a clot of blood in his hand. His name was Temüjin. By the time he had devastated half of Europe and a good part of Asia, the world had already began to call him Genghis Khan (Universal Ruler).

APPENDIX TWO

HISTORICAL FAUX PAS BY ASTRONOMERS

Introduction
Below we shall present a few rather glaring historical misrepresentations, included in the work of Astronomy professionals. Chastising the Astronomers is not the purpose of the exercise, because *errare humanum est* and no scientist can hope to infallibility. But since one of the tasks of this study is to defend several religious and philosophical positions espoused by the generations which preceded us, pointing out our modern society's errors in judgment and/or lack of historical knowledge, may move our contemporaries to a better appreciation of the overall contributions of our ancestors.

A statement appearing in books by Astronomers will be reproduced by identifying only the initials of the title of the book, its year of publication, and the relevant pages. Then a 'different' version of the same story, written by an established Historian and/or linguist, will be supplied. The readers may draw their own conclusions.

Example no. 1:
Title: T. N. Y. T. G. t. t. R. o. H. C., YOP: 1985, pp. 50-51:

"It has been asserted by some that, during wartime, Pope Calixtus III went so far as to excommunicate Halley's Comet (...). Others contend that what he really did was ask that God protect the Christians from "the devil, the Turks and the comet." The reference to the Turks was an allusion to a bloody fight. The Turks were threatening Europe. They had captured Constantinople and were now turning on Belgrade. Scientists later confirmed that Halley's Comet did appear at a crucial stage in the war and brightly lighted up the night over the battle of Belgrade. The Europeans, believing the comet foretold disaster, could not decide what to fear more, the Turks or the comet. As History shows, the Turks won the battle. Subsequently, however, they were defeated, and Europe was saved. Whether it was because the menacing comet had now headed back out to the harmless reaches of the Solar System, or because of the pope's intercession or other factors, is, of course, not known."

Robert Payne, *The History of Islam*, p. 266:

"(...) The attempt to conquer Europe went on unabated. In 1456 the Sultan marched against Belgrade with 150,000 men and 300 cannon, together with some 200 galleys which were rowed up the Danube and moored outside the city walls. Muhammad II boasted that he would reduce the city in fifteen days, but the Franciscan Friar John Capistrano and the aging John Hunyadi were determined to put an end to the invasion. The Turkish fleet was destroyed. The friar led a thousand Crusaders against the Turkish batteries, captured them and turned the guns against the Turks, who fled. Muhammad fought with his troops, but could not stem the advance of the people of Belgrade. In the rout the Sultan was carried off by his attendants, and 24,000 of his army were left dead on the battlefield. (...) Muhammad had been wounded in the battle of Belgrade, and was more than ever determined to inflict punishment on the Europeans."

My comment: The entire History of Europe from 1456 to at least 1913 A.D. is a living proof that Europe was **not** saved at Belgrade. (To this very day, Eastern Thrace is a part of Turkey). Consequently, the wording of example no. 1 merely attests to a historical ignorance that extends much beyond the ignorance of the Belgrade events.

Example no. 2:
Title: C., YOP: 1976, p. 14:
Anaxagoras (c. 500-426 B.C.) had remarkable insight and believed the sun to be a red-hot stone larger than the Peloponnesus, the peninsula upon which Athens stands, (...).

Title: P.M's H. o. A., YOP: 6th revised edition 1983, p. 3:
Anaxagoras of Clazomenae, born about 500 B.C., is the next major character in the story. He was a flat-earth supporter, but at least he was bold enough to suggest that the Sun is a red-hot body larger than the peninsula upon which Athens stands. (...)

My comment:
In the above case of double jeopardy, a Geographer would be more useful than a Historian. Since Anaxagoras explicitly mentioned Peloponnesus, we can safely conclude that the 6th revised edition of 1983 was not revised enough. Furthermore, what Anaxagoras said was that the sun is larger than the Peloponnesus, he did not specify by how much... ὑπερέχειν δὲ τὸν ἥλιον μεγέθει τὴν Πελοπόννησον.[4]

---

[4] For a better researched account on Anaxagoras, see also G. S. Kirk & J.E. Raven, [1975]); Milton C. Nahm, [1964]; and other authors. Unfortunately, Anaxagoras's work has reached us only in fragments. A sentence here and there, or a paragraph taken out of context cannot give us a full and unequivocal opinion

Example no. 3:
Title: C.I., YOP: 1986, p. 169:
Following the tradition of naming astronomical objects after figures from mythology, it may be appropriate to name this new asteroid Damocles, after the courtier of **Dionysus** who, having displeased his master, was set at a banquet with a naked sword suspended above his head by a single thread.

A short historical portrait of Damocles after the Roman Philosopher Cicero:[5] Damocles was one of the flatterers of **Dionysius the Elder**, (Tyrant of Syracuse) in Sicily. He admired the tyrant's wealth and pronounced him the happiest man on earth. Dionysius prevailed upon him to undertake for a while the charge of royalty, and be convinced of the happiness which a sovereign enjoyed. Damocles ascended the throne, and while he gazed upon the wealth and splendor that surrounded him, he perceived a sword hanging over his head by a horse hair. This so terrified him that all his imaginary felicity vanished at once, and he begged Dionysius to remove him from a situation which exposed his life to such fears and dangers.

A comment: Apparently the above author had confused god Dionysus with the Tyrant of Syracuse Dionysius. In the same book he further maintained that *Nemesis was the Greek goddess who persecuted the rich and the powerful*. In all reality, however, she was not partial at all. She was the goddess of vengeance, always prepared to punish impiety and at the same time liberally reward goodness and virtue. She was also supposed to defend the relics and the memory of the dead from all insult. Furthermore, her power transcended the confines of this world and reached far into the afterlife, where she searched for the most effectual and rigorous means of correction.[6]

I trust that the above examples help make the point: Our overall education regarding the ancients is deficient already. Ralph Waldo Emmerson said that *the use of History is to give value to the present hour*. There are a few hours left, and there may still be time to undo some of this self-inflicted

---

on someone's scientific edifice.

[5] (See also *Lemprière's Classical Dictionary*, pp. 190-191).

[6] By virtue of the famous dictum by Lord Acton that *power corrupts and absolute power corrupts absolutely*, the rich and mighty are more vulnerable to the temptations of power; hence, one may say, statistically speaking, that on the average Nemesis did persecute the rich and the powerful with greater frequency.

damage.

<u>A final remark</u>:
The word *superstition* has a great currency among many contemporaries of ours who tend to look down upon the ancients' 'peculiar' beliefs. But the word is loaded with multiple meanings and ought to be used sparingly. For one thing, the Latin etymology of the verb *superstito* implies
1)   to preserve alive;
2)   to stand over and above (and consequently, stay there, not depart therefrom, insist, persist in a certain belief and position).
Consequently, *superstitio-onis* also implies
1)   superstitious fear, fanaticism;
2)   a binding, awe-inspiring oath;
3)   an external religious observance and/or ceremony.

To make matters a bit more complicated, the arguably premier economist of the 20th century, Friedrich August von Hayek (1899-1992), Nobel Prize in Economics, 1974, in his *Law, Legislation and Liberty* defined superstition as *the belief that we know more than we actually do*. He consequently predicted that the 20th century will go down in History as the age of superstition, par excellence. (As good examples buttressing his thesis, he identified *Marx and Freud and the ways scientific error destroyed our indispensable human values*). Professor von Hayek lived long enough to see his theories triumph over both Marx and Freud. His cautioning us against Cartesian rationalism has been vindicated by this century's events. Of all the competing versions for the most accurate rendition of 'superstition' I personally feel that the one proposed by von Hayek is the most transferable into the next century.

APPENDIX THREE

THE GREEK TEXT OF THE PROPHECIES EMANATING FROM THE EAST (COLLECTED FROM VARIOUS CHAPTERS)

From the SibOr Book VIII, The Acrostic Poem on Jesus Christ

ΙΗΣΟΥΣ ΧΡΕΙΣΤΟΣ ΘΕΟΥ ΥΙΟΣ ΣΩΤΗΡ ΣΤΑΥΡΟΣ.

Ἱδρώσει δέ χθών, κρίσεως σημεῖον ὅτ'ἔσται.
Ἥξει δ'οὐρανόθεν βασιλεὺς αἰῶσιν ὁ μέλλων,
Σάρκα παρὼν πᾶσαν κρῖναι καὶ κόσμον ἅπαντα.
Ὄψονται δὲ θεὸν μέροπες πιστοὶ καὶ ἄπιστοι
Ὕψιστον μετὰ τῶν ἁγίων ἐπὶ τέρμα χρόνοιο.
Σαρκοφόρων δ'ἀνδρῶν ψυχὰς ἐπὶ βήματι κρίνει,
Χέρσος ὅταν ποτὲ κόσμος ὅλος καὶ ἄκανθα γένηται.
Ῥίψουσιν δ'εἴδωλα βροτοὶ καὶ πλοῦτον ἅπαντα.
Ἐκκαύσει δὲ τὸ πῦρ γῆν οὐρανὸν ἠδὲ θάλασσαν
Ἰχνεῦον, ῥήξει τε πύλας εἰρκτῆς Ἀΐδαο.
Σὰρξ τότε πᾶσα νεκρῶν ἐς ἐλευθέριον φάος ἥξει
Τῶν ἁγίων· ἀνόμους δὲ τὸ πῦρ αἰῶσιν ἐλέγξει.
Ὁππόσα τις πράξας ἔλαθεν, τότε πάντα λαλήσει·
Στήθεα γὰρ ζοφόεντα θεὸς φωστῆρσιν ἀνοίξει.
Θρῆνος δ'ἐκ πάντων ἔσται καὶ βρυγμός ὀδόντων.
Ἐκλείψει σέλας ἠελίου ἄστρων τε χορεῖαι.
Οὐρανὸν εἰλίξει· μήνης δέ τε φέγγος ὀλεῖται.
Ὑψώσει δέ φάραγγας, ὀλεῖ δ'ὑψώματα βουνῶν,
Ὕψος δ'οὐκέτι λυγρόν ἐν ἀνθρώποισι φανεῖται.
Ἴσα δ'ὄρη πεδίοις ἔσται καὶ πᾶσα θάλασσα
Οὐκέτι πλοῦν ἕξει. γῆ γὰρ φρυχθεῖσα τότ'ἔσται
Σὺν πηγαῖς, ποταμοί τε καχλάζοντες λείψουσιν.
Σάλπιγξ δ'οὐρανόθεν φωνήν πολύθρηνον ἀφήσει
Ὠρύουσα μύσος μελέων καί πήματα κόσμου.
Ταρτάρεον δὲ χάος δείξει τότε γαῖα χανοῦσα.
Ἥξουσιν δ'ἐπί βῆμα θεοῦ βασιλῆος ἅπαντες.
Ῥεύσει δ'οὐρανόθεν ποταμὸς πυρὸς ἠδὲ θεείου.
Σῆμα δέ τοι τότε πᾶσι βροτοῖς, σφρηγὶς ἐπίσημος
Τὸ ξύλον ἐν πιστοῖς, τὸ κέρας τὸ ποθούμενον ἔσται,
Ἀνδρῶν εὐσεβέων ζωή, πρόσκομμα δὲ κόσμου,
Ὕδασι φωτίζον κλητούς ἐν δώδεκα πηγαῖς·
Ῥάβδος ποιμαίνουσα σιδηρείη γε κρατήσει.
Οὗτος ὁ νῦν προγραφεὶς ἐν ἀκροστιχίοις θεὸς ἡμῶν
Σωτὴρ ἀθάνατος, βασιλεύς, ὁ παθὼν ἔνεχ'ἡμῶν.

**Excerpts from the Epistle of Sunday
of Our Lord Jesus Christ**

Εἰ δὲ καὶ ταῦτα οὐ μὴ ποιήσετε, οὐ μὴ πέμψω ἄλλην ἐπιστολήν, ἀλλὰ ἀνοίξει θέλω τοὺς οὐρανοὺς καὶ βρέξει θέλω πῦρ, χάλαζαν, ὕδωρ καχλάζον, ὅτι οὐ γινώσκει ἄνθρωπος, καὶ ποιήσω σεισμοὺς φοβεροὺς καὶ βρέξει θέλω αἷμα καὶ στακτήν Ἀπριλίῳ καὶ ἅπαν σπέρμα, ἀμπελῶνα καὶ φυτὰ ἐξαλείψω καὶ πρόβατα καὶ κτήνη ὑμῶν ἀφανίσω διὰ τὴν ἁγίαν κυριακήν. Καὶ πέμψειν ἔχω θηρία πτερωτά, ἵνα φάγωσιν τὰς σάρκας ὑμῶν, ἵνα εἴπητε· Ἀνοίγετε τὰ μνημεῖα, οἱ ἀπ'αἰῶνος κεκοιμωμένοι καὶ κρύψατε ἡμᾶς ἀπὸ τὴν ὀργὴν τοῦ Παντοκράτορος Κυρίου τοῦ Θεοῦ· καὶ σκοτίσω τὸ φῶς τοῦ ἡλίου καὶ ποιήσω σκότος, καθὼς τὸ ἐποίησα τοῖς Αἰγυπτίοις ποτὲ διὰ Μωϋσῆ δούλου μου. Καὶ πέμψει θέλω τὸν Ἰσμαηλίτην λαόν, τοῦ δουλεύειν αὐτῶν καὶ κακῷ θανάτῳ καὶ μαχαίρᾳ ἀπολέσει, καὶ κλαύσετε καὶ μετανοήσετε. Καὶ οὕτω ἀποστρέψω τὸ πρόσωπόν μου τοῦ μὴ ἀκούσειν ὑμᾶς, καὶ διὰ τὴν ἁγίαν κυριακήν·

St. Methodius of Patara (4th century A.D.)

... καὶ ἐξελεύσεται τὸ σπέρμα τοῦ Ἰσμαὴλ ἐκ τῆς ἐρήμου... καὶ προπορεύσονται αὐτῷ ἐπὶ τῆς γῆς τέσσαρες πληγαί, ὄλεθρος καὶ ἀπώλεια, καὶ φθορὰ καὶ ἐρήμωσις, καὶ οὐχ ὅτι ἀγάπη αὐτούς ὁ Θεός δίδωσιν δυναστείαν, τοῦ κρατῆσαι τῆς γῆς τῶν Χριστιανῶν, ἀλλά διὰ τήν ἀνομίαν αὐτῶν.

Καί κρατήσει ἐπὶ τήν Ἑπτάλοφον τὸ ξανθόν γένος ἕξ ἢ πέντε μῆνας (μῆνας πέντε καὶ ἡμέρας 27?) καὶ φυτευθήσονται ἐν αὐτῇ λάχανα, καὶ φάγονται ἐξ αὐτῶν πολλοί εἰς ἐκδίκησιν τῶν Ἁγίων. κρατήσουσι δέ ἐπί τήν Ἀνατολήν προνοηταί τρεῖς... καὶ μετὰ τούτους ἐγερθήσεται αὐτόνομος καὶ μετὰ τοῦτον ἕτερος λύκος ἀγριώδης... καὶ ταραχθήσονται καὶ τὰ καθήμενα ἔθνη, ἅτινα εἰσίν ἐπὶ τὰ βόρεια μέρη, κινήσουσι μετὰ μεγάλης βίας καὶ δριμύτητος θυμοῦ, καὶ χωριστήσονται εἰς τέσσαρας ἀρχάς, καὶ ἡ μέν πρώτη χειμάσει εἰς Ἔφεσον, ἡ δέ δευτέρα εἰς Μελάγια, ἡ τρίτη ἐν ἀκροκάμπῳ ἤγουν εἰς Πέργαμον, καὶ ἡ τετάρτη εἰς Βυθινίαν... τότε ταραχθήσονται τὰ ἔθνη καθήμενα ἐπί νότου γωνίας, καὶ ἐγερθήσεται ὁ Μέγας Φίλιππος μετὰ γλωσσῶν δέκα ὀκτώ καὶ συναχθήσονται ἐν τῇ Ἑπταλόφῳ καὶ συγκροτήσουσι πόλεμον, οἷος οὐ γέγονε πώποτε· καὶ δρομοῦσιν εἰς τάς ἐμβολάς καὶ τάς ῥύμας τῆς Ἑπταλόφου καὶ ὁ φόνος τῶν ἀνθρώπων ὡς ποταμός κινήσει, καὶ θολωθήσεται ἡ θάλασσα ἐκ τοῦ αἵματος ἕως τὰ βάθη τῆς Ἀβύσσου. Τότε βοῦς βοήσει καὶ ξηρόλοφος θρηνήσει· καὶ τότε σταθῶσιν οἱ ἵπποι καὶ φωνή ἐξ οὐρανοῦ κράζει, στῶμεν, στῶμεν, εἰρήνη ὑμῖν· ἀρκεῖ ἡ ἐκδίκησις ἐπὶ τούς ἀπειθεῖς καὶ ἀνυκόους καὶ ἀπέλθετε ἐπί τὰ δεξιά τὰ μέρη τῆς Ἑπταλόφου καὶ ἐκεῖ εὑρήσετε ἄνθρωπον ἐπὶ δύο κίονας ἱστάμενον ἐν κατηφείᾳ πολλῇ (ἔσται λαμπρός τὸ εἶδος, δίκαιος, ἐλεήμων, φορῶν πενιχρά, τῇ ὄψει αὐστηρός καὶ τῇ γνώμῃ πραΰς) ἔχοντα ἐπί τόν δεξιόν αὐτοῦ πόδα καλάμου ἧλον καὶ φωνή ὑπό τοῦ ἀγγέλου κηρυχθήσεται, στήσατε αὐτόν Βασιλέα, καὶ δώσουν αὐτῷ εἰς τήν δεξιάν χεῖρα ῥομφαίαν λέγοντες αὐτῷ· ἀνδρίζου Ἰωάννη καὶ ἴσχυε καὶ νίκα τούς ἐχθρούς σου· καὶ ἐπάρας τήν ρομφαίαν παρά τοῦ ἀγγέλου πατάξει τούς Ἰσμαηλίτας, Αἰθίοπας καὶ πᾶσαν γενεάν ἄπιστον. Τούς δέ Ἰσμαηλίτας μερίσει εἰς τρία μέρη, καὶ τήν μέν πρώτην ἐν ρομφαία, τήν δέ δευτέραν βαπτίσει, καὶ τήν τρίτην καταδουλώσεται ἐν τῇ Ἀνατολῇ· καὶ ἐν τῷ ὑποστρέφεσθαι αὐτόν, ἀνοιχθήσονται οἱ θησαυροί τῆς γῆς καὶ πάντες πλουτήσουσι καὶ οὐδείς ἐξ αὐτῶν πένης, καὶ ἡ γῆ δώσει τόν καρπόν αὐτῆς ἑκατονταπλασίονα· τά δέ ὅλα τά πολεμικά γενήσονται εἰς ἄροτρα καὶ δρέπανα· καὶ βασιλεύσει ἔτη τριάκοντα πέντε".

Saint Tarasius (Ἅγιος Ταράσιος)
...Τούτου γενομένου ἐγερθήσεται πόλεμος ἐμφύλιος, καὶ ἀπολεσθήσεται πᾶς ὁ λαός ὁ ἄπιστος· Καί τότε ἐξυπνήσει ὁ "Αγιος Βασιλεύς ὁ ἐν ἀρχῇ τοῦ ὀνόματος αὐτοῦ Ι καὶ ἐν τῷ τέλει Σ...

Leo VI Emperor of the East (Leo the Philosopher, Λέων ὁ Σοφός)
Περί τοῦ θρυλουμένου πτωχοῦ καὶ ἐκλεκτοῦ βασιλέως, τοῦ γνωστοῦ καὶ ἀγνώστου, τοῦ κατοικοῦντος ἐν τῇ ἄκρα τῆς Βυζαντίδος. Ὁ ἀληθινός βασιλεύς... ὅν ἐδίωξαν τῆς οἰκίας αὐτοῦ οἱ ἄνθρωποι... εἰς τό τέλος τῶν Ἰσμαηλιτῶν ἀποκαλυφθήσεται... ἐν ἡμέρα παρασκευῇ, ὥρα τρίτη... ἀποκαλυφθήσεται... Ὁ μέλλων ἀποκαλυφθῆναι διὰ τόξων καὶ σημείων φανήσεται. Ἐνηχηθῇ παρά τοῦ ὁρωμένου ἀγγέλου τοῦ ἀποκαλυφθεντος ὡς ἀνθρώπου λευκοφόρου εὐνούχου, καὶ εἰς τό οὖς αὐτοῦ εἴπῃ αὐτοῦ καθεύδοντος, καὶ τῆς δεξιᾶς αὐτοῦ λαβόμενος εἴπῃ. "Εγειραι ὁ καθεύδων καὶ ἀνάστα... καὶ ἐπιφαύσει σοι ὁ Χριστός. Προσκαλεῖται γάρ σε τοῦ ποιμαίνειν λαόν περιούσιον· καὶ ἐκ δευτέρου αὐτῷ εἴπῃ· ἔξελθε ὁ κεκρυμμένος, μηκέτι κρύπτου, πολλοί σέ ζητοῦσι... καὶ ἐκ τρίτου δώσει αὐτῷ πλάκας λιθίνας, ἐν αἷς ἐγκεχάρακται ἐντολαί δύο· ἐκδικῆσαι καὶ ἐθνοποιῆσαι χρηστά· καὶ ἀσέβειαν ἐκδιῶξαι καὶ τούς σοδομιτικά ἔργα ποιοῦντας περικαύστους ποιῆσαι· ὡσαύτως καὶ τούς κακούς ἱερεῖς ἐκ τοῦ ἱεροῦ ἐκδιῶξαι καὶ τούς ἀξίους εἰς τό δεῖον ἀποκαταστῆσαι. "Εχει δέ οὗτος σημεῖα. Ὁ ὄνυξ τοῦ μεγάλου δακτύλου τοῦ δεξιοῦ ποδός τήλωμα ἔχων... καὶ σταυρούς πορφυρούς ἔχων ἐπί τάς δύο ὠμοπλάτας... τό δέ ὄνομα τοῦ βασιλέως κεκρυμμένον ἐν τοῖς ἔθνεσι... Ἐπιθήσει Κύριος τήν χεῖρα αὐτοῦ ἐπί τήν κορυφήν αὐτοῦ... Ἐν ταῖς ἡμέραις ἐκείναις θλιβήσονται οἱ ἄνθρωποι, καὶ δώσουσι τά πρόσωπα αὐτῶν ἐπί τῆς γῆς, καὶ χοῦν πάσουσιν ἐπί τάς κεφαλάς αὐτῶν, καὶ βοήσουσι πρός Κύριον τόν Θεόν τοῦ οὐρανοῦ καὶ τῆς γῆς, καὶ τότε εἰσακούσεται Κύριος τάς δεήσεις αὐτῶν καὶ θήσει τά ὦτα ἐπί τούς κατοικοῦντας τήν γῆν, καὶ ἀποστελεῖ τόν ἀρχάγγελον αὐτοῦ σχήματι ἀνθρώπου καὶ αὐλισθήσεται ἐν ταῖς νήσοις. Καί εὑρήσει τόν ἅγιον αὐτοῦ, τόν εἰλημμένον παρ'οὐδενός βλεπόμενον καὶ παρά μηδενός γνωριζόμενον... ὁ τοῖς πᾶσι σκοτεινός καὶ ἀφανής, τῷ δέ Θεῷ καὶ ἑαυτῷ φανερός· ἐκ μοίρας δουκικῆς καὶ ἐκ γένους βασιλικοῦ καταγόμενος... καὶ ἅγιος τῷ Κυρίῳ... Ἀποκαλύψει ὁ Θεός καὶ ἐμφανίσει καὶ χρίσει αὐτόν ἔλαιον εἰς τά τέλη τῶν ἡμερῶν... Ἀποκαλυφθήσεται δέ οὕτως· φανήσεται γάρ ἀστήρ ἡμέρας τρεῖς, καὶ νυκτός ὥρας γ' μέσον τῆς πόλεως ἕω τῆς μητρός τοῦ Ὑψίστου. Ὁ δέ ἀστήρ οὐκ ἔστιν ἐκ τῶν πλανητῶν, ἀλλ'ἤ ὡς ἐμφαίνει εἰς τήν

392

σωτηρίαν γέννησιν τοῦ Χριστοῦ. Καί κήρυξ βοῶν τρανῶς ἐν ταῖς τρισίν ἡμέραις ἀνακαλῶν καί ἀνακαλύπτων τόν ἐλπιζόμενον. Τότε ὁ δῆμος ὁρῶν καί ἀκούων τήν τοῦ κηρύγματος βροντώδην φωνήν ἐκπλαγήσονται. Καί ἐξεστηκότες ἅμα τῇ χαρᾷ καί τῷ φόβῳ βοήσωσιν ἀγνοεῖν τόν ἐλπιζόμενον. Τότε ὁρώντων πάντων καί τό <u>Κύριε ἐλέησον</u> θερμῶς ἐκτενῶς βοώντων· καί τά μέτωπα αὐτῶν εἰς γῆν κρούσαντες καί χοῦν εἰς τήν κεφαλήν αὐτῶν πάσαντες καί στενάξαντες καί δάκρυα χύσαντες διά τήν ἐπιοῦσαν αὐτοῖς θλῖψιν, παρακληθήσεται τό θεῖον καί εὐμενῶς δέξεται τήν δέησιν αὐτῶν, καί ἱλέῳ ὄμματι ἐπιβλέψει ἐπί τούς κατοικοῦντας τήν γῆν· διά τούς καταλειφθέντας τότε ἐκλεκτούς γνωσθήσεται ὁ ἐκλεκτός. Ὁραθήσεται ἐν τῷ οὐρανῷ νεφῶδες στερέωμα τοῦ ἡλίου ἔχον μέγεθος ὥσπερ ἅλωνος θερινῆς ἁλώντων βοῶν ἕξ. κάτωθεν κρεμασθήσεται σταυρός, εὐωνύμως δέ τοῦ σταυροῦ τοῦ πορφυροῦ, ἐκτεταμένον τόξον, οἷον διέθεττο τοῖς πατράσιν ἡμῶν εἰς διαθήκην αἰώνιον, ἀγνοούντων δέ πάντων τόν ἐλπιζόμενον, ἀνακλασθήσεται τό τόξον διά τοῦ νοτιαίου μέρους ὅ ἔστιν εὐτελούμενον ἐν τῷ εἰλήματι (σκεπάσματι) τοῦ οὐρανοῦ καί δειχθήσεται τῇ θέσει τῆς καλιᾶς τοῦ ἀληθινοῦ βασιλέως. Τότε οἱ λαοί δόντες δόξαν τῷ Θεῷ δρομαίως σπεύσουσι ἐπί τό ἄκρον τοῦ τόξου· καί λαβόντες τόν πολύτιμον καί γηραιόν ἀνακτορίδην μετά λαμπάδων καί βαΐων καί ὠφραδῶν· ὅτι ποικίλως φέρουσι ἄν αὐτόν ἐν τῇ μεγάλη Σιών... Καί κήρυξ βροντοφωνῶν καί μή φαινόμενος, ἀπό τοῦ Οὐρανοῦ πρός τόν λαόν εἴπῃ· ἀρεστός ὑμῖν αὐτός ἐστι; Τότε λήψεται πάντας φόβος καί τρόμος καί ἔκστασις εἰς τήν τοῦ κηρύγματος βροντιαίαν φωνήν. Καί εἴθ' οὕτως τύπτοντες τά στήθη μετά δακρύων καί στεναγμῶν, τάς χεῖρας εἰς τόν οὐρανόν ἄραντες εἴπωσι: Ναί Κύριε, ὅτι σύ ἔδωκας αὐτόν, ἀρεστός ἡμῖν καί προσκυνήσαντες αὐτόν ἀνάξουσιν αὐτόν εἰς τήν μεγάλην Σιών. Καί προσευξάμενος καί σφαγίσας τάς Πύλας ἀνοιχθήσονται... οἱ δέ ἐκεῖσε ὄντες φύγωσι μετά πολλοῦ φόβου, καί προσευξάμενοι ἀναβιβάσαντες ἐφ'ὑψηλοῦ τόπου καλέσουσιν αὐτῶν βασιλέα... Καί οὕτως ἄξουσιν ἐν τῷ παλατίῳ νυκτός καί ἀλλοιωθήσονται τά σημεῖα. Ὁδηγήσουσι δέ αὐτόν δύο ἄγγελοι ἐν ὁμοιώματι ἀνθρώπου λευκοφόρου εὐνούχου· καί εἰς τά ὦτα αὐτοῦ λαλήσουσι τί μέλλειν πράττειν.

The Oracles by Leo the Philosopher

Οἱ Χρησμοί:

3β'. Ἐξουσία:

Οὐαί σοι πόλις ἑπτάλοφε, ὅταν τό εἰκοστόν
στοιχεῖον εὐφημίζεται εἰς τά τείχη σου.
Τότε ἤγκικεν ἡ πτῶσις καί ἡ ἀπώλεια
τῶν δυνατῶν σου, καί τῶν ἐν ἀδικίᾳ κρινόντων,
ὅς ἔχει τούς δακτύλους αὐτοῦ δρεπανωτούς.
ὅ ἐστι δρέπανον τῆς ἐρημώσεως
καί ἐν τῷ Ὑψίστῳ βλασφημία.

393

3γ. Εὐλάβεια:

Ὁ νεκρός ἤδη καὶ θέᾳ λελησμένος·
οἴδασι πολλοὶ κἄν μηδεὶς τοῦτον βλέπῃ·
ὡς ἐκ μέθης δὲ φανεὶς ἀθρόως,
σκῆπτρα κρατήσει τῆσδε τῆς βασιλείας.
Στῦλος γὰρ ὀφθεὶς ἐν πόλῳ κεκλωσμένος
κήρυξ ἀφανὴς τρὶς ἀνακράξει μέγα·
Ἄπιτε σπουδῇ τῇ πρὸς δυσμὰς Ἑπταλόφου
Εὕρητε δ' ἄνδρα οἰκέτην ἐμόν φίλον·
Ἄξατε τοῦτον εἰς βασιλείας δόμους,
Μηνόκρανον, μειλίχιον, πραΰν, ὑψίνουν,
τὸ μέλλον ὀξύτατον εἰδέναι μᾶλλον.
καὶ πάλιν ἕξεις, Ἑπτάλοφε, τὸ κράτος. (Ἐπίσης τὸ ἴδιο καὶ στὸ
Τρομερά, Λέοντος Σοφοῦ ΠΓ 107, 1137)

3δ.:

Βύζαντος αὐλή, ἑστία Κωνσταντίνου
Ρώμη, Βαβυλὼν καὶ Σιὼν ἄλλη νέα,
τρὶς τρὶς ἑκατόν καὶ σὺ συνάρξεις κράτος
Μιᾶς ἐν αὐτοῖς ὑστερούσης εἰκάδος.
Ὡς χοῦν ἀθροίσεις τῶν ἐθνῶν τὸ χρυσίον
καὶ πάσας ἄρξεις τάς πέριξ φυλαρχίας.
Ἀλλὰ σὲ πυρίστατον καὶ ξανθόν γένος
πᾶσαν τεφρώσει καὶ τὸ σὸν λύσει κράτος.
Ἔσῃ πάλιν γὰρ ὥσπερ οὐδ' ἀρξαμένη.
Ἕως Θεοῦ δάκτυλος ὀφθεὶς ἐξ Ἕω.
Χειρὸς ῥυείσης δακτύλους πλήξῃ δύο
αἰχμὰς φέροντας αὔρας ὡς ἐκ καμίνου
αἷς τὸν πατρῷον ἐκδικήσουσι μόρον.
Ἥξουσιν δ' αὖθις κυκλῶθεν τὰ σὰ τέκνα
εὐθείας, ὥσπερ ἐκ κύκλου πρός κεντρίον
ἐφ' οἷς δικαίοις ἐκβιβάσει πρός δίκην
καινή τὸ λοιπὸν ἡ καινὴ πάλιν ἔσῃ
καὶ κρεῖττον ἄρξεις τῶν ἐθνῶν, ἤπερ πάλαι.
Δόξης γὰρ οἶκος τοῦ Θεοῦ χρηματίσεις,
τοῖς ἴχνεσί σου προσπεσόντων τῶν πέλας.

Additional Byzantine Era Prophecies
(St. Andrew the Fool-For-Christ):

...Κλινεῖ Κύριος ὁ Θεὸς ὁ Παντοκράτωρ τὸ τόξον αὐτοῦ καὶ τὸν ἄκρατον θυμὸν αὐτοῦ. Καί σεισθήσεται ἡ πόλις καὶ ἀνυψωθῇ εἰς ὕψος ὡς μῆλον γυροβολούμενον". Καί, ἀφοῦ ταχέως καταρριφθῇ, θὰ κατακλύσουν καὶ θὰ κατακαλύψουν αὐτήν τὰ ὕδατα, καὶ οὕτω θὰ παραπεμφθῇ "τῷ φοβερῷ καὶ ἀχανεῖ πελάγει τῆς ἀβύσσου". (ΠΓ 111, 864-865). Τοσοῦτος θὰ εἶναι ὁ καταποντισμὸς τῆς πόλεως, ὥστε μετὰ τοῦτον θὰ ἐξέχῃ τῶν ὑδάτων "μόνος ὁ ἐν τῷ φόρῳ στῦλος, καθότι κέκτηται τοὺς τιμίους ἥλους", δι' ὦν ἐσταυρώθη ὁ Κύριος. "Αὐτός γὰρ μόνος μενεῖ καὶ σωθήσεται, ὥστε παραγενόμενα τὰ πλοῖα καὶ ἐν τούτῳ τοὺς σχοίνους αὐτῶν ἀποδήσαντες" οἱ ναυτικοὶ "κλαύσωσι καὶ θρηνήσωσι τήν Βαβυλῶνα ταύτην".[1]

Ieronymous Agathangelos

Ἱερώνυμος Ἀγαθάγγελος (ἐγράφη τὸ ἔτος 1279 ΜΧ):
Ἀγαθάγγελε δοῦλε Θεοῦ, σύναψον τήν ὅρασιν ταύτην μέ τάς τῶν προφητῶν... σκόπησον τὸ ὅραμα τοῦ Ἰεζεκιήλ, καὶ Ἡσαΐου, ἐννόησον ὅπερ ἐκεῖ λείπει εἰς ἀναπλήρωμα τοῦ λη' καὶ λθ' κεφ. ὀφειλομένου ἐν τῷ ἰδίῳ καιρῷ αὐτοῦ συμβῆναι, ἔπειτα συνάρμοσον ἐκεῖνο τῇ ὀπτασίᾳ τοῦ υἱοῦ Ζεβεδαίου καὶ παράβαλε τήν ἀποκάλυψίν σου μεθ'ὧν ἐκεῖνοι εἶδον καὶ εἶπον καὶ ἔγραψαν πρός τόν λαόν τῶν Ἑβραίων οὕτω καὶ σύ γράψον ταύτην πρός νουθεσίαν τοῦ χριστωνύμου λαοῦ ὅν τῷ ἰδίῳ αἵματι ἐξηγόρασε, ὡς ἡ νέα διάταξις φανεροῖ καὶ διδάσκει σε, ἵνα μή ὑπέρ τοῦ μέλλοντος ἀμφιβάλλῃς.

Ἀνάγνωθι, υἱέ ἀνθρώπου, τήν κατά τῆς ἁμαρτίας τοῦ λαοῦ τοῦ Θεοῦ Θείαν ἀπόφασιν καὶ κρίσιν, καὶ σύνες ἀκριβῶς, ὅτι ἡ ἁμαρτία τοιούτου ἀγνώμονος λαοῦ βοᾷ ἐνώπιον τοῦ θρόνου τοῦ Θεοῦ, ἧς ἕνεκα βιάζεται ὁ Θεός αὐτόν κολάσαι.

Κωνσταντῖνος ἤρξατο, καὶ Κωνσταντῖνος ἀπωλέσει τῆς Ἀνατολῆς τὸ Βυζαντινόν Βασίλειον· υἱέ ἀνθρώπου, ἀρίθμησον ἀπό τοῦ πρώτου Κωνσταντίνου ἕως τοῦ δωδεκάτου ἀριθμοῦ τοῦ ὁμοίου ὀνόματος, καὶ εὑρήσεις τόν ἀριθμόν ἐφ'ᾧ συμβήσεται. Ὁ Θεός ἀπεφάσισε καὶ ἡ ὁρισθεῖσα ἐξηκριβωμένως θεία Βουλή ἀμετάθετος ἔσται. Ἀποπληρωθήσεται μέν κατά τήν τετάρτην ἑκατοντάδα ἀπό τοῦ πεντηκοστοῦ δευτέρου ἕως τοῦ τρίτου, ἐφ'ᾧ ἔτει ἐκπεσεῖται τὸ ὑπέρογκον βασίλειον εἰς χεῖρας τῶν Σαρακηνῶν· ἔσονται δέ αἱ οἰκίαι διεφθαρμέναι, οἱ ἱεροί Ναοί μεμιασμένοι, καὶ οἱ πιστοί καταδεδιωγμένοι ἕως τῆς ὀγδόης ἑκατοντάδος ἀποφασιστικῶς, ἐπειδή θέλει ὁ Θεός ἵνα γνῷ ὁ λαός τήν δικαιοσύνην Του καὶ αἰσθανθῇ τὸ βάρος τῆς παντοδυνάμου αὐτοῦ χειρός, καὶ μετανοήσῃ καὶ ἀναδράμῃ πρός Αὐτόν, καὶ εὐδόκιμος εἶτα καὶ εὐπρόσδεκτος γένηται... καὶ ὥσπερ ὁ Ἰσραηλητικός λαός ἦν ὑπήκοος τῷ Ναβουχοδονόσορι, οὕτως ἔσται ὁ λαός οὗτος ὑποτασσόμενος τοῖς ἀσεβέσιν ἀγαρηνοῖς, ἕως τοῦ διωρισμένου καιροῦ, καὶ διαμενεῖ αἰχμάλωτος ὑπό τόν ζυγόν ἕως τετάρτης ὁλοπληροῦς σχεδόν ἑκατοντάδος.

Ὁ τρομερός αἰών προσοίσει τόν χρυσοδέκατον ἀριθμόν· εἶτα ρεύσει μέλι καὶ γάλα κατά πάντα, λήξωσιν αἱ ζάλαι, καὶ ὁλοπληρῆ πεντήκοντα ἔτη βασιλεύσει ἡ εἰρήνη· ἡ ἀλήθεια θριαμβεύσει, καὶ ὁ οὐρανός χαρήσεται τῇ ἀληθεῖ δόξῃ· ἀνυψωθήσεται ἡ Ὀρθόδοξος Πίστις καὶ σκιρτήσει αὕτη ἐξ Ἀνατολῆς πρός Δυσμάς ἵνα

---

[1] See also Delimpassis, op. cit., manuscript reference, ΠΓ 111, 868.

μακαρίζηται· φρίξουσιν οἱ βάρβαροι καὶ ὅλως τρέμοντες κατὰ κεφαλὴν ταχέως ἀποφεύξονται, ἐγκαταλείποντες τὴν μητρόπολιν τοῦ κόσμου· τότε ὁ Θεὸς ἔσται δοξαζόμενος καὶ ὄψονται οἱ ἄνθρωποι τὰ ἔργα τῆς παντοδυναμίας Αὐτοῦ. Οὕτω γένοιτο, καὶ οὕτως ἔσται ἀμήν.

Ὁ μονοσύλλαβος χρυσοῦς ἀριθμὸς τὸν ὅρον διαλύει· ὀφθήσεται εἰρήνη ἐπὶ τῆς γῆς· ἀκολουθεῖ ἡ φθορὰ τῶν ἐκ τῆς Ἄγαρ, ἔπειτα θριαμβεύσει ἡ Ἀποστολικὴ Ἐκκλησία. Ἐν πέντε καὶ πεντήκοντά ἐστιν ἐπηγγελμένον τὸ τέλος τῶν θλίψεων· τῇ δὲ ἑβδόμῃ, οὐκέτι ἐξόριστοι, οὐκέτι ταλαίπωροι...

... Καί ἔπειτα, ὑπὸ τῶν πατρικῶν φωλεῶν ἐπάξω ὑμᾶς εἰς τὴν αὐτάρκειαν.

... Ἀλλ᾽ ὅμως, υἱὲ ἀνθρώπου, μὴ φοβοῦ ἐπιστραφήσεται νεόθεν πρὸς τὴν χάριν, καὶ ἔσται τῆς προτέρας ἐνδοξότερος καὶ ὑφ᾽ αὐτὸ τὸ τοῦ κόσμου κράτος ὃ διαφθαρήσεται, μέλλει ὁ Θεὸς ὑποτάξαι πάλιν νέα ἄπειρα ἔθνη, καὶ πλεῖστα τῶν πρώτων.

...Ρωσσία, ξύπνησον, γοῦν ἐκ τοῦ ὕπνου... Ἰδού τὰ ἀριστοπολεμικά σου ὄργανα πληροῦσι τὸν αἰθέρα μελωδίας... ὦ ἀδελφή μου πορεύθητι, συνηγόρησον τὴν ἐξ αὐτοῦ αἰώνιον ἀλήθειαν· εἰς σὲ γὰρ ἐτηρεῖτο τὸ σημεῖον τῆς τοσαύτης φωταυγοῦς δόξης.

... Συνθήκας ποιεῖν δοκεῖτε, ἀλλ᾽ εἰς μάτην κοπιῶσι. Σύντομον ἐκεχειρίαν ἐγὼ ποιῶ, ὑπὲρ ἀληθοῦς εἰρήνης οὐ λογίζομαι. Ὁ Ἄρης ἀπειλεῖται τρομερὸν ὄλεθρον, ταχινὴ δοκεῖται τοῦ σύμπαντος ἡ τελείωσις.

... Ὦ κενόδοξος πόλις! (Ρώμη) πάντως ἐβάφης ἀνθρωπίνῳ αἵματι· οἱ βασιλεῖς σου ἔχεον ποταμοὺς αἱμάτων διὰ τοῦ δικαίου μαρτυρίου, καὶ οἱ πιστοὶ τοῦ Χριστοῦ ὡς θύματα ἐν μακελλείῳ ἀγεληδὸν ἔτρεχον· ποῦ ἔστι νῦν ἡ εὐσέβειά σου; ποῦ ὁ ζῆλος σου; Ὁ Θεός σὲ ἐγκατέλειπεν, ὁ Χριστός σὲ ἀπορρίπτει, καὶ ὁ Διάβολος σὲ κυριεύσει· αὐτός ἐστίν ὑπερήφανος ὥσπερ σὺ καὶ ψεύστης. Σὺ γέγονας ἄλωμα ἐκείνου, θυγάτηρ αὐτοῦ καὶ παλλακίς. Διὰ τοῦτο, ὦ ἀσελγής, ἔσῃ καταπορνευμένη ἡ Ἀνατολή ταπεινώσει σε, ἔσῃ αὐτῆς αἰχμάλωτος καὶ ὑποτεταγμένη τέρας καταχθόνιον· ἡ πορφύρα σου ἔσεται ὑπ᾽ αὐτῶν διερρηγμένη, ἡ τιάρα ἀπερριμμένη ὑπὸ τοὺς πόδας, ὅτι ἔκρυψας τὴν αἰώνιον ἀλήθειαν καὶ ψεύδει ταύτην ἐχρωμάτισας· κατεφρόνησας τὴν ἁγιότητά μου, ἥν ἐθεμελίωσα ἐν τῇ Ἀνατολῇ, ἐστράφης εἰς οἰνοπωλεῖον τῆς ἀπωλείας καὶ σπήλαιον ληστῶν, ἔθηκας νεωτερίσματα ἐν τῇ πίστει τῶν ἀνθρώπων, καὶ ἐπτώχευσας τὴν Ἐκκλησίαν μου· ναί, ναί, λίθος ἐπὶ λίθον ἐπὶ τὰ τείχη σου οὐκ ἐπιμενεῖ, καὶ ἔσῃ ἐρημωμένη ὡς ἡ ἁγία πόλις Δαυΐδ, ἡ Ἀνατολή μὲν ἐκλάμψει ἐπὶ σοί, σὺ δὲ διὰ πυρὸς ἔσῃ δεδοκιμασμένη, καὶ χρηματίσεις λίθος ἀκρογωνιαῖος· αὕτη ταπεινώσει τὸν ἀλαζόνα τράχηλόν σου· προσκυνοῦσα ἀπελεύσῃ λατρεῦσαι μετὰ τοῦ κυριεύσαντος τὸ ἐν Βυζαντίῳ θυσιαστήριόν μου ἀμήν, ἀμήν. Κρίκος σκληροῦ σιδήρου διαβήσεται τὸ ἴσθμιον τῶν μυκτήρων σου, καὶ τὸ χεῖλος τὸ ἀνόσιόν σου σταλάξει ἰόν ὀλέθριον· ἔχιδνα... ὕδρα ἑπτακέφαλος, βαβυλώνιος πύργος, τὸ αἰώνιον "Ον ἐκνικήσει σε καὶ θανατώσει σε. 'Αμήν.

... Τὸ ἀσεβὲς τοῦ Διαβόλου σχολεῖον, τὸ ἐν ἀνθρώποις φαινόμενον ὅσιον, ἰδοὺ πάμπαν ἀφανισθήσεται· τότε ὑπέρλαμπρον σύνταγμα Θείας Προνοίας διαυγάσει εἰς τὸν κόσμον. ... Καὶ ἰδοὺ λίθος Τρίγωνος, ἀπεδοκιμασμένος ἀπὸ τῶν οἰκοδόμων ἐγεννήθη εἰς κεφαλὴν γωνίας. Πένητες! ὑψώσατε τὸ ὄνομα Κυρίου τοῦ Θεοῦ ἡμῶν, ψάλλατε τῷ Μεγάλῳ Βασιλεῖ τῶν αἰώνων, δότε δόξαν, δεῦτε, δεῦτε, ὦ γένος εὐσεβές: Ψάλλατε καὶ ὑμεῖς οἱ ἐφευρέται τῶν διεστραμμένων αἱρέσεων τῷ Κυρίῳ, ὅτι ἀγαθός, ὅτι εἰς τόν αἰῶνα τὸ ἔλεος Αὐτοῦ. 'Αμήν: Καὶ ἰδοὺ πλῆθος μέγα στρατιᾶς οὐρανίου ἤγαγον τὸν μέγα δράκοντα, καὶ ἔδησαν δειναῖς νευραῖς καὶ ἔρριψαν αὐτόν ἐν τῷ Ταρτάρῳ τῆς καμίνου τοῦ πυρός.

St. Neilos the Myrrh-Gusher's prophecy, ('Άγιος Νεῖλος ὁ Μυροβλύτης)
"...Κατὰ δὲ τὴν ἐποχὴν ἐκείνην, θέλει γίνει καὶ ἡ τελευταία 8η Σύνοδος ἡ ὁποία θέλει τὴν φιλονικίαν τῶν αἱρετικῶν, καὶ νὰ καθαρίσῃ τὸν σῖτον ἀπὸ τὰ ζιζάνια, τὴν 'Ορθοδοξίαν ἀπὸ τὴν κακοδοξίαν, καὶ νὰ γίνῃ εἰρήνη ἐπ'ὀλίγον διάστημα (ἔτη 50) εἰς τοὺς ἀνθρώπους. "Επειτα πάλιν μετατραπήσονται εἰς τὸ κακὸν πορευόμενοι εἰς τὴν ἀπώλειαν."[2]

From General Makriyannis's Visions
'Απὸ τὸ βιβλίο του, μὲ τίτλο 'Οράματα καί Θάματα.
α) Σελὶς 197,
'Αφοῦ αὐτείνη τὴν μεγάλη λάψην ὅπου εἶδα τὸ βράδυ, τοῦ ἀφεντός μας καὶ τῆς βασιλείας του, ὅπου δὲν μπορῶ νὰ σᾶς τὴν παραστήσω, ἀνάμεσα τὸν ἀφέντη μας καὶ εἰς τὸν Χριστὸν ἐφάνη ἕνας σταυρός· τὸν ἐπῆρε ὁ Χριστὸς εἰς τὸ χέρι, καὶ εὐτὺς βγαίνει ἕνας καὶ εἶχε μιὰν μεγάλη τρομπέτα καὶ τὴν ἔβαλε εἰς τὸ στόμα του καὶ φώναξε πρῶτα ἀριστερὰ καὶ δεύτερα δεξιά, καὶ εὐτὺς κίνησαν δύο καβαλαραῖγοι μὲ τὶς σημαῖες, καὶ συχρόνως ὁ σταυρός, καὶ ἀκολουθοῦσαν μαζί τους ἀπὸ πίσω στρατέματα· ὕστερα ἄρχισε μιά θάλασσα καὶ γιομάτη ὅλο καράβια, μεγάλα καὶ τρανά, μὲ διάφορες σημαῖες, καὶ πλῆθος ἀπό αὐτά, πνιμένη ὅλη ἡ θάλασσα, ὅλο διάβαιναν· ὕστερα ἄρχισαν μυρμήγκοι στρατευμάτων, μαῦροι, κόκκινοι καὶ τὰ ἑξῆς. Διαβαίνοντας καὶ αὐτὰ πολλὴ ὥρα, παρουσιάζεται μία σὰν ἀντάρα, καπνὸς πολύς, καὶ ἕνας μεγάλος ποταμὸς ὅλο αἷμα· καὶ

---

[2] "Καί σέ ἄλλο κεφάλαιο λέγει ὅτι "μετὰ τὰ 1913 μένουν 79 ἔτη, εἰς τὰ ὁποῖα μέλλουν νὰ γενοῦν τὰ ὅσα κακὰ προεγράψαμεν." Ή 'Ερχομένη 'Οξεία καὶ Δίστομος 'Ρομφαία, p. 45.

τελειώνοντας αὐτά, ἄρχισαν τούρκικα γράμματα· ὁ τουράς τους πρωτοβῆκε καὶ κίνησε ὁμπρός, καὶ κοντὰ τὰ γράμματα. Τελειώνοντας αὐτά, περνοῦν γράμματα δικά μας, ἔλεγαν "Παίρνει τέλος". Ύστερα περνοῦν ψηφιὰ μὲ ἀριθμοὺς πλῆθος. Πάλε βλέπω: "Παίρνει τέλος τὸ βασίλειον". Ἐσκοτίστηκα καὶ ἀπὸ νοῦ καὶ ἀπὸ μάτια καὶ ἀπ'οὖλα μου τὰ ἥπατα, καὶ αὐτὸ μόνον μπόρησα νὰ βγάλω. (...)

β) σελίς 198,
Δι'αὐτὸ τῆς Τουρκίας, εἶναι καιρὸς ὁπού 'δα εἰς τὸν ὕπνο μου ὅτι ἕνας λαμπροφορεμένος ὡς δεσπότης μοῦ δίνει δύο χαρτιὰ τούρκικα καὶ μοῦ λέγει: Δῶσ'τα τοῦ Σπυρίδωνα, ὅτι εἶναι τὰ παλιὰ προικοσύφωνα τῆς Τουρκίας, καὶ νὰ τῆς τὰ δώσει, ὅτι ἐγὼ ἔκαμα νέα. (...)

γ) σελίς 200-201,
(...) εὐτὺς βλέπω τὸν ἀφέντη μας καὶ ὅλη του τὴν βασιλείαν· (...) ἔφεξε ὁ τόπος ὅλος· εἰς τὸ δεξιὸν τοῦ ἀφεντός μας ὁ Χριστὸς καὶ ἡ Θεοτόκο καὶ ὅλοι οἱ ἅγιοι στὴν σειρά τους· βγαίνει ἡ τρομπέτα καὶ τὴν λαλεῖ ἕνας γύρα τὸ ἕνα μέρος καὶ τ'ἄλλο ἀρκετὴ ὥρα, γύρα τρεῖς φορές· τότε ἄρχισαν καὶ γράμματα τούρκικα μὲ τὸν τουρά τους καὶ ἄρχισαν πλῆθος στρατέματα κοκκινοφορεμένα, ἄλλων λογιῶν φορέματα, καὶ βγαῖναν πεζούρα καὶ καβαλαρία καὶ ἐρχόταν δεξιὸν καὶ μπαῖναν μέσα ἀμάξια πλῆθος καὶ ἀναγκαῖα τοῦ πολέμου· αὐτὸ βάσταξε πολὺ· ἔρχόταν ὅμως σὰν σκιασμένοι καὶ ἀπογάλια, καὶ γιόμωσε ὁ τόπος, ἐπνίγηκε ἀπὸ αὐτούς. Τότε ὀλίγοι ἄνθρωποι ἀσπροφορεμένοι καὶ ἄλλοι πολλὰ ὀλίγοι εἰς αὐτὸν τὸν μεγάλον πληθυσμὸν καὶ κινοῦνε ἀνάντίον τους, ἡ Θεοτόκο μ'ἕναν λαμπρὸν σταυρὸν εἰς τὸ χέρι καὶ οἱ ἅγιοι καὶ δύο καβαλαραῖγοι μὲ λαμπρὲς σημαῖες, καὶ περνοῦν ὁμπρὸς αὐτὸν τὸν χείμαρρον καὶ δὲν ἔβλεπε ἕνας τὸν ἄλλον· κατασυντρίβονταν. (...)

δ) σελίς 205-206,
(...) καὶ χάνεται ἀπὸ σᾶς ὅλους τῆς οἰκογενείας σας καὶ ὅλων τῶν δυτικῶν αὐτείνή ἰδέα καὶ ἀπαίτησι διὰ πάντα ἀπὸ τὴν ὀρθοδοξίαν. Εἶναι νέον οἰκοδόμισμα, θέληση δική μου καὶ τῆς βασιλείας μου νά'χουν αὐτὸ ὁπού ματὰ τὸ εἶχαν· ἐγὼ τὸ σήκωσα καὶ ἐγὼ τὸ δίνω ὀπίσου· κανένα ἔθνος ἀπὸ σᾶς νὰ μὴ ματατολμήσει νά'χει αὐτείνη τὴν ἀπαίτησιν καὶ οὔτε καὶ οὔτε καὶ αὐτείνη ἡ Ρωσία, ὅτι ὅποιος φανταστεῖ αὐτά, εἶναι ἡ δίκια μου ὀργὴ εἰς αὐτὸν καὶ ὅσοι φανταστοῦν νὰ τὸν συνδράμουν δι'αὐτό· εἶναι ἡ βασιλεία τοῦ μονογενοῦ μου καὶ τῆς βασιλείας τῆς ἐδικῆς μου, καὶ διορίζω πίτροπον αὐτοῦ τὸν Γιωάννη Πρόδρομον, καὶ τῆς γενεὰ αὐτοῦ εἰς γενεὰ πρὸς γενεὰ ἀπάντους αἰῶνες δίνω αὐτό. Αὐτείνη εἶναι ἡ θέλησή μου καὶ εὐκαρίστησή μου. Ἐσὺ Γιάννη, πιστὲ εἰς ἐμὲ καὶ εἰς τὴν βασιλείαν μου, καὶ ἡ γενεά σου νὰ μιμηθοῦν ἐσένα, καὶ εἰς τοῦ Κωσταντίνου τὸ σπίτι εἶναι ἡ κατοικία σου καὶ τῶν ἀπογόνων σου, ὄχι ἀλλοῦ. (...)

Ανωνύμου Προφητεία (1053 Μ.Χ.)

1. Μέγας Εύρωπαϊκός πόλεμος.
2. Ήττα τής Γερμανίας, καταστροφή Ρωσσίας καί Αύστρίας.
3. Ήττα τών 'Αγαρηνών ύπό 'Ελλήνων.
4. Ένίσχυσις 'Αγαρηνών ύπό Δυτικών λαών καί ήττα τών 'Ελλήνων ύπό τής "Αγαρ.
5. Σφαγή 'Ορθοξόξων λαών.
6. Καί μεγάλη άνησυχία 'Ορθοδόξων λαών.
7. Εἰσβολή ξένων στρατευμάτων ἐξ 'Αδριατικοῦ πελάγους. Οὐαί εἰς τούς κατοικοῦντας ἐπί τῆς γῆς, ὁ ἅδης ἕτοιμος.
8. Πρός στιγμήν ὁ 'Αγαρηνός μέγας.
9. Νέος εὐρωπαϊκός πόλεμος.
10. Ένωσις 'Ορθοδόξων λαών μετά τῆς Γερμανίας.
11. Ήττα Γάλλων ύπό Γερμανῶν.
12. Έπανάστασις τών 'Ινδιῶν καί χωρισμός αὐτῶν άπό τῆς 'Αγγλίας.
13. 'Αγγλία εἰς μόνους Σάξωνας.
14. Νίκη 'Ορθοδόξων λαών καί γενική σφαγή 'Αγαρηνών ύπό 'Ορθοδόξων.
15. 'Ανησυχία κόσμου.
16. Γενική άπελπισία ἐπί τῆς γῆς.
17. Μάχη ἑπτά κρατῶν εἰς Κωνσταντινούπολιν. Τρία ἡμερονύκτια σφαγή. Νίκη τοῦ μεγαλυτέρου κράτους κατά τῶν ἕξ κρατῶν.
18. Συμμαχία ἕξ κρατῶν κατά τοῦ ἑβδόμου κράτους, τρία ἡμερονύκτια σφαγή.
19. Παῦσις πολέμου ύπό άγγέλου καί παράδοσις πόλεως τοῖς "Ελλησι.
20. 'Υπόκυψις Λατίνων εἰς άλάνθαστον Πίστιν 'Ορθοδόξων.
21. Έξωθήσεται 'Ορθόδοξος Πίστις άπό 'Ανατολῶν μέχρι Δυσμῶν.
22. Φόβος καί τρόμος βαρβάρων ὑπ'αὐτῆς.
23. Παῦσις τοῦ Πάπα καί κήρυξις ἑνός Πατριάρχου δι'ὅλην τήν Εὐρώπην.
24. Ἐν πέντε καί πεντήκοντα ἕτη τό τέλος τῶν θλίψεων· τήν δέ ἑβδόμην οὐκ ἔστι ταλαίπωρος, οὐκ ἔστι ἐξόριστος, ἐπανερχόμενος εἰς τάς άγκάλας τῆς Μητρός άγαλλομένης. Οὕτως ἔσται καί οὕτω γένοιτο.
'Αμήν. 'Αμήν. 'Αμήν.
Ἐγώ εἰμί τό Α καί τό Ω.
Πρῶτος καί ἔσχατος.
Τέλος μία ποίμνη καί εἰς ποιμήν ἔσται ἐκ τῆς άληθοῦς όρθοδόξου πίστεως.
Αὐτό γένοιτο.
'Αμήν. 'Αμήν. 'Αμήν.
Δοῦλος Χριστοῦ 'Αληθινοῦ Θεοῦ.

Prophecy of St. Andrew the Fool-For-Christ
'Η πόλις αὔτη ἡ ἐπάνω πολλῶν ἐθνῶν προκαθεζομένη άνάλωτος

399

(ἀπόρθητος) ἔθνεσι γενήσεται, καὶ ἀχείρωτος· ἡ γὰρ Θεοτόκος, ἐν σκέπῃ τῶν ἰδίων πτερύγων ταύτην ἐφύλαξε· καὶ ταῖς πρεσβείαις αὐτῆς ἄτρωτος διαφυλαχθήσεται... Λόγος δέ τις φέρεται εἰσιέναι τὸ γένος τῶν Ἀγαρηνῶν καὶ ἱκανὰ πλήθη τῇ μαχαίρᾳ αὐτῶν κατασφάξουσιν· ἐγὼ δέ φημί, ὅτι καὶ τὸ ξανθὸν γένος εἰσελεύσεται οὗτινος ἡ προσηγορία πρόκειται ἐν τῷ ἑπτακαιδεκάτῳ στοιχείῳ τῶν εἰκοσιτεσσάρων στοιχείων ἀνακεφαλαιωμένων, ἀλλ'εἰσελεύσεται μέν καὶ τὰ κῶλα τῶν ἁμαρτωλῶν ἐπὶ ἐδάφους καταστρώσουσιν, οὐαί δέ αὐτοῖς ἀπὸ τῶν δύο ὁρπήκων ὧν αἱ ῥομφαῖαι αὖραι καὶ ὀξεῖαι δρέπανοι, πυρὸν ἐν θέρει συγκόπτουσαι καὶ εἰς τὰ ὀπίσω οὐ μὴ ἀνθυποστρέψουσιν οὐκέτι, οὐδ'οὗ μὴ ἐνταῦθα καταλειφθήσονται... Ἐν γὰρ ταῖς ἐσχάταις ἡμέραις ἀναστήσει Κύριος ὁ Θεὸς βασιλέα ἀπὸ πενίας καὶ πορεύσεται ἐν δικαιοσύνῃ, καὶ γενήσεται δι'ἐλεημοσύνης τοῖς πᾶσιν εὐάρεστος, πάντα δέ πόλεμον καταπαύσει, καὶ τοὺς πένητας πλουσίους ἀπεργάσηται, καὶ ἔσται εἰρήνη ὃν τρόπον ἐπὶ τῶν ἡμερῶν Νῶε, διὰ τὸ μὴ ποιεῖν πόλεμον πώποτε. Ἔσονται γὰρ οἱ ἄνθρωποι πλούσιοι ἐν ταῖς ἡμέραις ἐκείναις σφόδρα, καὶ ἐν εἰρήνῃ καὶ ἐν γαλήνῃ βαθείᾳ ἐσθίοντες καὶ πίνοντες, γαμοῦντες καὶ ἐκγαμίζοντες, ἐν ἀδείᾳ πολλῇ πορευόμενοι καὶ ἀμερίμνως τοῖς γηΐνοις ἐπαναπαυόμενοι, καὶ ἐν τῷ μὴ εἶναι πόλεμον ἐπὶ τῆς γῆς συγκόψουσι τὰς σπάθας αὐτῶν εἰς ζυβίνας καὶ εἰς δρέπανα καὶ εἰς ἐργαλεῖα γεωργικά. Καί μετὰ ταῦτα δώσει τὸ πρόσωπον αὐτοῦ ἐπὶ ἀνατολὰς καὶ ταπεινώσει τοὺς υἱοὺς Ἄγαρ· ὀργισθήσεται γάρ αὐτοῖς ὁ Κύριος διὰ τὴν βλασφημίαν αὐτῶν ἣν ἐβλασφήμησαν εἰς τόν Κύριον ἡμῶν Ἰησοῦν Χριστόν καὶ διὰ τὴν τῶν Σοδόμων ἀσέλγειαν ἣν κατεργάζονται· πολλοὶ δέ ἐξ αὐτῶν τὸ ἅγιο βάπτισμα κομισάμενοι εὐάρεστοι γενήσονται καὶ τιμηθήσονται παρὰ τοῦ εὐσεβοῦς βασιλέως ἐκείνου, τοὺς δέ λοιποὺς ὀλέσει καὶ ἐμπυρίσει καὶ βιαίῳ θανάτῳ παραδώσει. Ἐν τοῖς καιροῖς ἐκείνοις ἀποκατασταθήσεται πᾶσα ἡ ὑφήλιος· καὶ τὸ Ἰλλυρικόν τῆς βασιλείας Ρωμαίων καὶ ἡ Αἴγυπτος κομίσει τὰ πάκτα αὐτῆς. Καί θήσει τὴν χεῖραν αὐτοῦ τὴν δεξιάν εἰς τὰ κύκλῳ ἔθνη· καὶ ἡμερώσει τὰ ξανθά ἔθνη καὶ τοὺς μισοῦντας αὐτὸν τροπώσεται· τριάκοντα καὶ δύο ἔτη κρατήσει τῆς βασιλείας. Δώδεκα ἔτη κῆνσον καὶ δόματα οὐ λήψεται. Ἀναστήσῃ δέ θυσιαστήρια τὰ συντετριμμένα καὶ ναούς ἁγίους ἀνοικοδομήσει. Δίκη οὐκ ἔσται ἐν ταῖς ἡμέραις ἐκείναις, ἀλλ'οὔτε ὁ ἀδικῶν ἢ ὁ ἀδικούμενος· πτήξει γὰρ ἀπὸ προσώπου αὐτοῦ πᾶσα ἡ γῆ, καὶ φόβῳ ποιήσει τοὺς υἱούς τῶν ἀνθρώπων σωφρονεῖν· καὶ τοὺς παρανόμους τῶν μεγιστάνων ἐξολοθρεύσει.

The Tombstone Prophecy

Τῇ πρώτῃ τῆς Ἰνδίκτου, ἡ Βασιλεία τοῦ Ἰσμαὴλ ὁ καλούμενος Μωάμεθ, μέλλει διὰ νὰ τροπώσῃ γένος τῶν Παλαιολόγων, τὴν Ἑπτάλοφον κρατήσει, ἔσωθεν βασιλεύσει, ἔθνη πάμπολλα κατάρξει, καὶ τάς νήσους ἐρημώσει μέχρι τοῦ Εὐξείνου Πόντου. Ἰστρογείτονας πορθήσει τῇ ὀγδόῃ τῆς Ἰνδίκτου. Πελοπόννησον κατάρξει, τῇ ἐνάτῃ τῆς Ἰνδίκτου, εἰς τὰ βόρεια τὰ μέρη μέλλει διὰ νὰ στρατεύσῃ· τῇ δεκάτῃ τῆς Ἰνδίκτου τοὺς Δαλμάτας τροπώσει, πάλιν ἐπιστρέψει ἔτι χρόνον, τοῖς Δαλμάταις πόλεμον ἐγείρει μέγαν μερικόν τε συντριβῆναι, καὶ

400

τὰ πλήθη καὶ τὰ φῦλα συνοδῇ τῶν Ἑσπερίων διά θαλάσσης καὶ ξηρᾶς τόν πόλεμον συνάψουν, καὶ τόν Ἰσμαήλ τροπώσουν, τὸ ἀπόγονον αὐτοῦ βασιλεύσει ἔλαττον μικρόν ὀλίγον. τὸ δέ ξανθόν γένον ἅμα μετά τῶν πρακτόρων ὅλον Ἰσμαήλ τροπώσουν, τήν Ἑπτάλοφον ἐπάρουν μετά τῶν προνομίων. τότε πόλεμον ἐγείρουν ἔμφυλον ἠγριωμένον, μέχρι τῆς πεμπταίας ὥρας. καὶ φωνή βοήσει τρίτον, στῆτε στῆτε μετά φόβου σπεύσατε πολλά σπουδαίως εἰς τά δεξιά τά μέρη ἄνδρα εὕρητε γενναῖον θαυμαστόν καὶ ρωμαλέον, τοῦτον ἕξετε Δεσπότην, φίλος γάρ ἐμοῦ ὑπάρχει καὶ αὐτόν παραλαβόντες, θέλημα ἐμόν πληροῦται.

Continuation of Agathangelos' prophecy on Protestantism

(...) ἀλλά γίνωσκε, ὅτι εἰς υἱός σου ἐκ τοῦ αὐτοῦ αἵματος ἐπί σέ ἐπιστρέφεται, καί ἀποβδελύττεται τό λατινικόν δόγμα, καί γίνεται κεφαλή τῶν αἱρετικῶν. Βλέπω τούς φίλους σου ἀπηλλοτριωμένους, ἐπεισάγοντας τοσαύτας νεοφανεῖς αἱρέσεις, ὅσα ἐστί τά τῶν πτερύγων χρώματα τοῦ λευκοῦ κύκνου. Βλέπω ἀπωθουμένας τάς ἑορτάς, χωλαίνουσαν τήν πίστιν, ἡ ἐκκλησία σου χωρίς ὁδηγοῦ, πλοιάριον ἄνευ πηδαλίου καί κυβερνήτου, καί ἡ πίστις σου ἄνευ βάσεως. Δεινόν τό πτῶμα, ὦ Θεέ. Θαύμασον ὅμως, υἱέ ἀνθρώπου. Ἐπειδή καί ἐξ αὐτῆς τῆς αἱρετικῆς Γερμανίας, καί δι'αὐτῆς ὑψωθήσεται μετά ταῦτα ἡ ἀλήθεια καί ἡ ἀψευδής λατρεία τῆς Ὀρθοδόξου πίστεως. Αὕτη μᾶλλον τῶν ἄλλων φυλῶν ἐκδικήσει σταθερώτατα τήν Ἀποστολικήν Ἀλήθειαν. Τό ἀνατολικόν δόγμα ἐν αὐτῇ ἀναλάμψει.

NAME INDEX

163-167, 179, 295-297, 331-333, 349, 350, 356, 372, 373, 376, 377

About the Author

Helen Tzima Otto was born and raised in Greece, where she received her Bachelor's Degree in Economics. Later she earned a MBA in Quantitative Management Science, a MA in International Economics and a Ph.D. in Economics from the University of Houston, Houston, Texas.

She has taught in academia and professional Business Schools in Houston Tx., Washington, D.C., Arlington, Va. and Madrid, Spain. She has worked in the private sector for several years. Whenever time permits, she assists her husband, Dr. Gordon H. Otto, in the consulting practice of Otto and Associates.

Dr. Otto's previous books are:

Essays in Verse and other Poems, 1990 and

Our Revelationary Age: The Prophecies for WWIII and the Year 2000, 1994.

EPILOGUE

Being an inveterate speculator in Futures, while the completed manuscript is lying ready before me, I cannot resist the temptation of advancing yet another speculation. I wish to invite the readers to synthesize all the information available to them through the study they just finished reading with the relevant testimony of the Most Holy Virgin Mary Theotokos during Her apparitions at Garabandal and Medjugorje.

The highlights of Her messages with respect to astral phenomena and generally all signs and wonders sent directly from God are given below. I tried to identify their underlying commonalities, combine them in the same sentences and draw their joint conclusions:

- The Holy Virgin said at Garabandal: ***Through the kiss I have bestowed on these objects my Son will perform miracles, wonders and prodigies before and after the Great Miracle.***

  Ergo, wonders and prodigies will occur before and after the Great Miracle. Thus, several signs and wonders are to be expected in the proximate future.

- There will be events on the earth as warnings to the world before the visible sign is given to humanity. The visible sign is the Miracle. The warning comes first. The warning is something that is first seen in the air, everywhere in the world and immediately is transmitted into the interior of our souls. It will last for a very little time, but it will seem a very long time because of its effect within us. We will see it and feel it within ourselves and it will be most clear that it comes from God.

- Satan will rule until the first secret is unfolded. (This comes from the Medjugorje testimony where 10 secrets were spoken of, in toto, namely, 10 events of global consequences, although some may be local in character.

- The third secret (spoken of at Medjugorje) will be a visible sign at Medjugorje, permanent, indestructible and beautiful. After the visible sign **those still alive** will have little time for conversion. The visible sign **is** the Miracle.

The expression *There will be events on the earth given as a warning to the world...* may very well involve the earthquakes, the volcanoes, the destructiveness wrought upon this planet by natural forces.

The third secret (spoken of during the apparitions at Medjugorje) coincides with the Great Miracle (un señal del milagro) spoken of at Garabandal. The Garabandal visionaries insist that 'something' will remain forever after over the physical location of the Holy Virgin's apparitions at Garabandal. *It will be possible to film or televise, but no one will be able to touch it.*

Those still alive, is a hint loaded with meaning: it tells us that by the time the permanent, indestructible and beautiful object appears in our skies, the world will have already gone through The Three Days Darkness and the great mortality this terrible event implies.

- *The miracle will coincide with an important event in the Church and on the feast day of a martyr of the Eucharist, in the evening, 8:30 p.m. between the 8th and 16th of April. Russia will be converted after the miracle. The reigning Pope will see the miracle from wherever he is. The miracle will take place within one year after the warning.* A permanent sign will remain forever as a result of the Great Miracle. It will be of a supernatural origin, never before seen on earth.

This last paragraph draws our attention once more to the hypothesis I have advanced in this study while analyzing the importance of Easter and Passover correlations for the years 1998 and 1999 A.D. I cannot prove it based on the data currently at my disposal, but I feel this important event in the Church is the Holiday of the **Life Giving**

Fountain, a day dedicated to the Mother of God, the first Friday after the Greek Easter. It may very well be that both years are most critical and both years will be connected with astral phenomena. Besides the comet spoken of so profusely in the prophecies, it appears most likely that also another heavenly body will become part and parcel of our proximate future. This one, will **remain forever** on our skies. It could be an Earth-Crossing Asteroid, caught by the gravitational pull of our planet or our satellite. Then, as the visionaries tell us, it will be seen by everybody on earth, and definitely it will be seen from Medjugorje and Garabandal; it can be photographed and televised but not touched, obviously; it will be indestructible and permanent and beautiful.

I invite the readers to keep on the alert and in great mental and spiritual preparedness from now on, and particularly as the month of April draws near every year, beginning with 1997 all the way till the Blessed Peace of Christ is established upon the earth. There are bound to be many signs and wonders in our heavens, and there is no law forbidding them from happening around April, in more than one year. It is quite possible that the *deviations of stars* spoken of in the Apocalypse of Daniel, (which as we saw covered also WWIII and the re-capture of Constantinople), referred to an Earth-Crossing Asteroid, deviating from its trajectory and becoming a satellite to our system. Considering that asteroids have stony and metallic compositions, an asteroid is a great candidate for a second Moon to our system. A comet, being of more volatile material could not survive long the gravitational pull, the continuous revolutions around our planet and through the sublimation process it would lose most of its material in a hurry. Therefore, it could never qualify for 'permanent' and 'indestructible' although temporarily it would be quite beautiful.